CAMBRIDGE LIBRARY COLLECTION

Books of enduring scholarly value

British and Irish History, Nineteenth Century

This series comprises contemporary or near-contemporary accounts of the political, economic and social history of the British Isles during the nineteenth century. It includes material on international diplomacy and trade, labour relations and the women's movement, developments in education and social welfare, religious emancipation, the justice system, and special events including the Great Exhibition of 1851.

The Principles of Political Economy

A friend, correspondent and intellectual successor to David Ricardo, John Ramsay McCulloch (1789–1864) forged his reputation in the emerging field of political economy by publishing deeply researched articles in Scottish periodicals and the Encyclopaedia Britannica. From 1828 he spent nearly a decade as professor of political economy in the newly founded University of London, thereafter becoming comptroller of the Stationery Office. Perhaps the first professional economist, McCulloch had become internationally renowned by the middle of the century, recognised for sharing his ideas through lucid lecturing and writing. First published in 1825, this textbook was an expanded version of an article originally written in 1822 for the Encyclopaedia Britannica. Reissued here is the 1830 enlarged second edition. In Britain and America the work reached many students, and was translated into multiple European languages. Several other works written or edited by McCulloch are also reissued in the Cambridge Library Collection.

Cambridge University Press has long been a pioneer in the reissuing of out-of-print titles from its own backlist, producing digital reprints of books that are still sought after by scholars and students but could not be reprinted economically using traditional technology. The Cambridge Library Collection extends this activity to a wider range of books which are still of importance to researchers and professionals, either for the source material they contain, or as landmarks in the history of their academic discipline.

Drawing from the world-renowned collections in the Cambridge University Library and other partner libraries, and guided by the advice of experts in each subject area, Cambridge University Press is using state-of-the-art scanning machines in its own Printing House to capture the content of each book selected for inclusion. The files are processed to give a consistently clear, crisp image, and the books finished to the high quality standard for which the Press is recognised around the world. The latest print-on-demand technology ensures that the books will remain available indefinitely, and that orders for single or multiple copies can quickly be supplied.

The Cambridge Library Collection brings back to life books of enduring scholarly value (including out-of-copyright works originally issued by other publishers) across a wide range of disciplines in the humanities and social sciences and in science and technology.

The Principles of Political Economy

With a Sketch of the Rise and Progress of the Science

J.R. McCulloch

CAMBRIDGE
UNIVERSITY PRESS

University Printing House, Cambridge, CB2 8BS, United Kingdom

Cambridge University Press is part of the University of Cambridge.
It furthers the University's mission by disseminating knowledge in the pursuit of education, learning and research at the highest international levels of excellence.

www.cambridge.org
Information on this title: www.cambridge.org/9781108078696

This edition first published 1830
This digitally printed version 2017

ISBN 978-1-108-07869-6 Paperback

THE PRINCIPLES OF POLITICAL ECONOMY:

WITH A SKETCH OF THE RISE AND PROGRESS OF THE SCIENCE.

By J. R. McCULLOCH, Esq.

PROFESSOR OF POLITICAL ECONOMY IN THE UNIVERSITY OF LONDON.

SECOND EDITION,

CORRECTED AND GREATLY ENLARGED.

"Non enim me cuiquam mancipavi, nullius nomen fero; multum magnorum virorum judicio credo, aliquid et meo vindico. Nam illi quoque, non inventa, sed quærenda, nobis reliquerunt."—*Seneca.*

LONDON:

PRINTED FOR WILLIAM TAIT, EDINBURGH;

LONGMAN, REES, ORME, BROWN, AND GREEN, LONDON;

AND W. CURRY AND CO. DUBLIN.

M.DCCC.XXX.

ADVERTISEMENT.

THIS Edition is very much enlarged, and, I hope I may add, considerably improved. Without, I trust, impairing the value of the work in a scientific point of view, I have endeavoured to give to it more of a practical character. For this purpose I have entered at considerable length into an examination of various important subjects of national policy, which, while they afford some striking illustrations of the application of the principles of the science, shew in how far they are liable to be modified in their operation by secondary or accidental causes. Wherever, indeed, an opportunity was afforded, I have been anxious to try every theoretical conclusion by the test of experience; and I am sanguine enough to believe, that the reader will find that the doctrines laid down, how defectively soever they may be explained, are at least consistent with the phenomena observed in the working of the machine of society.

London, February 1830.

PREFACE

[illegible] I have [illegible] the [illegible] [illegible]

For this purpose [illegible] material [illegible] and [illegible] of [illegible] examples of [illegible] to [illegible] but [illegible] I have been [illegible] the [illegible] of [illegible] and I [illegible] enough to [illegible] that [illegible] from [illegible] they may be [illegible] consistently [illegible] the [illegible] of [illegible]

[illegible]

CONTENTS.

INTRODUCTION.

RISE AND PROGRESS OF THE SCIENCE.

PART I.

PRODUCTION AND ACCUMULATION OF WEALTH.

CHAPTER I.

CHAPTER II.

CHAPTER III.

CHAPTER IV.

CHAPTER V.

CHAPTER VI.

CHAPTER VII.

CHAPTER VIII.

CHAPTER IX.

CHAPTER X.

PART II.

VALUE AND PRICE.

CHAPTER I.

CHAPTER II.

CHAPTER III.

CHAPTER IV.

PART III.

DISTRIBUTION OF WEALTH.

CHAPTER I.

CHAPTER II.

CHAPTER VIII.

PART IV.

CONSUMPTION OF WEALTH.

PRINCIPLES

OF

POLITICAL ECONOMY.

INTRODUCTION.

RISE AND PROGRESS OF THE SCIENCE.

Definition of the Science—its Importance—Causes of its being neglected in Greece and Rome, and in the Middle Ages—Evidence on which its Conclusions are founded—Rise of the Science in Modern Europe—Mercantile System—System of M. Quesnay and the French Economists—Publication of the "Wealth of Nations"—Distinction between Politics and Statistics and Political Economy.

Political Economy* may be defined to be the science of the laws which regulate the production, accumulation, distribution, and consumption of those articles or products that are necessary, useful, or agreeable to man, and which at the same time possess exchangeable value.

* *Economy*, from οἶκος, a house, or family, and νόμος, a law—*the government of a family*. Hence Political Economy may be said to be to the State what domestic economy is to a family.

When it is said that an article or product is possessed of *exchangeable value*, it is meant that there are individuals disposed to give a certain quantity of labour, or a certain quantity of some other article or product, obtainable only by means of labour, in exchange for it.

The power or capacity which particular articles or products have of satisfying one or more of the various wants and desires of which man is susceptible, constitutes their *utility*, and renders them objects of demand.

An article may be possessed of the highest degree of utility, or of power to minister to our wants and enjoyments, and may be universally made use of, without possessing exchangeable value. This is an attribute or quality of those articles only which it requires some portion of voluntary human labour to produce, procure, or preserve. Without the possession of utility of some species or other, no article can ever become an object of demand; but how necessary soever any particular article may be to our comfort, or even existence, still, if it be a spontaneous production of nature — if it exist independently of human agency — and if every individual can command indefinite quantities of it without any voluntary exertion or labour, it is destitute of value, and can afford no basis for the reasonings of the economist. A commodity, or a product, is not valuable, merely because it is useful or desirable; but it is valuable when, besides being possessed of these qualities, it can only be procured through the intervention of labour. It cannot justly be said, that the food with which we appease the cravings of hunger, or the clothes by which we defend ourselves from the inclemency of the weather, are more useful than atmospheric air; and yet they are possessed of that exchangeable value of which the latter is totally destitute. The reason is, that food and clothes are not, like air, gratuitous products; they cannot be had at all times, and in any quantity, without exertion; on the contrary, labour is always required for their production, or appropriation, or both; and as no one will voluntarily sacrifice the fruits of his industry without receiving an equivalent, they are truly said to possess exchangeable value.

The economist does not investigate the laws which determine the production and distribution of such articles as exist, and may be obtained in unlimited quantities, independently of all voluntary human agency. The results of the industry of man form the only subjects about which he is conversant. Political Economy might, indeed, be defined to be the *science of values;* for, nothing which is not possessed of exchangeable value, or which will not be received as an equivalent for something else which it has taken some labour to produce or obtain, can ever properly be brought within the scope of its inquiries.

The word *value* has been very frequently employed to express, not only the exchangeable worth of a commodity, or its capacity of exchanging for other commodities, but also its *utility*, or capacity of satisfying our wants, or of contributing to our comforts and enjoyments. But it is obvious, that the utility of commodities — that the capacity of bread, for example, to appease hunger, and of water to quench thirst — is a totally different and distinct quality from their capacity of exchanging for other commodities. Dr. Smith perceived this difference, and shewed the importance of carefully distinguishing between utility, or, as he expressed it, "*value in use*," and value in exchange. But he did not always keep this distinction in view, and it has been very often lost sight of by subsequent writers. There can be no doubt, indeed, that the confounding of these opposite qualities has been one of the principal causes of the confusion and obscurity in which many branches of the science, not in themselves difficult, are still involved. When, for instance, it is said that water is highly valuable, a very different meaning is attached to the phrase from what is attached to it when it is said that gold is valuable. Water is indispensable to existence, and has therefore a high degree of utility, or of "value in use;" but as it can generally be obtained in large quantities, without much labour or exertion, it has, in most places, but a very low value in exchange. Gold, on the other hand, is of comparatively little utility; but as it exists only in limited quantities, and requires a great deal of labour in its production, it has a comparatively high exchangeable value, and may be exchanged or bartered for a proportionally large quantity of most other commodities. To confound qualities so different must evidently lead to the most erroneous conclusions. And hence, to avoid all chance of error from mistaking the sense of so important a word as *value*, I shall not use it except to signify exchangeable worth, or value in exchange; and shall always use the word *utility* to express the power or capacity of an article to satisfy our wants, or gratify our desires.

Political Economy has sometimes been termed "the science which treats of the production, distribution, and consumption of *wealth*;" and if by wealth be meant those useful or agreeable articles or products which possess exchangeable value, the definition would seem to be unexceptionable. If, however, the term wealth be understood in either a more enlarged or contracted sense, it will be faulty. Mr. Malthus, for example, has supposed wealth to be identical with "those *material* objects which are necessary, useful, and agreeable to man."* But the inaccuracy of this definition

* "Principles of Political Economy," p. 28.

is evident, though we should wave the objections which may perhaps be justly taken to the introduction of the qualifying epithet *material.* In proof of this, it is sufficient to mention, that atmospheric air, and the heat of the sun, are both material, necessary, and agreeable products; though their independent existence, and their incapacity of appropriation, by depriving them of exchangeable value, places them, as has been already seen, without the pale of the science.

Dr. Smith nowhere explicitly states the precise meaning he attaches to the term wealth; but he most commonly describes it to be "the annual produce of land and labour." Mr. Malthus, however, has justly objected to this definition, that it refers to the sources of wealth before it is known what wealth is, and that it includes all the useless products of the earth, as well as those appropriated and enjoyed by man.

The definition previously given does not seem open to any of these objections. By confining the science to a discussion of the laws regulating the production, accumulation, distribution, and consumption of articles or products possessed of exchangeable value, we give it a distinct and definite object. When thus properly restricted, the researches of the economist occupy a field which is exclusively his own. He runs no risk of wasting his time in inquiries which belong to other sciences, or in unprofitable investigations respecting the production and consumption of articles which cannot be appropriated, and which exist independently of human industry.

Capacity of appropriation is indispensably necessary to constitute an article wealth. And I shall endeavour invariably to employ this term to distinguish such products only as are obtained by the intervention of human labour, and which, consequently, may be appropriated by one individual, and enjoyed exclusively by him. A man is not said to be wealthy, because he has an indefinite command over atmospheric air, or over such articles as nature gratuitously furnishes to him, in common with others, without any voluntary exertion on his part; for, this being a privilege which he enjoys along with every one else, can form no ground of distinction: but he is said to be wealthy, according to the degree in which he can afford to command those necessaries, conveniences, and luxuries, that are not the gifts of nature, but the products of human industry.

The object of Political Economy is to point out the means by which the industry of man may be rendered most productive of those necessaries, comforts, and enjoyments, which constitute *wealth;* to ascertain the circumstances most favourable for its accumulation; the proportions in which it is divided among the different classes of the community; and the mode in which it may be most advantageously consumed. The intimate connexion of such a science with all the best interests of society is abundantly obvious. There is no other, indeed, which comes so directly home to the every-day occupations and business of mankind. The consumption of wealth is indispensable to existence; but the eternal law of Providence has decreed, that wealth can only be procured by industry,—that man must earn his bread in the sweat of his brow. This twofold necessity renders the production of wealth the constant and principal object of the exertions of the vast majority of the human race; has subdued the natural aversion of man from labour; given activity to indolence; and armed the patient hand of industry with zeal to undertake, and patience to overcome, the most irksome and disagreeable tasks.

But when wealth is thus necessary, when the desire to acquire it is sufficient to make us submit to the greatest privations, the science which teaches the means by which its acquisition may be best promoted, by which we may obtain the greatest possible amount of wealth with the least possible difficulty,—must certainly deserve to be carefully studied and meditated. There is no class of persons to whom it can be considered as either extrinsic or superfluous. There are some, doubtless, to whom it may be of more advantage than to others; but it is of the utmost consequence to all. The prices of all sorts of commodities—the profits of the farmer, manufacturer, and merchant—the rent of the landlord—the employment and wages of the labourer—the influence of regulations affecting the freedom of industry—the incidence and effect of taxes and loans—all depend on principles which it belongs to this science to ascertain and elucidate.

Neither is wealth necessary only because it affords the means of subsistence: without it we should never be able to cultivate and improve our higher and nobler faculties. Where wealth has not been amassed, individuals, constantly occupied in providing for their immediate wants, have no time left for the culture of their minds; so that their views, sentiments, and feelings, become alike contracted, selfish, and illiberal. The possession of a decent competence, or the power to indulge in other pursuits than those which directly tend to satisfy our animal wants and desires, is necessary to soften the selfish passions; to improve the moral and intellectual character; and to ensure any considerable proficiency in liberal studies and pursuits. And hence, the acquisition of wealth is not desirable merely as the means of procuring immediate and direct gratifications, but is indispensably necessary to the advancement of society in civilisation and refinement. Without the tranquillity and leisure afforded by the possession of accumulated wealth, those speculative and elegant studies which expand and enlarge our views, purify our taste, and lift us higher in the scale of being, can never be successfully prosecuted. Barbarism and refinement depend far more on the amount of their wealth than on any other single circumstance in the condition of a people. It is impossible, indeed, to name a nation, distinguished either in philosophy or the fine arts, that has not been, at the same time, celebrated for its riches. The age of Pericles and Phidias was the flourishing age of Grecian, as the age of Petrarch and Raphael was of Italian commerce. The influence of wealth is, in this respect, almost omnipotent. It raised Venice from the bosom of the deep; and made the desert and sandy islands on which she is built, and the unhealthy swamps of Holland, the favoured abodes of literature, of science, and of art. In our own country its effects have been equally striking. The number and eminence of our philosophers, poets, scholars, and artists, have ever increased proportionally to the increase of the public wealth, or to the means of rewarding and honouring their labours.

The possession of wealth being thus indispensable to individual existence and comfort, and to the advancement of nations in civilisation, it may justly excite our astonishment, that so few efforts have been made to investigate its sources; and that the study of this science is not even yet considered as forming a principal part in a comprehensive system of education. A variety of circumstances might be mentioned, as occasioning its unmerited neglect; but the institution of *domestic slavery* in the ancient world, and the darkness of the period when the plan of education in the universities of modern Europe was first formed, seem to have had the greatest influence.

The citizens of Greece and Rome considered it degrading to engage in those occupations which form the principal business of the inhabitants of modern Europe. Instead of endeavouring to enrich themselves by their own exertions, they trusted to the reluctant labour of slaves, or to subsidies extorted from conquered countries. In some of the Grecian states, the citizens were prohibited from engaging in either manufactures or commerce; and though this prohibition did not exist in Athens and Rome, these employments were, notwithstanding, regarded as unworthy of freemen, and were, in consequence, exercised only by slaves, or by the very dregs of the people. Even Cicero, who had mastered all the philosophy of the ancient world, and raised himself above many of the prejudices of his age and country, does not scruple to affirm, that there can be nothing ingenuous in a workshop; that commerce, when conducted on a small scale, is mean and despicable; and when most extended, barely tolerable—*non admodum vituperanda!** Agriculture, indeed, was treated with more respect. Some of the most distinguished characters in the earlier ages of Roman history had been actively engaged in rural affairs; but, notwithstanding their example, the cultivation of the soil, in the flourishing period of the Republic, and under the Emperors, was most commonly carried on by slaves, belonging to the landlord, and employed on his account. The mass of Roman citizens was either engaged in the military service,† or derived a precarious and dependent subsistence from the supplies of corn furnished by the conquered provinces. In such a state of society the relations subsisting in modern Europe between landlords and tenants, and masters and servants, were nearly unknown; and the ancients

* "Illiberales autem et sordidi questus mercenariorum, omniumque quorum operæ, non quorum artes emuntur. Est enim illis ipsa merces auctoramentum servitutis. Sordidi etiam putandi, qui mercantur à mercatoribus quod statim vendant, *nihil enim proficiunt, nisi admodum mentiantur!* Opificesque omnes in sordidâ arte versantur, *nec enim quidquam ingenuum potest habere officina.* * * * Mercatura autem, si tenuis est, sordida putanda est; sin autem magna et copiosa, multa undique apportans, multisque sine vanitate impertiens, non est admodum vituperanda."—*De Officiis*, lib. i. sect. 42.

† "Rei militaris virtus præstat cæteris omnibus; hæc populo Romano, hæc huic urbi æternam gloriam peperit."—Cicero *pro Murenâ.*

were, in consequence, entire strangers to those interesting and important questions arising out of the rise and fall of rents and wages, which form so important a branch of economical science. The spirit of the philosophy of antiquity was also extremely unfavourable to the cultivation of Political Economy. The luxurious or more refined mode of living of the rich was regarded by the ancient moralists as an evil of the first magnitude.* They considered it as subversive of those warlike virtues which were the principal objects of their admiration; and they, therefore, denounced the passion for accumulating wealth as fraught with the most injurious consequences. It was impossible that this science could become an object of attention to minds imbued with such prejudices; or that it could be studied by those who contemned its objects, and vilified the labour by which wealth is produced.

At the establishment of our universities, the clergy being almost the exclusive possessors of the little knowledge then in existence, it was natural that their peculiar feelings and pursuits should have a marked influence on the plans of education they were employed to frame. Grammar, rhetoric, logic, school divinity, and civil law, comprised the whole course of study. To have

* "Paulatim," says Tacitus, speaking of the effects of the increasing wealth of the Romans, "discessum ad delinamenta vietorum, balnea, et conviviorum elegantiam, *idque apud imperitos humanitas vocatur.*"—Annal. lib. ii.

appointed professors to explain the principles of commerce, and the means by which labour might be rendered most effective, would have been considered as at once superfluous and degrading to the dignity of science. The ancient prejudices against commerce, manufactures, and luxury, retained a powerful influence in the middle ages. None then possessed any clear ideas as to the true sources of national wealth, happiness, and prosperity. The intercourse among states was extremely limited, and was maintained rather by marauding incursions and piratical expeditions in search of plunder, than by a commerce founded on the gratification of real and reciprocal wants.

These circumstances sufficiently account for the late rise of the science, and the little attention paid to it down to a very recent period. And since it has become an object of more general attention and inquiry, the differences which have subsisted among the most eminent of its professors have proved exceedingly unfavourable to its progress, and have generated a disposition to distrust its best-established conclusions.

It is clear, however, that those who distrust the conclusions of Political Economy, because of the variety of systems that have been advanced to explain the phenomena about which it is conversant, might on the same ground distrust the conclusions of almost every other science. The discrepancy between the various systems that have successively been sanctioned by the ablest physicians, chemists, natural philosophers, and moralists, is quite as great as the discrepancy between those advanced by the ablest economists. But who would therefore conclude, that medicine, chemistry, natural philosophy, and morals, rest on no solid foundation, or that they are incapable of presenting us with a system of well-established and consentaneous truths? We do not refuse our assent to the demonstrations of Newton and Laplace, because they are subversive of the hypotheses of Ptolemy, Tycho Brahé, and Descartes; and why should we refuse our assent to the demonstrations of Smith and Ricardo, because they have subverted the false theories that were previously advanced respecting the sources and the distribution of wealth? Political Economy has not been exempted from the fate common to the other sciences. None of them has been instantaneously carried to perfection; more or less of error has always insinuated itself into the speculations of their earliest cultivators. But the errors with which this science was formerly infected are now fast disappearing; and a very few observations will suffice to shew, that it really admits of as much certainty in its conclusions as any science founded on *fact and experiment* can possibly do.

The principles on which the production and

accumulation of wealth and the progress of civilisation depend, are not the offspring of legislative enactments. Man must exert himself to produce wealth, because he cannot exist without it; and the desire implanted in the breast of every individual, of rising in the world and improving his condition, impels him to save and accumulate. The principles which form the basis of this science make, therefore, a part of the original constitution of man, and of the physical world; and their operation may, like that of the mechanical principles, be traced by the aid of observation and analysis. There is, however, a material distinction between the physical and the moral and political sciences. The conclusions of the former apply in *every* case, while those of the latter apply only in the *majority* of cases. The principles which determine the production and accumulation of wealth are inherent in our nature, and exert a powerful, but not always the *same*, degree of influence over the conduct of every individual; and the theorist must, therefore, satisfy himself with framing rules to explain their operation in the majority of instances, leaving it to the sagacity of the observer to modify them so as to suit individual cases. Thus, it is an admitted principle in Morals, as well as Political Economy, that by far the largest portion of mankind have a much clearer view of what is conducive to their own interests, than it is possible for any other man or select number of men to have; and, consequently, that it is sound policy to allow each individual to follow the bent of his inclination, and to engage in any branch of industry he may think proper. This is the general theorem; and it is one which is established on the most comprehensive experience. It is not, however, like the laws which regulate the motions of the planetary system,—it will hold in nineteen out of twenty instances, but the twentieth may be an exception. But it is not required of the economist, that his theories should quadrate with the peculiar biasses of particular persons. His conclusions are drawn from observing the principles which are found to determine the conduct of mankind, as presented on the large scale of nations and empires. He has to deal with man in the aggregate—with states, and not with families—with the passions and propensities which actuate the great bulk of the human race, and not with those which are occasionally found to influence a solitary individual.

It should always be kept in view, that it is never any part of the business of the economist to inquire into the means by which the fortunes of individuals have been increased or diminished, except to ascertain their general operation and effect. The *public interests* should always form the exclusive objects of his attention. He is not to frame systems, and devise schemes, for increasing the wealth and enjoyments of particular classes;

but to apply himself to discover the sources of *national wealth* and *universal prosperity*, and the means by which they may be rendered most productive.

Nothing, indeed, is more common than to hear it objected to some of the best-established truths in political and economical science, that they are at variance with such and such facts, and that, therefore, they must be rejected. But it is certain that these objections most frequently originate in an entire misapprehension of the nature of the science. It would be easy to produce a thousand instances of individuals who have been enriched by monopolies, as they are sometimes by robbery and plunder; though it would be not a little rash thence to conclude, without further inquiry, that the community can be enriched by such means! This, however, is the single consideration to which the economist has to attend. The question never is, whether a greater or smaller number of persons may be enriched by the adoption of a particular measure, or by a particular institution, but whether its tendency be to enrich *the public*. Admitting that monopolies and restrictive regulations frequently enable individuals to accumulate ample fortunes, instead of this being, as is often contended, any proof of their real advantageousness, it is quite the reverse. It has been demonstrated again and again, that if monopolies and exclusive privileges enrich the *few*, they must, to the same extent, impoverish the *many;* and are, therefore, as destructive of that NATIONAL WEALTH, to promote which ought to be the principal object of every institution, as they are of the freedom of industry.

To arrive at a well-founded conclusion in this science, it is not, therefore, enough to observe results in particular cases, or as they affect particular individuals ; we must further inquire whether these results are *constant* and *universally applicable*—whether the same circumstances which have given rise to them in one instance, would in every instance, and in every state of society, be productive of the same or similar results.—A theory which is inconsistent with a *uniform* and *constant* fact must be erroneous ; but the observation of a particular result at variance with our customary experience, especially if we have not had the means of discriminating the circumstances attending it, ought not to induce us hastily to modify or reject a principle which accounts satisfactorily for the greater number of appearances.

The example of the few arbitrary princes who have been equitable, humane, and generous, is not enough to overthrow the principle which teaches that it is the nature of irresponsible power to debauch and vitiate its possessors—to render them haughty, cruel, and suspicious : nor is the example of those who, attentive only to present enjoyment, and careless of the future, lavish their fortunes in boisterous dissipation or vain expense, sufficient to invalidate the conclusion, that the passion for accumulation is infinitely stronger and more universally operative than the passion for expense. Had this not been the case, mankind could never have emerged from the condition of savages. The multiplied and stupendous improvements made in different ages and nations—the forests that have been cut down—the marshes and lakes that have been drained and subjected to cultivation—the harbours, roads, and bridges, that have been constructed—the cities and edifices that have been raised—are *all* consequences of a saving of income; and establish, in despite of a thousand particular instances of prodigality, the vast ascendency and superior force of the accumulating principle.

It is from the want of attention to these considerations that much of the error and misapprehension with which the science has been infected, has arisen. Almost all the absurd theories and opinions that have successively appeared have been supported by an appeal to facts. But a knowledge of facts, without a knowledge of their mutual relation—without being able to shew why the one is a cause and the other an effect—is, to use the illustration of M. Say, really no better than the indigested erudition of an almanack-maker, and can afford no means of judging of the truth or falsehood of a principle.

Neither should it be forgotten, that the alleged facts so frequently brought forward to shew the fallacy of general principles, are, in most cases, so carelessly observed, and the circumstances under which they have taken place so indistinctly defined, as to be altogether unworthy of attention. To observe accurately, requires a degree of intelligence and acuteness, a freedom from prejudice, and a patience of investigation, belonging to a few only. "There is," to use the words of the celebrated Dr. Cullen, "a variety of circumstances tending to vitiate the statements dignified with the name of experience. The simplest narrative of a case almost always involves some theories. It has been supposed that a statement is more likely to consist of unsophisticated facts, when reported by a person of no education; but it will be found an invariable rule, that the lower you descend in the medical profession, the more hypothetical are the prevailing notions. Again, how seldom is it possible for any case, however minutely related, to include all the circumstances with which the event was connected! Indeed, in what is commonly called experience, we have only a rule transferred from a case imperfectly known, to one of which we are equally ignorant. Hence, that most fertile source of error, the applying deductions drawn from the result of one case to another case, the circumstances of which are not precisely similar. *Without principles deduced from* *analytical reasoning, experience is a useless and a blind guide.*"*

Every one who has had occasion to compare the discordant statements of the mass of common observers, with respect to the practical bearing and real operation of any measure affecting the public economy, must be convinced that Dr. Cullen's reasoning is still more applicable to political and economical science than to medicine. Circumstances which altogether escape the notice of ordinary observers, often exercise the most powerful influence over national prosperity; and those again which strike them as being most important, are often comparatively insignificant. The condition of nations, too, is affected by so many circumstances, that without the greatest skill and caution, joined to a searching and refined analysis, and a familiar command of scientific principles, it is in most cases quite impossible to discriminate between cause and effect, and to avoid ascribing results to one set of causes that have been occasioned by another set. No wonder, therefore, when such is the difficulty of observing, that "the number of false facts afloat in the world, should infinitely exceed that of the false theories."† And after all, however carefully an *isolated* fact may be observed, still, for the reasons already stated, it can never form a

* Cullen's MS. Lectures. † A remark of Dr. Cullen.

foundation for a theorem either in the moral or political sciences. Those, indeed, who bring forward theories resting on so narrow a basis, are almost invariably *empirics*, whose vanity or interest prompts them to set up conclusions drawn from their own limited range of observation, in opposition to those that have been sanctioned by the general experience of mankind.

But although we are not to reject a received principle because of the apparent opposition of a few results, with the particular circumstances of which we are unacquainted, we should place no confidence in its solidity except when it has been deduced from a very comprehensive and careful induction. The economist will not arrive at a true knowledge of the laws regulating the production, accumulation, distribution, and consumption of wealth, unless he draw his materials from a very wide surface. He should study man in every different situation — he should have recourse to the history of society, arts, commerce, and civilisation — to the works of legislators, philosophers, and travellers — to every thing, in short, that can throw light on the causes which accelerate or retard the progress of nations: he should mark the changes which have taken place in the fortunes and condition of the human race in different regions and ages of the world: he should trace the rise, progress, and decline of industry: and, above all, he should carefully analyse and compare the effects of different institutions and regulations, and discriminate the various circumstances wherein an advancing and declining society differ from each other. These investigations, by disclosing the real causes of national opulence and refinement, and of poverty and degradation, furnish the economist with the means of giving a satisfactory solution of all the important problems in the science of wealth; and of devising a scheme of public administration calculated to ensure the continued advancement of the society.

Such inquiries cannot fail to excite the deepest interest in every ingenuous mind. The laws by which the motions of the celestial bodies are regulated, and over which man cannot exercise the smallest influence, are yet universally allowed to be noble and rational objects of study. But the laws which regulate the movements of human society—which cause one people to advance in opulence and refinement, at the same time that another is sinking into the abyss of poverty and barbarism—have an infinitely stronger claim on our attention; both because they relate to objects which exercise a direct influence over human happiness, and because their effects may be, and in fact are, continually modified by human interference. National prosperity does not depend nearly so much on advantageous situation, salubrity of climate, or fertility of soil, as on the adoption of measures fitted to excite the inventive powers of genius, and to give perseverance and activity to industry. The establishment of a wise system of public economy can compensate for every other deficiency: it can render regions naturally inhospitable, barren, and unproductive, the comfortable abodes of an elegant and refined, a crowded and wealthy population: but where it is wanting, the best gifts of nature are of no value; and countries possessed of the greatest capacities of improvement, and abounding in all the materials necessary for the production of wealth, with difficulty furnish a miserable subsistence to hordes distinguished only by their ignorance, barbarism, and wretchedness.

Those who reflect on the variety and extent of knowledge required for the construction of a sound theory of Political Economy, will cease to feel any surprise at the errors into which economists have been betrayed, or at the discrepancy of the opinions that are still entertained on some important points. Political Economy is of very recent origin. Though various treatises of considerable merit had previously appeared on some of its detached parts, it was not treated as a whole, or in a scientific manner, until about the middle of last century. This circumstance is of itself enough to account for the number of erroneous systems that have since appeared. Instead of deducing their general conclusions from a comparison of particular facts, and a careful examination of the phenomena attending the operation of different principles, and of the same principles under different circumstances, the first cultivators of almost every branch of science have begun by framing their theories on a very narrow and insecure basis. Nor is it really in their power to go to work differently. Observations are scarcely ever made, or particulars noted, for their own sakes. It is not until they begin to be sought after, as furnishing the only test by which to ascertain the truth or falsehood of some popular theory, that they are made in sufficient numbers, and with sufficient accuracy. It is, in the peculiar phraseology of this science, the effectual demand of the theorist that occasions the production of the facts or raw materials he is afterwards to work into a system. The history of the science strikingly exemplifies the truth of this remark. Being, as already observed, entirely unknown to the ancients, and but little attended to by our ancestors down to a comparatively late period, most of those circumstances which would have enabled us to judge of the wealth and civilisation of the most celebrated states of antiquity, and of Europe during the middle ages, have either been thought unworthy of notice by the historian, or have been very imperfectly and carelessly detailed. Those, therefore, who first began to trace its general principles, had but a comparatively limited and scanty experience on which to build their conclusions. Nor did they even avail themselves of the few historical facts with which they might easily have become acquainted; but, for the most part, confined their attention to such as happened to come within the sphere of their own observation.

The once prevalent opinion, that wealth consists exclusively of Gold and Silver, naturally grew out of the circumstance of the money of all civilised countries consisting almost entirely of these metals. Having been used both as standards by which to measure the value of different commodities, and as the equivalents for which they were most frequently exchanged, they acquired an artificial importance, not in the estimation of the vulgar only, but in that of persons of the greatest discernment. The simple and decisive consideration, that to buy and sell is really nothing more than to barter one commodity for another—to exchange a certain quantity of corn or cloth, for example, for a certain quantity of gold or silver, and *vice versâ*—was entirely overlooked. The attention was gradually transferred from the *money's worth* to the money itself; and the wealth of individuals and of states was measured, not by the abundance of their disposable products—by the quantity and value of the commodities with which they could afford to purchase the precious metals—but by the quantity of these metals actually in their possession. And hence the policy, as obvious as it was universal, of attempting to increase the amount of national wealth by forbidding the exportation of gold and silver, and encouraging their importation.

It appears from a passage in Cicero, that the exportation of the precious metals from Rome had been frequently prohibited during the existence of the Republic;* and this prohibition was repeatedly renewed, though to very little purpose, by the Emperors.† Neither, perhaps, has there been a state in modern Europe which has not expressly forbid the exportation of gold and silver. It is said to have been interdicted by the law of England previously to the Conquest; and reiterated statutes were subsequently passed to the same effect; one of which (3d Henry VIII. cap. 1), enacted so late as 1512, declared, that all persons carrying over sea any coins, plate, jewels, &c. should, on detection, forfeit double their value.

The extraordinary extension of commerce

* "*Exportari aurum non oportere, cum sæpe antea senatus, tum me consule, gravissime judicavit.*"—Orat. pro L. Flacco, cap. 28.

† Pliny, when enumerating the silks, spices, and other Eastern products imported into Italy, says, "*Minimâque computatione millies centena millia sestertiûm annis omnibus, India et Seres, peninsulaque illa (Arabia) imperio nostro adimunt. Tanto nobis deliciæ et fœminæ constant.*"—Hist. Nat. lib. xii. cap. 18.

during the fifteenth and sixteenth centuries occasioned the substitution of a more refined and complex system for increasing the supply of the precious metals, in place of the coarse and vulgar one that had previously obtained. The establishment of a direct intercourse with India by the Cape of Good Hope, seems to have had the greatest influence in effecting this change. The precious metals have always been among the most advantageous articles of export to the East: and, notwithstanding the old and deeply-rooted prejudices against their exportation, the East India Company obtained, when first instituted, in 1600, leave annually to export foreign coins, or bullion, of the value of 30,000*l.*; on condition, however, of their importing, within six months after the termination of every voyage, except the first, as much gold and silver as they exported. But the enemies of the Company contended, that this condition was not complied with; and that it was besides *contrary to all principle*, and highly injurious to the public interests, to permit gold and silver to be sent out of the kingdom. The merchants, and others interested in the support of the Company, could not controvert the reasonings of their opponents, without openly impugning the ancient policy of absolutely preventing the exportation of the precious metals. They did not, indeed, venture to contend, even if it really occurred to them, that the exportation of bullion to India was advantageous, on the ground that the commodities purchased by it were of greater value in England; but they contended, that its exportation was advantageous, because the commodities brought from India were chiefly re-exported to other countries, from which a greater amount of bullion was obtained than had been originally required for their payment in the East. Mr. Thomas Mun, the ablest of the Company's advocates, ingeniously compares the operations of the merchant in conducting a trade carried on by the exportation of gold and silver, to the seed-time and harvest of agriculture. "If we only behold," says he, "the actions of the husbandman in the seed-time, when he casteth away much good corn into the ground, we shall account him rather a madman than a husbandman. But when we consider his labours in the harvest, which is the end of his endeavours, we shall find the worth and plentiful increase of his actions."*

Such was the origin of what has been called the MERCANTILE SYSTEM: and, when compared with the previous prejudice—for it hardly de-

* "Treasure by Foreign Trade," orig. ed. p. 50.—This work was published in 1664, a considerable period after Mr. Mun's death. Most probably it had been written about 1635 or 1640. Mun had previously advanced the same doctrines, nearly in the same words, in his Defence of the East India Trade, originally published in 1621, and in a petition drawn up by him, and presented by the East India Company to Parliament, in 1628.

serves the name of system—which wholly interdicted the exportation of gold and silver, it must be allowed that its adoption was a considerable step in the progress to sounder opinions. The supporters of the mercantile system, like their predecessors, held that gold and silver alone constituted wealth; but they thought that sound policy dictated the propriety of allowing their exportation to foreigners, provided the commodities imported in their stead, or a portion of them, were afterwards sold to other foreigners for more bullion than had been sent abroad to purchase them; or provided the importation of the foreign commodities caused the exportation of so much more native produce than would otherwise have been exported, as would more than equal their cost. These opinions necessarily led to the celebrated doctrine of the *Balance of Trade*. It was obvious that the precious metals could not be imported into countries destitute of mines, except in return for exported commodities; and the grand object of the supporters of the mercantile system being the monopoly of the largest possible supply of the precious metals, they adopted various complex schemes for encouraging the exportation, and restraining the importation of almost all products, except gold and silver, that were not intended for future exportation. When the value of the exports exceeded that of the imports, the *excess* was denominated a *favourable balance;* and was regarded as forming, at one and the same time, the sole cause and measure of the progress of countries in the career of wealth: for, it was taken for granted, that the equivalent of the balance must inevitably be brought home in gold and silver, or in those metals which were then believed to be the only real riches individuals or nations could possess.

These principles and conclusions, though absolutely false and erroneous, afford a tolerable explanation of a few very obvious phenomena; and what did more to recommend them, they were in perfect unison with the popular prejudices on the subject. The merchants and practical men, who founded the mercantile system, did not consider it necessary to subject the principles they assumed to any very refined analysis or examination. But reckoning them sufficiently established by the common consent and agreement of mankind, they applied themselves to the discussion of the practical measures calculated to give them the greatest efficacy.

"Although a kingdom," says Mr. Mun, "may be enriched by gifts received, or by purchase taken, from some other nations; yet these are things uncertain, and of small consideration when they happen. The ordinary means, therefore, to increase our wealth and treasure, is by foreign trade; wherein we must ever observe this rule—*to sell more to strangers yearly than we consume of* *theirs in value.* For, suppose, that when this kingdom is plentifully served with cloth, lead, tin, iron, fish, and other native commodities, we do yearly export the overplus to foreign countries to the value of 2,200,000*l.*, by which means we are enabled, beyond the seas, to buy and bring in foreign wares for our use and consumption to the value of 2,000,000*l.*: by this order duly kept in our trading, we may rest assured that the kingdom shall be enriched yearly 200,000*l.*, which must be brought to us as so much treasure; because that part of our stock which is not returned to us in wares must necessarily be brought home in treasure."*

The gain on foreign commerce is here supposed to consist wholly of the gold and silver which, it is assumed, must be brought home in payment of the excess of exported products. Mr. Mun lays no stress whatever on the circumstance of foreign commerce reducing the price of almost every description of commodities, by giving birth to the *territorial division of labour* amongst different countries; and of its also enabling each particular people to obtain an infinite variety of useful and agreeable products, of which they would, otherwise, have been wholly ignorant. We are desired to consider all this accession of wealth—all the vast additions made by com-

* "Treasure by Foreign Trade," p. 11.

merce to the motives which stimulate, and the comforts and enjoyments which reward the labour of the industrious, as *nothing*,—and to fix our attention exclusively on the balance of 200,000*l.* of gold and silver! This is much the same as if we were desired to estimate the comfort and advantage derived from a suit of clothes, by the number and glare of the metal buttons by which they are fastened. And yet Mr. Mun's rule for estimating the advantageousness of foreign commerce was long regarded, by most merchants, writers, and practical statesmen, as infallible; and such is the inveteracy of ancient prejudices, that we are still, every now and then, congratulated on the excess of our exports over our imports!

There were many circumstances, however, besides the erroneous notions respecting the precious metals, which led to the enactment of regulations restricting the freedom of industry, and secured the ascendency of the mercantile system. The feudal governments established in the countries that had formed the western division of the Roman Empire, early sunk into a state of confusion and anarchy. The princes, unable of themselves to restrain the usurpations of the greater barons, or to control their violence, endeavoured to strengthen their influence and consolidate their power, by attaching the inhabitants of cities and towns to their interests. For this purpose, they granted them charters, enfranchising the inhabitants, abolishing every existing mark of servitude, and forming them into corporations, or bodies politic, governed by a council and magistrates of their own selection. The order and good government that were, in consequence, established in the cities and towns, and the security of property enjoyed by their inhabitants, while the rest of the country was a prey to rapine and disorder, stimulated their industry, and gave them a decided superiority over the cultivators of the soil. It was from them that the princes derived the greater part of their supplies of money; and it was by their co-operation that they were enabled to subdue the pride and independence of the barons. But the citizens did not render this continued assistance to their sovereigns merely by way of compensation for the original gift of their charters. They were continually soliciting new privileges. And it was not to be expected that those whom they had laid under so many obligations, and who justly regarded them as forming the most industrious and deserving portion of their subjects, should feel any great disinclination to gratify their wishes. They either obtained or usurped the privilege of preventing any individual from exercising any branch of industry till he had obtained leave from them. That they might obtain cheap provisions, and be able to carry on their industry under the most favourable circumstances, the exportation of corn, and of the raw materials of their manufactures, was strictly prohibited; at the same time that heavy duties and absolute prohibitions prevented the importation of manufactured articles from abroad, and secured the monopoly of the home-market to the native manufacturers. These, together with various subordinate regulations intended to force the importation of the raw materials required in manufactures, and the exportation of manufactured goods, form the principal features of the system of public economy adopted, in the view of encouraging domestic industry, in every country of Europe, in the fourteenth, fifteenth, sixteenth, and seventeenth centuries. The freedom of intercourse, that had been partially recognised by their ancient laws, was almost totally destroyed; and the spirit of invention was restrained still more, perhaps, by vicious systems of legislation than by the real difficulties that opposed its development. To such an excess was the protective system at one time carried, that it was not uncommon to forbid the use of new manufactures, even when produced at home, lest they might interfere with those already established. So late as 1721, the wearing of calicoes was prohibited, for the avowed purpose of encouraging the woollen and silk manufactures, by the imposition of a penalty of 20*l.* on the seller, and of 5*l.* on the wearer. In 1736 this law was repealed as to British calicoes, provided, however, that the warp were of linen yarn. It is almost superfluous to add, that had these absurd statutes not been wholly repealed, the cotton manufacture could not have made any progress amongst us.

But the exclusion of all competition, and the monopoly of the home-market, were not enough to satisfy the manufacturers and merchants. Having obtained all the advantage they could from the public, they next attempted to prey on each other. Such of them as possessed most influence procured the privilege of carrying on particular branches of industry to the exclusion of every one else. This abuse was carried to a most oppressive height in the reign of Elizabeth, who granted an infinite number of new patents: and the grievance became at length so insupportable as to induce all classes to join in petitioning for its abolition; which, after much opposition on the part of the Crown, by whom the power of erecting monopolies was considered a very valuable branch of the prerogative, was effected by an act passed in 1624. This act has been productive of the greatest advantage; but it touched none of the fundamental principles of the mercantile or manufacturing system; and the privileges of all bodies-corporate were exempted from its operation.

In France the interests of the manufacturers were warmly espoused by the celebrated M. Colbert, minister of finance during the most splendid period of the reign of Louis XIV.; and the year

1664, when the famous tariff, compiled under his direction, was promulgated, has been sometimes considered, by the continental writers, though, as has been seen, erroneously, as the era of the mercantile system.*

The restrictions in favour of the manufacturers were all zealously supported by the advocates of the mercantile system and the balance of trade. The facilities given to the exportation of goods manufactured at home, and the obstacles thrown in the way of importation from abroad, seemed peculiarly well fitted for making the exports exceed the imports, and procuring a favourable balance. Instead, therefore, of regarding these regulations as the offspring of a selfish, monopolising spirit, they looked on them as having been dictated by the soundest policy. The interests of the manufacturers and merchants were thus supposed to be identified, and were held to be the same with those of the public. The acquisition of a favourable balance of payments was the grand *object* in view; and heavy duties and restrictions on importation, and bounties and premiums on exportation, were the *means* by which this object was to be attained. It cannot excite our surprise, that a system having so many popular prejudices in its favour, and which afforded a plausible apology for the exclusive privileges

* See Mengotti, "Dissertazione sul Colbertismo," cap. xi.

enjoyed by many numerous and powerful classes, should have early attained, or that it should still preserve, notwithstanding the overthrow of its principles, much practical influence.*

"It is no exaggeration to affirm," says a late foreign writer, "that there are very few political errors which have produced more mischief than the mercantile system. Armed with power, it has commanded and forbid, where it should only have *protected*. The regulating mania which it has inspired has tormented industry in a thousand ways, to force it from its natural channels. It has made each particular nation regard the welfare of its neighbours as incompatible with its own; hence the reciprocal desire of injuring and impoverishing each other; and hence that spirit of commercial rivalry which has been the immediate or remote cause of the greater number of modern wars. This system has stimulated nations to employ force or cunning to extort commercial treaties, productive of no real advantage to themselves, from the weakness or ignorance of others. It has formed colonies, that the mother country might enjoy the monopoly of their trade, and force them to resort only to her markets. In short, where this system has been productive of

* Melon and Forbonnais in France,—Genovesi in Italy,—Mun, Sir Josiah Child, Dr. Davenant, the authors of the British Merchant, and Sir James Steuart, in England,—are the ablest writers who have espoused, some with more, and some with fewer exceptions, the leading principles of the mercantile system.

the least injury, it has retarded the progress of national prosperity; every where else it has deluged the earth with blood, and has depopulated and ruined some of those countries whose power and opulence it was supposed it would carry to the highest pitch."*

The shock given to previous prejudices and systems by those great discoveries and events, which will for ever distinguish the fifteenth and sixteenth centuries, and the greater attention which the progress of civilisation and industry naturally drew to the sources of national power and opulence, prepared the way for the downfal of the mercantile system. The advocates of the East India Company, whose interests had first prompted them to question the prevailing doctrines as to the exportation of bullion, gradually assumed a higher tone; and at length boldly contended that bullion was nothing but a commodity, and that it was for the public advantage that its exportation should be rendered perfectly free. Similar opinions were soon after avowed by others. Many eminent merchants began to look with suspicion on several of the received maxims; and acquired more correct and comprehensive views in respect of the just principles of commercial intercourse. The new ideas ultimately made their way into the House of Commons; and in 1663, the statutes pro-

* Storch, "Cours d'Economie Politique," tom. i. p. 102. Paris edition.

hibiting the exportation of *foreign* coin and bullion were repealed; full liberty being given, not only to the East India Company, but also to private traders, to export them in unlimited quantities.

In addition to the controversy about the East India trade, the discussions respecting the foundation of colonies in America and the West Indies, the establishment of a compulsory provision for the support of the poor, the prohibition against exporting wool and importing cattle from Ireland, &c. attracted, in the seventeenth century, an extraordinary portion of the public attention to questions connected with the domestic policy of the country. In its course, a more than usual number of tracts were published on commercial and economical subjects. And although the authors of the greater number were strongly tinctured with the prevailing spirit of the age, it cannot be denied, that several amongst them have emancipated themselves from its influence, and have an unquestionable right to be regarded as the founders of the modern theory of commerce — as the earliest expositors of those sound and liberal doctrines, by which it has been shewn, that the prosperity of states can never be promoted by restrictive regulations, or by the depression of their neighbours — that the genuine spirit of commerce is inconsistent with the dark, selfish, and shallow policy of monopoly—

and that the *self-interest* of mankind, not less than their duty, requires them to live in peace, and to cultivate a fair and friendly intercourse with each other.

Besides Mr. Mun, Sir Josiah Child,* (whose work, though founded on the principles of the mercantile system, contains many sound and liberal views), Sir William Petty,† and Sir Dudley North, are the most distinguished of the economical writers of the seventeenth century. The latter not only rose above the established prejudices of the time, but had sagacity enough to detect the more refined and less obvious errors that were newly coming into fashion. His tract, entitled, " Discourses on Trade, principally directed to the Cases of Interest, Coinage, Clipping, and Increase of Money," published in 1691, contains a far more able statement of the true principles of commerce than any that had then appeared. He is throughout the intelligent and consistent advocate of commercial freedom. He is not, like the most eminent of his predecessors, well informed on one subject, and erroneous on another. His system is consentaneous in its parts, and complete. He shews, that in commercial matters, nations have the same

* " A New Discourse of Trade," first published in 1668; but greatly enlarged and improved in the second edition, published in 1690.

† " Quantulumcunque," published in 1682; " Political Anatomy of Ireland," published in 1672; and other works.

interests as individuals; and forcibly exposes the absurdity of supposing, that any trade which is advantageous to the merchant can be injurious to the public. His opinions respecting the imposition of a seignorage on the coinage of money, and the expediency of sumptuary laws, then very popular, are equally enlightened.

I subjoin, from the preface to this tract, an abstract of the general propositions maintained in it: —

" *That the world as to trade is but as one nation or people, and therein nations are as persons.*

" That the loss of a trade with one nation is not that only, separately considered, but so much of the trade of the world rescinded and lost, for all is combined together.

" *That there can be no trade unprofitable to the public; for if any prove so, men leave it off; and wherever the traders thrive, the public, of which they are a part, thrive also.*

" That to force men to deal in any prescribed manner may profit such as happen to serve them; but the public gains not, because *it is taken from one subject to give to another.*

" That no laws can set prices in trade, the rates of which must and will make themselves. But when such laws do happen to lay any hold, it is so much impediment to trade, and therefore prejudicial.

" That money is a merchandise, whereof there

may be a glut, as well as a scarcity, and that even to an inconvenience.

"That a people cannot want money to serve the ordinary dealing, and more than enough they will not have.

"That no man will be the richer for the making much money, nor have any part of it, but as he buys it for an equivalent price.

"That the free coynage is a perpetual motion found out, whereby to melt and coyn without ceasing, and so to feed goldsmiths and coyners at the public charge.

"That debasing the coyn is defrauding one another, and to the public there is no sort of advantage from it; for that admits no character, or value, but intrinsick.

"That the sinking by alloy or weight is all one.

"That exchange and ready money are the same, nothing but carriage and re-carriage being saved.

"That money exported in trade is an increase to the wealth of the nation; but spent in war, and payments abroad, is so much impoverishment.

"In short, that *all favour to one trade, or interest, is an abuse, and cuts so much of profit from the public.*"

Unluckily, this admirable tract never obtained any considerable circulation. There is good reason, indeed, for supposing that it was designedly suppressed.* At all events, it speedily became excessively scarce; and I am not aware that it has ever been referred to by any subsequent writer on commerce.

The same enlarged and liberal views that had found so able a supporter in Sir Dudley North, were afterwards advocated to a greater or less extent by Locke,† the anonymous author of a pamphlet on the East India Trade,‡ Vanderlint,|| Sir Matthew Decker,§ Hume,¶ and Harris.** But their efforts were ineffectual to the subversion of the mercantile system. Their notions respecting the nature of wealth were confused and contradictory; and as they neither attempted to investigate its sources, nor to trace the causes of national opulence, their arguments in favour of a

* See the Honourable Roger North's "Life of his Brother, the Honourable Sir Dudley North," p. 179.

† "Considerations on the Lowering of Interest and Raising the Value of Money," 1691; and "Further Considerations on Raising the Value of Money," 1695.

‡ "Considerations on the East India Trade," 1701. This is a very remarkable pamphlet. The author has successfully refuted the various arguments advanced in justification of the prohibition against importing East Indian manufactured goods; and has given a very striking illustration of the effects of the division of labour.

|| "Money answers all Things," 1734.

§ "Essay on the Causes of the Decline of Foreign Trade," 1744.

¶ "Political Essays," 1752.

** "Essay on Money and Coins," 1757.

liberal system of commerce had somewhat of an empirical aspect, and failed of making that impression which is always made by reasonings logically deduced from well-established principles, and shewn to be consistent with experience. The opinions entertained by Mr. Locke, as to the paramount influence of labour in the production of wealth, were at once original and correct; but he did not prosecute his investigations in the view of elucidating the principles of the science, and made no reference to them in his subsequent writings. And though Mr. Harris adopted Mr. Locke's views, and deduced from them some practical inferences of great importance, his general principles are merely introduced by way of preface to his Treatise on Money; and are not explained at any length, or in that logical and systematic manner necessary in scientific investigations.

But, what the English writers had left undone, was now attempted by a French philosopher, equally distinguished for the subtlety and originality of his understanding, and the integrity and simplicity of his character. This was the celebrated M. Quesnay, a physician attached to the court of Louis XV. He has the merit of being the first who attempted to investigate and analyse the sources of wealth, with the intention of ascertaining the fundamental principles of Political Economy; and who thus gave it a systematic form, and raised it to the rank of a science. His father was a small proprietor; and, having been educated in the country, Quesnay was naturally inclined to regard agriculture with more than ordinary partiality. At an early period of his life he had been struck with its depressed state in France, and had set himself to discover the causes which had prevented its making that progress which the industry of the inhabitants, the fertility of the soil, and the excellence of the climate, seemed to insure. In the course of this inquiry he speedily discovered that the prevention of the exportation of corn to foreign countries, and the preference given by the regulations of Colbert to manufactures and commerce over agriculture, formed the most powerful obstacles to the progress and improvement of the latter. But Quesnay was not satisfied with exposing the injustice of this preference, and its pernicious consequences. His zeal for the interests of agriculture led him, not merely to place it on the same level with manufactures and commerce, but to raise it above them, by endeavouring to shew that it is the only species of industry which contributed to increase the riches of a nation. Founding on the indisputable fact, that every thing which either ministers to our wants or desires, must be originally derived from the earth, Quesnay assumed as a self-evident truth, and as the basis of his system, that the *earth is the only source of wealth;* and held that labour is altogether incapable of producing any new value, except when employed in agriculture, including under that term fisheries and mines. His observation of the striking effects of the vegetative powers of nature, and his inability to explain the real origin and causes of *rent,* confirmed him in this opinion. The circumstance, that of all who engage in industrious undertakings, none but the cultivators of the soil pay rent for the use of *natural agents,* appeared to him an incontrovertible proof, that agriculture is the only species of industry which yields a nett surplus (*produit net*) over and above the expenses of production. Quesnay allowed that manufacturers and merchants are highly useful; but, as they realise no nett surplus in the shape of rent, he contended that they do not add any greater value to the raw material of the commodities they manufacture, or carry from place to place, than is equivalent to the value of the capital or stock consumed by them during the time they are engaged in these operations. These principles once established, Quesnay proceeded to divide society into three classes; the *first,* or *productive* class, by whose agency all wealth is produced, consists of the farmers and labourers engaged in agriculture, who subsist on a portion of the produce of the land reserved to themselves as the wages of their labour, and as a reasonable profit on their capital: the *second,* or *proprietary* class, consists of those who live on the rent of the land, or on the *nett surplus produce* raised by the cultivators after their necessary expenses have been deducted: and the *third,* or *unproductive* class, consists of manufacturers, merchants, menial servants, &c., whose labour, though exceedingly useful, adds nothing to the national wealth, and who subsist entirely on the wages paid them by the other two classes. It is obvious, supposing this classification made on just principles, that all taxes must fall on the landlords. The third, or unproductive class, have nothing but what they receive from the other two classes; and if any deduction were made from the fair and reasonable profits and wages of the husbandmen, or *productive class,* it would have the effect of paralysing their exertions, and consequently of spreading poverty and misery throughout the land, by drying up the only source of wealth. Hence it necessarily follows, on M. Quesnay's theory, that the entire expenses of government, and the various public burdens, must, howsoever imposed, be ultimately defrayed out of the *produit net,* or rent of the landlords; and consistently with this principle, he proposed that all the existing taxes should be repealed, and that a single tax (*impôt unique*), laid directly on the nett produce, or rent, of the land, should be imposed in their stead.

But, however much impressed with the importance of agriculture over every other species of industry, Quesnay did not solicit for it any exclusive favour or protection. He successfully contended, that the interests of the agriculturists, and of all the other classes, would be best promoted by establishing a system of perfect freedom. "Qu'on maintienne," says he, in one of his general maxims, "l'entière liberté du commerce; *car la police du commerce intérieur et extérieur la plus sure, la plus exacte, la plus profitable à la nation et à l'état, consiste dans* LA PLEINE LIBERTÉ DE LA CONCURRENCE."* Quesnay shewed that it could never be for the interest of the proprietors and cultivators of the soil to fetter or discourage the industry of merchants, artificers, and manufacturers; for the greater the liberty they enjoy, the greater will be their competition, and their services will, in consequence, be rendered so much the cheaper. Neither, on the other hand, can it ever be for the interest of the unproductive classes to harass and oppress the agriculturists, either by preventing the free exportation of their products, or by any sort of restrictive regulations. When the cultivators enjoy the greatest degree of freedom, their industry, and, consequently, their nett *surplus produce*—the only fund from which any accession of national wealth can be derived—will be carried to the greatest possible extent.

* "Physiocratie," première partie, p. 119.

According to this "liberal and generous system,"* the establishment of perfect liberty, perfect security, and perfect justice, is the only, as it is the infallible, means of securing the highest degree of prosperity to all classes.

"On a vu," says the ablest expositor of this system, M. Mercier de la Rivière, "qu'il est de l'essence de l'ordre que l'intérêt particulier d'un seul ne puisse jamais être séparé de l'intérêt commun de tous; nous en trouvons une preuve bien convaincante dans les effets que produit naturellement et necessairement la plénitude de la liberté qui doit régner dans le commerce, pour ne point blesser la propriété. L'intérêt personnel, encouragé par cette grande liberté, presse vivement et perpétuellement chaque homme en particulier de perfectionner, de multiplier les choses dont il est vendeur; de grossir ainsi la masse des jouissances qu'il peut procurer aux autres hommes, afin de grossir, par ce moyen, la masse des jouissances que les autres hommes peuvent lui procurer en échange. *Le monde* alors *va de lui-même;* le désir de jouir, et la liberté de jouir, ne cessant de provoquer la multiplication des productions et l'accroissement de l'industrie, ils impriment à toute la société un mouvement qui devient une tendance perpetuelle vers son meilleur état possible."†

* "Wealth of Nations," vol. iii. p. 134, my edition.

† "L'Ordre Nat. et Essent. des Sociétés Politiques," ii. 444.

As other opportunities will be afforded of examining the principles of this very ingenious theory, it is sufficient at present to remark, that, in assuming agriculture to be the only source of wealth, because the matter of which commodities are formed is originally derived from the earth, M. Quesnay and his followers mistook altogether the nature of production, and really supposed wealth to consist of matter; whereas, in its natural state, matter is very rarely possessed of any immediate or direct utility, and *is invariably destitute of value.* It is only by means of the *labour* required to appropriate matter, and to fit and prepare it for our use, that it acquires exchangeable value, and becomes wealth. Human industry does not produce wealth by making any additions to the matter of our globe; this being a quantity susceptible neither of augmentation nor diminution. Its real and only effect is to produce wealth *by giving utility to matter already in existence;* and it will be afterwards shewn, that the labour employed in manufactures and commerce is to the full as productive of utility, and consequently of wealth, as the labour employed in agriculture. Neither is the cultivation of the soil, as M. Quesnay supposed, the only species of industry which yields a surplus produce after the expenses of production are deducted. When agriculture is most productive, that is, when none but the best of the good soils are cultivated, no rent, or *produit net*, is obtained from the land; and it is only after recourse has been had to poorer soils, and when, consequently, the productive powers of the labour and capital employed in cultivation begin to diminish, that rent begins to appear: so that, instead of being a consequence of the superior productiveness of agricultural industry, rent is really a consequence of its becoming comparatively less productive than others!

The "Economical Table," containing a set of formulæ constructed by M. Quesnay, and intended to exhibit the various phenomena accompanying the production of wealth, and its distribution among the productive, proprietary, and unproductive classes, was published at Versailles, with accompanying illustrations, in 1758; and the novelty and ingenuity of the theory which it expounded, its systematic and scientific shape, and the liberal system of commercial intercourse which it recommended, speedily obtained for it a very high degree of reputation.* It is to be regretted, that the friends and disciples of Quesnay, among whom we have to reckon the Marquis de Mirabeau, Mercier de la Rivière, Dupont de Nemours, Saint Peravy, Turgot, and other distinguished individuals in France, Italy, and Germany, should, in their zeal for his peculiar doctrines, which they enthusias-

* See Appendix, Note A., for some further remarks on the economical theory.

tically exerted themselves to defend and propagate, have exhibited more of the character of partisans, than of (what there is the best reason to think they really were) sincere and honest inquirers after truth. Hence it is that they have always been regarded as a sect, known by the name of *Economists*, or *Physiocrats;* and that their works are characterised by an unusual degree of sameness.*

But, in despite of their defects, there can be no question that the labours of the *Economists* powerfully contributed to accelerate the progress of the science. In reasoning on subjects connected with national wealth, it was now found to be necessary to subject its sources, and the laws which regulate its production and distribution, to a more accurate and searching analysis.

* The following are the principal works published by the French Economists: —

"Tableau Economique, et Maximes Générales du Gouvernement Economique," par François Quesnay. 4to, Versailles, 1758.

"Théorie de l'Impôt," par M. de Mirabeau. 4to and 12mo, 1760.

"La Philosophie Rurale," par M. de Mirabeau. 4to, and 3 tom. 12mo, 1763.

"L'Ordre Naturel et Essentiel des Sociétés Politiques," par Mercier de la Rivière. 4to, and 2 tom. 12mo, 1767.

"Sur l'Origine et Progrès d'une Science Nouvelle," par Dupont de Nemours. 1767.

"La Physiocratie, ou Constitution Naturelle du Gouvernement le plus avantageux au Genre Humain; Recueil des Principaux Ouvrages Economiques de M. Quesnay," rédigé et publié par Dupont de Nemours, deux parties. 1767.

In the course of this examination, it was speedily ascertained that both the mercantile and economical theories were erroneous and defective; and that, to establish the science on a firm foundation, it was necessary to take a much more extensive survey, and to seek for its principles, not in a few partial and distorted facts, or in metaphysical abstractions, but in the connexion and relation subsisting among the various phenomena manifested in the progress of civilisation. The Count di Verri, whose "Meditations on Political Economy" were published in 1771, demonstrated the fallacy of the opinions entertained by the *Economists* respecting the superior productive-

"Lettres d'un Citoyen à un Magistrat, sur les Vingtièmes et les autres Impôts," par l'Abbé Baudeau. 12mo, 1768.

"Mémoire sur les Effets de l'Impôt indirect; qui a remporté le Prix proposé par la Société Royale d'Agriculture de Limoges," (par Saint Peravy). 12mo, 1768.

"Réflexions sur la Formation et la Distribution des Richesses," par Turgot. 8vo, 1771. This is the best of all the works founded on the principles of the *Economists;* and is, in some respects, the best work on the science published previously to the "Wealth of Nations."

The "Journal d'Agriculture," and the "Ephémérides du Citoyen," contain a variety of valuable articles contributed by Quesnay and other leading *Economists.* The "Ephémérides" was begun in 1767, and was dropped in 1775: it was first conducted by the Abbe Baudeau, and then by Dupont.

The reader will find a pretty full account of the life of M. Quesnay, a life which, unlike that of most literary men, abounded in incident and adventure, in the "Supplement to the Encyclopædia Britannica."

ness of the labour employed in agriculture; and shewed that all the operations of industry really consist of *modifications of matter already in existence.** But Verri did not trace the consequences of this important principle; and possessing no clear and definite notions of what constituted wealth, did not attempt to discover the means by which labour might be facilitated. He made some valuable additions to particular branches of the science, and had sufficient acuteness to detect errors in the systems of others; but the task of constructing a better system in their stead required talents of a far higher order.

At length, in 1776, our illustrious countryman, Adam Smith, published the "Wealth of Nations"—a work which has done for Political Economy what the Essay of Locke did for the philosophy of mind. In this work the science was, for the first time, treated in its fullest extent; and the fundamental principles on which the *production* of wealth depends, established beyond the reach of cavil and dispute. In opposition to the

* "*Accostare e seperare* sono gli unici elementi che l' ingegno umano ritrova analizando l' idea della riproduzione; e tanto è riproduzione di valore e di richezza se la terra, l' aria, e l' aqua ne' campi si trasmutino in grano, come se colla mano dell' uomo il gluttine di un insetto si trasmuti in velluto, o vero alcuni pezzetti di metallo si organizzino a formare una ripetizione."—*Meditazioni sulla Economia Politica*, § 3.

Economists, Dr. Smith has shewn that *labour* is the only source of wealth, and that the wish to augment our fortunes and to rise in the world—a wish that comes with us from the womb, and never leaves us till we go into the grave—is the cause of wealth being saved and accumulated: he has shewn that labour is productive of wealth when employed in manufactures and commerce, as well as when it is employed in the cultivation of the land; he has traced the various means by which labour may be rendered most effective; and has given a most admirable analysis and exposition of the prodigious addition made to its powers by its *division* among different individuals and countries, and by the employment of accumulated wealth, or *capital,* in industrious undertakings. He has also shewn, in opposition to the commonly received opinions of the merchants, politicians, and statesmen of his time, that wealth does not consist in the abundance of gold and silver, but in the abundance of the various necessaries, conveniences, and enjoyments of human life; that it is in every case sound policy to leave individuals to pursue their own interest in their own way; that, in prosecuting branches of industry advantageous to themselves, they necessarily prosecute such as are, at the same time, advantageous to the public; and that every regulation intended to force industry into particular channels, or to determine the species of commercial intercourse to be carried on between different parts of the same country, or between distant and independent countries, is impolitic and pernicious—injurious to the rights of individuals—and adverse to the progress of *real* opulence and lasting prosperity.

The fact that the distinct statement of several of the most important of these principles, and that traces of them all, may be found in the works of previous writers, does not detract in any, or but in a very inconsiderable degree, from the real merits of Dr. Smith. In adopting the discoveries of others, he has made them his own; he has demonstrated the truth of principles on which his predecessors had, in most cases, stumbled by chance; has separated them from the errors by which they were encumbered, traced their remote consequences, and pointed out their limitations; has shewn their practical importance and real value, their mutual dependence and relation; and has reduced them into a consistent, harmonious, and beautiful system.

But, however excellent in many respects, still it cannot be denied that there are errors, and those too of no slight importance, in the "Wealth of Nations." Dr. Smith does not say that, in prosecuting such branches of industry as are *most advantageous* to themselves, individuals necessarily prosecute such as are, at the same time, MOST *advantageous to the public*. His leaning to the system of M. Quesnay—a leaning perceptible in every part of his work—made him so far swerve from the sounder principles of his own system, as to admit that the preference shewn by individuals in favour of particular employments is not always a *true test* of their public advantageousness. He considered agriculture, though not the only productive employment, as the most productive of any; the home trade as more productive than a direct foreign trade; and the latter than the carrying trade. It is clear, however, that these distinctions are all fundamentally erroneous. A state being nothing but a collection of individuals, it follows, that whatever is most for their advantage must be most for the advantage of the state; and it is obvious, that the self-interest of those concerned will always prevent them from engaging in manufacturing and commercial undertakings, unless they yield as large profits, and are, consequently, as publicly beneficial, as agriculture. Dr. Smith's opinion with respect to the unproductiveness of all labour not realised in a fixed and vendible commodity, appears, at first sight, to rest on no better foundation than the opinion of the *Economists* as to the unproductiveness of commerce and manufactures; and I flatter myself that its fallacy will be fully established in the sequel of this work. Perhaps, however, the principal defect of the " Wealth of Nations" consists in the erroneous doctrines laid down with respect to the invariable value of corn, and the effect of fluctuations in wages and profits on prices. These have prevented Dr. Smith from acquiring clear and accurate notions respecting the nature and causes of rent, and the laws which govern the rate of profit; and have, in consequence, vitiated the theoretical conclusions in those parts of his work which treat of the distribution of wealth and the principles of taxation.

But, after every allowance has been made for these defects, enough still remains to justify us in considering Dr. Smith as the real founder of the modern theory of Political Economy. If he has not left us a perfect work, he has, at all events, left us one which contains a greater number of useful truths than have ever been given to the world by any other individual; and he has pointed out and smoothed the route, by following which, subsequent philosophers have been enabled to perfect much that he had left incomplete, to rectify the mistakes into which he had fallen, and to make many new and important discoveries. Whether, indeed, we refer to the soundness of its leading doctrines, to the liberality and universal applicability of its practical conclusions, or to the powerful and beneficial influence it has had on the progress and perfection of the science, and still more on the policy and conduct of nations, Dr. Smith's work must be placed in the foremost rank of those that have helped to liberalise, enlighten, and enrich mankind.

Political Economy was long confounded with politics; and it is undoubtedly true that they are very intimately connected, and that it is frequently impossible to treat those questions which strictly belong to the one, without referring more or less to the principles and conclusions of the other. But in their leading features they are sufficiently distinct. The laws which regulate the production and distribution of wealth are the same in every country and stage of society. Those circumstances which are favourable or unfavourable to the increase of riches and population in a republic, may equally exist, and will have exactly the same effects, in a monarchy. That security of property, without which there can be no steady and continued exertion—that freedom of engaging in every different branch of industry, so necessary to call the various powers and resources of human talent and ingenuity into action—and that economy in the public expenditure, so conducive to the accumulation of national wealth—are not attributes which belong exclusively to a particular species of government. If free states generally make the most rapid advances in wealth and population, it is an indirect rather than a direct consequence of their political constitution: it results more from the greater probability that the right of property will be held sacred, that the freedom of industry will be less fettered and restricted, and that the public income will be more judiciously levied and expended, under a popular government, than from the circumstance merely of a greater proportion of the people being permitted to exercise political rights and privileges: give the same securities to the subjects of an absolute monarch, and they will make the same advances. Industry does not require to be stimulated by extrinsic advantages: the additional comforts and enjoyments which it procures have always been found sufficient to insure the most persevering and successful exertions; and whatever may have been the form of government, those countries have always advanced in the career of improvement, in which the public burdens have been moderate, the freedom of industry maintained, and every individual allowed peaceably to enjoy the fruits of his labour, to cultivate his mind, and communicate his ideas to others. It is not, therefore, so much on its political organisation, as on the talents and *spirit* of its rulers, that the wealth of a country is principally dependent. Economy, moderation, and intelligence, on the part of those in power, have frequently elevated absolute monarchies to a very high degree of opulence and prosperity; while all the advantages derived from a more liberal system of government have not been able to preserve free states from being impoverished and exhausted by the extravagance, intolerance, and short-sighted policy of their rulers.

The sciences of Politics and Political Economy are, therefore, sufficiently distinct. The politician examines the principles on which government is founded; he endeavours to determine in whose hands the supreme authority may be most advantageously placed; and unfolds the reciprocal duties and obligations of the governing and governed portions of society. The political economist does not take so high a flight. It is not of the constitution of the government, but of its ACTS only, that he is called upon to judge. Whatever measures affect the production or distribution of wealth, necessarily come within the scope of his observation, and are freely canvassed by him. He examines whether they are in unison with the principles of the science. If they *are*, he pronounces them to be advantageous, and shews the nature and extent of the benefits of which they will be productive; if they *are not*, he shews in what respect they are defective, and to what extent their operation will be injurious. But he does this without inquiring into the constitution of the government by which these measures have been adopted. The circumstance of their having emanated from the privy council of an arbitrary monarch, or the representative assembly of a free state, though in other respects of supreme importance, cannot affect the immutable principles by which he is to form his opinion upon them.

Besides being confounded with Politics, Political Economy has sometimes been confounded with Statistics; but they are still more easily separated and distinguished. The object of the statistician is to describe the condition of a country at some given period; while the object of the economist is to discover the causes which have brought it into that condition, and the means by which its wealth and riches may be indefinitely increased. He is to the statistician what the physical astronomer is to the mere observer. He takes the facts furnished by the researches of the statistician, and after comparing them with those furnished by historians and travellers, he applies himself to discover their relation. By a patient induction — by carefully observing the circumstances attending the operation of particular principles, he discovers the effects of which they are really productive, and how far they are liable to be modified by the operation of other principles. It is thus that the various general laws which regulate and connect the apparently conflicting, but really harmonious interests of every different order in society, have been discovered, and established with all the certainty of demonstrative evidence.

PRINCIPLES

OF

POLITICAL ECONOMY.

PART I.

PRODUCTION AND ACCUMULATION OF WEALTH.

CHAPTER I.

Definition of Production—Labour the only Source of Wealth.

ALL the operations of nature and art are reducible to, and really consist of, *transmutations*, — of changes of form and of place. By production, in this science, we are not to understand the production of matter, for that is the exclusive attribute of Omnipotence, but the production of *utility*, and consequently of exchangeable value, by appropriating and modifying matter already in existence, so as to fit it to satisfy our wants, and contribute to our enjoyments.* The labour which is thus employed is the only

* This point has been strongly and ably stated by M. Destutt Tracy. "Non-seulement," says he, "nous ne créons jamais rien, mais il nous est même impossible de concevoir ce que c'est que *créer* ou *anéantir*, si nous entendons rigoureusement par ces mots, *faire quelque chose de rien*, ou *reduire quelque chose à rien;* car nous n'avons jamais vu un être quelconque sortir du néant ni y rentrer. De-là cet axiome admis par toute l'antiquité,—rien ne vient de *rien*, et ne peut redevenir *rien*. Que faisons-nous donc par notre travail, *par notre action sur tous les êtres qui nous entourent?* Jamais rien, qu'opérer dans ces êtres des changemens de forme ou de lieu qui les approprient à notre usage, qui les rendent utiles à la satisfaction de nos besoins. Voilà ce que nous devons entendre

source of wealth. Nature spontaneously furnishes the matter of which all commodities are made; but, until labour has been applied to appropriate that matter, or to adapt it to our use, it is wholly destitute of value, and is not, nor ever has been, considered as forming wealth.* Place us on the banks of a river, or in an orchard, and we shall infallibly perish, either of thirst or hunger, if we do not, *by an effort of industry*, raise the water to our lips, or pluck the fruit from its parent tree. It is seldom, however, that the mere appropriation of matter is sufficient. In the vast majority of cases, labour is required not only to appropriate it, but also to convey it from place to place, and to give it that peculiar shape, without which it may be totally useless, and incapable of ministering either to our necessities or our comforts. The coal used in our fires is buried deep in the bowels of the earth, and is absolutely worthless until the labour of the miner has extracted it from the mine, and brought it into a situation where it can be made use of. The stones and mortar of which our houses are built, and the rugged and shapeless materials from which the various articles of convenience and ornament with which they are furnished have been prepared, were, in their original state, alike destitute of value and utility. And of the innumerable variety of animal, vegetable, and mineral products, which form the materials of our food and clothes, none was originally ser-

par *produire;* c'est *donner aux choses une utilité qu'elles n'avoient pas.* Quel que soit notre travail, s'il n'en résulte point d'utilité, il est infructueux; s'il en résulte, il est *productif.*"—*Traité d'Economie Politique*, p. 82.

* The writer of an article in the "Quarterly Review," (No. 60, Art. 1) contends that the *earth* is a source of wealth, because it supplies us with the matter of commodities. But this, it is obvious, is the old error of the economists reproduced in a somewhat modified shape. It would, in truth, be quite as correct to say that the earth is a source of pictures and statues, because it supplies the materials made use of by painters and statuaries, as to say that it is a source of wealth, because it supplies the matter of commodities.

viceable, while many were extremely noxious to man. It is his *labour* that has given them utility, that has subdued their bad qualities, and made them satisfy his wants and minister to his comforts and enjoyments. "Labour was the first price, the original purchase-money that was paid for all things. It was not by gold or by silver, but by labour, that all the wealth of the world was originally purchased."*

Those who observe the progress, and trace the history of the human race, in different countries and states of society, will find that their comfort and happiness have been always very nearly proportioned to the power which they possessed of rendering their labour effective in appropriating the raw products of nature, and in fitting and adapting them to their use. The savage, whose labour is confined to the gathering of wild fruits, or the picking up of shell-fish on the sea-coast, is placed at the very bottom of the scale of civilisation, and is, in point of comfort, decidedly inferior to many of the lower animals. The *first* step in the progress of society is made when man learns to hunt wild animals, to feed himself with their flesh, and clothe himself with their skins. But labour, when confined to the chase, is extremely barren and unproductive. Tribes of hunters, like beasts of prey, whom they closely resemble in their habits and modes of subsistence, are but thinly scattered over the surface of the countries which they occupy; and notwithstanding the fewness of their numbers, any unusual deficiency in the supply of game never fails to reduce them to the extremity of want. The *second* step in the progress of society is made when the tribes of hunters and fishers learn to apply their labour, like the ancient Scythians and modern Tartars, to the domestication of wild animals and the rearing of flocks. The subsistence of herdsmen

* "Wealth of Nations," vol. i. p. 54. My edition is uniformly quoted.

and shepherds is much less precarious than that of hunters, but they are almost entirely destitute of those comforts and elegancies which give to civilised life its chief value. The *third* and most decisive step in the progress of civilisation — in the great art of producing the necessaries and conveniences of life — is made when the wandering tribes of hunters and shepherds renounce their migratory habits, and become agriculturists and manufacturers. It is then that man begins fully to avail himself of his productive powers. He then becomes laborious, and, by a necessary consequence, his wants are then, for the first time, fully supplied, and he acquires an extensive command over the articles necessary for his comfort as well as his subsistence.*

The importance of labour in the production of wealth was very clearly perceived both by Hobbes and Locke. At the commencement of the 24th chapter† of the "Leviathan," published in 1651, Hobbes says, "The *nutrition* of a commonwealth consisteth in the *plenty* and *distribution* of *materials* conducing to life.

"As for the plenty of matter, it is a thing limited by nature to those commodities which, from (the two breasts of our common mother) *land* and *sea*, God usually either freely giveth, or for labour selleth to mankind.

"For the matter of this nutriment, consisting in animals, vegetables, minerals, God hath freely laid them before us, in or near to the face of the earth ; so as there

* This progress has been pointed out by Varro:—"Gradum fuisse naturalem, cùm homines viverunt ex iis rebus quæ inviolata ultrò ferret terra. Ex hâc vitâ in secundam descendisse pastoritiam, cùm, propter utilitatem, ex animalibus quæ possent sylvestria, deprehenderent, ac concluderent, et mansuescerent. In queis primùm, non sine causâ, putant oves assumptas, et propter utilitatem et propter placiditatem. Tertio denique gradu, à vitâ pastorali ad agriculturam descenderunt; in quâ ex duobus gradibus superioribus retinuerunt multa, et quò descenderunt ibi processerunt longè, dum ad nos perveniret." — *De Re Rusticâ*, lib. ii. cap. 1.

† "Of the Nutrition and Procreation of a Commonwealth."

needeth no more but the labour and industry of receiving them. Insomuch that *plenty dependeth* (next to God's favour) *on the labour and industry of man.*"

But Mr. Locke had a much clearer apprehension of this doctrine. In his "Essay on Civil Government," published in 1689, he has entered into a lengthened, discriminating, and able analysis, to shew that it is from labour that the products of the earth derive almost all their value. "Let any one consider," says he, "what the difference is between an acre of land planted with tobacco or sugar, sown with wheat or barley, and an acre of the same land lying in common, without any husbandry upon it, and he will find that the improvement of labour makes the far greater part of the value. I think it will be but a very modest computation to say, that of the products of the earth useful to the life of man, *nine-tenths* are the effects of labour; nay, if we will rightly consider things as they come to our use, and cast up the several expenses about them, what in them is purely owing to nature, and what to labour, we shall find, that in most of them *ninety-nine hundredths* are wholly to be put on the account of labour.

"There cannot be a clearer demonstration of any thing, than several nations of the Americans are of this, who are rich in land, and poor in all the comforts of life; whom nature having furnished as liberally as any other people with the materials of plenty, *i. e.* a fruitful soil apt to produce in abundance what might serve for food, raiment, and delight; yet, for *want of improving it by labour,* have not one-hundredth part of the conveniences we enjoy; and the king of a large and fruitful territory there, feeds, lodges, and is clad worse than a day-labourer in England.

"To make this a little clearer, let us but trace some of the ordinary provisions of life through their several progresses, before they come to our use, and see how much they receive of their value from human industry. Bread, wine, and cloth, are things of daily use and great plenty; yet, notwithstanding, acorns, water, and leaves or skins, must be our bread, drink, and clothing, did not labour furnish us with these more useful commodities; for, whatever bread is more worth than acorns, wine than water, and cloth or silk than leaves, skins, or moss, that is solely owing to labour and industry; the one of these being the food and raiment which unassisted nature furnishes us with; the other provisions which our industry and pains prepare for us; which how much they exceed the other in value, when any one hath computed, he will then see how much labour makes the far greatest part of the value of things we enjoy in this world; and the ground which produces the materials is scarce to be reckoned in as any, or, at most, but a very small part of it; so little, that even amongst us, land that is wholly left to nature, that hath no improvement of pasturage, tillage, or planting, is called, as indeed it is, *waste;* and we shall find the benefit of it amount to little more than nothing.

" An acre of land that bears here twenty bushels of wheat, and another in America which, with the same husbandry, would do the like, are, without doubt, of the same natural intrinsic value (utility). But yet, the benefit mankind receives from the one in a year is worth five pounds, and from the other possibly not worth a penny, if all the profit an Indian received from it were to be valued and sold here; at least, I may truly say, not $\frac{1}{1000}$. 'Tis labour, then, which puts the greatest part of value upon land, *without which it would scarcely be worth any thing.* 'Tis to that we owe the greatest part of all its useful products; for all that the straw, bran, bread, of that acre of wheat, is more worth than the product of an acre of as good land which lies waste, is all the effect of labour. For 'tis not barely the ploughman's pains, the reaper's and thrasher's toil, and the baker's sweat, is to be counted into the bread we eat; the labour of those who broke the oxen, who digged and wrought the iron and stones, who felled and framed the timber employed about the plough, mill, oven, or any other utensils, which are a vast number, requisite to this corn, from its being seed to be sown, to its being made bread, must all be charged on the account of *labour*, and received as an effect of that: nature and the earth furnishing only the almost worthless materials as in themselves. 'Twould be a strange *catalogue of things that industry provided and made use of about every loaf of bread,* before it came to our use, if we could trace them. Iron, wood, leather, barks, timber, stone, bricks, coals, lime, cloth, dyeing-drugs, pitch, tar, masts, ropes, and all the materials made use of in the ship that brought away the commodities made use of by any of the workmen, to any part of the work; all which 'twould be almost impossible, at least too long, to reckon up."*

Mr. Locke has here all but established the fundamental principle on which the science rests. Had he carried his analysis a little further, he could not have failed to perceive that neither water, leaves, skins, nor any one of the spontaneous productions of nature, has any *value,* except what it owes to the labour required for its appropriation. The utility of such products causes them to be demanded; but it does not give them value. This

* "Of Civil Government," book ii. §§ 40, 41, 42, and 43. This is a very remarkable passage. It contains a far more distinct and comprehensive statement of the fundamental doctrine, that labour is the constituent principle of value, than is to be found in any other writer previous to Dr. Smith, or than is to be found even in the "Wealth of Nations." But Mr. Locke does not seem to have been sufficiently aware of the real value of the principle he had elucidated, and has not deduced from it any important practical conclusion. On the contrary, in his tract on "Raising the Value of Money," published in 1691, he lays it down broadly, that all taxes, howsoever imposed, must ultimately *fall on the land;* whereas it is plain he ought, consistently with the above principle, to have shewn, that they would fall, not exclusively on the produce of land, but generally on *produce of industry*, or on all species of commodities.

is a quality which can be communicated only through the agency of voluntary labour of some sort or other. An object which it does not require any portion of labour to appropriate or adapt to our use, may be of the very highest utility; but, as it is the free gift of nature, it is utterly impossible that it can possess the smallest value.*

That commodities could not be produced without the co-operation of the powers of nature, is most certain. I am very far, indeed, from attempting to depreciate the obligations we are under to our common mother, or from endeavouring to exalt the benefits man owes to his own exertions by concealing or underrating those which he enjoys by the bounty of nature. But it is the distinguishing characteristic of the services rendered by the latter that they are gratuitous. They are infinitely useful, and they are, at the same time, infinitely cheap. They are not,

* Bishop Berkeley entertained very just opinions respecting the source of wealth. In his "Querist," published in 1735, he asks,—"Whether it were not wrong to suppose *land* itself to be wealth? And whether the *industry of the people* is not first to be considered, as that which constitutes wealth, which makes even land and silver to be wealth, neither of which would have any value, but as means and motives to industry? Whether, in the wastes of America, a man might not possess twenty miles square of land, and yet want his dinner, or a coat to his back?"—*Querist*, Numbers 38 and 39.

M. Say appears to think ("Discours Préliminaire," p. 37) that Galiani was the *first* who shewed, in his treatise "Della Moneta," published in 1750, that labour was the only source of wealth. But the passages now laid before the reader prove the erroneousness of this opinion. Galiani has entered into *no analysis or argument to prove the correctness of his statement;* and as it appears from other parts of his work that he was well acquainted with Mr. Locke's "Tracts on Money," a suspicion naturally arises that he had seen the "Essay on Civil Government," and that he was really indebted to it for a knowledge of this principle. This suspicion derives strength from the circumstance of Galiani being still less aware than Mr. Locke of the value of the discovery. —See *Trattato della Moneta*, p. 39, ediz. 1780.

like human services, sold for a price; they are merely appropriated. When a fish is caught, or a tree is felled, do the nereids or wood-nymphs make their appearance, and stipulate that the labour of nature in producing it should be paid for before it is carried off and made use of by man? When the miner has dug his way down to the ore, does Plutus prevent him from appropriating it? Nature is not, as so many would have us suppose, frugal and grudging. All her rude products, and all her capacities and powers, are offered freely to man. She neither demands nor receives a return for her favours. Her services are of inestimable *utility;* but being granted freely and unconditionally, they are wholly destitute of value, and are consequently without the power of communicating that quality to any thing.

The utility of water, or its capacity to slake thirst, is equal at all times and places; but as this quality is communicated to it by nature, it adds nothing to its value, which is, in all cases, measured by the labour required for its appropriation. A very small expenditure of labour being required to raise water from a river to the lips of an individual on its banks, its value, under such circumstances, is very trifling indeed. But when, instead of being upon its banks, the consumers of the water are five, ten, or twenty miles distant, its value, being increased proportionally to the greater expenditure of labour upon its conveyance, may become very considerable. This principle holds universally. The utility of coal, or its capacity of furnishing heat and light, makes it an object of demand; but this utility, being a free gift of nature, has no influence on its value or price: this depends entirely on the labour required to extract the coal from the mine, and to convey it to where it is to be consumed.

"Si je retranche," to use a striking illustration of this doctrine given by M. Canard, "de ma montre, par la pensée, tous les travaux qui lui ont été successivement appliqués, il ne restera que quelques grains de minéral placés dans l'intérieur de la terre, d'où on les a tirés, et où ils n'ont aucune valeur. De même, si je décompose le pain que je mange, et que j'en retranche successivement tous les travaux successifs qu'il a reçus, il ne restera que quelques tiges d'herbes graminées, eparses dans des déserts incultes, et sans aucune valeur."*

Those who contend, as almost all the continental economists do, that the agency of natural powers adds to the value of commodities, uniformly confound utility and value—that is, as was formerly observed, they confound the power or capacity of articles to satisfy our wants and desires with the quantity of labour required to produce them, or the quantity for which they would exchange. These qualities are, however, as radically different as those of weight and colour. To confound them is to stumble at the very threshold of the science. It is but too clear, that those who do so have yet to make themselves acquainted with its fundamental principles.

It is true that natural powers may sometimes be appropriated or engrossed by one or more individuals to the exclusion of others, and those by whom they are so engrossed may exact a price for their services; but does that shew that these services cost the engrossers any thing? If A has a waterfall on his estate, he may, probably, get a rent for it. It is plain, however, that the work performed by the waterfall is as completely gratuitous as that which is performed by the wind that acts on the blades of a windmill. The only difference between them consists in this,—that all individuals having it in their power to avail themselves of the services of the wind, no one can intercept the bounty of nature, and exact a price for that which she freely bestows; whereas A, by appropriating the waterfall, and consequently acquiring a command over it, has it in his power to prevent its being used at all, or to sell its services. He can oblige

* "Principes d'Economie Politique," p. 6.

B, C, and D, to pay for liberty to use it; but as they pay for that which costs him nothing, he gains the *whole* that they lose; so that the services rendered by the waterfall are still so much clear gain — so much work performed gratuitously for society.

It is to labour, therefore, and to it only, that man owes every thing possessed of exchangeable value. Labour is the talisman that has raised him from the condition of the savage — that has changed the desert and the forest into cultivated fields — that has covered the earth with cities, and the ocean with ships — that has given us plenty, comfort, and elegance, instead of want, misery, and barbarism. What was said of the enchantress Enothea, may be truly applied to labour:

> Quicquid in orbe vides, paret mihi. Florida tellus,
> Cùm volo, fundit opes; scopulique, atque horrida saxa
> Niliades jaculantur aquas.

The fundamental principle, that it is only through the agency of labour that the various articles and conveniences required for the use and accommodation of man can be obtained, being thus established, it necessarily follows, that the great practical problem involved in that part of the science which treats of the *production* of wealth, must resolve itself into a discussion of the means by which labour may be rendered most efficient, or by which *the greatest amount of necessary, useful, and desirable products may be obtained with the least possible outlay of labour.* Every measure that has any tendency to add to the power of labour, or, which is the same thing, to reduce the cost of commodities, must add proportionally to our means of obtaining wealth and riches; while every measure or regulation that has any tendency to waste labour, or to raise the cost of commodities, must equally lessen these means. This, then, is the simple and decisive test by which we are to judge of the expediency of all measures affecting the wealth of the country, and of the value of all inventions. If they render labour more productive—if they tend, by reducing the value of commodities, to render them more easily obtainable, and to bring them within the command of a greater portion of society, they must be advantageous; but if their tendency be different, they must as certainly be disadvantageous. Considered in this point of view, that great branch of the science which treats of the *production* of wealth will be found to be abundantly simple, and easily understood.

Labour, according as it is applied to the raising of raw produce—to the fashioning of that raw produce, when raised, into articles of utility, convenience, or ornament—or to the conveyance of raw and wrought produce from one country or place to another—is said to be agricultural, manufacturing, or commercial. An acquaintance with the particular processes and most advantageous methods of applying labour in each of these grand departments of industry, forms the peculiar and appropriate study of the agriculturist, manufacturer, and merchant. It is not consistent with the objects of the political economist to enter into the details of particular businesses and professions. He confines himself to an investigation of the means by which labour in general may be rendered most productive, and how its powers may be increased in *all* the departments of industry.

Most writers on Political Economy have entered into lengthened discussions with respect to the difference between what they have termed productive and unproductive labour. I cannot, however, I confess, discover any real ground for most of those discussions, or for the distinctions that have frequently been set up between one sort of labour and another. The subject is not one in which there is apparently any difficulty. It is not at the species of labour carried on, but at its *results*, that we should look. So long as an individual employs himself in any way not detrimental to others, and accomplishes the object he has in view, his labour is obviously productive; while, if he do not accomplish it, or obtain some sort of equivalent advantage from the exertion of the labour, it is as obviously unproductive. This definition seems clear, and leads to no perplexities; and it will be shewn, in another chapter, that it is not possible to adopt any other without being involved in endless difficulties and contradictions.

In thus endeavouring to exhibit the importance of labour, and the advantages which its successful prosecution confers on man, it must not be supposed that reference is made to the labour of the hand only. This species, indeed, comes most under our observation; it is that, too, without which we could not exist, and which principally determines the value of commodities. It is questionable, however, whether it be really more productive than the labour of the mind. The hand is not more necessary to execute than the head to contrive. Some very valuable discoveries have no doubt been the result of accident; while others have naturally grown out of the progress of society, without being materially advanced by the efforts of any single individual. These, however, have not been their only, nor, perhaps, their most copious sources; and every one, how little soever he may be acquainted with the history of his species, is aware that we are indebted to the labour of the mind, to patient study and long-continued research, for numberless inventions, some of which have made almost incalculable additions to our powers, and changed, indeed, the whole aspect and condition of society.

CHAPTER II.

Progressive Nature of Man — Means by which the Productive Powers of Labour are increased. — SECTION I. *Security of Property.* — SECTION II. *Division of Employments.* — SECTION III. *Accumulation and Employment of Capital — Definition and Source of Profit — Circumstances most favourable for the Accumulation of Capital.*

IT is the proud distinction of the human race, that their conduct is determined by reason, which, though limited and fallible, is susceptible of indefinite improvement. In the infancy of society, indeed, being destitute of that knowledge which is the result of long experience and study, without that dexterity which is the effect of practice, and without the guidance of those instincts which direct other animals, man seems to occupy one of the lowest places in the scale of being. But the faculties of most animals come rapidly to maturity, and admit of no further increase or diminution; whereas, the human species is naturally progressive. In addition to the necessity which obliges man to exert himself to provide subsistence, he is, almost uniformly, actuated by a wish to improve his condition; and he is endowed with sagacity to enable him to devise the means of gratifying this desire. By slow degrees, partly by the aid of observation, and partly by contrivances of his own, he gradually learns to augment his powers, and to acquire an increased command over the necessaries, conveniences, and enjoyments of human life. Without the unerring instinct of the ant, the bee, or the beaver, he becomes, from a perception of their advantage, the greatest storemaster and builder in the world; and without the strength of the elephant, the swiftness of the hound, or the ferocity of the tiger, he subjects every animal to his power. Having felt the advantages resulting from improved accommodations, he becomes more desirous to extend them. The attainment of that which seemed, at the commencement of the undertaking, to be an object beyond which his wishes could not expand, becomes an incentive to new efforts. "Man never is, but always to be blessed." The gratification of a want or desire is merely a step to some new pursuit. In every stage of his progress, he is destined to contrive and invent, to engage in new undertakings, and, when these are accomplished, to enter with fresh energy upon others. "Even after he has attained to what, at a distance, appeared to be the summit of his fortune, he is in reality only come to a point at which new objects are presented to entice his pursuits, and towards which he is urged with the spurs of ambition, while those of necessity are no longer applied. Or, if the desire of any thing better than the present should at any time cease to operate on his mind, he becomes listless and negligent, loses the advantages he had gained, whether of possession or skill, and declines in his fortune, till a sense of his own defects and his sufferings restore his industry."*

It has been said that nations, like individuals, have their periods of infancy, maturity, decline, and death. But though the comparison strikes at first, and history affords many apparent instances of its truth, it is, notwithstanding, inapplicable. The human body is of frail contexture and limited duration; but nations are perpetually renovated; the place of those who die is immediately filled up by others, who, having succeeded to the arts, sciences, and wealth, of those by whom they were preceded, start with unprecedented advantages in their career. It is plain, therefore, that if the principle of improvement were not counteracted by hostile aggression, vicious institutions, or some other adventitious circumstance, it would

* Ferguson's "Principles of Moral and Political Science," vol. i. p. 56.

always operate, and would secure the constant advancement of nations.

Powerful, however, as is the passion to rise — to ascend still higher in the scale of society — the advance of the arts has not been left wholly to depend on its agency. Had such been the case, it is reasonable to suppose that the earlier inventions and discoveries would, by rendering others of comparatively less importance, have slackened the progress of civilisation. But in the actual state of things, no such relaxation can ever take place. The principle of increase implanted in the human race is so very powerful, that population never fails of speedily expanding to the limits of subsistence, how much soever they may be extended. Indeed, its natural tendency is to exceed these limits, or to increase the number of people faster than the supplies of food and other necessary accommodations provided for their support. This tendency, as will be afterwards shewn, is, in some degree, checked in civilised societies, by the prudential considerations to which the difficulty of bringing up a family necessarily gives rise. But, in despite of their influence, the principle of increase is at all times, and under every variety of circumstances, so very strong as to call forth unceasing efforts to increase the means of subsistence. It forms, in fact, a constantly operating principle to rouse the activity and stimulate the industry of man. The most splendid inventions and discoveries do not enable him to intermit his efforts ; — if he did, the increase of population would speedily change his condition for the worse, and he would be compelled either to sink to a lower station, or to atone for his indolence by renewed and more vigorous exertions. The continued progress of industry and the arts is thus secured by a double principle : man is not merely anxious to advance; he dares not, without manifest injury to himself, venture to stand still. But, because such is our lot, because we are constantly seeking an imaginary repose and felicity we are never destined to realise, are we, therefore, as some have done, to arraign the wisdom of Providence? Far from it. In the words of the profound and eloquent philosopher whom I have just quoted, "We ought always to remember that these labours and exertions are themselves of principal value, and to be reckoned amongst the foremost blessings to which human nature is competent; that mere industry is a blessing apart from the wealth it procures; and that the exercises of a cultivated mind, though considered as means for the attainment of an external end, are themselves of more value than any such end whatever."*

In tracing the progress of mankind from poverty and barbarism to wealth and civilisation, there are three circumstances, the vast importance of which must strike even the most careless observer; and without whose conjoined existence and co-operation, labour could not have become considerably productive, nor society made any perceptible progress. The *first* is the *security of property*, or a lively and well-founded conviction in the mind of every individual that he will be allowed to dispose at pleasure of the fruits of his labour. The *second* is the introduction of exchange or barter, and the consequent appropriation of particular individuals to particular employments. And the *third* is the accumulation and employment of the produce of previous labour, or, as it is more commonly termed, of capital, or stock. All the improvements that have ever been made, or that ever can be made, in the great art of producing the necessaries, comforts, and conveniences of human life, may be classed under some one or other of these three heads. It is, therefore, indispensable that principles so important, and which lie at the very bottom of the science, should be well understood.

SECT. I.—SECURITY OF PROPERTY.

Security of property is the first and most indispensable requisite to the production of wealth. Its utility in this

* Ferguson's "Principles of Moral and Political Science," vol. i. p. 250.

respect is, indeed, so obvious and striking, that it has been more or less respected in every country, and in the earliest and rudest periods. All have been impressed with the reasonableness of the maxim which teaches that those who sow ought to be permitted to reap—that the labour of a man's body and the work of his hands are to be considered as exclusively his own. No savage horde has ever been discovered in which the principle of *meum* and *tuum* was not recognised. Nothing, it is plain, could ever tempt any one to engage in a laborious employment—he would neither domesticate wild animals, nor clear and cultivate the ground, if, after months and years of toil, when his flocks had become numerous, and his harvests were ripening for the sickle, a stranger were to be allowed to rob him of the produce of his industry. No wonder, therefore, that the utility of laws or institutions, securing to every individual the peaceable enjoyment of the produce he had raised, and of the ground he had cultivated and improved, suggested itself to the first lawgivers. The author of the book of Job places those who removed their neighbour's land-marks at the head of his list of wicked men; and some of the earliest profane legislators subjected those who were guilty of this offence to a capital punishment.*

Dr. Paley has said that the *law of the land* is the real foundation of the right of property. But the obvious *utility* of securing to each individual the produce raised by his industry, undoubtedly formed the irresistible reason that induced every people emerging from barbarism to establish this right. It is, in fact, the foundation on which almost all the other institutions of society rest; and Cicero has truly stated, that it was chiefly for the protection of property that civil government was instituted. *Hanc enim ob causam maximè, ut sua tuerentur, respublicæ civitatesque constitutæ sunt. Nam etsi duce naturæ, congregabantur homines, tamen spe custodiæ rerum suarum,*

* Goguet, "De l'Origine des Loix," &c. tom. i. p. 30, 4to. ed.

*urbium præsidia quærebant.** Until property had been publicly guaranteed, men must have looked on each other as enemies rather than friends. The idle and improvident are always desirous of seizing on the earnings of the laborious and frugal; and, were they not restrained by the strong arm of the law — were they permitted to prosecute their attacks—they would, by generating a feeling of insecurity, effectually check both industry and accumulation, and sink all classes to the same level of hopeless misery as themselves. The security of property is, indeed, quite as indispensable to accumulation as to production. No man ever denies himself an immediate gratification when it is within his power, unless he thinks that by doing so he has a fair prospect of obtaining a greater accession of comforts and enjoyments, or of avoiding a probable evil, at some future period. Where property is protected, an individual who has produced as much by one day's labour as is sufficient to maintain him two days, is not idle during the second day, but accumulates the surplus above his wants as a reserve stock; the increased consequence and enjoyments which the possession of such stock or capital brings along with it, being, in the great majority of cases, more than sufficient to counterbalance the desire of immediate gratification. But, wherever property is insecure, we look in vain for the operation of this principle. "It is plainly better for us," is then the invariable language of the people, "to enjoy while it is in our power, than to accumulate property which we shall not be permitted to use, and which will either expose us to the extortion of a rapacious government, or to the unrestrained depredations of those who exist only by the plunder of their more industrious neighbours."

But it must not be imagined that the security of property is violated only when a man is deprived of the power of peaceably enjoying the fruits of his industry: it

* "De Officiis," lib. ii. cap. 21.

is also violated, and perhaps in a still more glaring and unjustifiable manner, when he is prevented from using the powers given him by nature, in any way, not injurious to others, that he considers most beneficial to himself. Of all the species of property which a man can possess, *the faculties of his mind and powers of his body* are most particularly his own. He ought, therefore, to be permitted to enjoy, that is, to use or exert, these powers at his discretion. And hence the right of property is as much infringed upon when a man is interdicted from engaging in a particular branch of business, as when he is forcibly bereft of the property he has produced or accumulated. Every monopoly which gives to a few individuals the exclusive power of carrying on certain branches of industry, is thus, in fact, established in direct violation of the property of all other individuals. It prevents them from using their natural capacities or powers in what they might have considered the best manner; and, as every man who is not a slave is justly held to be the best, and, indeed, only judge of what is advantageous for himself, the most obvious principles of justice and the right of property are both subverted when he is excluded from any employment. In like manner, the right of property is violated whenever any regulation is made to force an individual to employ his labour or capital in a particular way. The property of a landlord is violated when he is compelled to adopt any system of cultivation, even though it were really preferable to that which he was previously following; the property of a capitalist is violated when he is obliged to accept a particular rate of interest for his stock; and the property of a labourer is violated when he is obliged to employ himself in any particular occupation, or for a fixed rate of wages.

The finest soil, the finest climate, and the finest intellectual powers, can prevent no people from becoming barbarous, poor, and miserable, if they have the misfortune to be subjected to a government which does not respect and maintain the right of property. This is the greatest of all calamities. The ravages of civil war, of pestilence, and famine, may be repaired ; but nothing can enable a nation to contend against the deadly influence of an established system of violence and rapine. It is the want of security—the want of any lively and well-founded expectation among the inhabitants of their being permitted freely to dispose of the fruits of their industry, that is the principal cause of the present wretched state of the Ottoman dominions, as it was of the decline of industry and arts in Europe during the middle ages. When the Turkish conquerors overran those fertile and beautiful countries in which, to the disgrace of the European powers, they are still permitted to encamp, they parcelled them among their followers, on condition of their performing certain military services, on a plan corresponding, in many important particulars, to the feudal system of our ancestors. But none of these possessions, except those which have been assigned to the church, is hereditary. They all revert, on the death of the present possessors, to the sultan, the sole proprietor of all the immovable property in the empire. The occupiers of land in Turkey, having, in consequence of this vicious system, no adequate security that their possessions will be allowed to descend, on their death, to their children or legatees, are comparatively careless of futurity; and as none can feel any interest in the fate of an unknown successor, no one ever executes any improvement of which he does not expect to be able to reap all the advantage during his own life. This is the cause that the Turks are so extremely careless about their houses: they never construct them of solid or durable materials; and it would be a gratification to them to be assured that they would fall to pieces the moment after they had breathed their last. Under this miserable government, the palaces have been changed into cottages and the cities into villages. The long-continued want of security has extinguished the very spirit of industry, and destroyed not only the power, but even the desire to emerge from barbarism.*

Had it been possible for arbitrary power to profit by the lessons of experience, it must long since have perceived that its own wealth, as well as the wealth of its subjects, would be most effectually promoted by maintaining the inviolability of property. Were the Turkish government to establish a vigilant system of police — to secure to each individual the unrestricted power of disposing of the fruits of his labour—and to substitute a regular plan of taxation in place of the present odious system of extortion and tyranny,—industry would revive, capital and population would be augmented, and moderate duties, imposed on a few articles in general demand, would bring a much larger sum into the coffers of the treasury than all that is now obtained by force and violence. The *stated* public burdens to which the Turks are subjected are light when compared with those imposed on the English, the Hollanders, or the French. But the latter know that when they have paid the taxes due to government, they will be permitted peaceably to enjoy or accumulate the remainder of their earnings; whereas the Turk has no security but that the moment after he has paid his stated contribution, the pacha, or one of his satellites, may strip him of every additional farthing he possesses! Security is the foundation — the principal element in every well-digested system of finance. When maintained inviolate, it enables a country to support, without much difficulty, a very heavy load of taxes; but where there is no security — where property is a prey to rapine and

* Thornton's "Account of the Turkish Empire," vol. ii. p. 63. "The Turks," says Denon, "bâtissent le moins qu'ils peuvent; ils ne réparent jamais rien: un mur menace ruine, ils l'étayent; il s'éboule, ce sont quelques chambres de moins dans la maison; ils s'arrangent à côté des décombres: l'édifice tombe enfin, ils en abandonnent le sol, où, s'ils sont obligés d'en déblayer l'emplacement, ils n'emportent le plâtras que le moins loin qu'ils peuvent."—Tom. i. p. 193.

spoliation — to the attacks of the needy, the powerful, or the profligate — the smallest burdens are justly regarded as oppressive, and uniformly exceed the means of the impoverished and spiritless inhabitant.

Mr. Brydone states, that it was customary for the more intelligent Sicilians with whom he had any conversation respecting the natural riches of their celebrated island and its capacities of improvement, to observe,—" Yes, if these were displayed, you would have reason, indeed, to speak of them. Take a look of these mountains, they contain rich veins of every metal, and many of the Roman mines still remain. But to what end should we explore them? *It is not we that should reap the profit.* Nay, a discovery of any thing very rich might possibly prove the ruin of its possessor. No, in our present situation, the hidden treasures of the island must ever remain a profound secret. Were we happy enough to enjoy the blessings of your constitution, you might call us rich indeed. Many hidden doors of opulence would then be opened, which now are not even thought of, and we should soon re-assume our ancient name and consequence."*

The Jews have been supposed to afford an instance of a people whose property has been long exposed to an almost uninterrupted series of attacks, and who have, notwithstanding, continued to be rich and industrious. But when rightly examined, it will be found that the case of the Jews forms no exception to the general rule. The strong prejudices which have been almost universally entertained against them, had long the effect of preventing their acquiring any property in land, and have excluded them from participating in the funds of the charitable institutions of the different countries over which they are scattered. Having, therefore, no adventitious support on which to depend, in the event of their becoming infirm or destitute, they had a powerful additional motive to save

* "Tour in Sicily and Malta," p. 351.

and accumulate; and being excluded from agriculture, they were of necessity compelled to addict themselves to commerce and the arts. In an age when the mercantile profession was generally looked upon as mean and sordid, and when, of course, they had comparatively few competitors, they must have made considerable profits; but these have been very greatly exaggerated. It was natural that those who were indebted to the Jews should represent their gains as enormous; for this inflamed the existing prejudices against them, and afforded a miserable pretext for defrauding them of their just claims. There are a few rich Jews in most of the large cities of Europe; but the majority of that race has ever been, and still is, as poor as its neighbours.

Let us not, therefore, deceive ourselves by supposing that it is possible for any people to emerge from barbarism, or to become wealthy, prosperous, and civilised, without the security of property. Security is indispensably necessary to the successful exertion of the powers of industry. Where it is wanting, it is idle to expect either riches or civilisation.* "The establishment of property is in fact," to borrow the statement of one of the greatest ornaments of the English church, "the source from which all the arts of civilisation proceed. Before this establishment takes place, the indolent suffer no inferiority, the active receive no gain; but from the date of the recognition of pro-

* "Ce n'est que là où les proprietés sont assurés, où l'emploi des capitaux est abandonné au choix de ceux qui les possèdent; ce n'est que là dis-je, que les particuliers seront encouragés à se soumettre aux privations les plus dures pour compenser par leurs épargnes les retards que la profusion du gouvernement peut apporter aux progrès de la richesse nationale. Si l'Angleterre, malgré ses guerres ruineuses, est parvenue à un haut degré d'opulence; si, malgré les contributions énormes dont le peuple y est chargé, son capital est pourtant accru dans le silence par l'économie des particuliers, il ne faut attribuer ces effets qu'à la liberté des personnes et à la sureté des proprietés qui y régnent, plus que dans aucun autre pays de l'Europe, la Suisse exceptée."—STORCH, *Cours d'Economie Politique*, tom. i. p. 260.

perty to the individual, each man is rich, and comfortable, and prosperous, setting aside the common infirmities which flesh is heir to, according to his portion of effective industry or native genius. From this period he is continually impelled by his desires from the pursuit of one object to another, and his activity is called forth in the prosecution of the several arts which render his situation more easy and agreeable."*

Rousseau and the Abbé Mably have made an objection to the institution of private property, which has been, in some measure, sanctioned by Beccaria and others.† They allow that this institution is advantageous for those who possess property; but they contend, that it is disadvantageous for those who are poor and destitute. It has condemned, they affirm, the greater portion of mankind to a state of misery, and has provided for the exaltation of the few by the depression of the many! The sophistry of this reasoning is so apparent, as hardly to require being pointed out. The right of property has not made *poverty*, but it has powerfully contributed to make *wealth*. Previously to its establishment, the nations which are now most civilised were sunk to the same level of wretchedness and misery as the savages of New Holland and Kamtschatska. All classes have been benefited by the change; and it is mere error and delusion to suppose that the rich have been benefited at the expense of the poor. The right of property gives no advantage to one over another. It deals out justice impartially to all. It does not say, labour, and I shall reward you; but it says, "*labour, and I shall take care that none shall be permitted to rob you of the produce of your exertions*." The protection afforded to property by all civilised

* Sumner's "Records of the Creation," 4th ed. vol. ii. p. 51.

† Speaking of theft, Beccaria calls it, "Il delitto di quella infelice parte di uomini, a cui *il diritto di proprietà (terribile, e forse non necessario diritto), non ha lasciato, che una nuda essistenza.*"— *Dei Delitti e delle Pene*, § 22.

societies, though it has not made all men rich, has done more to produce that effect than all their other institutions put together. But, the truth is, that differences of fortune are as consonant to the nature of things, and are as really a part of the order of Providence, as differences of sex, complexion, or strength. No two individuals will ever be equally fortunate, frugal, and industrious; and supposing an equality of fortunes were at any time forcibly established, it could not be maintained for a week: some would be more inclined to spend than others; some would be more laborious and inventive; and some would have larger families. By establishing a right of property, we enable industry and forethought to reap their due reward; but they do this without the smallest imaginable injury being in consequence inflicted upon any one else. There may, no doubt, be institutions which tend to increase those inequalities of fortune that are natural to society, but the right of property is not one of them. Its effects are altogether beneficial. It is, in fact, a rampart raised by society against its common enemies — against rapine and violence, plunder and oppression. Without its protection, the rich would become poor, and the poor would be totally unable to become rich—all would sink to the same bottomless abyss of barbarism and poverty. "It is the security of property," to use the just and forcible expressions of an able writer, "that has overcome the natural aversion of man from labour, that has given him the empire of the earth, that has given him a fixed and permanent residence, that has implanted in his breast the love of his country and of posterity. To enjoy immediately—to enjoy without labour, is the natural inclination of every man. This inclination must be restrained; for its obvious tendency is to arm all those who have nothing against those who have something. The law which restrains this inclination, and which secures to the humblest individual the quiet enjoyment of the fruits of his industry, is the most splendid achievement of legislative wisdom—the noblest triumph of which humanity has to boast."*

Sect. II.—Division of Employments among Individuals.

The division of employments can only be imperfectly established in rude societies and thinly-peopled countries. But in every state of society—in the rudest as well as the most improved—we can trace its operation and effects. The various physical powers, talents, and propensities, with which men are endowed, fit them for different occupations; and a regard to mutual interest and convenience naturally leads them, at a very early period, to establish a system of barter and a division of employments. It was speedily seen, that by separating and combining their efforts so as to bring about some desirable end, they might, with ease, accomplish tasks that could not otherwise be attempted. Even in the simplest businesses this co-operation is required; neither hunting nor fishing, any more than agriculture or manufactures, can be advantageously carried on by solitary individuals. Man is the creature of society; and is compelled, in every stage of his progress, to depend for help on his fellows. *Quò alio fortes sumus, quàm quòd mutuis juvamur officiis?* Instead of trusting to his own unaided efforts for a provision of the various articles required for his subsistence, comfort, and security, he instinctively associates himself with others, and finds in this association the principal source of his superior power. Perceiving that he can obtain an incomparably greater command of all that he deems useful or desirable by applying himself in preference to some one department of industry, he limits his attention to it only. As society advances, this division extends itself on all sides: one man becomes a tanner, or dresser of skins; another a shoemaker; a third a weaver; a fourth a

* Bentham, "Traité de Législation," tom. ii. p. 37.

house-carpenter; a fifth a smith, and so on; one undertakes the defence of the society, and one the distribution of justice; and each endeavours to cultivate and bring to perfection whatever talent or genius he may possess for the particular calling in which he is engaged: the wealth and comforts of all classes are, in consequence, prodigiously augmented. In countries where the division of labour is carried to a considerable extent, agriculturists are not obliged to spend their time in clumsy attempts to manufacture their own produce; and manufacturers cease to interest themselves about the raising of corn and the fattening of cattle. The facility of exchanging is the vivifying principle of industry: it stimulates agriculturists to adopt the best system of cultivation and to raise the largest crops, because it enables them to exchange whatever portion of the produce of their lands exceeds their own wants, for other commodities contributing to their comforts and enjoyments; and it stimulates manufacturers and merchants to increase and improve the quantity, variety, and quality of their goods, that they may thereby obtain greater supplies of raw produce. A spirit of industry is thus universally diffused; and that apathy and languor which characterise a rude state of society, entirely disappear.

But the facility of exchanging, or the circumstance of being able readily to barter the surplus produce of our own labour for such parts of the surplus produce of other people's labour as we may desire to obtain and they may choose to part with, is not the only advantage of the separation of employments. Besides enabling each individual to addict himself in preference to those departments which suit his taste and disposition, it adds very largely to the efficacy of his powers, and enables him to produce a much greater quantity of useful and desirable articles than he could do were he to engage indiscriminately in different businesses. Dr. Smith, who has treated this subject in the most masterly manner, has classed the circumstances which conspire to increase the productive powers of industry, when labour is divided, under the following heads:—*First;* the increased skill and dexterity of the workmen; *second,* the saving of time which is commonly lost in passing from one employment to another; and, *third,* the circumstance of the division of employments having a tendency to facilitate the invention of machines and processes for abridging and saving labour. A few observations on each of these heads are subjoined.

1st, *With respect to the improvement of the skill and dexterity of the labourer:*— It is sufficiently plain, that when a person's whole attention is devoted to one branch of business, when all the energies of his mind and powers of his body are made to converge, as it were, to a single point, he must attain to a degree of proficiency in that particular branch, to which no individual engaged in a variety of occupations can be expected to reach. A peculiar play of the muscles, or *sleight of hand,* is necessary to perform the simplest operation in the best and most expeditious manner; and this can only be acquired by habitual and constant practice. Dr. Smith has given a striking example, in the case of the nail-manufacturer, of the extreme difference between training a workman to the precise occupation in which he is to be employed, and training him to a similar and closely allied occupation. "A common smith," says he, "who, though accustomed to handle the hammer, has never been used to make nails, if, upon some particular occasion, he is obliged to attempt it, will scarce, I am assured, be able to make above two or three hundred nails in a day, and those, too, very bad ones. A smith who has been accustomed to make nails, but whose sole or principal business has not been that of a nailer, can seldom, with his utmost diligence, make more than eight hundred or a thousand nails in a day. But I have seen several boys, under twenty years of age, who had never exercised any other trade but that of making nails, and who, when they exerted themselves, could make, each of them, upwards of *two thousand three hundred nails in a day*;"* or nearly three times the number of the smith who had been accustomed to make them, but who was not entirely devoted to that particular business!

2d, The effect of the division of labour in preventing that *waste of time in moving from one employment to another*, which must always take place when an individual is engaged in different occupations, is even more obvious than the advantage derived from the improvement of the skill and dexterity of the labourer. When the same individual carries on different employments, in different and perhaps distant places, and with different sets of tools, it is plainly impossible he can avoid losing a considerable portion of time in passing between them. If the different businesses in which a labourer is to be engaged could be carried on in the same workshop, the loss of time would be less, but even in that case it would be considerable. "A man," as Dr. Smith has justly observed, "commonly saunters a little in turning his hand from one sort of employment to another. When he first begins the new work, he is seldom very keen and hearty; his mind, as they say, does not go along with it, and for some time he rather trifles than applies to good purpose. The habit of sauntering and of indolent careless application, which is naturally, or rather necessarily acquired by every country workman, who is obliged to change his work and his tools every half hour, and to apply his hand in twenty different ways almost every day of his life, renders him almost always slothful and lazy, and incapable of any vigorous application, even on the most pressing occasions. Independent, therefore, of his deficiency in point of dexterity, this cause alone must always reduce considerably the quantity of work which he is capable of performing."†

3d, With regard to the effect of the division of em-

* "Wealth of Nations," vol. i. p. 22. † Ib. vol. i. p. 23.

ployments in *facilitating the invention of machines and processes for abridging and saving labour*:—It is obvious that those engaged in any branch of industry must be more likely to discover easier and readier methods of carrying it on, when the whole attention of their minds is devoted exclusively to it, than if it were dissipated among a variety of objects. But it is a mistake to suppose, as has been sometimes done, that it is the inventive genius of workmen and artificers only that is whetted and improved by the division of labour. As society advances, the study of particular branches of science and philosophy becomes the principal or sole occupation of the most ingenious men. Chemistry becomes a distinct science from natural philosophy; the physical astronomer separates himself from the astronomical observer, the political economist from the politician; and each, meditating exclusively or principally on his peculiar department of science, attains to a degree of proficiency and expertness in it which the general scholar seldom or never reaches. And hence, in labouring to promote our own ends, we all necessarily adopt that precise course which is most advantageous for all. Like the different parts of a well-constructed engine, the inhabitants of a civilised country are all mutually dependent on, and connected with each other. Without any previous concert, and obeying only the powerful and steady impulse of self-interest, they universally conspire to the same great end; and contribute, each in his respective sphere, to furnish the greatest supply of necessaries, luxuries, conveniences, and enjoyments.

But it is necessary to observe, that the advantages derived from the division of labour, though they may be, and in fact are, partially enjoyed in every country and state of society, can only be carried to their full extent where there is a great power of exchanging, or an *extensive market*. There are an infinite variety of employments which cannot be separately carried on without the precincts of a large city; and, in all cases, the division becomes more perfect, according as the demand for the produce is extended. It is stated by Dr. Smith, that ten labourers, employed in different departments in a pin manufactory, can produce 48,000 pins a day; but it is evident that if the demand were not sufficient to take off this quantity, ten men could not be constantly employed in the pin-making business; and the division of employments in it could not, of course, be carried so far. The same principle holds universally. A cotton mill could not be constructed in a small country having no intercourse with its neighbours. The demand and competition of Europe and America have been necessary to carry the manufactures of Glasgow, Manchester, and Birmingham, to their present state of improvement.

The effect of the division of labour in increasing the quantity and perfection of the products of industry, had been noticed by several of the writers who preceded Dr. Smith, especially by Mr. Harris and M. Turgot; but none of them did what Dr. Smith has done. None of them has fully traced its operation, or shewn that the power of engaging in different employments depends on the *power of exchanging;* and that, consequently, the advantages derived from the division of labour are necessarily dependent upon, and regulated by, the extent of the market. This is a principle of very great importance, and by establishing it Dr. Smith shed a new light on the whole science, and laid the foundation of many important practical conclusions. "Présentée de cette manière," says M. Storch, "l'idée de la division du travail étoit absolument neuve; et l'effet qu'elle a fait sur les contemporains de Smith, prouve bien qu'elle l'était réellement pour eux. Telle qu'elle se trouve indiquée dans les passages que je viens de citer, elle n'a fait aucune impression. Développée par Smith, cette idée a d'abord saisi tous ses lecteurs; tous en ont senti la vérité et l'importance; et cela suffit pour lui en assurer tout l'honneur, lors même que son génie eut été guidé par les indications de ses devanciers."*

Sect. III.—Definition of Capital—Mode in which it contributes to the Formation of Wealth—Circumstances most favourable for its Accumulation.

The capital of a country may be defined to be *that portion of the produce of industry existing in it, which can be made* DIRECTLY *available, either to the support of human existence, or to the facilitating of production.* This definition differs from that of Dr. Smith, which has been adopted by most economists. He divides the whole produce of industry belonging to a country, or its *stock,* into *capital* and *revenue;* the first consisting exclusively of such portions of stock as are employed with the intention of producing some species of commodities; and the second consisting of whatever is employed to maintain or gratify the inhabitants, without any ulterior object. According to Dr. Smith, all this latter part is unproductively consumed, and contributes nothing to the increase of wealth. But these distinctions seem to be for the most part imaginary. Portions of stock employed without any immediate view to production, are often by far the most productive. Consistently with Dr. Smith's definition, the stock that Arkwright and Watt made use of themselves, must be said to have been employed unproductively, or as *revenue;* and yet no one will deny that, by enabling them to subsist and continue their operations, it contributed infinitely more to increase their wealth, and that of the country, than any equal amount of stock expended on the artisans in their service. It is always extremely difficult to say when any portion of stock is, or is not, productively employed; and any definition of capital which involves the determination of such a point, can serve

* Tom. iv. p. 9.

only to embarrass and obscure a subject that is otherwise abundantly simple. In my view of the matter, it is enough to constitute an article capital, that it can directly contribute to the support of man, or assist him in appropriating or producing commodities. It may not, it is true, be employed for either of these purposes, and though it were, it might not produce the anticipated results. But the questions as to the mode of employing an article, and the consequences of that employment, ought, surely, to be held to be, what they obviously are, perfectly distinct from the question, whether that article is capital. For any thing that we can *à priori* know to the contrary, a horse yoked to a gentleman's coach may be quite as productively employed as if he were yoked to a brewer's dray; but whatever difference may obtain in the cases, the identity of the horse is not affected—he is equally possessed, in the one and the other, of the capacity to assist in production; and, so long as he possesses that capacity, he ought to be viewed, independently of all other considerations, as a part of the capital of the country.

It is usual to suppose capital distributed into two great divisions, the one denominated *circulating*, and the other *fixed* capital. But though this distinction be convenient for some purposes, it is one that cannot be made with any considerable accuracy. By circulating capital is commonly meant those portions of capital that are most rapidly consumed, such as food, clothes, and other articles necessary for the subsistence of man, the corn used as seed and in the feeding of horses, coal, &c.; while the lower animals, the houses, and the various instruments and machines, that are either actually employed, or may be employed, in production, are ranged under the head of fixed capital. Without circulating capital, or food, clothes, &c., it would plainly be impossible to engage in any sort of undertaking where the return was not almost immediate; and without fixed capital, or tools, engines, &c. there are very few sorts of labour that could be carried on at all, or with any advantage. But the progressive nature of man, his foresight and invention, lead him, even in the earliest ages, to provide a reserve of food, and to contrive tools and instruments to assist him in his operations. The hunter avails himself of the aid of a club and a sling to abridge his labour, and facilitate the acquisition of game; and the same principle which prompted him to resort to and construct those rude instruments, never ceases to operate: it is always producing some new improvement; and in an advanced and refined period, gives us ships for canoes, muskets for slings, steam-engines for clubs, and cotton-mills for distaffs.

Hence it is only by the employment and co-operation of both descriptions of capital, that wealth can be largely produced, and universally diffused. An agriculturist might have an ample supply of carts and ploughs, of oxen and horses, and, generally, of all the instruments and animals used in his department of industry; but were he destitute of *circulating* capital, or of food and clothes, he would not be able to avail himself of their assistance, and instead of tilling the ground, would have to resort immediately to some species of appropriative industry: and, on the other hand, supposing an agriculturist were abundantly supplied with provisions, what could he do without the assistance of *fixed* capital, or tools? What could the most skilful husbandman perform were he deprived of his spade and his plough?—a weaver were he deprived of his loom?—a carpenter were he deprived of his saw, his hatchet, and his planes?

The division of labour cannot be carried to any considerable extent without the previous accumulation of capital. Before labour can be divided, "a stock of goods of different kinds must be stored up somewhere, sufficient to maintain the labourer, and to supply him with materials and tools. A weaver cannot apply himself entirely to his peculiar business, unless there is beforehand stored up somewhere, either in his own possession or in that of some other person, a stock sufficient to maintain him, and to supply him with the materials and tools of his work, till he has not only completed but sold his web. This accumulation must, evidently, be previous to his applying himself for so long a time to such a peculiar business."*

As the accumulation of capital must have preceded the extensive division of labour, so its subsequent division can only be perfected as capital is more and more accumulated. Accumulation and division act and re-act on each other. The quantity of work which the same number of people can perform increases in a great proportion with every fresh subdivision of labour; and according as the operations of each workman are reduced to a greater degree of identity and simplicity, he has, as already explained, a greater chance of discovering machines and processes for facilitating his separate task. The quantity of industry, therefore, not only increases in every country with the increase of the stock or capital which sets it in motion; but, in consequence of this increase, the division of labour is extended, new and more powerful implements and machines are invented, and the same quantity of labour is made to produce an infinitely greater quantity of commodities.

Besides enabling labour to be divided, capital contributes to facilitate labour and produce wealth in the three following ways:—

First,—It enables work to be executed that could not be executed, or commodities to be produced that could not be produced, without it.

Second,—It saves labour in the production of almost every species of commodities.

Third,—It enables work to be executed better, as well as more expeditiously.

* "Wealth of Nations," vol. ii. p. 2.

With regard to the *first* of these modes in which we are benefited by the employment of capital, or to the circumstance of its *enabling commodities to be produced that could not be produced without it*, it is plain, as has been already observed, that the production of such commodities as require a considerable period for their completion, could not be attempted unless a stock of circulating capital, or of food and clothes sufficient for the maintenance of the labourer while employed on them, was previously provided. But the possession of fixed capital, or of tools and machines, is frequently as necessary to the production of commodities as the possession of circulating capital. It would, for example, be quite impossible to produce a pair of stockings without the aid of wires; and, although the ground might be cultivated without the aid of a plough, it could not be cultivated without the aid of a spade or a hoe. If we run over the vast catalogue of the various arts practised in a polished and civilised country, it will be found that there are extremely few that can be carried on by the mere employment of the fingers, or rude tools with which man is furnished by nature. It is almost always necessary to provide ourselves with the results of previous industry and invention, and to strengthen our feeble hands by arming them, if I may so speak, "with the force of all the elements."

In the *second* place, the employment of capital not only enables many species of commodities to be produced that could not be produced without its co-operation, but it also occasions a *saving of labour in the production of many others*; and thus, by lowering their cost, brings them within the reach of a far greater number of consumers. We have been so long accustomed to avail ourselves of the services of the most commodious and powerful machines, that it requires a considerable effort of abstraction to become fully aware of the advantages derived from them. But if we compare the state of the arts practised alike by civilised man and the savage, we can hardly fail of being convinced that it is to their employment that we owe a very large proportion of our superior comforts and enjoyments. Suppose we were like the Peruvians, and many other people of the New as well as the Old World, destitute of iron,* and unacquainted with the method of domesticating and employing oxen and horses, how prodigious a change for the worse would be made in our condition! It was customary, in some countries, to make cloth by taking up thread after thread of the warp, and passing the woof between them by the unassisted agency of the hand; so that years were consumed in the manufacture of a piece which by the aid of the loom we are enabled to produce in as many days.† It will be afterwards shewn, that nothing, perhaps, has contributed so much to accelerate the progress and diffuse the blessings of civilisation, as the establishment of a commercial intercourse between different and distant nations. But how could this have been effected without the invention and construction of vessels? And if we compare the early navigators, creeping timidly along the shore in canoes, formed out of trees partly hollowed by fire, and partly by the

* Mr. Locke has the following striking observations on the use of iron:—"Of what consequence the discovery of one natural body, and its properties, may be to human life, the whole great continent of America is a convincing instance; whose ignorance in useful arts, and want of the greatest part of the conveniences of life, in a country that abounded with all sorts of natural plenty, I think may be attributed to their ignorance of what was to be found in a very ordinary, despicable stone, I mean the mineral of *iron*. And whatever we think of our parts, or improvements, in this part of the world, where knowledge and plenty seem to vie with each other; yet, to any one that will seriously reflect upon it, I suppose it will appear past doubt, that, were the use of iron lost among us, we should in a few ages be unavoidably reduced to the wants and ignorance of the ancient savage Americans, whose natural endowments and provisions came no way short of those of the most flourishing and polite nations; so that he who first made use of that one contemptible mineral, may be truly stiled the father of arts and author of plenty."—*Essay on the Understanding*, book iv. cap. 12.

† Ulloa, "Voyage de l'Amérique," tom. i. p. 336. Ed. Amst. 1752.

aid of a stone hatchet, or the bone of some animal, with those who now boldly traverse the trackless ocean in noble ships laden with the produce of every climate, we shall have a faint idea of the advance of the arts, and of what we owe to machinery. Those who have distinguished themselves in this career, though they have rarely met with that gratitude and applause from their fellow-citizens to which they had so just a claim, have been the great benefactors of the human race. By pressing the powers of nature into our service, and subjecting them to our control, they have given us almost omnipotent power, and rendered us equal to the most gigantic undertakings. Without their assistance we should have been poor indeed! Such as the naked and half-famished savage of New Holland is at this day, such would the Athenian, the Roman, and the Englishman, have been, but for the invention of machinery, and the employment of natural agents in the great work of production.

The *third* advantage derived from the employment of capital consists in the circumstance of its enabling work to be done *better*, as well as more expeditiously, than it could be done without it. Cotton, for example, might be spun by the hand; but the admirable machines invented by Hargraves, Arkwright, and others, besides enabling us to spin a hundred or a thousand times as much yarn as could be spun by means of a common spindle, have also improved its quality, and given it a degree of fineness and of evenness, or equality, in its parts, which was never previously attained. A painter would occupy months, or it might be years, in painting with a brush the cottons, or printed cloths, used in the hanging of a single room; and it would be very difficult, if not impossible, for the best artist to give the same perfect identity to his figures that is given to them by the machinery now made use of for that purpose. Not to mention the other and more important advantages of which the invention of movable types and printing has been productive, it is certain that the most perfect manuscript — one on which years of patient and irksome labour have been expended — is unable, in point of delicacy and correctness, to match a well-printed work, executed in the hundredth part of the time, and at a hundredth part of the expense. The great foreign demand for English manufactured goods results no less from the superiority of their manufacture than from their greater cheapness; and for both these advantages we are principally indebted to the excellence of our machinery.

There are other considerations which equally illustrate the extreme importance of the accumulation and employment of capital. The produce of the labour of a nation cannot be increased otherwise than by an increase in the number of its labourers, or in their productive powers; but without an increase of capital, it is in most cases impossible to employ another workman with advantage. If the food and clothes destined for the support of the labourers, and the tools and machines with which they are to operate, be all required for the maintenance and efficient employment of those already in existence, there can be no additional demand for others. Under such circumstances, the rate of wages cannot rise; and if the number of inhabitants be increased, they must be worse provided for. Neither is it at all probable that the powers of the labourer should be augmented, except capital be previously increased. Without the better education and training of workmen, the greater subdivision of their employments, or the improvement of machinery, their productive energies can never be materially increased; and in almost all these cases, additional capital is required. It is seldom, unless by its means, that workmen can be better trained, or that the undertaker of any work can either provide them with better machinery, or make a more proper distribution of labour among them. Should the work to be done consist of a number of parts, to keep a workman constantly employed in one only requires a much larger stock than when he is occasionally employed in every different part. "When," says Dr. Smith, "we compare the state of a nation at two different periods, and find that the annual produce of its land and labour is evidently greater at the latter than at the former, that its lands are better cultivated, its manufactures more numerous and more flourishing, and its trade more extensive; we may be assured that its capital must have increased during the interval between these two periods, and that more must have been added to it, by the good conduct of some, than had been taken from it, either by the private misconduct of others, or by the public extravagance of government."* It is therefore apparent, that no country can ever reach the stationary state, so long as she continues to accumulate additional capital. While she does this, she will always have a constantly increasing demand for labour, and will be constantly augmenting the mass of necessaries, luxuries, and conveniences, and consequently also the numbers of her people. But with every diminution of the rate at which capital had been previously accumulating, the demand for labour will decline. When no additions are made to capital, no more labour will be, or, at least, can be advantageously, employed. And should the national capital diminish, the condition of the great body of the people would deteriorate; the wages of labour would be reduced; and pauperism, with its attendant train of vice, misery, and crime, would spread its ravages throughout society.

Having thus endeavoured to shew what capital is, the importance of its employment, and the manner in which it operates to facilitate production; I shall proceed to explain its origin, and the circumstances most favourable for its accumulation.

Had it been a law of nature that the quantity of

* "Wealth of Nations," vol. ii. p. 116.

produce obtained from industrious undertakings should merely suffice to replace that which had been expended in carrying them on, society could have made no progress, and man must have continued in the state in which he was originally placed. But such is not the established order of things. It is so constituted that, in the vast majority of cases, more wealth or produce is obtained through the agency of a given quantity of labour, than is required to enable it to be performed. This surplus, or excess of produce, has been denominated *profit;* and it is from it that all capital has been derived. Man is naturally provident: it is not enough that his immediate wants are supplied; he looks forward to the future. Even the savage who kills more game in a day than he can consume, does not throw the surplus away; experience has taught him that he may be less fortunate on another occasion; and he, therefore, either preserves it as a reserve against any future emergency, or barters it with his fellow-savages for some article belonging to them. Neither could experience be long in suggesting, that the previous accumulation of a stock of provisions was indispensable to enable individuals to engage in undertakings which, though productive in the end, required some considerable time before they made any return. No doubt, therefore, the principle which prompts to save and amass, which leads man to sacrifice an immediate gratification for the sake of an increase of security, or a greater enjoyment at some future period, manifested itself in the earliest ages. At first, indeed, its operation must have been comparatively feeble. But it gathered fresh strength and consistency, according as the many advantages of which it is productive gradually disclosed themselves. The dried fish, canoes, and spears of the wretched inhabitants of Terra del Fuego exhibit the first fruits of that powerful passion, to which we owe all the accumulated riches of the world.

Seeing, therefore, that capital is formed out of the excess of the produce realised by those who engage in industrious undertakings over and above the produce necessarily expended in carrying them on; it plainly follows, that the *means* of amassing capital will be greatest where this excess is greatest; or, in other words, that they will be greatest where the rate of profit is greatest. This is so obvious a proposition as hardly to require illustration. The man who can produce a bushel of wheat in *two* days has it evidently in his power to accumulate twice as much as the man who, either from a deficiency of skill, or from his being obliged to cultivate a bad soil, is forced to labour *four* days to produce the same quantity; and the capitalist who can invest stock so as to yield a profit of ten *per cent* has it equally in his power to accumulate twice as fast as the capitalist who cannot find a mode of investment that will yield more than five *per cent.** It is true that high profits only give the means of amassing capital—that, if men had always lived up to their incomes, that is, if they had always consumed the whole produce of their industry in the gratification of their immediate wants, or desires, there could have been no such thing as capital in the world. But experience shews, that while high profits afford greater means of saving, they, at the same time, give additional force to the parsimonious principle. Economy is in no respect different from the other virtues; and it would be unreasonable to expect that it should be strongly manifested, where it does not bring along with it a corresponding reward. Before a man can accumulate, he must live: and if the sum that remains to him, after his necessary expenses are deducted, be but small and trifling, the probability is, that he will rather choose to consume it immediately, than to hoard it up in the expectation, that, by the addition of farther savings, it may, at some future and

* This is in reality understated. It is plain, inasmuch as all parties must live on their profits, that those who gain double could accumulate more than twice as fast as the others.

very distant period, become the means of making a small addition to his income. But wherever profits are high, and there is a great power of accumulation, we deny ourselves immediate gratifications, because we have a certain prospect that, by doing so, we shall speedily attain to a state of comparative affluence; and that our future means of obtaining an increased supply of conveniences and luxuries will be greatly increased by our present forbearance. Give to any people the power of accumulating, and you may depend upon it they will not be disinclined to use it effectively. Those who inquire into the circumstances which have determined the state of the different countries of the world, will find that the power of accumulation, or, which is the same thing, the rate of profit, has uniformly been greatest in those which have made the most rapid advances. In the United States, for example, the rate of profit is commonly twice as high as in Great Britain or Holland; and it is to its greater magnitude that the comparatively quick progress of that republic in wealth and population is wholly to be ascribed. The desire of adding to our fortune, and improving our condition, is inherent in the human constitution, and is the fundamental principle, the *causa causans,* of all the improvements that have ever been made. It is impossible to specify a single instance of any people having missed an opportunity of amassing. Whenever the bulk of the citizens have the power of adding to their stock, they never fail to do so. "No measure of fortune, or degree of skill, is found to diminish the supposed necessities of human life; refinement and plenty foster new desires, while they furnish the means or practise the methods to gratify them."*

Perhaps it will be said, in opposition to these statements, that the rate of profit is high in Eastern countries, and that they are, notwithstanding, either retrograding or

* Ferguson's "Essay on Civil Society," p. 360.

advancing only by imperceptible degrees. It may be questioned, however, whether the rate of profit be really higher in them than in Europe. No doubt the rate of *interest* is higher; but that is a consequence of the hazard to which the principal is exposed, because of the prejudices against usury, and the vicious and defective nature of Eastern governments. All taking of interest is prohibited by the Koran; and this is really one of the chief reasons why it is so very high in the countries which respect its authority. "L'usure," says Montesquieu, "augmente dans les pays Mahometans á proportion de la sévérité de la défense. Il faut que le prêteur s'indemnise du peril de la contravention."* It is not meant, however, to affirm, that great productiveness of industry, or a high rate of profit, is necessarily, and in every instance, accompanied by a great degree of prosperity. Countries with every imaginable capability for the profitable employment of industry and stock may have the misfortune to be subjected to an arbitrary government, which does not respect the right of property; and the insecurity thence resulting may be sufficient to paralyse all the exertions of those who are otherwise placed in the most favourable situation for the accumulation of capital and wealth. But I believe it may be laid down as a principle, from which there is really no exception, that if any two or more countries have governments that are about equally tolerant and liberal, and give equal protection to property, their prosperity will be in proportion to the rate of profit in each. Wherever profits are high, capital is rapidly augmented, and there is a comparatively rapid increase of wealth and population; but, on the other hand, wherever profits are low, the means of employing additional labour are comparatively limited, and the progress of society rendered so much the slower.

* "Esprit des Loix," liv. xxi. chap. 19.

It is not, therefore, by the absolute amount of its capital, but by *its power of employing that capital with advantage*—a power which, in all ordinary cases, is correctly measured by the common and average rate of profit—that the capacity of any country to increase in wealth and population is to be estimated. Before the laws regulating the rate of profit and the increase of capital had been thoroughly investigated, the great wealth and commercial prosperity of Holland, where profits, from 1650 downwards, were comparatively low, were considered by Sir Josiah Child, and many later writers, as the natural result, and were consequently regarded by them as a convincing proof, of the superior advantages of low profits and interest. But this was really, as will be afterwards shewn, mistaking the *effect of heavy taxation* for the *cause of wealth!* A country where profits are considerably lower than in others, may, notwithstanding, abound in wealth, and be possessed of immense capital; but it is the height of error to suppose, that this lowness of profits could have facilitated their accumulation. The truth is, that the low rate of profit in Holland during the 18th century was at once a cause and a symptom of her decline. Sir William Temple mentions, in his Observations on the Netherlands, written about 1670, that the trade of Holland had then passed its zenith; and it is certain, that the vast capitals of the Dutch merchants had been principally amassed previously to the wars in which the republic was successively engaged with Cromwell, Charles II., and Louis XIV., and when the rate of profit was much higher than at any subsequent period.

But without referring to the case of America, Holland, or any other country, the smallest reflection on the motives which induce men to engage in any branch of industry is sufficient to shew that the advantages derived from it are always supposed to be *directly as the rate of profit*. What is the object which every man has in view when he employs either his capital, or his personal powers, in any industrious undertaking? Is it not to gain the greatest possible amount of profit on his capital, or the greatest possible reward for his labour? One branch of industry is said to be peculiarly advantageous, for the single and sufficient reason that it yields a comparatively large profit; and another is, with equal propriety, said to be peculiarly disadvantageous, because it yields a comparatively small profit. It is always to this *standard*—to the high or low rate of profit which they yield—that every individual refers in judging of the comparative benefits of different undertakings;—and what is true of individuals, must be true of states.

No certain conclusion respecting the prosperity of any country can ever be drawn from the magnitude of its commerce or revenue, or the state of its agriculture or manufactures. Every branch of industry is liable to be affected by secondary or accidental causes. They are always in a state of flux or reflux; and some of them are frequently seen to flourish when others are very much depressed. The AVERAGE RATE OF PROFIT is the best barometer—the best criterion of national prosperity. A rise of profits is, speaking generally, the effect of industry having become *more* productive; and it shews that the power of the society to amass capital, and to add to its wealth and population, has been increased, and its progress accelerated: a fall of profits, on the contrary, is the effect of industry having become *less* productive, and shews that the power to amass capital has been diminished, and that the progress of the society has been clogged and impeded.* However much a particular, and it may be an important, branch of industry is depressed,

* I am here only laying down the leading principles on the subject. In the chapter on the "Circumstances which determine the Rate of Profit," I shall endeavour to investigate the influence of fluctuations in the value of money, of loans to government, &c., on profits. The doctrine advanced in the text is meant only to apply in cases where these disturbing causes are not in operation.

still, if *the average rate* of profit be high, we may be assured that the depression cannot continue, and that the condition of the country is really prosperous. On the other hand, though there should be no distress in any particular branch—though agriculture, manufactures, and commerce, should be carried to a greater extent than they have ever been carried before—though a nation should have numerous, powerful, and well-appointed armies and fleets, and though the style of living among the higher classes should be more than ordinarily sumptuous,—still, if the rate of profit have become comparatively low, we may pretty confidently affirm, that the condition of such a nation, however prosperous in appearance, is bad and unsound at bottom; that the plague of poverty is secretly creeping on the mass of her citizens; that the foundations of her power and greatness have been shaken; and that her decline may be anticipated, unless measures be devised for relieving the pressure on the national resources, by adding to the productiveness of industry, and consequently, to the rate of profit.

It has been wisely ordered, that the principle which prompts to save and amass should be as powerful as it is advantageous. "With regard to profusion," says Dr. Smith, "the principle which prompts to expense is the passion for present enjoyment; which, though sometimes violent, and very difficult to be restrained, is in general only momentary and occasional. But the principle which prompts to save, is the desire of bettering our condition; a desire which, though generally calm and dispassionate, comes with us from the womb, and never leaves us till we go into the grave. In the whole interval which separates these two moments, there is scarce, perhaps, a single instant in which any man is so perfectly and completely satisfied with his situation as to be without any wish of alteration or improvement of any kind. An augmentation of fortune is the means by which the greater part of men propose and wish to better their condition.

It is the means the most vulgar and the most obvious; and the most likely way of augmenting their fortune is to save and accumulate some part of what they acquire, either regularly and annually, or upon some extraordinary occasion. Though the principle of expense, therefore, prevails in almost all men upon some occasions, and in some men upon almost all occasions, yet in the greater part of men, taking the whole course of their life at an average, the principle of frugality seems not only to predominate, but to predominate very greatly."*

It is this principle which carries society forward. The spirit of parsimony, and the efforts which the frugal and industrious classes make to improve their condition, in most instances balance not only the profusion of individuals, but also the more wasteful profusion and extravagance of governments. This spirit has been happily compared by Smith to the unknown principle of animal life—the *vis medicatrix naturæ*—which frequently restores health and vigour to the constitution, in spite both of disease and of the injudicious prescriptions of the physician. So powerful indeed is its influence, that, notwithstanding the many hundreds of millions that have been spent in warlike enterprises by this country since the Revolution, and particularly during the late war, it is certain that the national capital was greater at the termination of the last, as of every preceding contest, than at its commencement.

But, however great the capacity of the principle of accumulation to repair the waste of capital, we must take care not to fall into the error of supposing, as very many have done, that its operations are in *all* cases promoted by a large public expenditure. To a certain extent, indeed, this is true. A moderate increase of taxation has the same effect on the habits and industry

* "Wealth of Nations," vol. ii. p. 112.

of a nation, that an increase of his family, or of his necessary and unavoidable expenses, has upon a private individual. Man is not influenced solely by hope; he is also powerfully operated upon by fear. Taxation brings this latter principle into the field. To the desire of rising in the world, inherent in the breast of every individual, an increase of taxation superadds the fear of being cast down to a lower station, of being deprived of conveniences and gratifications which habit has rendered almost indispensable; and the combined influence of the two principles produces efforts that could not be produced by the unassisted agency of either. They stimulate individuals to endeavour, by increased efforts of industry and economy, to repair the breach taxation has made in their fortunes; and it not unfrequently happens that their efforts do more than this, and that, consequently, the national wealth is increased through the increase of taxation. But we must be on our guard against the abuse of this doctrine. To render an increase of taxation a cause of greater exertion, economy, and invention, its increase should be slow and gradual; and it should never be carried to such a height as to incapacitate individuals from making the sacrifices it imposes on them, by such a moderate degree of increased exertion and economy as it may be in their power to make without requiring any very violent change in their habits. The increase of taxation must not be such as to render it impracticable to overcome its influence, or to induce the belief that it is impracticable. Difficulties that are seen to be surmountable sharpen the inventive powers, and are readily grappled with; but an apparently insurmountable difficulty, or such an excessive weight of taxation as it was deemed impossible to meet, would not stimulate but destroy exertion. Instead of producing new efforts of ingenuity and economy, it would produce only despair. Whenever taxation becomes so heavy that the produce it takes from individuals can no longer be replaced by fresh efforts, such efforts uniformly cease to be made;

the population becomes dispirited; industry is paralysed; and the country rapidly declines.

A striking illustration of the truth of what has now been stated, may be derived from observing what takes place with respect to the occupation of land by farmers. It might seem, on a superficial view of the matter, that the circumstance of a farm being low rented would not occasion any decline of the tenant's industry, seeing that every thing he could make it produce, over and above the rent, by diligence and economy, would belong to himself. Such, however, is not found to be really the case; and it is very difficult to say whether the over or under renting of land be most injurious. If a farm be too high rented, that is, if no exertion of skill, or reasonable outlay on the part of the tenant, can enable him to pay his rent and obtain a fair return for his trouble, he gets dispirited. The farm is in consequence ill managed; scourging crops are resorted to; and ultimately it is thrown on the landlord's hands, in an impoverished and deteriorated condition. But the disadvantages attending the under-renting of land are hardly less obvious. To make farmers leave those routine practices to which they are very strongly attached, and become really industrious and enterprising, they must not only have the power of rising in the world, but their rents must be such as to impress them with a conviction, that if they do not make the necessary exertions their ruin will assuredly follow. Estates that are under-rented are, uniformly almost, farmed in a very inferior style to those that are let at their fair value; and the tenants are comparatively poor. "I have not," says Mr. Young, "seen an instance of rent being very low, and husbandry, at the same time, being good. Innumerable are the instances of farmers living miserably, and even breaking, on farms at very low rents, being succeeded by others, on the same land, at very high rents, who make fortunes. Throughout my journey I have universally observed, that such farms as were the most wretchedly managed were very much under-let."*

What an increase of rent is to the farmers, an increase of taxation is to the public. If it be carried beyond due bounds, or to such an extent that it cannot be fully balanced by increased efforts to produce and save, it is productive only of national poverty and decline; but so long as it is confined within moderate limits, it acts as a powerful stimulus to industry and economy, and most commonly occasions the production of more wealth than it abstracts.

That capital is formed out of profit, and that profit is itself the surplus obtained from industrious undertakings, after the produce expended in carrying them on has been fully replaced, is a proposition, which, though universally true, is at variance with the common notions on the subject. Instead of supposing profits to originate in the manner now stated, they are almost uniformly supposed to depend on the sale of the produce, and to be made at the expense of the purchaser. Thus, to take a familiar instance, the hat-maker who sells a hat for thirty shillings, which cost him twenty-five shillings of outlay, believes himself, and is universally believed by others, to have made the five shillings of profit at the expense of the individual who bought the hat. In truth and reality, however, he has done no such thing. He produced, in a given time, a hat equivalent to, or worth, in silver, thirty shillings, while the various expenses necessarily incurred in its manufacture only amounted to twenty-five shillings. But then it must be borne in mind that, speaking generally, the various individuals who deal with the hat-maker are placed in

* Young's "Tour in the North of England," vol. iv. p. 376. See also "Analysis of the Statistical Account of Scotland," part i. p. 258, &c. for proofs of the same principle.

the same situation: the farmer, the clothier, the bootmaker, &c. are all making the same profits in their respective businesses; or, in other words, they are all producing quantities of corn, cloth, boots, &c., equal to thirty shillings, by an outlay of twenty-five shillings. It is clear, therefore, that in exchanging the precious metals for commodities, or in exchanging one sort of commodities for another, the one party gains nothing at the expense of the other. Profit is in all cases the result of more being produced in a given period than has been consumed in that period. The introduction of exchanges would not be advantageous, if it merely enabled one set of individuals to prey upon some other set. This, however, is not its effect. By enabling labour to be divided, it gives individuals the means of employing themselves in preference in some one pursuit, and consequently causes commodities to be produced and distributed in the best and cheapest manner; but it does nothing more.

If the popular opinions with respect to the source of profits were well founded, it would inevitably follow, inasmuch as they take for granted that all producers make their profits at the expense of some one else who buys their commodities, not only that no additions could be made to capital, but that the capital now in the world would be very soon annihilated. If such were really a correct view of the circumstances under which mankind are placed, our lot would be any thing but enviable. Happily, however, this is not our situation. The produce of the labour we exert during any given time, is almost always greater than the produce we are obliged to consume during the same time; and the surplus or profit being accumulated, becomes, in its turn, an instrument of vast power, and adds prodigiously to the productiveness of industry.

It is clear, therefore, that there is really no class of industrious individuals who live at the expense of any other class. The retail dealer, for example, is in no respect more indebted to his customers than they are to him. It is not *his*, but *their own*, interest that they have in view, when they resort to his shop. Society is, in truth, as M. Destutt Tracy has remarked, nothing but a continued series of exchanges ;* but they are exchanges in which full equivalents are always given for whatever is received. Profits are a consequence of the bounty of nature ; and do not in any degree depend on the superior acuteness of those who sell, or on the weakness and simplicity of those who buy. The advantages observed to result from the separation of employments has occasioned the division of society into particular classes, who exchange the surplus produce of their own labour for the surplus produce of the labour of others ; and the intercourse thence arising is one by which, from the greater facility with which it renders all sorts of useful and desirable commodities obtainable, all individuals are mutually benefited. This, however, it must always be kept in view, is the whole effect of the division of labour, and of the introduction of a system of exchanges. To whatever extent that division may be carried, it is still true that profits depend not on it, or on exchanges, but on the excess of the commodities produced in a given period, over those that are consumed in the same period.

However extended the sense previously attached to the term capital may at first sight appear, I am disposed to think that it might be interpreted still more comprehensively. Instead of understanding by capital all that portion of the produce of industry extrinsic to man, which may be made applicable to his support, and to the facilitating of production, there does not seem to be any good reason why man himself should not, and very many why he should, be considered as forming a part of the national capital. Man is as much the produce of previous outlays

* "Economie Politique," p. 78.

of wealth expended on his subsistence, education, &c. as any of the instruments constructed by his agency; and it would seem, that in those inquiries which regard only his mechanical operations, and do not involve the consideration of his higher and nobler powers, he should be regarded in precisely the same point of view. Every individual who has arrived at maturity, though he may not be instructed in any particular art or profession, may yet, with perfect propriety, be viewed, in relation to his natural powers, as a machine which it has cost twenty years of assiduous attention, and the expenditure of a considerable capital, to construct. And if a farther sum be expended in qualifying him for the exercise of a business or profession requiring unusual skill, his value will be proportionally increased, and he will be entitled to a greater reward for his exertions; as a machine becomes more valuable when new powers are given to it by the expenditure of additional capital or labour in its construction.

Dr. Smith has fully admitted the justice of this principle, though he has not reasoned consistently from it. He states, that the acquired and useful talents of the inhabitants ought to be considered as forming a portion of the national capital. "The acquisition of such talents," he justly observes, "during the education, study, or apprenticeship of the acquirer, always costs a real expense, which is a capital fixed and realised, as it were, in his person. Those talents, as they make a part of his fortune, so do they likewise of that of the society to which he belongs. The improved dexterity of a workman may be considered in the same light as a machine or instrument of trade, which facilitates and abridges labour, and which, though it costs a certain expense, repays that expense with a profit."*

Instead, then, of being entirely overlooked, as is most fréquently the case, the dexterity, skill, and intelligence

* Vol. ii. p. 12.

of the mass of its inhabitants ought to be most particularly attended to in estimating the capital and productive capacities of a country. Much stress is uniformly and justly laid on the power and efficacy of the machines which man has constructed to assist him in his undertakings; but man is himself the most important of all machines, and every addition made to his skill and dexterity is an acquisition of the utmost consequence. The discrepancies that actually obtain in the physical organisation and capacities of the various races of men, are comparatively trifling; and yet, how vast is the difference, in other points of view, between an American Indian or an African, and an Englishman or a Frenchman! The former, ignorant and uninstructed, is poor and miserable, though placed in countries blessed with a soil of exhaustless fertility and a genial climate; the latter, intelligent and educated, is wealthy, prosperous, and happy, though placed under comparatively unfavourable circumstances. Lord Bacon's aphorism, that *knowledge is power*, is true as well in a physical as a moral sense. It not only enables its possessors to obtain an ascendancy over their less-instructed neighbours, but it makes immeasurable additions to their productive capacities. An ignorant and uneducated people, though they may possess all the materials and powers necessary for the production of wealth, are uniformly sunk in poverty and barbarism. And until their mental powers have begun to expand, and they have been taught to exercise the empire of mind over matter, the avenues to improvement are shut against them, and they have neither the power nor the wish to emerge from their low and degraded condition.

It has been said, and perhaps truly, that it was the rapid growth and extension of the cotton manufacture that bore us triumphantly through the late dreadful contest, and gave us wealth and power sufficient to overcome the combined force of almost all Europe, though wielded by a chief of consummate talent. But, what is the cotton manufacture? Is it not wholly the result of the discoveries and inventions of Hargraves, Arkwright, Crompton, Cartwright, and a few others?* It was their sagacity that discovered and explored this mighty channel for the profitable employment of millions upon millions of capital, and of thousands upon thousands of workmen; so that all the various and innumerable benefits and advantages we have derived from it, are to be ascribed to them as to their original authors and inventors.

To those who are impressed with a conviction of the truth of the principles thus briefly stated — who are duly sensible of the vast importance of science to the advancement of nations, nothing can be more gratifying than the progress made of late years in diffusing instruction among the great mass of the community. The discoveries of Bell and Lancaster, and the schools founded on their principles, have had a powerful influence in spreading a knowledge of the elementary branches of instruction; while the Mechanics' Institutions formed in the metropolis, and other great towns, afford the labouring part of the population an opportunity of perfecting themselves in their respective arts, by making them acquainted with the principles on which they depend, and from the better application of which every new improvement must be derived. It is impossible to form any accurate estimate of the beneficial influence of this general instruction on the future fortunes of the empire; but it is abundantly certain that it must be very great. More discoveries will be made, according to the degree in which more individuals are placed in a situation to make them. And it is neither impossible, nor at all improbable, that the lustre which now attaches to the names of Arkwright and Watt may be dimmed, though it can never be wholly effaced, by the more numerous, and, it may be, more important

* For an account of the rise, progress, and present state of the cotton manufacture, see the "Edinburgh Review," no. xci.

discoveries, that will, at no distant period, be made by those who would have passed from the cradle to the tomb in the same obscure and beaten track that had been trodden by their unambitious ancestors, had not the education now so generally diffused, served to elicit and ripen the seeds of genius implanted in them for the common advantage of mankind.*

* There are some striking and useful remarks on the influence of observation and knowledge on production, in Mr. Hodgskin's work, entitled "Popular Political Economy."

CHAPTER III.

Definition and Growth of Credit — Contributes to facilitate Production by distributing Capital in the most advantageous manner — Circulation of Bills, &c.

HAVING seen, in the last chapter, the effects resulting from the accumulation and employment of capital, our attention is next called to the subject of credit. This is most commonly represented as a very effective agent in the production of wealth; and though its influence has been, in this respect, a good deal exaggerated, it is, notwithstanding, of very considerable importance.

Credit is the term used to express the trust or confidence placed by one individual in another when he assigns him property in loan, or without stipulating for the immediate payment of its price. The party who lends is said to give credit, and the party who borrows to obtain credit.

In the earlier stages of society credit is in a great measure unknown. This arises partly from the circumstance of very little capital being then accumulated, and partly from government not having the means, or not being sufficiently careful, to enforce that punctual attention to engagements so indispensable to the existence of confidence or credit. But as society advances, capital is gradually accumulated, and the observance of contracts is enforced by the public authority. Credit then begins to grow up. On the one hand, individuals who have either more capital than they can conveniently employ, or who are desirous of withdrawing from business, are disposed to lend, or to transfer a part or the whole of their capital to others, on condition of their obtaining a certain stipulated premium or interest for its use, and what they consider sufficient security for its repayment; and on the other hand, there are always individuals to be met with disposed to borrow, partly and principally in order to extend their businesses beyond the limits to which they can be carried by means of their own capital, or to purchase commodities on speculation, and partly to defray debts already contracted. These different classes of individuals mutually accommodate each other. Those desirous of being relieved from the fatigues of business, find it very convenient to lend their capital to others; while those who are anxious to enlarge their businesses, obtain the means of prosecuting them to a greater extent.

Now, it is in the effects resulting from this transference of capital from those who are willing to lend to those who are desirous to borrow, that we must seek for the advantages derivable from credit. The immediate and direct effect of all the operations carried on by its agency, how extensive and complicated soever they may appear, is merely to occasion a change in the actual holders or employers of stock. Nothing, indeed, is more common than to hear it stated, that commodities are produced, and the most expensive operations carried on, by means of credit or confidence; but this is an obvious mistake. Wealth cannot be produced, nor can any sort of industrious undertaking be entered upon or completed, without the aid of labour and capital; and all that credit does, or can do, is, by facilitating the transfer of capital from one individual to another, to bring it into the possession of those who, it is most probable, will employ it to the greatest advantage. A few remarks will render this apparent.

It is plain, that to whatever extent the power of the borrower of a quantity of produce, or a sum of money, to extend his business, may be increased, that of the lender must be equally diminished. The same portion of capital cannot be employed by two individuals at the same time. If A transfer his capital to B, he necessarily, by so doing, deprives himself of a power or capacity of production which B acquires. It is most probable, indeed, that this capital will be more productively employed in the hands of B than of A; for the fact of A having lent it, shews that he either had no means of employing it advantageously, or was disinclined to take the trouble; while the fact of B having borrowed it, shews that he conceives he can advantageously employ it, or that he can invest it so as to make it yield an interest to the lender and a profit to himself. It is obvious, however, that except in so far as credit has the effect of thus bringing capital into the possession of those who, it may be fairly presumed, will employ it most beneficially, it can contribute nothing to the increase of wealth.

The most common method of making a loan is by selling commodities on credit, or on condition that they shall be paid at some future period. The price is increased proportionally to the length of credit given; and if any doubt be entertained with respect to the punctuality or solvency of the buyer, a farther sum is added to the price, in order to cover the risk that the seller or lender runs of not recovering the price, or of not recovering it at the stipulated period. This is the usual method of transacting business where capital is abundant and confidence general; and there can be no manner of doubt that the amount of property lent in Great Britain, the Netherlands, and most other commercial countries, in this way, is infinitely greater than all that is lent in all other ways.

When produce is sold in the way now described, it is usual for the buyers to give their bills to the sellers for the price, payable at the period when the credit is to expire; and it is in the effects consequent to the negotiation of such bills that much of that *magical* influence that has sometimes been ascribed to credit is believed to consist. Suppose, to illustrate this, that a paper-maker, A, sells to a printer, B, a quantity of paper, and that he gets his bill for the sum, payable at twelve months after date: B could not have entered into the transaction had he been obliged to pay ready money; but A, notwithstanding he has occasion for the money, is enabled, by the facility of negotiating or discounting bills, to give the requisite credit, without disabling himself from prosecuting his business. In a case like this, both parties are said to be supported by credit; and as cases of this sort are exceedingly common, it is contended that half the business of the country is really carried on by its means. All, however, that such statements really amount to is, that a large proportion of those engaged in industrious undertakings do not employ their own capital, but that of others. In the case in question, the printer employs the capital of the paper-maker, and the latter employs that of the banker or broker who discounted the bill. This person had, most likely, the amount in spare cash lying beside him, which he might not well know what to make of; but the individual into whose hands it has now come will immediately apply it to useful purposes, or to the purchase of the materials, or the payment of the wages of the workmen employed in his establishment. It is next to certain, therefore, that the transaction will have been advantageous. But still it is essential to bear in mind that it will have been so, not because credit is of itself a means of production, or because it can give birth to capital not already in existence; but because, through its agency, capital finds its way into those channels in which it has the best chance of being profitably employed.

The real advantage derived from the use of bills and bank-notes as money, consists, as will be afterwards shewn, in their substituting so cheap a medium of exchange as paper, in the place of one so expensive as gold, and in the facilities which they give to the transacting of commercial affairs. If a banker lend A a note for 100*l*. or 1,000*l*., he will be able to obtain an equivalent portion of the land or produce of the country in exchange for it; but that land or produce was already in existence. The issue of the note did not give it birth. It was previously in some one's possession; and it will depend wholly on the circumstance of A's employing it more or less advantageously than it was previously employed, whether the transaction will, in a public point of view, be profitable or not. On analysing any case of this kind, we shall *invariably* find that all that the highest degree of credit or confidence can do, is merely to change the distribution of capital — to transfer it from one class to another. These transfers are occasionally too productive of injurious results, by bringing capital into the hands of spendthrifts: this, however, is not a very common effect; and there can be no doubt that they are, in the majority of instances, decidedly beneficial.

The following extract from the evidence of Mr. Ricardo before the Committee appointed by the House of Lords in 1819, to inquire into the expediency of the resumption of cash payments by the Bank of England, sets the principles I have been endeavouring to establish in a very clear point of view.

"Do you not know," Mr. Ricardo was asked, "that when there is a great demand for manufactures, the very credit which that circumstance creates enables the manufacturer to make a more extended use of his capital in the production of manufactures?" To this Mr. Ricardo answered, "I have no notion of credit being at all effectual in the production of commodities; commodities can only be produced by labour, machinery, and raw materials; and if these are to be employed in one place, they must necessarily be withdrawn from another. Credit is the means, which is alternately transferred from one to another, to make use of capital actually existing; it does not create capital; it determines only by whom that capital shall be employed: the removal of capital from one employment to another may often be very advantageous, and it may also be very injurious."

Mr. Ricardo was then asked, "May not a man get credit from a bank on the security of his capital which is profitably employed, whether vested in stock or land; and may he not, by means of that credit, purchase or create an additional quantity of machinery and raw materials, and pay an additional number of labourers, without dislodging capital from any existing employment in the country?" To this Mr. Ricardo answered, "Impossible! an individual can purchase machinery, &c. with credit; he can never create them. If he purchase, it is always of some one else; and consequently he displaces some other from the employment of capital."*

* "Lords' Report," p. 192.

CHAPTER IV.

Circumstances which led to the Introduction and Use of Money—Qualities which a Commodity used as Money should possess—Use of Coinage—Variations in the Value of Money—Introduction and Use of Paper Money.

WHEN the division of labour was first introduced, commodities were directly bartered for each other. Those, for example, who had a surplus of corn, and were in want of wine, endeavoured to find out those who were in the opposite circumstances, or who had a surplus of wine and wanted corn, and then exchanged the one for the other. It is obvious, however, that the power of exchanging, and, consequently, of dividing employments, must have been subjected to perpetual interruptions, so long as it was restricted to mere barter. A carries produce to market, and B is desirous to purchase it; but the produce belonging to B is not suitable for A. C, again, would like to buy B's produce, but B is already fully supplied with the equivalent C has to offer. In such cases, and they must be of constant occurrence wherever money is not introduced, no direct exchange could take place between the parties; and it might be very difficult to bring it about indirectly.*

The extreme inconvenience attending such situations must early have forced themselves on the attention of every one. Efforts would, in consequence, be made to avoid them; and it would speedily appear that the best or rather the only way in which this could be effected, was to exchange either the whole or a part of one's

* The difficulties that would arise on such occasions, and the devices that would be adopted to overcome them, have been very well illustrated by Colonel Torrens, in his work on the "Production of Wealth," p. 291.

surplus produce for some commodity of known value, and in general demand; and which, consequently, few persons would be inclined to refuse to accept as an equivalent for whatever they had to dispose of. After this commodity had begun to be employed as a means of exchanging other commodities, individuals would become willing to purchase a greater quantity of it than might be required to pay for the products they were desirous of immediately obtaining; knowing that should they, at any future period, want a further supply either of these or other articles, they would be able readily to procure them in exchange for this universally desired commodity. Though at first circulating slowly and with difficulty, it would, as the advantages arising from its use were better appreciated, begin to pass freely from hand to hand. Its value, as compared with other things, would thus come to be universally known; and it would at last be used not only as the common medium of exchange, but as a standard by which to measure the value of other things.

Now this commodity, whatever it may be, is *money*.

An infinite variety of commodities have been used as money in different countries and periods. But none can be advantageously used as such, unless it possess several very peculiar qualities. The slightest reflection on the purposes to which it is applied, must, indeed, be sufficient to convince every one that it is indispensable, or, at least exceedingly desirable, that the commodity selected to serve as money should (1) be divisible into the smallest portions; (2) that it should admit of being kept for an indefinite period without deteriorating; (3) that it should, by possessing great value in small bulk, be capable of being easily transported from place to place; (4) that one piece of money of a certain denomination, should always be equal, in magnitude and quality, to every other piece of money of the same denomination; and (5) that its value should be comparatively steady, or as little subject to variation as possible. Without the *first* of these qualities, or the capacity of being divided into portions of every different magnitude and value, money, it is evident, would be of almost no use, and could only be exchanged for the few commodities that might happen to be of the same value as its indivisible portions, or as whole multiples of them: without the *second*, or the capacity of being kept or hoarded without deteriorating, no one would choose to exchange commodities for money, except only when he expected to be able speedily to re-exchange that money for something else: without the *third*, or facility of transportation, money could not be conveniently used in transactions between places at any considerable distance: without the *fourth*, or perfect sameness, it would be extremely difficult to appreciate the value of different pieces of money: and without the *fifth* quality, or comparative steadiness of value, money could not serve as a standard by which to measure the value of other commodities; and no one would be disposed to exchange the produce of his industry for an article that might shortly decline considerably in its power of purchasing.

The union of the different qualities of comparative steadiness of value, divisibility, durability, facility of transportation, and perfect sameness, in the precious metals, doubtless, formed the irresistible reason that has induced every civilised community to employ them as money. The value of gold and silver is certainly not invariable, but, generally speaking, it changes only by slow degrees; they are divisible into any number of parts, and have the singular property of being easily re-united, by means of fusion, without loss; they do not deteriorate by being kept; and, from their firm and compact texture, they are very difficult to wear. Their cost of production, especially that of gold, is so considerable, that they possess great value in small bulk, and can, of course, be transported with comparative facility; and an ounce of pure gold or silver, taken from the mines in any quarter of the world, is precisely equal, in point of quality, to an ounce of pure gold or silver dug from the mines in any other quarter. No wonder, therefore, when all the qualities necessary to constitute money are possessed in so eminent a degree by the precious metals, that they have been used as such, in civilised societies, from a very remote era. "They became universal money," as M. Turgot has observed, "not in consequence of any arbitrary agreement among men, or of the intervention of any law, but by the nature and force of things."

When first used as money, the precious metals were in an unfashioned state, in bars or ingots. The parties having agreed about the quantity of metal to be given for a commodity, that quantity was then weighed off. But this, it is plain, must have been a tedious and troublesome process. Undoubtedly, however, the greatest obstacle that would be experienced in early ages to the use of gold and silver as money, would be found to consist in the difficulty of determining the degree of their purity with sufficient precision; and the discovery of some means by which their weight and fineness might be readily and correctly ascertained, would be felt to be indispensable to their extensive use as money. Fortunately, these means were not long in being discovered. The fabrication of coins, or the practice of impressing pieces of the precious metals with a stamp indicating their weight and purity, belongs to the remotest antiquity.* And it may safely be affirmed, that there have been very few inventions of greater utility, or that have done more to accelerate the progress of improvement.

It is material, however, to observe that the introduction and use of coined money make no change whatever in the *principle* on which exchanges were previously conducted. The coinage saves the trouble of weighing and assaying gold and silver, but it does nothing more. It declares the weight and purity of the metal in a coin; but the *value*

* Goguet, "De l'Origine des Loix," &c. tom. i. p. 269.

of that metal or coin is in all cases determined by precisely the same principles which determine the value of other commodities, and would be as little affected by being recoined with a new denomination, as the burden of a ship by a change of her name.

Inaccurate notions with respect to the influence of coinage seem to have given rise to the opinion, so long entertained, that coins were merely the *signs* of values! But it is clear that they have no more claim to this designation than bars of iron or copper, sacks of wheat, or any other commodity. They exchange for other things, because they are desirable articles, and are possessed of real intrinsic value. A draft, check, or bill, may not improperly, perhaps, be regarded as the sign of the money to be given for it. But that money is nothing but a commodity; it is not a sign, it is the thing signified.*

Money, however, is not merely the universal equivalent, or *marchandise bannale*, used by the society: it is also the *standard* used to compare the values of all sorts of products; and the stipulations in the great bulk of contracts and deeds, as to the delivery and disposal of property, have all reference to, and are commonly expressed in, quantities of money. It is plainly, therefore, of the utmost importance that its value should be preserved as invariable as possible. Owing, however, to improvements in the arts, the exhaustion of old mines and the discovery of new ones, the value of the precious metals is necessarily inconstant; though, if we except the effects produced in the sixteenth century by the discovery of the American mines, it does not appear to have varied so much at other times as might have been anticipated. Great mischief has, however, been repeatedly occasioned by the changes that have been made in most countries in the weight, and sometimes also in the purity of coins;

* The Count di Verri was one of the first economists who shewed clearly what money is, as well as what it is not.—See "Meditazioni sulla Economia Politica," § 2.

and since the impolicy of these changes has been recognised, similar, and perhaps still more extensive, disorders have sprung from the improper use of substitutes for coins. It is, indeed, quite obvious, that no change can take place in the value of money, without proportionally affecting the pecuniary conditions in all contracts and agreements. Much, however, of the influence of a change depends on its direction. An increase in the value of money is, for reasons that will afterwards be stated, uniformly more prejudicial in a public point of view than its diminution; the latter, though injurious to individuals, may sometimes be productive of national advantage, but such can never be the case with the former.*

No certain estimate can ever be formed of the quantity of money required to conduct the business of any country; this quantity being, in all cases, determined by the value of money itself, the services it has to perform, and the devices used for economising its employment. Generally, however, it is very considerable; and when it consists wholly of gold and silver, it occasions a very heavy expense. There can indeed be no doubt that the wish to lessen this expense has been one of the chief causes that have led all civilised and commercial nations to fabricate a portion of their money of some less valuable material. Of the various substitutes resorted to for this purpose, paper is, in all respects, the most eligible. Its employment seems to have grown naturally out of the circumstances incident to an advancing society. When government becomes sufficiently powerful and intelligent to enforce the observance of contracts, individuals possessed of written promises from others, that they will pay certain sums at certain specified periods, begin to assign them to those to whom they are indebted; and when the subscribers are persons of fortune, and of whose solvency no doubt can be enter-

* See Chapter on Profits.

tained, their obligations are readily accepted in payment of debts. But when the circulation of promises, or bills, in this way has continued for a while, individuals begin to perceive that they may derive a profit by issuing them in such a form as to fit them for being readily used as a substitute for money in the ordinary transactions of life. Hence the origin of bank-notes. An individual in whose wealth and discretion the public have confidence, being applied to for a loan, say of 5,000*l.*, grants the applicant his bill or note, payable on demand, for that sum. Now, as this note passes, in consequence of the confidence placed in the issuer, currently from hand to hand as cash, it is quite as useful to the borrower as if it had been gold; and supposing that the rate of interest is five per cent, it will yield, so long as it continues to circulate, a revenue of 250*l.* a year to the issuer. A banker who issues notes, coins, as it were, his credit. He derives the same revenue from the loan of his written promise to pay a certain sum, that he could derive from the loan of the sum itself, or of an equivalent amount of produce! And while he thus increases his own income, he, at the same time, contributes to increase the wealth of the public. The cheapest species of currency being substituted in the place of that which is most expensive, the superfluous coins are either used in the arts, or are exported in exchange for raw materials or manufactured goods, by the use of which both wealth and enjoyments are increased. Ever since the introduction of bills, almost all great commercial transactions have been carried on by means of paper only. Notes are also used to a very great extent in the ordinary business of society; and while they are readily exchangeable at the pleasure of the holder for coins, or for the precise quantities of gold or silver they profess to represent, their value is maintained on a par with the value of these metals; and all injurious fluctuations in the value of money are as effectually avoided as if it consisted wholly of the precious metals.*

In common mercantile language, the party who exchanges money for a commodity is said to buy; the party who exchanges a commodity for money being said to sell. Price, unless where the contrary is distinctly mentioned, always means the value of a commodity estimated or rated in money.

* For an account of the measures necessary to be adopted to insure the ready conversion of paper into the precious metals, see Chapter on the Interference of Government.

CHAPTER V.

Division of Employments among different Countries, or Commerce—Wholesale and Retail Dealers—Influence of improved Means of Communication—Mode in which Commerce contributes to increase Wealth—Restrictions on Commerce—Injurious Operation of these Restrictions.

BESIDES enabling each individual in a limited society to confine himself to some one employment, there is another and most important branch of the division of labour, which not only enables particular individuals, but the inhabitants of entire districts, and even nations, to addict themselves, in preference, to certain branches of industry. It is on this *territorial division of labour*, as it has been appropriately termed by Colonel Torrens, that the commerce carried on between different districts of the same country, and between different countries, is founded. The various soils, climates, and capacities of production, possessed by the different provinces of an extensive country, fit them for being appropriated, in preference, to certain species of industry. A district where coal is abundant, which has an easy access to the ocean, and a considerable command of internal navigation, is the natural seat of manufactures. Wheat and other species of grain are the proper products of rich arable soils; and cattle, after being reared in mountainous districts, are most advantageously fattened in meadows and low grounds. It is clearly as little for the advantage of the inhabitants of different districts, as it would be for that of an individual, to engage indiscriminately in every possible employment. Who can doubt that vastly more manufactured goods, corn, cattle, and fish, are produced by the people of Lancashire confining their principal attention to manufactures, those of Kent to agriculture, those of Argyleshire to the raising of cattle, and those of the Shetland Isles to the catching of fish, than if each had endeavoured directly to supply themselves with these or similar productions, without the intervention of an exchange?

The commercial intercourse between the inhabitants of different countries and districts, and even between those of the same district, is most commodiously carried on by a distinct class of individuals denominated merchants, from that *commutatio mercium* which forms their business. This class is, for the most part, subdivided into two subordinate classes—the *wholesale dealers* and the *retailers*. The business of the first principally consists in conveying commodities from places where they are relatively cheap to those where they are relatively dear. Generally speaking, they buy at the first hand, or from the producers; but instead of selling directly to the consumers, they most commonly sell to the retailers. The business of the latter is to keep assortments of such goods as are wanted in the places where they reside; serving them out to their customers, or the public, in such quantities, and at such times, as may best suit their convenience. This subdivision is exceedingly beneficial for all parties. It would be next to impossible for a wholesale merchant to retail the goods he has collected in distant markets; but, supposing he were to attempt it, he would, it is clear, have to establish agents in different parts of the country: so that, besides requiring an additional capital, he would be compelled, from inability to give that unremitting attention to any single department of his business, so indispensable to secure its being conducted with due economy and in the best way, to lay a higher price on his goods. The objections that have sometimes been made to the intervention of retailers between the wholesale dealers, or the producers, and the consumers, are plainly, therefore, without the slightest foundation. It is essential that goods should be retailed.

Of what use would it be to bring a cargo of salt from Liverpool, or of beef from Cork, to London, were it not to be divided and sold in such portions as might suit the wants of the citizens? And it admits of demonstration, that this necessary business will be done best and cheapest by a class distinct from the wholesale dealers.

It is frequently, indeed, alleged, that the number of retailers is in most places unnecessarily great, and that, in order to subsist, they charge an enormous profit. But it is easy to see, that there can be no real ground for these statements. A regard to their own interest will always prevent too many individuals from entering into the retail trade, as it prevents them from entering into any other employment; at the same time that the competition to which they are exposed will effectually hinder them from realising more than the ordinary rate of profit. That they sometimes appear to realise more than this rate, is, no doubt, true—but this arises from confounding wages and profits. An individual, besides deriving a profit from the capital which he employs, should, in the event of his superintending its employment, obtain, in addition, a remuneration or wages for that superintendence. Suppose, for the sake of illustration, that a grocer in a small country town employs a capital of 1,000*l*., that profits are 10 per cent, and that he could earn, by hiring himself to another, 50*l*. a year of salary. In this case it is plain the goods must be sold at 15 per cent advance, that being the lowest rate that will yield 10 per cent of profits and 50*l*. of wages. Had the grocer been able to employ a capital of 2,000*l*. he would have obtained the same profits and wages by selling his goods at an advance of 12½ per cent. Hence the difference in the price of goods when retailed in large and small towns. In the former there is scope for the employment of large capitals in the business of retailing, so that a comparatively small per centage over and above the customary rate of profit, is sufficient to defray the wages of those engaged in carrying it on; while, in the latter, owing to the limited field for the employment of capital, a comparatively large per centage is necessary as wages. Profits are, evidently, the same in both cases.

It is plain, from these statements, that the formation of a separate mercantile class adds very greatly to the advantages resulting from commerce. It is they, in fact, who give an uninterrupted motion to the plough and the loom. The intervention of the wholesale and retail dealers enables every one to apply himself exclusively to his particular calling. Agents and warehouses being established all over the country for the purchase and sale of commodities, the agriculturists and manufacturers, knowing where they may always dispose of their peculiar productions at the current prices of the day, and where they may obtain whatever they wish to buy, devote their whole time and energies to their proper businesses. Continuity is, in consequence, given to their exertions; and the powers of production are augmented to an extent that could not have been conceived possible previously to the rise of the mercantile class.

The formation of roads and canals, or of easy methods of communication between different parts of a country, contributes powerfully to facilitate commercial operations, and is in the highest degree beneficial. A diminution of the expenses of conveyance, has, it is evident, the same direct influence on prices as a diminution of the expenses of production; perhaps, however, its indirect influence is more advantageous. The great workshops, (for so we may truly call Manchester, Leeds, Birmingham, Sheffield, Glasgow, Paisley, &c.) with which Great Britain is studded, could not exist without improved roads and canals; but while the latter enable their inhabitants to obtain all the bulky products of the soil and the mines almost as cheap as if they lived in the country, and give them the means of carrying on their employments on a large scale, and of perfecting and subdividing every branch of industry, they also afford the means of distributing their productions throughout the country at an extremely small advance of price. Roads and canals are thus productive of a double benefit— cheapening, at one and the same time, raw produce to the inhabitants of towns, and manufactures to those of the country. In a moral point of view, their effects are equally salutary. They give to every different part of a widely extended empire the same common interest; and by promoting their intercourse, and consequently exciting a spirit of emulation and competition amongst the citizens of the remotest districts, impart new life and vigour to society.

It is easy to see that foreign trade, or the territorial division of labour between different and independent countries, contributes to increase their wealth in precisely the same manner that the internal trade contributes to increase the wealth of the different provinces of the same kingdom. There being a far greater variety in the productive powers with which nature has endowed different and distant countries than there is in those of the provinces of any one country, it would seem that a free intercourse between them must be proportionally more advantageous. It would, it is evident, cost infinitely more to raise the wines of France, the fruits of Spain, or the sugars of Jamaica, in England, than to make Yorkshire yield the same products as Devonshire. Indeed, there are myriads of products, and some of them of the greatest utility, that cannot be raised except in particular countries. Were it not for foreign commerce, we should be wholly destitute of tea, coffee, raw cotton, raw silk, spices, gold bullion, and a thousand other equally useful and valuable commodities. Providence, by giving different soils, climates, and natural productions, to different countries, has evidently intended that they should be mutually serviceable to each other. If no artificial obstacles were thrown in the way of their intercourse, each people would naturally engage, in preference, in those employments in which it has a superiority, exchanging such parts of its produce as it could spare for the productions it could more advantageously bring from others. And thus, by exciting industry, rewarding ingenuity, and using most efficaciously the peculiar powers bestowed by nature, commerce distributes labour as best suits the genius and capacities of every country. By making us acquainted with various productions to which we should otherwise have been entire strangers, it gives us new tastes and new appetites, at the same time that it affords the means, and excites the desire, of gratifying them. It enables each particular people to profit by the inventions and discoveries of all the rest; while, by bringing the home producers into competition with foreigners, it stimulates their industry and invention, and forces routine to give way to emulation. The division of labour is carried to its farthest extent; the mass of necessary and useful products is vastly augmented; and opulence generally diffused. Nor is the influence of commerce, in other points of view, less powerful and salutary. It is the grand engine by which the blessings of civilisation are diffused, and the treasures of knowledge and of science conveyed to the remotest corners of the habitable globe; while, by making the inhabitants of each country dependent on the assistance of those of others for a large share of their comforts and enjoyments, it forms a powerful principle of union, and binds together the universal society of nations by the common and powerful ties of mutual interest and reciprocal obligation.

"Combien," to use the words of a late French writer, "le spectacle de tous les travaux concourant à la production de la richesse, sans autre préeminence ni distinction que celle que leur assure l'échange de leurs produits, est encourageant pour les classes laborieuses, stimulant pour les peuples, favorable à la civilisation, honorable pour l'humanité ! Dans ce système tous les hommes suivent leur penchant, développent, perfectionnent leurs facultés, s'encouragent par une noble émulation, sont avertis à chaque instant du besoin qu'ils ont les uns des autres, se lient entre eux par des rapports habituels, s'attachent par leurs intérêts réciproques, et renouent les liens de la grande famille du genre humain que la séparation des familles nationales avoit brisés. Ces familles, éparses sur le globe, ne sont plus étrangères entre elles, travaillent l'un pour l'autre, et correspondent ensemble malgré les gouffres des mers et l'aspérité des climats, les montagnes inaccessibles, et les déserts inhospitaliers. Grâces au génie du commerce, et aux inépuisables ressources de l'industrie, tous les perils sont bravés, toutes les difficultés sont vaincues, tous les obstacles sont surmontés, et les bienfaits du travail général circulent dans le monde entier."*

It cannot indeed be denied, that mistaken views of commerce, like those so frequently entertained of religion, have been the cause of many wars and of much bloodshed. But the folly of the monopoly system, and the ruinous nature of the contests to which it has given rise, have been made obvious. It has been fully and clearly demonstrated, that nothing can be more irrational and absurd, than that dread of the progress of others in wealth and civilisation that was once so prevalent; and that the true glory and real interest of every people will be more certainly advanced by endeavouring to emulate and outstrip their neighbours in the career of science and civilisation, than by engaging in schemes of conquest and aggression.

The influence of foreign commerce in giving increased efficacy to labour, and augmenting national wealth, may

* Ganilh, "des Systèmes d'Economie Politique," tom. i. p. 173. Ed. 1821.

be easily illustrated. The superiority of our wool, for example, our command of coals, of skilful workmen, of improved machinery, and of all the instruments and means of manufacturing industry, enable us to produce cloth at a much cheaper rate than the Portuguese; while, on the other hand, the soil and climate of Portugal being peculiarly favourable for the cultivation and growth of the vine, she can produce wine incomparably cheaper than it could be produced here. And hence it is obvious, that if we confine ourselves to the manufacture of cloth, and exchange it with the Portuguese for wine, we shall obtain a far larger supply of that desirable beverage than if we attempted to cultivate the vine at home; at the same time that the Portuguese, by exchanging wine for English cloth, will, on their part, obtain much more cloth, for a much less price, than they would do were they to counteract the intention of nature, and convert a portion of their capital and industry from the culture of the vine, in which they have so great an advantage, to the manufacture of cloth, in which the advantage is wholly on the side of others.

What has been already stated is sufficient to expose the sophism involved in the reasoning of the *Economists*, who contended, that as an equivalent must be always given for such commodities as are obtained from foreigners, it was impossible foreign commerce could add any thing to national wealth. How, they asked, can the wealth of a country be increased by giving equal values for equal values? They admitted that commerce made a better distribution of the wealth of the world; but as it did nothing more than exchange one sort of wealth for another, they denied that it could make any addition to its amount. At first sight, this sophistical and delusive statement appears sufficiently conclusive; but a very few words will be sufficient to demonstrate its fallacy. Those who suppose that commerce cannot be a means of increasing the wealth of both parties, and that if one of them gains any thing, it must be at the expense of the other, entirely misconceive its nature and objects. It may have cost as much to produce the cloth with which the English purchase the wine of Portugal, as it did to produce the latter; or it may have cost even more. But then it must be observed, that in making the exchange, the value of the wine is estimated by what it takes to produce it in Portugal, which has peculiar capabilities for that species of industry, and not by what it would take to produce it in England were the trade put an end to; while, in like manner, the value of the cloth is estimated by what it takes to produce it in England, and not by what it would cost to produce it in Portugal. The advantage of the intercourse consists in its enabling each country to obtain commodities, which it could either not produce at all, or which it would cost a comparatively large sum to produce directly at home, for what it costs to produce them under the most favourable circumstances, and with the least possible expense. In no respect, therefore, can the gain of the one be said to be a loss to the other. Their intercourse is evidently productive of mutual advantage. Through its means each is supplied with produce for which it has a demand, by a far less sacrifice of labour and expense than would otherwise be required; so that the wealth of both parties is not only better distributed, but is, at the same time, vastly augmented, by thus judiciously availing themselves of each other's peculiar capacities and powers.

To set this important principle in a clearer point of view, let us suppose that with a certain outlay we may either manufacture 10,000 yards of cloth or raise 1,000 quarters of wheat, and that with the same outlay the Poles can manufacture 5,000 yards of cloth or raise 2,000 quarters of wheat. Under these circumstances it is plain, that with a free intercourse established between the two countries, we should be able, by manufacturing cloth and exporting it to Poland, to obtain *twice* the quantity of corn in exchange for any given sum that we should obtain by employing it in the cultivation of land at home; at the same time that the Poles would get *twice* as much cloth in exchange for their corn as they would have got had they tried to manufacture it. How ridiculous, then, to contend that commerce is not a means of adding to the productiveness of labour, and, consequently, of increasing wealth! Were our intercourse with Portugal and the West Indies put an end to, it would be impossible, perhaps, to produce port-wine, sugar, and coffee, directly in this country; and though it were not impossible, it would, at any rate, require a hundred or a thousand times the expense to produce them here that it does to produce the equivalents exported to pay for them.

The influence of foreign commerce in stimulating industry by multiplying its rewards, is also of very great importance. Did our command of wealth extend only over that which is produced in a particular district or province, we should be far less industrious, because we should have far fewer motives to prompt our industry. A man might with comparatively little difficulty procure a sufficient supply of corn, of cloth, and of beer; and if the utmost exertions of skill and economy could only procure him additional supplies of these articles, such exertions would very soon cease to be made. No sooner, however, is a commercial intercourse established with foreigners, than conveniences and accommodations of all sorts are prodigiously multiplied. In addition to the products of its immediate vicinity, every considerable market is then abundantly supplied with those of all the countries and climates of the world. Nor is there any fortune so great that its owner can be without a motive to increase it still more, seeing the immeasurable variety of desirable objects it may be employed to obtain.

To form a faint idea of what we owe to foreign commerce, imagine it prohibited, and then reflect for a moment on the deduction that would be made from our means of subsistence, comfort, and enjoyment. The cotton and silk trades would be annihilated; instead of breakfasting on the products of China and the West Indies, we should have to content ourselves with the pottage of our ancestors; beer would take the place of burgundy, and gin of champagne; when our crops were redundant, the surplus would be comparatively useless, and when deficient, there would be no foreign supplies with which to stay the ravages of famine. Our maritime preponderance would fall with the fall of our commerce; and from occupying the most prominent place in the first rank among nations, we should immediately sink to the level of Spain or Portugal.

I shall not imitate the example of most writers on commerce, by entering into a lengthened examination of the question, whether the home or foreign trade be most advantageous. It is indeed quite obvious that it admits of no satisfactory solution. Without some species of home trade, it would be altogether impossible to divide and combine employments, or to emerge from barbarism; and without foreign trade, and the innumerable productions, arts, and improvements, which it brings along with it, the progress made by society would be comparatively trifling. The former might, perhaps, have raised us to the condition of our ancestors in the days of Richard II.; but we are mainly indebted to the latter for the almost incredible advances we have since made, as well as for those we are yet destined to make.

It would be superfluous, even if it were not inconsistent with the objects and limits of this work, to enter on a detailed investigation of the policy of the various restrictions that have been imposed, at different periods, on the freedom of commerce. Those which were intended to increase the importation, or to hinder the exportation of the precious metals, have been admitted, almost universally, to be founded on erroneous principles, and have either fallen into disuse or been repealed. I shall therefore confine myself, in what I am now to state, to a few observations on the policy of those restrictions that are intended to promote the industry and employment of particular countries, by partially or wholly preventing the importation of such articles from abroad as may be produced at home.

If either the whole or any considerable portion of an article in extensive demand be imported from foreign countries, no one can doubt that the prevention of such importation will give an immediate advantage to the home producers of the article. It can hardly, however, be necessary to say, that the legislator has nothing to do with the interests of any one class, unless in the view of rendering them conducive to those of the society. The circumstance of a restriction being advantageous to a greater or smaller number of individuals, is no proof whatever of its expediency. To establish this, it must also be shewn that it is advantageous, or at least not injurious, to the public—that it does not sacrifice the interests of the community to those of a favoured few. No particular system of commercial policy deserves any preference to another, except in so far as it may be better calculated to advance the welfare of the nation. If a restricted trade will do this more effectually than a free and unfettered one, it ought to be adopted, to the exclusion of the latter; but if it will not do this, it ought as certainly to be put down. Neither freedom nor prohibition is, in itself, good or bad. The influence which each exercises over the *public* is the only thing to be attended to. The supply of its wants is the real end and purpose of all sorts of industrious undertakings; and the interests of those engaged in them should occupy the attention of government only, when it is believed that they may be made, through its interference, more subservient to their legitimate object.

We have already seen, that the number of workmen employed in a country must always be limited to the number which its capital can feed and maintain. But it is plain that no regulation can directly add any thing to that capital. It may, and indeed most frequently does, divert a portion of it into channels into which it would not otherwise have flowed. This, however, is its *only effect;* and the real question for consideration is—Whether the artificial direction which is thus given to a portion of the national capital, renders it more or less productive than it would have been, had it been left at liberty to seek out channels of employment for itself?

In discussing this question it may be observed, in the *first* place, that every individual is constantly exerting himself to find out the most advantageous methods of employing his capital and labour. It is true that it is his own advantage, and not that of the society, which he has in view; but a society being nothing more than a collection of individuals, it is plain that each, in steadily pursuing his own aggrandisement, is following that precise line of conduct which is most for the public advantage. It is a consequence of this principle, that if no particular branches of industry were encouraged more than others, those would be preferred which naturally afforded the greatest facilities for acquiring fortunes, and, consequently, for increasing the capital of the country. Self-interest is the most powerful stimulus that can be applied to excite the industry, and to sharpen the intellect and ingenuity of man; and no proposition can be more true, than that each individual can, in his local situation, judge better what is advantageous and useful for himself than any other person. "The statesman," says Dr. Smith, "who should attempt to direct private people in what manner they ought to employ their capitals, would not only load himself with a most unnecessary attention, but assume an authority which could safely be trusted, not only to no single person, but to no council or senate whatever, and which would no where be so dangerous as in the hands of a man who had folly and presumption enough to fancy himself fit to exercise it."*

But, in the *second* place, it is evident, that the prevention of the importation of foreign produce has in effect the consequence, so justly censured by Dr. Smith, of dictating to individuals in what manner they shall employ their capital and labour. It prevents them from obtaining those articles which cannot be raised at home; and it compels them to pay a higher price for such as may be raised at home, though with comparative difficulty. But to prohibit an individual from using any article merely because it is the product of another country, or to compel him to pay an unnecessarily enhanced price for it, is at once oppressive and impolitic. If restrictions on importation did not exist, no produce would ever be raised in any country that could be imported at a cheaper rate from another. The conduct of societies would then be regulated by the same principles that regulate the conduct of individuals in private life; and it is the maxim of every prudent master of a family, not to attempt to make at home what it would cost more to make than to buy. The tailor, as Dr. Smith has remarked, does not attempt to make his own shoes, but buys them from a shoemaker; the shoemaker, on his part, does not attempt to make his own clothes, but employs a tailor; and the farmer makes neither the one nor the other, but obtains them in exchange for corn and cattle. In all civilised societies, each individual finds it for his advantage to employ himself in some particular business, and to exchange a part of his peculiar produce for such parts of the produce of others as he may have occasion for. And it has not yet been shewn how that conduct which is universally admitted to be wise and proper in individuals, should be foolish and

* "Wealth of Nations," vol. ii. p. 280.

absurd in the case of a state,—that is, in the case of the total number of individuals inhabiting a particular tract of country!

It must be remembered, that the total absence of restrictions will not give foreigners the power of supplying those commodities that are as cheaply produced at home as abroad. Home producers have always great advantages over others. The price of their commodities is not so much enhanced by the expense of conveyance; and they are intimately acquainted with the language, laws, fashions, and credit of those with whom they deal. A foreigner has none of these circumstances in his favour; and, consequently, comes into the home market under disadvantages with which nothing but the comparative cheapness of his goods could enable him to contend. But if a Frenchman, or an American, can supply us with any article cheaper than we can raise it, why should we not buy it from him? Why should we not extend the same principle to foreigners that is found to be so extremely advantageous in conducting our intercourse with our immediate neighbours? Though our ports were open for the reception of all the commodities of all the commercial nations in the world, none would be purchased unless the purchasers concluded it to be for their advantage,—that is, unless they obtained the article from the foreigners at a *less* price than they could have obtained it for from their own countrymen.

The fact that we are able to obtain a commodity in a particular foreign market at a lower price than it can be raised for here, or imported from any other place, shews that some of our peculiar productions fetch a higher price in that market than any where else. The price of a commodity is merely the quantity of money, or of some other commodity, given for it. No one doubts that we can buy claret cheaper in Bordeaux than in any other place; or, which is the same thing, that we are able to dispose of the produce given for claret to greater advantage there than we can do elsewhere. There is no test of high or low price, except the quantity of produce for which an article exchanges. And thus it is evident, that when we prohibit buying in the cheapest markets, we, at the same time, and by the same act, prohibit selling in the dearest markets. Suppose that, by sending a certain quantity of cottons or hardware to Brazil, we might get in exchange 150 hogsheads of sugar; and that the same quantity, if sent to Jamaica, would only fetch 100 hogsheads; is it not obvious, that by preventing the importation of the former we force our goods to be sold for *two-thirds* of the price they would otherwise have brought? To suppose that a commercial system productive of such results can be a means of increasing national wealth, is to suppose what is evidently contradictory and absurd.

When a restriction is laid on the importation of any description of commodities, their price rises, and the home producers get an immediate advantage: but what they gain in this way is of very trifling importance. For, as additional capital is drawn to the business, prices are speedily reduced to the level that barely affords the ordinary rate of profit. This level may be either identical with that at which prices previously stood, or it may be higher. If the former should happen to be the case, little, though something, will have been lost, but nothing whatever will have been gained by the restriction. Capital will have been transferred from one employment to another; and while a greater quantity of the produce formerly imported from abroad will henceforth be produced at home, there will be a corresponding diminution in the production of that which had been exported to the foreigners in payment of the imports. But, in the vast majority of cases, the price is not the same after a prohibition has been enacted, but is permanently raised; for, when an article may be as cheaply produced at home as abroad, its prohibition would be unnecessary, and would not be thought of. Suppose that an article imported from the foreigner, for which we paid a million, is excluded, and that it costs a million and a half to raise it at home: it is clear that the effect of the prohibition on the consumers of the article is precisely the same as if, supposing the trade to have continued free, a direct and peculiar tax of 500,000*l.* a year had been laid on them. But it will be observed, that had such a tax been imposed, its produce would have come into the hands of government, and would have formed a portion of the national income; whereas, the increased cost of the article is, under the circumstances supposed, *occasioned by an increased difficulty of production,* and is, therefore, of no advantage to any one.

It consequently results, that even in those rare cases in which a restrictive regulation has no tendency to raise prices, it is hurtful, by changing the natural distribution of capital, and lessening the foreign demand for the produce of industry to the same extent that it increases the home demand. But in that incomparably more numerous class of cases in which a restriction occasions a rise in the price of the article which it affects, it is infinitely more injurious. Besides the mischief arising from varying the natural distribution of capital, and circumscribing the foreign trade of the country, such restriction has the effect of imposing a heavy burden on the people, for no purpose of general or public utility, but to produce a certain and grievous injury, by tempting individuals to withdraw from really advantageous businesses, to engage in those that cannot be prosecuted without great national loss, and which must be abandoned the moment the prohibition ceases to be enforced.

It has been said, though, perhaps, without due consideration, that had it not been for restrictions on importation, several manufactures that now furnish employment to a considerable population, would most probably never have had any existence amongst us. But, supposing this statement to be admitted, it would not form any valid objection to the principles now laid down. It is quite as much for the interest of communities as of single families, to respect the principle of the division of labour. Every people will always find it for their advantage to addict themselves, in preference, to those branches of industry in which they have a superiority over others: for, it is by this means only that they can ever fully avail themselves of their peculiar facilities of production, or employ their capital, and the labour of their husbandmen and artisans, most beneficially.

It is certainly true, that, after an artificial system has been long acted upon, its abolition seldom fails of producing considerable temporary embarrassment and hardship; and for this reason, no prudent government will ever rashly adopt any measure, however unexceptionable in point of principle, that might occasion any immediate and serious injury to a considerable class of its subjects. Every change in the public economy of a great nation ought to be cautiously and gradually effected. Those who have capital employed in businesses, carried on under the protection of a restrictive regulation, ought to be afforded a reasonable time and every facility, either to withdraw from them or to prepare to withstand the free competition of foreigners. But this is *all* they can justly claim. The fact of a departure having been made, on one or more occasions, from the sound principle of the freedom of industry, can never be alleged as a sufficient reason for obstinately persevering in a course of policy which has been ascertained to be most inimical to the public interests, or for refusing to embrace the earliest opportunity of reverting to a better system. To act on such a principle would be to perpetuate the worst errors and absurdities, and would be a proceeding utterly inconsistent with all the ends and objects of government.

It is abundantly certain, too, that the loss and inconvenience which unavoidably follow every change in a long-established system of commercial policy, have been very greatly exaggerated. But, whatever may be the case in this respect in other countries, such is our superiority in the arts, that the free importation of foreign products would drive but a very inconsiderable portion of our people from the employments they now carry on. Admitting, however, that the total abolition of the prohibitive system might force a few thousand workmen to abandon their present occupations, it is material to observe that *equivalent new ones* would, in consequence, be opened to receive them; and that the total aggregate demand for their services would not be in any degree diminished. Suppose that, under a system of free trade, we imported a part of the silks and linens we now manufacture at home: it is quite clear, inasmuch as neither the French nor Germans would send us their commodities gratis, that we should have to give them an equal amount of British commodities in exchange; so that such of our artificers as had been engaged in the silk and linen manufactures, and were thrown out of them, would, in future, obtain employment in the production of the articles that must be exported as equivalents to the foreigner. We may, by giving additional freedom to commerce, change the species of labour in demand, but we cannot lessen its quantity. Should our imports this year amount to ten or twenty millions more than they did last year, we shall, it is certain, have to pay them by exporting an equally increased amount of our peculiar products. And, therefore, if *exportation* be a good thing, and the most ardent admirers of the restrictive system admit it to be such, *importation* must also be a good thing — for the two are indissolubly connected; and to separate them, even in imagination, implies a total ignorance of the most obvious principles. All commerce, whether carried on between individuals of the same or of different countries, is founded on a fair principle of reciprocity. Buying and selling are in it what action and re-action are in physics, *equal and contrary*. Those who will not buy from others, render it impossible for others to buy from them. Every sale infers an equal purchase, and every purchase an equal sale. Hence, to prohibit buying is exactly the same thing, in effect, as to prohibit selling. No merchant would ever export a single bale of goods, were he prevented from importing a greater value in its stead. But it is impossible that he can do this, if foreign commodities be excluded. In whatever degree, therefore, an unrestricted trade might lead us to receive commodities from other countries, in the same degree it would render them customers for our commodities — would promote our manufactures, and extend our trade. To suppose that commerce may be too free, is to suppose that labour may be turned into too productive channels — that the objects of demand may be too much multiplied, and their price too much reduced; it is like supposing that our agriculture may be too much improved and our crops rendered too luxuriant!

The principles now established, demonstrate the groundless nature of the complaints so frequently set up of the injury arising from the prevalence of a taste for foreign commodities. We get nothing from abroad except in exchange for something else; and the individual who uses only Polish wheat, Saxon cloth, and French silks and wine, gives, by occasioning the exportation of an equal amount of British produce, precisely the same encouragement to industry here, that he would give were he to consume nothing not directly produced amongst us. The Portuguese will not send us a single bottle of port, unless we send to them, or to some one to whom they are indebted, its worth in cottons, hardware, or some sort of produce; so that whether we use the wine, or its equivalent, is, except as a matter of taste, of no importance whatever.

What has now been stated goes far to settle the disputed question as to the influence of absentee expenditure. If an English gentleman, living at home, and using none but foreign articles in his establishment, gives the same encouragement to industry that he would do were he to use none but British articles, he must, it is obvious, do the same thing should he go abroad. Whatever he may get from the foreigner, when at Paris or Brussels, must be paid for, directly or indirectly, in British articles, quite in the same way as when he resided in London. Nor is it easy to imagine any grounds for pronouncing his expenditure in the latter more beneficial to this country than in the former.*

Arguments similar to those now so briefly stated, to shew the benefits of commercial freedom, and the impolicy of attempting to promote industry at home by laying restraints on importation from abroad, have been

* I do not mean, by any thing now stated, nor did I ever mean, by any thing I have stated on other occasions, to maintain that absenteeism may not be, in several respects, injurious. It would be easy, indeed, to shew that both England and Scotland have been largely benefited by the residence of the great landed proprietors on their estates. No one can doubt that they have been highly instrumental in introducing the manners, and in diffusing a taste for the conveniences and enjoyments of a more refined society; and that the improved communications between different places, the expensive and commodious farm-buildings, and the plantations with which the country is sheltered and ornamented, are to be, in a great degree, ascribed to their residence. It may be doubted, however, considering the circumstances under which most Irish landlords acquired their estates, the difference between their religious tenets and those of their tenants, the peculiar tenures under which the latter hold their lands, and the political condition of the country, whether their residence would have been of any considerable advantage. But, whatever conclusion may be come to as to this point, cannot affect what has been stated in the text. The question really at issue refers merely to the *spending* of revenue, and has nothing to do with the improvement of estates; and, notwithstanding all that has been said to the contrary, I am not yet convinced that absenteeism is, in this respect, at all injurious.

repeatedly advanced. The superior advantages resulting from the freedom of commerce were exhibited, as already stated, in a very striking point of view, by Sir Dudley North, nearly one hundred and forty years since; and Sir Matthew Decker, Mr. Hume, and others, subsequently illustrated and enforced the same principles, and shewed the ruinous consequences of the prohibitive system. But its complete overthrow was reserved for Dr. Smith, who has examined and refuted the various arguments in favour of commercial restrictions in the most able and masterly manner, and with an amplitude of illustration that leaves nothing to be desired. Such, however, and so powerful, were the prejudices in favour of the prohibitive system, and such the obstacles opposed to the progress of more enlarged and liberal opinions, that, notwithstanding Dr. Smith's work has been in general circulation for about half a century, it is only within these very few years that statesmen and merchants have given a practical assent to its doctrines, and have attempted to act on them. But, fortunately a new era has at length begun—*novus sæclorum nascitur ordo!* The principles of free trade are no longer viewed as barren and unprofitable speculations—as the visions of theorists, dreaming in their closets of public happiness never to be realised. They have received the sanction of the Parliament of England. To the glory of being the first to promulgate and demonstrate the truth of this just and beneficent system, we can now claim the higher praise of being the first to give it a practical bearing and real effect. It is true, that monopoly is still deeply ingrafted on our commercial policy, and that we allow some most important branches of trade to labour under oppressive and vexatious restraints. But it is a great deal to have commenced the return to a better system; and to have publicly declared our conviction, that freedom of commerce is productive alike of private happiness and public prosperity. "And if," to use the words of a distinguished statesman, "in the long and honourable career which is still open to the adversaries of commercial restrictions, monopoly, and preference, the same spirit shall animate, the same resolution uphold, the country and the legislature — if full and uncompromising effect be finally given to a system confirmed by experience, and sanctioned by public applause, not this age, nor this country alone, will have reason to bless our exertions. There is no period so remote, there is no nation so barbarous, in which we may not confidently anticipate that these successful researches of British philosophy, this auspicious example of British policy, will become, under the favour of Providence, a pure and ample source of continually increasing human happiness." *

* "Lord Grenville's Speech at the Dissolution of the Levant Company," 11th February, 1825.

CHAPTER VI.

Different Employments of Capital and Labour—Agriculture, Manufactures, and Commerce, equally advantageous—The investment of Capital in different Businesses determined by the Rate of Profit which they respectively yield—Manufactures not productive of increased Mortality—Influence of Commerce on Public Spirit.

In treating of the accumulation of capital, it was shewn, that the ratio of its increase is the circumstance which chiefly determines national prosperity; that an augmentation of capital is equivalent to an augmentation of the means of supporting and employing additional labourers—and that its diminution equally diminishes the comforts and enjoyments, and perhaps also the necessaries, of the labouring classes, and diffuses poverty and misery over a country; and it was also shewn, that the increase or diminution of the rate of profit is the great cause of the increase or diminution of capital. Now, if such be the case, it seems impossible to resist coming to the conclusion, that those employments which yield the *greatest profit*, or in which industry is most productive, are the most advantageous. But Dr. Smith, Mr. Malthus, and others, have objected to this standard. They admit that if two capitals yield equal profits, the employments in which they are engaged are equally beneficial to those who carry them on; but they contend, that, if one of these capitals be employed in agriculture, it will be productive of greater public advantage. It is not difficult, however, to discover that this opinion rests on no good foundation; and to shew that the *average rate of profit* is, under all circumstances, the single and infallible test by which we are to judge which employment is most and which is least advantageous.

A capital may be employed in four different ways; either, *first*, in the production of raw produce; or, *secondly*, in manufacturing and preparing raw produce for use and consumption; or, *thirdly*, in transporting the raw and manufactured products from one place to another according to the demand; or, *fourthly*, in dividing particular portions of either into such small parcels as may suit the convenience of those who want them. The capitals of all those who undertake the improvement or cultivation of lands, mines, or fisheries, are employed in the first of these ways; the capital of all master-manufacturers is employed in the second; that of all wholesale merchants in the third; and that of all retailers in the fourth. It is difficult to conceive that a capital can be employed in any way which may not be classed under one or other of these heads.

On the importance of the employment of capital in the acquisition of raw produce, and especially in the cultivation of the soil, it is unnecessary to enlarge. It is from the soil, including under that term mines and fisheries, that the *matter* of all commodities that minister to our necessities, comforts, or enjoyments, is originally derived. The industry which appropriates the raw productions of the earth, as they are offered to man by nature, preceded every other. But these spontaneous productions are always extremely limited. And it is by agriculture only, or by the application of labour and capital to the cultivation of the ground, that large supplies of those raw products, which form the principal part of the food of man, can be obtained. It is not quite certain that any species of grain, as wheat, barley, rye, oats, &c. has ever been discovered growing spontaneously. But, although this must originally have been the case, still the extreme scarcity of such spontaneous productions in every country with which we are acquainted, and the labour required to raise them in considerable quantities, prove beyond all question that it is to agriculture that we are almost exclusively indebted for them. The transition from the pastoral to the agricultural mode of life is decidedly the most important step in the progress of society. Whenever, indeed, we compare the quantity of food, and of other raw products, obtained from a given surface of a well-cultivated country, with those obtained from an equal surface of an equally fertile country occupied by hunters or shepherds, the powers of agricultural industry in increasing useful productions appear so striking and extraordinary, that we cease to feel surprise at the preference so early and generally given to agriculture over manufactures and commerce; and are disposed to subscribe without hesitation to the panegyric of Cicero, when he says, "*Omnium autem rerum ex quibus aliquid acquiritur, nihil est agriculturâ melius, nihil uberius, nihil dulcius, nihil homine libero dignius.*"

But are there really any just grounds for this preference? Are not manufactures and commerce equally advantageous as agriculture? Without agriculture we could never possess any considerable supply of the *materials* out of which food and clothes are made; but were we unacquainted with the arts by which these materials, when procured, are converted into food and clothes, the largest supply of them would be of little or no service. The labour of the miller who grinds the corn, and of the baker who bakes it, is as necessary to the production of bread, as that of the husbandman who tills the ground. It is the business of the agriculturist to raise flax and wool; but if the labour of the spinner and weaver had not given them utility, and fitted them for being made into a comfortable dress, they would have been nearly, if not entirely worthless. Without the labour of the miner who digs the mineral from the bowels of the earth, we could not have obtained the matter out of which many of our most useful implements and splendid articles of furniture have been made; but if we compare the ore when dug from the mine with the finished articles, we shall certainly be convinced that the labour of the purifiers and refiners of the ore, and of the artists by whom it was converted to useful purposes, has been quite as advantageous as that of the miner.

Not only, however, is manufacturing industry, or that species of industry which fits and adapts the raw products of nature to our use, requisite to render their acquisition of any considerable value; but it is also certain, that without its assistance they could not be obtained in any considerable quantity. The mechanic who fabricates the plough contributes as efficaciously to the production of corn as the husbandman who guides it. But the ploughwright, the mill-wright, the smith, and all those artisans who prepare tools and machines for the husbandman, are really manufacturers, and differ in no respect from those employed to give utility to wool and cotton, except that they work on harder materials. Tools and machines of all sorts are the product of the labour of the tool and engine manufacturer; and without their aid, it is impossible that agricultural labour, or that any other sort of labour, should ever become considerably productive.

" Distinguer," says the Marquis Garnier, " le travail des ouvriers de l'agriculture d'avec celui des autres ouvriers, est une abstraction presque toujours oiseuse. Toute richesse, dans le sens dans lequel nous la concevons, est nécessairement le résultat de ces deux genres de travail, et la consommation ne peut pas plus se passer de l'un que de l'autre. Sans leur concours simultanée il ne peut y avoir de chose consommable, et par conséquent point de richesse. Comment pourrait-on donc comparer leurs produits respectifs, puisque, en séparant ces deux espèces de travail, on ne peut plus concevoir de véritable produit, de produit consommable et ayant une valeur réelle ? La valeur du blé sur pied résulte de l'industrie du moissonneur qui recueillera, du batteur qui le séparera de la paille, du meunier et du boulanger qui le convertiront successivement en farine et en pain, tout comme elle résulte du travail du laboureur et du semeur. Sans le travail du tisserand, le lin n'aurait pas plus le droit d'être compté au nombre des richesses, que l'ortie ou tout autre végétal inutile. A quoi pourrait-il donc servir de rechercher lequel de ces deux genres de travail contribue le plus à l'avancement de la richesse nationale? N'est-ce pas comme si l'on disputait pour savoir lequel, du pied droit ou du pied gauche, est plus utile dans l'action de marcher?"*

In fact, there is not at bottom any real distinction between agricultural and manufacturing industry. It is, as has already been shewn, a vulgar error to suppose that the operations of husbandry add any thing to the stock of matter already in existence. All that man can do, and all that he ever does, is merely to give to matter that particular form which fits it for his use. But it was contended by M. Quesnay and the *Economists*, and their opinions have in this instance been espoused by Dr. Smith, that the husbandman is powerfully assisted, in adapting matter to our use, by the aid derived from the vegetative powers of nature, while the manufacturer has to perform every thing himself without any such co-operation. — "No equal quantity of productive labour or capital employed in manufactures," says Dr. Smith, "can ever occasion so great a reproduction as if it were employed in agriculture. *In them nature does* NOTHING, *man does* ALL; and the reproduction must always be proportioned to the strength of the agents that occasion it. The capital employed in agriculture, therefore, not only puts into motion a greater quantity of productive labour than any equal capital employed in manufactures, but in proportion, too, to the quantity of productive labour which it employs, it adds a much greater value to the annual produce of

* See page 58 of the "Discours Préliminaire" to the second edition of the translation of the "Wealth of Nations," by the Marquis Garnier.

the land and labour of the country, to the real wealth and revenue of its inhabitants. *Of all the ways in which a capital can be employed it is by far the most advantageous to the society.*"*

This is perhaps the most objectionable passage in the "Wealth of Nations;" and it is really astonishing that so acute and sagacious a reasoner as Dr. Smith should have maintained a doctrine so manifestly erroneous. It is indeed true, that nature powerfully assists the labour of man in agriculture. The husbandman prepares the ground for the seed and deposits it there; but it is nature that unfolds the germ, that feeds and ripens the growing plant, and brings it to a state of maturity. But does not nature do as much for us in every department of industry? The powers of water and of wind which move our machinery, support our ships, and impel them over the deep,—the pressure of the atmosphere, and the elasticity of steam, which enable us to work the most stupendous engines, are they not the spontaneous gifts of nature? Machinery is advantageous only because it gives us the means of pressing some of the powers of nature into our service, and of making them perform the principal part of what we must otherwise have wholly performed ourselves. In navigation, is it possible to doubt that the powers of nature—the buoyancy of the water, the impulse of the wind, and the polarity of the magnet, contribute fully as much as the labour of the sailor to waft our ships from one hemisphere to another? In bleaching and fermentation, the whole processes are carried on by natural agents. And it is to the effects of heat in softening and melting metals, in preparing our food, and in warming our houses, that we owe many of our most powerful and convenient instruments, and that these northern climates have been made to afford a comfortable habitation. So far, indeed, is it from being true that

* "Wealth of Nations," vol. ii. p. 149.

nature does much for man in agriculture, and nothing in manufactures, that the fact is more nearly the reverse. There are no limits to the bounty of nature in manufactures; but there are limits, and those not very remote, to her bounty in agriculture. The greatest possible amount of capital might be expended in the construction of steam-engines, or of any other sort of machinery, and after they had been multiplied indefinitely, the last would be as powerful and efficient in producing commodities and saving labour as the first. Such, however, is not the case with the soil. Lands of the first quality are speedily exhausted; and it is impossible to apply capital indefinitely even to the best soils, without obtaining from it a constantly diminishing rate of profit. The rent of the landlord is not, as Dr. Smith conceived it to be, the recompense of the work of nature remaining, after all that part of the product is deducted which can be regarded as the recompense of the work of man. But it is, as will be afterwards shewn, the excess of produce obtained from the best soils in cultivation, over that which is obtained from the worst —it is a consequence not of the increase, but of the diminution of the productive power of the labour employed in agriculture.

If, however, the giving of utility to matter be, as it really is, the exclusive object of every species of industry, it is plain that the capital and labour employed in carrying commodities from where they are produced to where they are to be consumed, and in dividing them into minute portions, so as to fit the wants of the consumers, are really as productive as if they were employed in agriculture or manufactures. The miner gives utility to matter — to coal for example — by bringing it from the bowels of the earth to its surface; but the merchant or carrier who transports this coal from the mine whence it has been dug to the city, or place where it is to be burned, gives it a further and perhaps a more considerable value. We do not owe our fires exclusively to the miner, or exclusively to the coal merchant. They are the result of the conjoined operations of both, as, also, of the operations of those who furnished them with the tools and implements used in their respective employments.

It is probably unnecessary to do more than refer to what has been previously stated with respect to the utility of retail dealers. But the following extract from the "Wealth of Nations" sets it in a somewhat different point of view:—"If," says Dr. Smith, "there was no such trade as a butcher, every man would be obliged to purchase a whole ox or a whole sheep at a time. This would generally be inconvenient to the rich, and much more so to the poor. If a poor workman was obliged to purchase a month's or six months' provisions at a time, a great part of the stock which he employs as a capital in the instruments of his trade, or in the furniture of his shop, and which yields him a revenue, he would be forced to place in that part of his stock which is reserved for immediate consumption, and which yields him no revenue. Nothing can be more convenient for such a person than to be able to purchase his subsistence from day to day, or even from hour to hour, as he wants it. He is thereby enabled to employ almost his whole stock as a capital. He is thus enabled to furnish work to a greater value, and the profit which he makes by it in this way much more than compensates the additional price which the profit of the retailer imposes upon the goods. The prejudices of some political writers against shopkeepers and tradesmen are altogether without foundation. So far is it from being necessary either to tax them, or to restrict their numbers, that they can never be multiplied so as to hurt the public interests, though they may so as to hurt one another. The quantity of grocery goods, for example, which can be sold in a particular town, is limited by the demand of that town and its neighbourhood. The capital, therefore, which can be employed in the grocery trade, cannot exceed what is sufficient to purchase that quantity. If this capital is divided between two different grocers, their competition will tend to make both of them sell cheaper than if it were in the hands of one only; and if it were divided among twenty, their competition would be just so much the greater, and the chance of their combining together in order to raise the price just so much the less. Their competition might, perhaps, ruin some of themselves; but to take care of this is the business of the parties concerned, and it may safely be trusted to their discretion. It can never hurt either the consumer or the producer; on the contrary, it must tend to make the retailers both sell cheaper and buy dearer, than if the whole trade was monopolised by one or two persons. Some of them, perhaps, may occasionally decoy a weak customer to buy what he has no occasion for. This evil is, however, of too little importance to deserve the public attention, nor would it necessarily be prevented by restricting their number."*

Thus it appears, that *all* the modes in which capital can be employed in productive industry, or, in other words, that the raising of raw produce, the fashioning of that raw produce after it is raised into useful and desirable articles, the carrying of the raw and manufactured products from place to place, and the retailing of them in such portions as may suit the public demand, are *equally* advantageous: that is, the capital and labour employed in any one of these departments contributes equally with that which is employed in the others, to increase the mass of necessaries, conveniencies, and luxuries. Without a previous supply of raw produce, we could have no manufactures; and without manufactures and commercial industry, the greater part of that raw produce would be entirely worthless. Manufacturers and

* "Wealth of Nations," vol. ii. p. 146.

merchants are to the body politic what the digestive powers are to the human body. We could not exist without food; but the largest supplies of food cannot lengthen our days when the machinery by which nature adapts it to our use, and incorporates it with our body, is vitiated and deranged. Nothing, therefore, can be more silly and childish than the estimates so frequently put forth of the comparative advantages of agricultural, manufacturing, and commercial industry. They are all inseparably connected, and depend upon, and grow out of each other. The agriculturists raise raw produce for the manufacturers and merchants, while the latter manufacture and import necessary, convenient, and ornamental articles for the use of the former. Whatever, consequently, contributes to promote or depress the industry and enterprise of one class, must have a beneficial or injurious influence upon the others. "Land and trade," to borrow the just and forcible expressions of Sir Josiah Child, "are TWINS, and have always, and ever will, *wax* and *wane together*. It cannot be ill with trade but land will fall, nor ill with land but trade will feel it."* Hence the obvious absurdity of attempting to exalt one species of industry, by giving it factitious advantages, at the expense of the rest. No preference can be given to agriculturists over manufacturers and merchants, or to the latter over the former, without occasioning the most mischievous consequences. Individuals ought, in all cases, to be allowed to follow their own inclinations in the employment of their stock and industry. Where industry is free, their interests can never be opposed to the interests of the public. When they succeed best in increasing their own wealth, they must necessarily also succeed best in increasing the wealth of the state of which they are subjects.

This mutual dependence of the different branches of

* "New Discourse of Trade." Glasg. ed. p. 15.

industry on each other, and the necessity of their co-operation to enable mankind to make any considerable progress in civilisation, have been ably illustrated in one of the early numbers of the "Edinburgh Review." "It may safely be concluded, that all those occupations which tend to supply the necessary wants, or to multiply the comforts and pleasures of human life, are equally productive, in the strict sense of the word, and tend to augment the mass of human riches, meaning, by riches, all those things which are necessary, or convenient, or delightful to man. The progress of society has been productive of a complete separation of employments originally united. At first, every man provided, as well as he could, for his necessities as well as his pleasures, and for *all* his wants, as well as *all* his enjoyments. By degrees, a division of these cares was introduced; the subsistence of the community became the province of one class, its comforts of another, and its gratifications of a third. The different operations subservient to the attainment of each of these objects were then intrusted to different hands; and the universal establishment of barter connected the whole of these divisions and subdivisions together—enabled one man to manufacture for all, without danger of starving by not ploughing or hunting, and another to plough or hunt for all, without the risk of wanting tools or clothes by not manufacturing. It has thus become as impossible to say exactly who feeds, clothes, or entertains the community, as it would be to say which of the many workmen employed in the manufacture of pins is the actual pin-maker, or which of the farm-servants produces the crop. All the branches of useful industry work together to the common end, as all the parts of each branch co-operate to its particular object. If you say that the farmer feeds the community, and produces all the raw materials which the other classes work upon, we answer, that unless those other classes worked up the raw materials, and supplied the farmer's necessities, he would be forced to allot part of his labour to this employment, whilst he forced others to assist in raising raw produce. In such a complicated system, it is clear that all labour has the same effect, and equally increases the whole mass of wealth. Nor can any attempt be more vain than theirs who would define the particular parts of the machine that produce the motion, which is necessarily the result of the *whole powers combined*, and depends on each particular one of the mutually connected members."*

Besides underrating the importance of manufactures in promoting the increase of national wealth, it has been said that they are most unfavourable to the health of the people. But this statement, though in accordance with popular prejudice, is certainly without any good foundation. The period during which manufactures have made the most astonishing progress amongst us, has been marked by an equally astonishing diminution of the rate of mortality. In 1780 the deaths, throughout England and Wales, amounted to about 1 in 40 of the population; in 1811 they had declined to 1 in 52; and in 1821 they had sunk to only 1 in 58. The improvement began about the middle of last century, and has, doubtless, been owing partly to the greater prevalence of habits of cleanliness and sobriety amongst the poor, and the meliorations that have been made in their diet, dress, and houses; partly to the improvement of the climate, resulting from the drainage of bogs and marshes; and partly, and since 1800 chiefly perhaps, to discoveries in medical science, and the extirpation of the small-pox. But to whatever causes this wonderfully increased healthiness may be ascribed, there is conclusive evidence to shew that they have not been counteracted by the extension of manufactures. Had such been the case, the improvement would have been greater in the country than in the towns, whereas it has been

* Vol. iv. p. 362.

decidedly less. The mortality in London, during the first half of last century, is supposed to have been as high as 1 in 20, while, at this time, it does not amount to 1 in 40. The rate of mortality in Manchester in 1770, as deduced from the careful observations made by Dr. Percival, was 1 in 28; whereas, notwithstanding the prodigious increase of manufacturing establishments that has taken place in the interval, the mortality is not supposed to exceed, at this moment, 1 in 45. According to Dr. Enfield, the population of Liverpool, in 1773, was found, by actual enumeration, to be 32,450; and dividing this number by 1,191, the annual burials at that period, we have the proportion of deaths to the whole population as 1 to 27¼. But in 1821, when the population of Liverpool and its environs amounted to 141,487, the deaths were only in the ratio of 44⅘; and excluding the environs, they were, to the population of the town, as 1 to about 41. At an average of the entire period from 1810 to 1820, there died in Birmingham 1 out of every 39·7 inhabitants; in Glasgow 1 out of every 45·6; in Leeds 1 out of every 47·6; and in Northampton 1 out of every 51.* In Lancashire, which may, almost without a metaphor, be regarded as one immense workshop, the average rate of mortality, as deduced from the returns obtained under the late census, was as low as 1 in 55; being only about *five* per cent more than the mortality in Westmorland, which has hardly any manufacturing establishments, and is occupied chiefly by small proprietors.

Besides supposing that the health of the population is injured by the extension of manufactures, it has been supposed that the extreme subdivision of labour in manufacturing establishments, and the undivided attention which every one employed in them must give to the single operation in which he is engaged, has a most pernicious influence over the mental faculties. The genius of the

* See "Edinburgh Review," no. xcvii. p. 18.

master is said to be cultivated, but that of the workman to be condemned to perpetual neglect. "Many mechanical arts," says Dr. Ferguson, "require no capacity; they succeed best under a total suppression of sentiment and reason; and ignorance is the mother of industry as well as of superstition. Reflection and fancy are subject to err; but a habit of moving the hand or the foot is independent of either. Manufactures, accordingly, prosper most where the head is least consulted, and where the workshop may, without any great effort of imagination, be considered as an engine, the parts of which are men."* Similar statements have been made by others. Even Dr. Smith, who has given so beautiful an exposition of the benefits derived from the division of employments, has, in this instance, concurred with the popular opinion, and has not hesitated to affirm that constant application to one particular occupation in a large manufactory, "necessarily renders the workman as *stupid and ignorant as it is possible to make a human being*." Nothing, however, can be more marvellously incorrect than these representations. Instead of its being true that the workmen employed in manufacturing establishments are less intelligent and acute than those employed in agriculture, the fact is distinctly and completely the reverse. The weavers and other mechanics of Glasgow, Manchester, and Birmingham, possess far more information than is possessed by the agricultural labourers of any county in the empire. And this is really what a less prejudiced inquiry into the subject would have led us to anticipate. The various occupations in which the husbandman has successively to engage, their constant liability to be affected by so variable a power as the weather, and the perpetual change in the appearance of the objects which daily meet his eyes, and with which he is conversant, occupy his attention, and render him a stranger to that ennui and desire for extrinsic and

* "Essay on Civil Society," p. 303.

adventitious excitement which must ever be felt by those who are constantly engaged in burnishing the point of a pin, or in performing the same endless routine of precisely similar operations. This want of excitement cannot, however, be so cheaply or effectually gratified in any way as it may be by cultivating, that is, by *stimulating*, the mental powers. Workmen in general have no time for dissipation; and if they had, the wages of labour are too low, and the propensity to save and accumulate too powerful, to allow of any very large proportion of them seeking to divert themselves by indulging in riot and excess. They are thus driven to seek for recreation in mental excitement; and their situation affords them every facility for amusing and diverting themselves in this manner. Agricultural labourers, spread over a wide extent of country, are without the means of assembling, except on some rare occasions, for the purpose either of amusement or instruction; but, by working together, those engaged in manufacturing establishments have constant opportunities of discussing all topics of interest and importance. They are thus gradually trained to habits of thinking and reflection; their intellects are sharpened by the collision of conflicting opinions; and a small contribution from each individual enables them to establish lectureships and libraries, and to obtain a large supply of newspapers and periodical publications. But whatever doubt may exist respecting the *cause*, whether it be ascribed to the better elementary instruction of the lower classes in towns and villages, or to the circumstances under which they are placed in after life, there can be none as to the *fact*, that the intelligence of manufacturing workmen has increased according as their numbers have increased, and as their employments have been more and more subdivided. There is not, I apprehend, any real ground for supposing that they were ever less intelligent than the agriculturists; though, whatever may have been the case formerly, none will now venture to affirm that they are inferior to them in intellectual acquirements, or that they are mere machines without sentiment or reason.

It has been further objected to the extension of manufactures, that when any thing occurs to give them a check, or to throw the immense population dependent on them out of employment, or when, owing to a scarcity, a sudden rise takes place in the price of provisions, public tranquillity and the security of property are apt to be endangered. Demagogues, it is said, and those workshop orators so frequently met with in the manufacturing districts, take advantage of the feverish excitement produced by the distress, to vilify the institutions of the country; and by representing the privations of the workmen as the effect of measures intended to advance the interests of the higher classes, and not as springing from accidental or uncontrollable causes, occasion outrages which can only be repressed by the employment of a large military force, and the adoption of measures that are not always very consistent with the principles of a free government. It would be useless to attempt to deny that there is a great deal of truth in this statement. But it will be afterwards shewn, that the greater number of those commercial revulsions which occasion so much distress in the manufacturing districts, and the great rise of price that invariably takes place when the home supply of grain is materially deficient, are principally to be ascribed to the operation of monopolies, or to the restraints laid on the freedom of commerce. They may, therefore, be expected to become less frequent and disastrous, according as a nearer approach is made to a free commercial system; and will, consequently, afford a less powerful incentive to popular commotions. In point of fact, however, the violent and unjustifiable proceedings of which the manufacturing population have occasionally been guilty, have resulted more from ignorance of their real interests than from any thing else. No sufficient pains have been taken to shew them how essential the security of property and the preservation of tranquillity are to the very existence of manufactures; and that when they either attack the establishments of their masters, or attempt to hinder the employment of machinery, or to obstruct their fellows who choose to work at reduced wages, they are acting in the very way that is most certain to involve themselves in ruin. Had the workmen been fully aware that such must be the inevitable result of violent proceedings on their part, is it to be doubted they would have been less common? It is fortunate, therefore, that the apathy which has so long existed as to the instruction of the poor in a knowledge of the circumstances which really determine their condition, is at length beginning to disappear. They cannot become better informed with respect to them, without, at the same time, becoming less under the influence of prejudice, and less disposed to second the designs of violent and seditious persons.

But admitting that a manufacturing population must be, in an unusual degree, violent, inflammable, and apt to be misled; these disadvantages seem, even in a political point of view, to be far more than overbalanced by advantages, for which we are exclusively indebted to the extension of manufactures. Turbulence, whatever may be its influence in other respects, produces an excitement that is favourable to the developement of the mental faculties, and hinders them from becoming inactive or torpid. It is, indeed, to be regretted, that measures intended and calculated to advance the public interests, should ever become, as they have frequently done, objects of popular indignation and attack. But were it not for the formation of cities and towns, or, in other words, for the growth of manufactures and commerce, the same tame acquiescence would, in most instances, be given to the most injurious as to the most beneficial measures. Men seldom entertain a just sense of their own importance, or acquire a knowledge of their rights, or are able to defend them with courage and effect, until they have been congregated into masses. An agricultural population, thinly distributed over an extensive country, and without any point of re-union, rarely opposes any vigorous resistance to the most oppressive and arbitrary measures. But such is not the case with the population of towns: their inhabitants are all actuated by the same spirit; they derive courage from their numbers and union; the bold animate the timid; the resolute confirm the wavering: the redress of an injury done to a single citizen becomes, in some degree, the business of the whole body: they take their measures in common, and prosecute them with a vigour and resolution that generally makes the boldest minister pause in an unpopular career. The most superficial, as well as the most profound reader of history, must acknowledge the truth of what is now stated; the introduction and establishment of extensive manufactures and commerce having every where been the era of public freedom, and of an improved system of government.

That hostility to commercial pursuits so generally entertained by the philosophers of antiquity, and which has descended from them to many of their successors in more modern times, seems to have originated principally in an idea that commerce was unfavourable to the patriotic virtues, and that those who were familiar with foreign countries ceased to entertain any very peculiar regard for their own. That there is some foundation for this statement is true; but it is not true that commerce tends to weaken that love of country which is founded upon just grounds. All that it does is to moderate the excessive preference of ourselves to all others, which is the surest proof of ignorance and barbarism: and in this respect it differs nothing from the acquaintance with foreigners obtained through the medium of books. The merchant who has visited a foreign country, and the individual who has read an account of it, will naturally be disposed to compare its institutions with those of his own country. When the latter seem to be the best calculated to promote the public interests, this comparison will not, certainly, render them less meritorious in his eyes; and when they are comparatively defective, can any thing be more desirable than to have the means of rectifying and amending them, not upon speculative or doubtful grounds, but according to the experience of other nations? A Turk, or a Spaniard, may be as intensely patriotic as an Englishman or an American; but the patriotism of the former is a blind indiscriminating passion, which prompts him to admire and support the very abuses that depress and degrade himself and his country; whereas the patriotism of the latter is of a comparatively sober and rational description. He prefers his country, not merely because it is the place of his birth, but because, upon contrasting it with others, he is satisfied, that though not faultless in every respect, its institutions are comparatively excellent, and are well fitted to secure private happiness and public prosperity.

The idea that the patriotism of those engaged in commercial pursuits is less ardent than that of the agricultural classes, never could have been entertained by any one who had the least acquaintance with history, or who was not blinded by prejudice. Were the Athenians or Corinthians less patriotic than the Spartans or Thebans? Alexander had more difficulty in conquering Tyre than in subduing the whole Persian empire; and Carthage had nearly arrested the Romans in their progress to universal dominion. But it is needless to go back to antiquity for examples to prove the beneficial influence of commerce on the patriotic virtues. The Hollanders and the English have been less distinguished among the nations of Europe for their vast commerce and wealth, than for the extraordinary sacrifices and exertions they have made for the sake of private freedom and national independence.

Thus, then, we arrive, by a different and more lengthened route, at the same result I have already endeavoured to establish. The inextinguishable passion for gain — the *auri sacra fames*—will always lead capitalists to employ their stocks in such branches of industry as yield, all things considered, the *highest rate of profit*. And it is clear to demonstration, that those which yield this highest rate are those in which it is most for the public interest that capital should be invested. The profits of a particular branch of industry are rarely raised except by an increased demand for its produce. Should the demand for cottons increase, there would be an increased competition for them; and their price being in consequence augmented, the manufacturers would obtain comparatively high profits. But the rate of profit has a natural tendency to equality; and, when monopolies do not interpose, it cannot continue either permanently higher or lower in one employment than in others. As soon as the price of cottons had risen, fresh capital would begin to be employed in their production. The manufacturers would endeavour to borrow additional quantities, and those engaged in less lucrative employments would gradually contract their businesses, and transfer a portion of their stock to where it would yield a larger return. The equilibrium of profit would thus be again restored. For the greater capital employed in the cotton trade, by increasing the supply according to the increased demand, would reduce prices to their old level. Such is the mode in which the interests of individuals are, in all cases, rendered subservient to those of the public. High profits attract capital; but high profits in particular businesses are the effect of high prices, and these are always reduced, and the commodities brought within the command of a greater number of purchasers, as soon as additional capital has been employed in their production. It is clear, therefore, that that employment of capital is the best which yields the greatest profit; and hence, if two capitals yield *equal* profits, it proves that the departments of industry in which they are respectively invested, how much soever they may differ in many respects, are equally beneficial to the country. Nothing, indeed, can be more nugatory than to apprehend that the freedom of industry should attract capital to a comparatively disadvantageous employment. If it flow to manufactures or commerce rather than agriculture, it is because it yields larger profits to the individual, and consequently to the state.

CHAPTER VII.

Improvements in Machinery similar in their Effects to Improvements in the Skill and Dexterity of the Labourer—Do not occasion a Glut of Commodities—Sometimes force Workmen to change their Employments—Have no Tendency to lessen, but most commonly increase the Demand for Labour—Case supposed by Mr. Ricardo—True Cause of Gluts—Error of those who ascribe them to a Deficiency of Money—Circumstances which occasion Miscalculations on the part of the Producers.

VARIOUS bad consequences have been supposed to result from the continued extension and improvement of machinery. But a presumption arises at the outset, that they must be in a great degree visionary, inasmuch as they would equally follow from the continued improvement of the skill and industry of the labourer. If the construction of a machine that would manufacture two pairs of stockings for the same expense that had previously been required to manufacture one pair, be under any circumstances injurious, the injury would, obviously, be equal were the same thing accomplished by increased dexterity and skill on the part of the knitters; were the females, for example, who have been in the habit of knitting two or three pairs in the week, able in future to knit four or six pairs. There is really no difference in the cases. And supposing the demand for stockings were already sufficiently supplied, M. Sismondi could not, consistently with the principles he has advanced,* hesitate about condemning such an improvement as a very great evil—as a means of throwing *half* the people engaged in the stocking manufacture out of employment. The question respecting the improvement of machinery is, therefore, at bottom, the same with the question respecting the improvement

* "Nouveaux Principes," tom. ii. p. 318.

of the science, skill, and industry of the labourer. The principles which regulate our decision in the one case, must also regulate it in the other. If it be advantageous that the manual dexterity of the labourer should be indefinitely extended — that he should be enabled to produce greater quantities of commodities with the same, or a less quantity of labour, it surely must be advantageous that he should avail himself of the assistance of such machines as may most effectually assist him in bringing about that result.

In order the better to appreciate the effects resulting either from the increased skill and dexterity of the labourer, or from an improvement in tools or machines, let us suppose that the productive powers of industry are universally augmented, and that the workmen engaged in every different employment can, with the same exertion, produce twice the quantity of commodities as at present: is it not evident that this increased facility of production would double the wealth and enjoyments of all individuals? The shoemaker who had formerly manufactured only *one* pair of shoes a day, would now be able to manufacture *two* pairs. But as an equal improvement is supposed to have taken place in every employment, he would be able to obtain twice the quantity of all other things in exchange for shoes. In a country thus circumstanced, every workman would have a great quantity of the produce of his own work to dispose of, beyond what he had occasion for; and as every other workman would be in the same situation, each would be enabled to exchange his own goods for a great quantity, or, what comes to the same thing, for the price of a great quantity, of those of others. The condition of such a society would be vastly improved. All the necessaries, luxuries, and conveniences of life, would be comparatively abundant.

It may, however, be asked, would the *demand* be sufficient to take off this increased quantity of commodities?

Would their extraordinary multiplication not cause such a glut of the market, as to force their sale at a lower price than would suffice to repay even the diminished cost of their production? But it is not necessary, in order to render an increase in the powers of production advantageous, that they should always be fully exerted. If the labourer's command over the necessaries and comforts of life were suddenly doubled, his consumption as well as his savings would doubtless be very greatly increased; but it is not at all likely that he would continue to exert his full powers. He would then be able, without endangering his means of subsistence, to devote a greater portion of his time to purposes of instruction and amusement. It is only where the powers of industry are feeble or very much loaded, where supplies of food have to be drawn from soils of inferior fertility, or where population is in excess, that workmen are compelled to make every possible exertion. High wages are advantageous only because of the increased comforts they bring along with them; and of these, an addition to the time which may be devoted to amusement is certainly not one of the least. Wherever wages are high, and little subject to fluctuation, the labourers are found to be active, intelligent, and industrious. But they rarely prosecute their employments with the same intensity as those who are obliged, by the pressure of necessity, to strain every nerve to the utmost. They are enabled to enjoy their intervals of ease and relaxation; and they would be censurable if they did not enjoy them.

Suppose, however, that the productive powers of industry are doubled; nay, suppose they are increased ten or ten thousand times, and that they are exerted to the utmost, it would not occasion any lasting glut of the market. It is true, that those individuals who are most industrious may produce commodities which those who are less industrious—who prefer indolence to exertion—may not have the means of purchasing, or for which they may not be able to furnish an equivalent. But the glut arising from such a contingency must speedily disappear. Every man's object, in exerting his productive powers, must be either to consume the entire produce of his labour himself, or to exchange it, or portions of it, for such commodities as he wishes to obtain from others. Suppose, now, that he directly consumes every thing he produces: it is obvious that in such a case there can be no glut or excess; for, to suppose that commodities, produced in order to be directly consumed by the individuals producing them, may be in excess, is equivalent to supposing that production may be carried on without any motive, or that there may be an effect without a cause! When individuals, instead of directly consuming the produce of their industry, offer it in exchange to others, their miscalculation may occasion a glut. Should A, for example, produce commodities, and offer them in exchange to B or C, who is unable to furnish him with those he is desirous to obtain, he will have miscalculated, and there will be a glut: he should, it is obvious, have either offered his commodities to others, or have applied himself to the production of those which he wanted. This, however, is an error that will speedily be rectified; for, if he find that he cannot attain his object by prosecuting his present employment, he will forthwith set about changing it, producing, in time to come, such commodities only as he can find a merchant for, or as he means to consume. It is clear, therefore, that a *universally* increased facility of production can never be the cause of a permanent overloading of the market. Suppose that the amount of capital and labour, engaged in every different employment, is adjusted according to the effectual demand, and that they are *all* yielding the same nett profit; if the productive powers of labour were universally increased, the commodities produced would all preserve the same relation to each other. Double or treble the quantity of one commodity would be given for double or treble the quantity of every other commodity. There would be a general augmentation of the wealth of the society, but there would be no excess of commodities in the market; the increased equivalents on the one side being precisely balanced by a corresponding increase on the other. But if, while one class of producers were industrious, another chose to be idle, there would be a temporary excess. It is clear, however, that this excess would be occasioned by the *deficient* production of the idle class. It would not be a consequence of production being too much, but of its being too little increased. Increase it more — make the idle class equally productive with the others, and then it will be able to furnish them with equivalents for their commodities, and the surplus will immediately disappear. It is in vain that Mr. Malthus attempts to defeat this reasoning by supposing the existence of an *indisposition to consume!* There is no such indisposition in any country in the world; not even in Mexico, to which Mr. Malthus has specially referred.* The indisposition is not to consume, but to produce. In Mexico, as elsewhere, no one is entitled to consume the products of the industry of others unless he furnish them with an equivalent; but the Mexican prefers indolence to the gratification derivable from the commodities he might procure by means of labour. Mr. Malthus has mistaken this indisposition to produce for an indisposition to consume; and has, in consequence, been led to deny the proposition, that effective demand depends upon production.

Mr. Malthus has justly stated, that the demand for a commodity depends "on the *will* combined with the *power* to purchase it;" that is, on the power to furnish an equivalent for it. But when did any one hear of a want of *will* to purchase commodities? If it alone could procure the necessaries and luxuries of life, every beggar

* "Principles of Political Economy," p. 382.

would become as rich as Crœsus, and the market would constantly be understocked with commodities. The *power* to purchase is the real desideratum. It is the incapacity of furnishing equivalents for the products necessary to supply our wants, that "makes calamity of so long life." The more, then, that this incapacity is diminished, or, which is the same thing, the more industrious every individual becomes, and the more the facility of production is increased, the more will the condition of society be improved.

It is quite visionary to suppose that a deficiency of foreign demand for the products of industry can ever be occasioned by an increase of productive power. Such want of demand, when it does occur, must proceed from one or other of the following causes:—It must either be a consequence of the comparatively high price of our commodities, or of the restrictions which have been imposed on the importation of British goods into foreign countries, and on the importation of foreign goods into Britain. Now it is obvious, that if the falling off in the foreign demand proceed from the former of these causes, it must have been infinitely greater had the cost of production continued undiminished. If, notwithstanding all the contrivances of our Arkwrights and Watts, to save labour and expense in the production of commodities, we are still in danger of being undersold by foreigners, it is certain that, without these contrivances, we should not have been able to withstand their competition for a single moment. It would be not a little inconsequential, first to complain that our goods were too high priced for the foreign market, and then to declaim against the only means by which their prices can be reduced and the demand increased!

It is not to increased facilities of production, but to the restraints imposed on the freedom of trade, that the difficulty we so frequently experience of disposing of our commodities in the foreign market, is, in most cases, to be ascribed. The Poles, Swedes, French, Chinese, Brazilians, &c. are desirous to exchange their corn, timber, iron, wine, silks, tea, sugar, &c. &c. for our products. These commodities, too, are particularly well fitted for our markets, and form, indeed, the very articles our merchants are most anxious to import. It is plain, therefore, that the decline that has occasionally taken place in the foreign demand for our products, has not been owing to their excessive supply—for the foreigners are both *able* and *willing* to purchase them—but to those impolitic and injurious regulations which fetter and restrict the freedom of importation and exportation in all commercial countries. It is not in our power, nor in that of any one country, to give universal freedom to commerce. But if we repealed our restrictive regulations—if, instead of forcing our people to build their houses of the inferior and expensive timber of Canada, we allowed them to use the better and cheaper timber of Norway and Sweden; and if, instead of forcing the cultivation of poor soils, that yield only a scanty and inadequate return, we imported the comparatively cheap corn of Poland and the United States, the foreign demand for our commodities would be astonishingly increased; and, what perhaps is of still more importance, it would become comparatively steady.

It is said, indeed, that any relief which we could derive from the adoption of a more enlarged commercial system, would only be temporary; that the power of production we possess is so vast, that our commodities would speedily glut even the market of the world! This, it must be confessed, is rather an improbable supposition; but, assuming that we could, by means of our improved machinery, manufacture a sufficient supply of cottons to serve every country, and even to sink their price below the cost of production, it could have no permanently bad consequence, but the reverse. The self-interest of the manufacturers would immediately suggest to them the advantage of withdrawing a part of their capital, and employing it in some other species of industry. If we reverted to the sound principle of free trade, the demand for commodities would be comparatively steady. It would no longer be materially affected by the circumstance of our harvests being more or less productive than ordinary, or by any of those contingencies which now exert so great an influence on our trade. And if it were found that, at an average of two or three years, we had not been able to dispose of our cottons, woollens, &c. with a sufficient profit, it would be a proof that their production had been carried too far; and as there could be no rational prospect of the demand being speedily increased, manufacturers would not be tempted, as at present, to linger on in a disadvantageous employment, but would transfer a portion of their capitals to other businesses; and the supply of goods being thus diminished, their price would rise to its proper level.

Still, however, it may be urged, that, under a free commercial system, we might not only be able to manufacture too much of one, but of all commodities demanded by foreigners. But, admitting that such were the case, still it would not afford any ground whatever for doubting, that an increase of the powers of production would even then be attended with great and unmixed advantage. If foreigners are unable or unwilling to furnish equivalents for the products we send abroad, we must relinquish the production of the exported commodities, and directly produce those we intended to import, or substitutes for them. Now, the real question comes to be—if a question can be raised on such a subject—Whether it is advantageous that we should be able to produce these commodities cheaply, or not? Foreign trade is beneficial, because a country, by exporting the produce of those branches of industry in which it has some peculiar advantage, is enabled to import the produce of those branches in which the advantage is on the side of the foreigner. But, to insure this benefit, it is not necessary that the whole capital of the country should be vested in those particular branches. England can furnish better and cheaper cottons than any other country; but it is not therefore contended that she ought to produce nothing but cottons. Were she able to furnish the same supply of cottons as at present with a tenth part of the capital and labour, is it not plain that her means of producing all other commodities would, in consequence, be prodigiously augmented?

But it is contended, that these means would not be put in requisition; and that it is impossible so great a saving of labour could take place in a branch of industry employing above a million of people, with any rational prospect of such an increase in the demand for labour in other employments, as would take up the hands that would be thrown idle. As this is an objection which has been reproduced in a thousand different shapes, and on which much stress has been laid, it will be proper to examine it somewhat in detail.

In the *first* place, it may be observed, that an improvement which had the effect of sinking the price of cottons nine-tenths,—that is, which enabled one-tenth of the capital and labour engaged in their manufacture to produce the same quantity of goods that is now produced, would not throw the other nine-tenths out of employment. The demand for cottons, instead of remaining stationary, would, under such circumstances, be very greatly increased. Those who subsist by their labour, and whose command over the necessaries and luxuries of life is always comparatively limited, form an immense majority of the population of every country. And any considerable reduction in the price of a commodity in general use, has uniformly almost been found to extend the demand for it in a much greater proportion. This has been eminently the case in the cotton manufacture itself. It is impossible, I believe, to name another branch of industry in which the powers of production have been so much increased; and yet it is certain, that the extension of the market consequent to every new invention for saving labour and expense, has always occasioned the employment of an additional number of hands. Such a reduction of price as has been supposed, would give a prodigious stimulus to the manufacture. Our cottons would obtain a still more incontestible superiority in every market than they now enjoy, and would be brought within the command of an immensely increased number of consumers. Foreign governments would in vain attempt to prohibit their introduction. Cheap goods never fail of making their way through every barrier—*per medios ire satellites amant.* In the words of Sir Josiah Child, "They that can give the best price for a commodity, shall never fail to have it by one means or other, notwithstanding the opposition of any laws, or interposition of any power by sea or land; of such force, subtilty, and violence, is the general course of trade."*

But in the *second* place, it is easy to shew that the advantages attending the introduction of machinery do not, as many suppose, at all depend on the circumstance of the market extending proportionally to the reduction in the price of commodities. They are equally great when no such extension can take place. Suppose the price of cottons were to sink to a tenth of what it is at this moment: if the demand for them were not at the same time extended, nine-tenths of those engaged in the manufacture would be thrown out of *that* employment; but it is demonstrable that there would be a corresponding extension of the demand for the produce of other branches of industry. The wealth of the buyers of cottons could not be impaired by their production being facilitated and their price reduced. They would still have the *same capital* to employ, and the *same revenue* to expend. The only difference would be, that

* "Discourse about Trade," p. 129. Ed. 1690.

one pound would purchase as large a supply of cottons in future as ten pounds did before; and that the remaining nine pounds would be applied to the purchase of other things. That they would be so applied is certain; for although we may have enough of a particular commodity, it is absolutely impossible that we can ever have what we should reckon a sufficient supply of *all* sorts of commodities. There are no limits to the passion for accumulation:

> Nec Crœsi fortuna unquam nec Persica regna
> Sufficient animo —

The portion of revenue that had been set free by the fall in the price of cottons would not be permitted to lie idle in our pockets. It would unquestionably be applied to purchase, either directly by the parties themselves, or indirectly by those to whom they might lend it, an additional quantity of something else. The *total* effective demand of the society for labour or the produce of labour would not, therefore, be in the slightest degree impaired. The capital and workmen disengaged from the cotton manufacture would henceforth be as profitably employed in the production of those commodities for which an equivalent increase of demand had taken place; so that, after the lapse of such a period as would permit of their transfer to those new employments being effected, labour would be in as great demand as before, while every individual would be able to obtain ten times the former quantity of cottons for the same quantity of labour, or of any other commodity whose real value had remained constant.

It has, however, been contended,* that when machinery is employed to perform work which has previously been performed by means of labourers, the price of the commodity is seldom or never diminished to such an

* Sismondi, "Nouveaux Principes," tom. ii. p. 325.

extent as to render the reduction of price equivalent to the wages of the labourers thrown out of employment. The invention of machinery, says M. Sismondi, by which cottons could be produced five per cent below the present prices, would occasion the dismissal of every cotton-spinner and weaver in England; while the increased demand for other commodities, occasioned by this trifling saving, would barely afford employment for five per cent, or *one-twentieth* part of the disengaged hands; so that were an improvement of this kind to take place, the vast majority of these persons must either be starved outright, or provided for in the workhouse. But, in making this statement, M. Sismondi has neglected one most important element—he has not told us how his machines are to be produced. If, as he has tacitly assumed, they cost nothing—if, like atmospheric air, they are the free gift of Providence, and do not require any labour to procure them—then, instead of prices falling five per cent, they will fall to *nothing;* and every farthing formerly applied to purchase cottons will be set at liberty, and made available to the purchase of other things. But if, by stating that the introduction of new machinery has reduced the price of cottons five per cent, M. Sismondi means, as he must do, that 20,000*l.* vested in an improved machine will produce the same quantity of cottons as 21,000*l.* employed in the payment of wages, or in the machinery now in use, it is plain, that twenty out of every twenty-one parts of all the capital and labour formerly employed in the cotton manufacture will henceforth be employed in the manufacture of machinery, and that the other twenty-first part will be employed in producing the commodities for which, owing to the fall of five per cent in the price of cottons, a proportionally greater demand must be experienced. In this case, therefore, it is plain that, instead of twenty out of every twenty-one labourers engaged in the cotton manufacture being thrown out of employment, there would not be a single individual in that situation. But as this reasoning proceeds on the supposition that the machines would last only *one* year, M. Sismondi might still contend, that if they were fitted to last *ten* or *twenty* years, there would be a deficiency of employment. The truth is, however, that the reverse holds; and that, instead of being diminished, the demand for labour would be increased, according to the greater durability of the machines. Suppose profits are ten per cent; when a capital of 20,000*l*. is vested in a machine fitted to last *one* year, the goods produced by it must sell for 22,000*l*., viz. 2,000*l*. as profits, and 20,000*l*. to replace the machine itself. But if the machine were fitted to last *ten* years, then the goods produced by it, instead of selling for 22,000*l*. would only sell for 3,254*l*. viz. 2,000*l*. as profits, and 1,254*l*. to accumulate as an annuity for ten years, to replace the original capital of 20,000*l*. Thus it appears, that by introducing a machine, constructed with an equal capital, which should last *ten* years instead of *one* year, the price of the commodities produced by it would be sunk to about *one-seventh* of their former price. Hence, the consumers of cottons would, by means of their equally increased demand for other articles, afford, in future, employment for *six-sevenths* of the disengaged labourers. Nor is this the only effect that would be produced. The proprietor of the machine would have, exclusive of the ordinary profit on his capital, at the end of the first year, an additional stock of 1,254*l*. or one-sixteenth of the value of his machine, which he must necessarily expend in some way or other in the payment of wages; at the end of the second year, this additional revenue or stock would be increased to about one-eighth of the value of the machine; and, in the latter years of its existence, it is plain that, instead of having declined, the demand for labour would have very nearly *doubled*.

But there is another circumstance which must not be lost sight of in treating this question. The reductions effected in the prices of commodities by the introduction of improved machinery, while they invariably occasion an increase of consumption, occasion also an increase of capital. A fall in the cost of producing an article in extensive demand, is really equivalent to an increase in the revenue of all classes ; and it is difficult to believe that the means of saving should be increased without a greater accumulation taking place. Persons belonging to the middle and upper classes, who have been pretty fully supplied with a high-priced article, do not, when its price is reduced, materially extend their purchases of it. Neither do they, generally speaking, lay out the whole saving on other articles required for immediate use. Many, no doubt, do this ; but the greater number accumulate a portion of the saving, and form out of it a fresh capital. In this way all considerable inventions and discoveries contribute powerfully to augment the stock of the country ; and their advantage consists as much, perhaps, in this as in any other circumstance.

It appears, therefore, that the construction of machines having a tendency to lower the price and to increase the supply of commodities, cannot diminish the demand for labour, or reduce the rate of wages. Their introduction into one employment, though it had no influence on the increase of capital, would occasion an equal or greater demand for the disengaged labourers in other employments. But, as has just been seen, the capital, and consequently the demand for labour, of most of those who buy goods whose price is reduced, are materially increased. Ultimately, therefore, the introduction of machines cannot fail of being highly advantageous to the labourer ; and even when first resorted to, they never impose on him any other hardship than that of occasionally forcing him to change his business. This, however, is seldom a very material one. A person trained to habits of industry and application, can be easily moved from one employment to another. All the great departments of industry have so many things in common, that an individual who has attained to any considerable proficiency in one, has seldom much difficulty in attaining to a like proficiency in some branch of another. It is easy for a weaver of cottons to become a weaver of woollens, or linen; and a very limited degree of instruction would suffice to teach the maker of a cart or plough to construct a thrashing-machine.*

Mr. Malthus, however, is not satisfied with this reasoning. "In withdrawing capital," he says, "from one employment, and placing it in another, there is almost always a considerable loss. Even if the whole of the remainder were directly employed, it would be less in amount. Though it might yield a greater produce, it would not command the same quantity of labour as before; and, unless more menial servants were used, many persons would be thrown out of employment; and thus the power of the whole capital to command the same quantity of labour would evidently depend upon the contingency of the vacant capitals being withdrawn, *undiminished, from their old occupations,* and finding immediately equivalent employment in others."† This statement implies, that, though the effective demand of the society would not be diminished by an increased facility of production—for it is distinctly admitted that no such diminution would take place—yet, unless the *whole fixed capital,* which had been rendered useless by the improvement, could be withdrawn, and vested in some other branch, there would be no means of supplying this demand, or of employing the same quantity of labour as before. But this view of the matter proceeds on a mistake, into which it is not a little surprising that an experienced economist should have fallen. A manufacturer's power

* See Note B, at the end of the Volume.

† "Principles of Political Economy," p. 404.

to employ labour does not depend on the entire amount of his capital, but on the amount of that portion only which is *circulating*. A capitalist possessed of a hundred steam-engines and of 50,000*l.* of circulating capital, has no greater demand for labour, and does not, in fact, employ a single workman more, than the capitalist who has no machinery, and only 50,000*l.* devoted exclusively to the payment of wages. All this portion could, however, be withdrawn; and as it determines the power to employ labour, it is not true, that, when capitals are transferred from one business to another, " many persons are thrown out of employment."

It is certainly true, that an individual who is obliged to transfer his capital from one business to another, loses all the profit he formerly derived from that portion which cannot be transferred. But the introduction of improved machinery is not to be prevented because the old clumsy machinery previously used may be superseded, and destroyed. A few individuals may lose; but the whole society is always sure to derive a great accession of wealth from the adoption of every device by which labour may be saved. It has been already shewn, that neither the power nor the will to purchase commodities is diminished by the introduction of machines facilitating production; and as the power to employ workmen depends on the amount of circulating capital which may, in all cases, be withdrawn without loss, it is plain it could not be diminished. The wages of labour would, therefore, continue as high as before, while the reduction in the price of commodities would cause these wages to exchange for a greater share of the necessaries and comforts of life, at the same time that it would occasion a more rapid accumulation of capital. Hence it appears, how much soever it may be at variance with the popular opinion, that improvements in machinery are always more advantageous to the labourer than the capitalist. In particular cases they may reduce the profits of the latter, and destroy a portion of his capital; but they cannot, in any case, diminish the wages of the labourer, while they must lower the value of commodities, and improve his condition.

It may be conceded that, were the foreign demand for cottons and hardware suddenly to cease, it might be difficult, perhaps impossible, to find equally advantageous employments for the capital and labour that would consequently be disengaged.* But although this is a good reason why we should be extremely cautious about the adoption of measures tending to stimulate our foreign customers to manufacture for themselves, or to exclude us from their markets, it is not easy to see why it should have led Mr. Malthus to question the advantage of improvements in machinery. It still appears to me, that an increased facility of production must be as advantageous in a country surrounded by Bishop Berkeley's wall of brass, as in one that maintains an extensive intercourse with others. Supposing, which is possible, that foreigners were to refuse to exchange the articles we wish to import for our cottons, hardware, &c., it is plain that, in such a case, we must either offer them other things, which they may be disposed to accept, or, if that be impossible, we must ourselves directly set about the production of the commodities we wish to obtain, or of substitutes for them. Now, in the event of our being compelled to have recourse to this latter alternative, and, instead of importing the wines of Portugal, the sugars of the West Indies, and the corn of Poland, being obliged to produce them or equivalent articles at home, is it possible to doubt that it would be of the greatest advantage were we to discover processes by which we might be able to obtain them, or their substitutes, as cheap or cheaper than before? It has indeed been said, that there are no grounds for supposing that such an

* Malthus's "Principles of Political Economy," p. 411.

improvement could take place; and I am not disposed to dissent from this opinion. But the question is not, whether the improvement can be made; but whether, if made, it would not be greatly and signally beneficial?—and whether every approach to it be not advantageous?

It will be observed, that, in arguing this question, it has been supposed throughout that the object which the person who constructs a machine has in view is, to lower the cost and increase the quantity of the commodities to be produced by its agency. But Mr. Ricardo has supposed* that a machine might be introduced, not in the view of reducing the cost of commodities, but that it might yield the same, or, at all events, only a very little more nett profit, than was derived from laying out the capital vested in it on labour; and in such a case, there can be no doubt that its introduction would be injurious to the labourer. To render this more intelligible, let us suppose that profits are 10 per cent, and that a capitalist has 10,000*l.* employed in paying the wages of workmen, who produce him as much cloth as sells at the end of a year for 11,000*l.*, that is 10,000*l.* to replace his capital, and 1,000*l.* as profits. Mr. Ricardo says, that this individual may, with equal advantage to himself, vest his capital in a very durable machine, that will produce only the *one-eleventh* part of the cloth, or as much as will yield the 1,000*l.* of profits; though, if he do this, it is obvious, that all the workmen he employed will be turned adrift, and there will no longer be either a demand for their services, or a fund for their maintenance. But though a case of this sort may be supposed, it may, at the same time, be safely affirmed, that it has never actually occurred, and that it is extremely unlikely it ever will occur. Capitalists resort to machines only when they expect

* "Principles of Political Economy and Taxation," 3d ed. p. 466.

to produce, by their means, the usual supply of commodities with less outlay. If they were to act in the way supposed by Mr. Ricardo, those who had been bringing 110,000 yards of cloth to market, of which 10,000 were profits, would, in future, bring only these 10,000: so that, under such circumstances, every fresh introduction of machinery would inevitably be followed by *a diminished supply of commodities, and a rise of prices!* But hitherto the opposite effects have, as every one knows, uniformly followed, and, it may be confidently predicted, will uniformly continue to follow, the extension of machinery. No man would choose to vest his capital in an engine from which it could not be withdrawn, were it only to yield the same, or but a little more profit, than it did when employed in supporting labourers; for this would inevitably expose his fortune to very considerable hazard from the caprices of fashion, at the same time that it would greatly lessen his influence and consideration in the country. The case under review is barely possible. In the actual business of the world, machines are never introduced to lessen, but always to augment *gross produce;* for they are introduced only when it is believed that they can be made to supply the existing demand at a cheaper rate than it was previously supplied; and it has been sufficiently proved, that while they do this, they cannot occasion the least injury to the labourer, but must, on the contrary, be highly beneficial to him.

It appears, therefore, that the utmost facility of production can never be injurious, but must always be attended with the greatest advantage. " Augmenter la reproduction annuelle, la porter aussi loin qu'elle peut aller, en débarrassant de toutes entraves, et en animant l'activité des hommes, voilà le *grand but* que doit se proposer le gouvernement."* An excess of one particular commo-

* Dignan, " Essai sur l'Economie Politique," p. 134.

dity, or of a few commodities, may be occasionally produced; but it is quite impossible that there can be an excess of every commodity. The fault is not in producing too much, but in producing commodities which either do not suit the tastes of those who we wish should buy them, or which we cannot ourselves consume. If we attend to these two grand requisites,—if we produce such commodities only as can be taken off by those to whom we offer them, or such as are directly available to our own use, we may increase the power of production a thousand or a million of times, and we shall be as free of all excess as if we diminished it in the same proportion. A glut never originates in an increase of production; but is in every case a consequence of the misapplication of productive power, or of the producers not having properly adapted their means to their ends. They wished for example, to obtain silks, and they offered cottons in exchange: the producers of silks were, however, already sufficiently supplied with cottons, but were in want of broad-cloths. Hence the cause of the glut. It consists not in over production, but in the production of cottons which were not wanted, instead of broad-cloths which were. Let this error be rectified, and the glut will disappear. Even though the producers of silks were not only supplied with cottons, but also with cloth, and every other commodity which it is in the power of the demanders to offer, the principle for which I am contending would not be invalidated. For, if those who want silks cannot obtain them in exchange for broad-cloths, or such other commodities as they are either possessed of or can produce, they have a resource — they may abandon the production of the commodities which they do not want, and apply themselves *directly to the production of those* which they do want, or of equivalent articles. In no case, therefore, can an increased facility of production be attended with inconvenience. We might with equal truth pretend, that an increased fertility of soil, and an increased salubrity of climate, were injurious. Such commodities as are carried to market, are produced only that they may be exchanged for others; and the fact of their being in excess, affords a conclusive proof that there is a corresponding deficiency in the supply of those they were intended to buy, or to be exchanged for. A universal glut of all sorts of commodities is impossible: every excess in one class must be compensated by an equal deficiency in some other class. "To suppose that there may be a production of commodities without a demand, provided these commodities be of the right species, is as absurd as to suppose that the revenues of the several individuals composing the society may be too great for their consumption."*

Before dismissing this subject, I may observe, that gluts are not unfrequently ascribed to a deficiency of money. But though the quantity of money in circulation determines the *price* of commodities, or their value estimated in money, it does not exercise the smallest influence over the quantity of other commodities for which any one in particular will exchange. It is, however, the acquisition of those others, and not of money, that is the *end* which every man has in view who carries any thing to market. The money that individuals receive for what they have to sell, is immediately laid out, either directly by themselves, or indirectly by those to whom they lend it, upon what they have to buy: and if it should so happen that the produce which one has to dispose

* "Sketch of the Advance and Decline of Nations," p. 82. M. Say was the first who shewed, in a full and satisfactory manner, that effective demand depends upon production (see his chapter *de Débouchés*); and that gluts are the result of the misapplication, and not of the increase, of productive power. But the same principle had been noticed by many previous writers: by Dean Tucker, in his "Queries on the Naturalisation Bill," p. 13, published in 1752; by Mengotti, in his "Dissertazione sul Colbertismo," p. 31, published in 1792; and still more distinctly in the tract just quoted, published in 1795.

of is redundant, while that which he wishes to procure is deficient, he will experience loss and inconvenience. But these, it is obvious, are circumstances that are wholly independent of the value of money. It is, no doubt, true, that changes in its value exert, in consequence of their affecting all previously existing contracts, a powerful temporary influence over every class of persons;* but whether money bear a permanently high or low value, is, as far as the occurrence of gluts is concerned, of no sort of importance.

It may further be observed, that though no complaint be more common, there is hardly one so uniformly ill-founded, as that of a scarcity of money. Like all other valuable products in universal demand, money will always be scarce to those who cannot afford to buy it, and who are destitute of credit. But if any one possessed of really valuable produce be at any time unable to get it disposed of, he will, in the vast majority of instances, find the cause in something else than a scarcity of money — in its having been produced in too great quantities, or in an actual, or an apprehended falling off in the demand, &c.; none of which circumstances would be in any degree affected by an increase of the currency. However rich individuals may be, they will purchase no more of any article than is required to supply their wants; and if more be produced, the surplus will either lie on the hands of the producers, or have to be sold at a reduced price. It is plainly, therefore, to no purpose to ascribe gluts and revulsions of the market to a deficiency of money. A whist-player might as well ascribe his losses to a deficiency of counters. The miscalculation of the producers is their real cause: if they produce such articles as others are able and willing to buy, or such as they can themselves make use of, there will be no glut;

* For an estimate of the effect of these changes, see the Chapter on Profits.

and if they do not, there will be a glut, though a Potosi should be discovered in every county.

Having thus ascertained that the miscalculation of producers, or the misapplication of productive power, is in every case the specific cause of gluts, we have next to inquire into the circumstances which most commonly occasion this miscalculation or misapplication. In a practical point of view this is an inquiry of much importance.

Miscalculations seem generally to originate in some previous change in the usual proportion between the supply and demand of commodities. Every exertion of industry involves a certain degree of speculation. The individual who buys raw cotton or raw silk, in the intention of manufacturing it into articles of dress or furniture, assumes that the article, when manufactured, will sell for such a price as will indemnify him for his expenses, and leave him the customary rate of profit on his capital. It is clear, however, that there is a good deal of risk in an adventure of this sort: if the fashion were to change while the articles were in preparation, it might be impossible to get them disposed of, except at a considerable loss; or if new facilities were in the interim to be given to the commerce with countries whence similar articles could be procured, or any discovery were to be made which might tend to facilitate their production, their price would certainly fall, and the speculation would turn out an unprofitable one. But how singular soever the statement may at first appear, it will be found that miscalculations and gluts are more frequently produced by an increase than by a decline in the demand for produce. Suppose that, owing either to the opening of new markets, to a change of fashion, or to any other cause, the demand for hardware were suddenly increased: the consequences of such increased demand would be, that its price would immediately rise, and that the manufacturers would obtain comparatively high profits. But the rate of profits cannot, unless monopolies interfere to prevent or counteract the operation of the principle of competition, continue for any considerable period either higher or lower in one employment than in others. As soon, therefore, as this rise in the price of hardware had taken place, additional capital would begin to be employed in its production. Those already engaged in the trade would endeavour to extend their business by borrowing fresh capital; while a number of those engaged in other businesses would withdraw from them, and enter into it. Unluckily, however, it is next to certain that this transference of capital would not stop at the point when it would suffice to produce the additional supply of hardware at the old prices, but that it would be carried so much farther as to produce a glut, and a consequent revulsion. A variety of causes conspire to produce this effect: the advantages which any class of producers derive from an increased demand for their peculiar produce, are uniformly exaggerated, as well by that portion of themselves who are anxious, in order to improve their credit, to magnify their gains, as by those engaged in other employments. The adventurous and sanguine — those who are particularly disposed to take *omne ignotum pro magnifico* — crowd into a business which they readily believe presents the shortest and safest road to wealth and consideration; at the same time that many of that generally numerous class who have their capitals lent to others, and who are waiting until a favourable opportunity occurs for vesting them in some industrious undertaking, are tempted to follow the same course. It occurs to few, that the same causes which impel one to enter into a department that is yielding comparatively high profits, are most probably impelling thousands. Confident in his own good fortune, the adventurer leaves a business to which he had been bred, and with which he was well acquainted, to enter as a competitor on a new and untried arena; while those who are already engaged in the advantageous business stretch their credit to the utmost, in order to acquire the means of extending their concerns, and of increasing the supply of the commodity in unusual demand. The result, that every unprejudiced observer would anticipate, almost invariably takes place. A disproportionate quantity of capital being attracted to the lucrative business, a glut of the market, and a ruinous depression of prices, unavoidably follow.

Those who investigate the history of industry, either in this or any other country, will find, that a period of *peculiar* prosperity in any one branch is the almost uniform harbinger of mischief. If we turn, for example, to the history of agriculture, the alternation between periods of high prices and great agricultural prosperity, and of low prices and great agricultural distress, is so striking, that it cannot fail to arrest the attention of every one. The high prices of 1800 and 1801 gave an extraordinary stimulus to agricultural industry. Nearly *double* the number of acts of parliament were passed in 1802 for the enclosure and drainage of land that had been passed in any previous year. A great extent of old grass fields was at the same time subjected to the plough. And in consequence of this extension of cultivation, and of the improvements that were then entered upon and completed, the supply of corn was so much increased in 1804, that prices sunk considerably below the previous level; and an act was then passed, in consequence of the representations made by the agriculturists of their distressed condition, granting them additional protection against foreign competition. The high prices of 1810, 1811, 1812, and 1813, had a precisely similar result. They attracted so much additional capital to the land, and occasioned such an extension of tillage, that we grew in 1812 and 1813 an adequate supply of corn for our own consumption. And, under such circumstances, it is certain that the price of corn must inevitably have fallen, in consequence of the unusually abundant harvest of 1814, though the ports had been entirely shut against importation from abroad.

The history of the West India trade may also be referred to as affording the most convincing proofs of the truth of this principle. The devastation of St. Domingo by the Negro insurrection, which broke out in 1792, by first diminishing, and in a very few years entirely annihilating, the supply of about 115,000 hhds. of sugar, which France and the Continent had previously drawn from that island, occasioned an extraordinary rise of prices, and gave a proportional encouragement to its cultivation in other parts. So powerful was its influence in this respect, that Jamaica, which, at an average of the six years preceding 1799, had exported only 83,000 hhds., exported in 1801 and 1802 upwards of 286,000, or 143,000 a year! But the duration of this prosperity was as brief as it was signal. The same rise of price which had produced such effects in the British islands, occasioned a similar, though less rapid, extension of cultivation in the colonies of the continental powers. The increased supplies of sugar and coffee that were in consequence obtained from Cuba, Porto-Rico, Martinique, Guadaloupe, Brazil, &c. became, in no very long time, not only sufficient to fill up the vacuum caused by the cessation of the supplies from St. Domingo, but actually to overload the continental market. The great foreign demand for British plantation sugar, which had been experienced after the destruction of the St. Domingo trade, gradually diminished until 1805 or 1806, when it almost entirely ceased; and the whole extra quantity raised in consequence of that demand, being thrown upon the home market, its price, which had been 66*s.* a cwt. in 1798, exclusive of duty, fell in 1806 to 34*s.*; a price which the Committee that was then appointed by the House of Commons to inquire into the distresses of the planters, states, was not only insufficient to yield them any profit, but even to indemnify them for their actual outlay. And I may add, that, owing to the ill-advised measures which were soon after adopted for creating a forced and unnatural demand for sugar, by substituting it in the place of barley in the distillery, its supply was prevented from being diminished in proportion to the diminution of the effective demand; so that, some short intervals only excepted, the planters have ever since been involved in difficulties.*

The history of the silk-trade, of distillation, and, indeed, of every branch of industry, furnishes but too many proofs of the constant operation of this principle of compensation. The greater and more signal the peculiar prosperity of any one department, the greater invariably is the subsequent recoil. Such an increased demand for any commodity as would raise its price 10 per cent above the common level, would certainly cause it to be produced in excess, and would in consequence occasion a revulsion. But were the price to rise 30 or 40 per cent above the common level, the temptation to employ additional capital in its production would be so very great, that the revulsion would both take place sooner, and be incomparably more severe.

Revulsions of the sort now described will necessarily continue to occur, to a greater or less extent, under all systems of public economy. But there is nothing that would tend so much to lessen their frequency and violence as a determination on the part of government to withhold all relief, except in cases of extreme necessity, from those who have the misfortune to be involved in them. It must be acknowledged that this seems, at first sight, rather a harsh doctrine; but, on examination, it will be found to be the only safe and really practicable line of conduct that government can follow. Almost all the restrictions and prohibitions which fetter our commerce

* Spence on the "Distresses of the West India Planters," pp. 7–26.

and enterprise have been occasioned by government stepping out of its proper province, and interfering for the relief of those who had got themselves entangled in difficulties. By this means, a very large proportion of the industry of the country was at one time placed on an insecure foundation; and, notwithstanding the reforms that have been effected, a great deal is still in that situation. Merchants and manufacturers have been, in this way, partially relieved from that natural responsibility under which every man ought to act, and tempted to trust to the support usually afforded by government in the event of their speculations giving way. Were it possible, indeed, to grant such assistance without injury to the rest of the community, none would object to it; but as this cannot be done, I confess it appears to me, not only that sound policy, but also that real humanity, would dictate the propriety of its being withheld in all but extreme cases.

The next best thing that could be done to prevent improvident speculations, would be the establishment of a perfectly free commercial system. Under such a system, we should engage only in those branches of industry for the prosecution of which we have some natural or acquired advantage, and which would, in consequence, be in a great measure secure against those unfavourable contingencies that are always affecting businesses fenced round with restrictions. Suppose, to illustrate this principle, that a really free trade were established in silks: we should, under such circumstances, export supplies of all those mixed fabrics of wool and silk, and of gloves and hosiery, in the production of which we have an advantage; at the same time that a considerable part of our demand for other descriptions of silk goods would most probably be supplied by the foreigner. If, on the one hand, therefore, the demand for silks should, in consequence of a change of fashion, or any other cause, suddenly increase, the competition of the foreign manufacturers would prevent prices attaining any very extravagant height, and would thereby prevent both the inordinate extension of the manufacture and the subsequent recoil: and if, on the other hand, the demand for silks in this country happened to decline, the various foreign markets resorted to by our manufacturers would give them the means of disposing of their surplus goods at a small reduction of price compared to what must take place when they are confined, as has hitherto been the case, to the home market.

This reasoning is consistent with the most comprehensive experience. Restrictions and prohibitions are, in all cases, productive of uncertainty and fluctuation. Every artificial stimulus, whatever may be its momentary effect on the department of industry to which it is applied, is immediately disadvantageous to others, and ultimately ruinous to that which it was intended to promote. No arbitrary regulation, no act of the legislature, can add any thing to the capital of the country; it can only force it into artificial channels. And, after a sufficient supply of capital has flowed into these channels, a *re-action* must commence. There can be no foreign vent for their surplus produce; so that whenever any change of fashion, or fluctuation in the taste of the consumers, occasions a falling off in the demand, the warehouses are sure to be filled with commodities which, in a state of freedom, would not have been produced. The ignorant and the interested always ascribe such gluts to the employment of machinery, or to the want of sufficient protection against foreign competition. The truth is, however, that they are the necessary and inevitable results of an artificial and exclusive system of policy, or of the application of those poisonous nostrums by which the natural and healthy state of the public economy is vitiated and deranged.

CHAPTER VIII.

Population proportioned to the Means of Subsistence — Influence of Moral Restraint — Capacity of the Principle of Population to repair the Ravages of Plagues and Famines—Comparative Increase of Capital and Population—Law of Increase a powerful Incentive to Industry—Contributes to promote the Civilisation and Happiness of Mankind—Practice of Infanticide— Foundling Hospitals.

THE circumstances most favourable for the production of wealth being thus traced and exhibited, I shall now shortly investigate those that appear to determine the increase and diminution of man himself.

From the remotest period down to our own times, it had been the policy of legislators to give an artificial stimulus to population, by encouraging early marriages, and bestowing rewards on those who brought up the greatest number of children.* But the researches of Mr. Malthus, who, though without any claim to the discovery of the tendency of population to outrun the means of subsistence, was certainly the first to establish it on an extensive induction of facts, and to point out some of its more important effects, have shewn the mischievous nature of such interferences. They have shewn, that every increase in the numbers of a people, occasioned

* By a singular contradiction, at the very moment that the Roman laws authorised the exposition of infants, and vested fathers with the power to decide whether they would bring up their children, the censors were instructed to impose a tax (*æs uxorium*) on bachelors; and different laws were passed, bestowing various privileges upon those who reared the greatest number of children. The famous *Lex Papia Poppæa* (so called from the consuls M. Papius Mutilus and Q. Poppæus Secundus, by whom it was introduced), enacted during the reign of Augustus, exempted such Roman citizens as had *three* children from all public charges and contributions.—TERASSON, "*Histoire de la Jurisprudence Romaine*," p. 58.

by artificial expedients, and which is not either preceded or accompanied by a corresponding increase of the means of subsistence, can be productive only of misery, or of increased mortality;—that the difficulty never is to bring human beings into the world, but to feed, clothe, and educate them when there;—that mankind *do* every where increase their numbers, till their multiplication is restrained by the difficulty of providing subsistence, and the poverty of some part of the society;—and that, consequently, instead of attempting to strengthen the principle of increase, we should invariably endeavour to control and regulate it.

If the extraordinary pains most governments have taken to encourage the increase of population were not positively pernicious, it is pretty evident that they were, at least, quite uncalled for and unnecessary. Man does not require any adventitious inducement to tempt him to enter into matrimonial connexions. He is impelled to engage in them by one of the most powerful instincts implanted in his nature. Still, however, this instinct or passion is, in civilised communities, controlled in a greater or less degree by prudential considerations. To occasion a marriage, it is not always enough that the parties should be attached to each other. The obligation of providing for the children that may be expected to spring from it, is one that cannot fail to awaken the forethought, and influence the conduct, of all but the most improvident and thoughtless. If the situation of those that might be disposed to enter into a matrimonial alliance be such as to preclude all reasonable expectation of their being able to bring up and educate their children, without exposing themselves to privations, or to the risk of being cast down to a lower place, they may not, improbably, either relinquish all thoughts of forming a union, or postpone it till a more convenient opportunity. No doubt, there are very many individuals in every country who are not affected by such considerations, and who, seeing the future through the deceitful medium of their passions, are not deterred from gratifying their inclinations by any fear of the consequences. Others, however, are more prudent; and it is abundantly certain, that the greater number of persons in the more elevated stations of life, as well as those who are peculiarly ambitious of rising in the world, and those of all ranks who have learned to look to the consequences of their actions, are invariably influenced, to some extent or other, by the circumstances alluded to. Hence, in civilised countries, the proportion of marriages to the population may fairly be expected, on general grounds, to depend, in a considerable degree, on the facility of acquiring subsistence, or of bringing up a family: and experience shews that such is the case; for it is found, that where food and other accommodations are abundant, marriages are at once early and numerous, and conversely. "*Partout*," says Montesquieu, "*où il se trouve une place où deux personnes peuvent vivre commodément, il se fait un mariage.* La nature y porte assez lorsqu'elle n'est point arrêtée par la difficulté de la subsistance."* The same principle has been laid down by Dr. Smith: "The demand for men," says he, "like that for any other commodity, necessarily regulates the production of men, quickens it when it goes on too slowly, and stops it when it advances too fast. It is this demand which regulates and determines the state of population in all the different countries of the world—in North America, in Europe, and in China; which renders it rapidly progressive in the first, slow and gradual in the second, and altogether stationary in the last."† The most comprehensive observation confirms the truth of this remark. Those who inquire into the past and present state of the world, will find that the population of all countries has been prin-

* "Esprit de Loix," liv. xxiii. cap. 10.

† "Wealth of Nations," vol. i. p. 133.

cipally determined by their means of subsistence. Whenever these means have been increased, population has also been increased, or been better provided for; and when they have been diminished, the population has been worse provided for, or has sustained an actual diminution of numbers, or both effects have followed.

But notwithstanding the influence of prudential considerations, or of the checks to marriage from the fear of not being able to provide for a family, the principle of increase is so very strong as not only to keep the population of the most favoured countries, and where industry is most productive, on a level with the means of subsistence, but to give it a tendency to exceed them. This arises partly and principally from the little attention paid by most individuals to whatever does not begin to be felt till some future and undefined period — a circumstance which leads them to engage in improvident unions, at the same time that it hinders them from making adequate provision, even when they have the means, against sickness and old age; partly from the violence of passion, occasionally subverting the resolutions of those who are otherwise most considerate; and partly from accident or misfortune, disappointing the expectations of those who married with a reasonable prospect of being able to support themselves and their families. The number of the poor may be diminished, but it were vain to expect that they should ever entirely "cease out of the land." Even in those countries that are making the most rapid advances, not a few of the inhabitants have to maintain a constant struggle with poverty, and are but insufficiently supplied with the articles indispensable to provide for the wants of a numerous family. But when the natural tendency to increase is so very powerful, it is not easy to believe that the application of any artificial stimulus to accelerate it can be otherwise than pernicious. Subsistence is the grand desideratum. If it be supplied in sufficient abundance, population may safely be left to take care of itself. Instead of there being the least risk of its falling below the means of subsistence, the danger is all on the other side. There are no limits to the prolific power of plants and animals. They are all endued with a principle which impels them to increase their numbers beyond the nourishment prepared for them. The whole surface of the earth might be gradually covered with shoots derived from a single plant; and though it were destitute of all other inhabitants, it might, in a few ages, be replenished from a single nation, or even from a single pair.

"Throughout the animal and vegetable kingdoms," says Mr. Malthus, "nature has scattered the seeds of life with a most profuse and liberal hand; but has been comparatively sparing in the room and nourishment necessary to rear them. The germs of existence contained in this earth, if they could freely develope themselves, would fill millions of worlds in the course of a few thousand years. Necessity, that imperious, all-pervading law of nature, restrains them within the prescribed bounds. The race of plants and the race of animals shrink under this great restrictive law, and man cannot by any efforts of reason escape from it."*

The effect of plagues and epidemic disorders illustrates the powerful operation of the principle of population in a very striking manner. However afflicting to humanity, there is no reason to suppose that the world would have been more populous than it really is had these scourges been entirely unknown. So long as the means of subsistence are not impaired, the principle of increase speedily fills up the vacuum caused by any unusual mortality. The diminution of the population improves the condition of those who survive. By lessening the number of people without usually lessening the capital that is to feed and maintain them, it gives

* "Essay on Population," vol. i. p. 3. 5th ed.

them an increased power over subsistence. The period of marriage is, in consequence, accelerated, and the number of births proportionally increased, while a greater number of those born attain to maturity. It appears from the tables given by M. Messance, in his valuable work on the population of France, that the ravages occasioned by the plague of Marseilles, in 1720, were very soon repaired; and that, notwithstanding the diminution of population, the marriages became more numerous, and were also more fruitful, immediately after the mortality had subsided. But the effects which followed the pestilence that desolated the Prussian dominions and the middle parts of Europe, in 1710 and 1711, are, in this respect, still more remarkable. Sussmilch, whose accuracy is well known, mentions, that, previously to its occurrence, the average annual number of marriages, in a district of Prussia which had been carefully surveyed, amounted to about 6,000; and though the pestilence is supposed to have swept off a full *third* of the inhabitants, yet, in the year immediately following this excessive mortality, the marriages amounted to double their former number, or to about 12,000!* It would be easy to produce a thousand similar instances of the prodigious activity of the principle of population, and of its capacity to repair the most dreadful ravages. It might, for example, have been supposed, that the massacres of the revolution, and the bloody wars in which France was constantly engaged for more than twenty years, would have made a serious inroad on her population. But, instead of being less, France was more populous at the restoration than at the expulsion of the Bourbons. The abolition of the feudal privileges of the nobility, and of the tithes, *gabelle, corvées,* and other partial and oppressive burdens, improved the condition and stimulated the industry of the people. The means of subsistence were

* "Malthus on Population," vol. ii. p. 170. 5th ed.

greatly increased; and the new impulse that was thus given to the principle of population, was sufficient, not only to repair the waste occasioned by the ravages of the guillotine and the sword, but to add, in the course of twenty-five years, about three millions to the numbers existing in 1789. The effects of the dreadful plague that raged in London in 1666, were not perceptible fifteen or twenty years afterwards. It may even be doubted whether Turkey and Egypt are, at an average, much less populous for the plagues which periodically lay them waste. They, no doubt, contain far fewer people now than formerly; but this is rather to be attributed to the tyranny and brutal oppression of their government, which destroys their industry, than to the losses they sustain by the plague. The traces of the most destructive famines in China, Hindostan, Egypt, and other countries, are very soon obliterated; and the most tremendous convulsions of nature, such as volcanic eruptions and earthquakes, if they do not happen so frequently as to frighten away the inhabitants or to destroy their industry, have been found to produce almost no effect on the average population.*

The extreme importance of controlling the principle of population by the influence of moral restraint, may be shewn by comparing the natural ratio of its increase with that of the increase of capital. It has been already seen, that that portion of the accumulated produce or capital of a country which consists of food and clothes, or of the articles directly available to the support of man, forms the only fund from which the inhabitants derive any part of their subsistence: and hence it is plain, that if capital have a tendency to increase faster than population, the condition of society must, generally speaking, become more and more prosperous. While, on the other hand, it is equally plain, that if population have a tendency

* Malthus, vol. ii. p. 198.

to increase faster than capital, and if this tendency be not counteracted by increased industry and economy, or checked by the prudence and forethought of the people, their condition must become gradually more and more wretched, until the portion of subsistence falling to the share of the majority be reduced to the lowest pittance that can support mere animal existence.

It is not possible to obtain any very accurate accounts of the amount of the capital of a country at different periods; but its capacity to feed and support human beings, and the rate of its increase, may, notwithstanding, be learned with sufficient accuracy for our purpose, by referring to the progress of population. It is clear, from statements previously made, that so long as the inhabitants of a country continue to have the same, or about the same, command of the necessaries and conveniences of life, their numbers must vary with the corresponding variations in the capital of the country. Whenever, therefore, we find the people increasing without any, or with but very little, variation taking place in their condition, it is a proof that capital has increased in the same, or very nearly the same proportion. Now, it has been ascertained, that the population of several of the states of North America has, after making proper deductions on account of immigrants, continued to double for a century past in so short a period as twenty, or at most twenty-five years; and as the quantity of necessaries and conveniences falling to the share of an inhabitant of the United States has not been materially increased or diminished during the last century, this increase of population is a proof that the capital of the country has advanced in a corresponding ratio. But in all old, settled countries, the increase of capital, and consequently of population, is much slower. The population of Scotland, for example, is supposed to have amounted to 1,050,000 in 1700; and as it amounted to 2,135,000 in 1820, it would follow, on the principle already stated, supposing the condition of the people to have been stationary, that the capital of that country had required about 120 years to double. Instead, however, of continuing nearly uniform, it is perhaps impossible to name any other people whose condition has been, in all respects, so much improved during the last century as that of the Scotch; which shews, beyond a doubt, that the capital of Scotland had far more than doubled during the period referred to. In like manner, the population of England and Wales amounted to 6,064,000 in 1740, and to 12,256,000 in 1821; and as the circumstances of the English people, though not nearly so much improved as those of the Scotch, have, notwithstanding, been decidedly amended, it follows that the capital applicable to the support of man in this division of the empire, or the supply of food, clothes, and other articles required for the support of human life, has doubled in less than *eighty* years, perhaps in not more than *sixty*. Now, as the last sixty years have been distinguished by many very great improvements in agriculture, and still more in manufactures, it may, one should think, be fairly presumed, that sixty years is about the *shortest* period in which the capital of an old settled and densely peopled country can be expected to double; and yet this is more than twice the period required for the doubling of capital in the United States.

The cause of this discrepancy in the rates at which capital and population advance in different countries, is to be found in the circumstance of industry being more productive in some than in others. It is obvious, that the increase of that portion of capital which consists of the food and other raw products required for the subsistence and accommodation of man, must be very materially influenced by the fertility of the soils under tillage. Suppose that the agriculture of two countries is equally advanced: if the fertility of the soils under cultivation were twice as great in the one as in the other, it is evident that the power of increasing supplies of food and other raw materials would be twice as great in the country where the soil was of the highest, as in that where it was of the lowest fertility. This principle enables us to account for the extraordinarily rapid increase of capital and population in the United States, and generally in all colonies planted in fertile and thinly-peopled countries. America possesses a boundless extent of fertile and unoccupied land; and her agriculturists, who are acquainted with all the arts and sciences of Europe, apply themselves to the cultivation of the finest soils only. Hence their industry is extremely well rewarded. Each farmer has a great deal more produce than is required for his own consumption, or that of his family; and as he accumulates the surplus as capital, it increases, and, consequently, population also, with proportional rapidity.

But the situation of Great Britain, and of all old, settled, and comparatively populous countries, is entirely different. Our most fertile lands have long since been brought under tillage; and we are now obliged to raise whatever additional supplies of food we require, either by forcing the more fertile lands, or by resorting to such as are of very inferior productive power. The consequence is, that agricultural industry is here comparatively ill rewarded. A given quantity of labour applied to the worst lands under tillage in England, does not probably yield above half the quantity of food, and other raw products, that it would yield were it applied to lands of the same degree of fertility as the worst that are under tillage in the western states of America; and hence it follows, that the undertaker of any work in England who should give the same quantity of produce to his men, as wages, that is given to labourers in these states, would have a far less quantity remaining for himself, and would have a proportionally small power of accumulating capital. It is true that, in the event of wages being reduced when tillage is extended over inferior soils, the share of the produce falling to the employers of workmen is not diminished to the same extent that production is diminished; but as the labourers must always obtain a supply of necessaries and conveniences sufficient to enable them to exist and continue their race, no very considerable reduction can, in most cases, be made from wages; and, in point of fact, it is invariably found, that wherever tillage is widely extended over inferior soils, both the quantity of produce, and the share of that produce falling to the capitalists, are very much diminished; and there is, in consequence, a comparatively slow increase of capital and population.

The powerful influence exercised by the quality of the soils under cultivation on the productiveness of industry, and consequently on the accumulation of capital, may be learned as well by tracing the progress of cultivation in the same country, as by comparing its state in different countries. It is stated, for example, by Messrs. Iveson, Harvey, Wakefield, and other intelligent witnesses examined by the Committee of the House of Commons, appointed, in 1822, to inquire into the state of agriculture, that the best lands under tillage in England yield from thirty-six to forty bushels of wheat per acre, while the worst only yield from eight to ten bushels. Hence, it is apparent, supposing the skill to have been equal, that a given quantity of labour would have yielded four times the quantity of produce when the best lands only were cultivated, that it will yield when applied to the culture of the worst lands at present under tillage; and had other things been about equal at the two periods, there would have been, in the first, *four times the power to accumulate capital,* and consequently to provide for the wants of a population increasing four times as fast as in the latter.

It is true, that the differences that have actually obtained in England between the rates at which capital and population have increased at different periods, have not been proportioned to the differences in the quality of the soils then under cultivation; and this because agriculture has not been stationary, but has been, all the while, making constant advances. It is obvious, however, had agricultural science remained in the same state, that our power to increase the supply of food required for a growing population would have varied with every variation in the qualities of the soils successively brought under cultivation.

But in countries situated like England and the United States, whose inhabitants speak the same language, and have an intimate intercourse with each other, all the arts and sciences extensively cultivated in them both, naturally approach nearly to an equality. No considerable discovery could be made in agricultural science in England without its being soon after communicated to America, nor in America without its communication to England: and therefore, if the lands last taken into cultivation in America be possessed of twice the productive power of those last taken into cultivation in England, there can be little doubt but that agricultural industry in the former will be about twice as productive as in the latter; and the power possessed by each country of increasing that portion of its capital which consists of food and other farm produce will be in the same proportion.

It appears, therefore, that the power or capacity of countries to add to their supplies of food, is very different at different stages of their progress. In the earlier periods, when population is comparatively limited, it being only necessary to cultivate the best lands, industry is comparatively productive, and there is a rapid increase both of capital and population: but the best lands, in every advancing country of moderate extent, are speedily exhausted; and, whenever this is the case, recourse must unavoidably be had to those of inferior fertility, to obtain the means of providing for an increasing population: and with every inferior quality of land brought under cultivation, a proportional diminution will be made in the productiveness of industry, and in the rate at which capital and population advance. Were cultivation so far extended in Kentucky and Louisiana as to render the lands last subjected to tillage in them of no greater fertility than those last cultivated in Great Britain, the progress of capital and population would be reduced to precisely the same level there and here.

But while the power of all countries to feed additional inhabitants is thus progressively diminished, according to the diminished fertility of the soils successively subjected to cultivation, the power of adding to their numbers undergoes no sensible change. That principle, or instinct, which impels man to propagate his species, has appeared in all ages and countries so nearly the same, that it may, in the language of mathematicians, be considered a *constant quantity*. The same power that has doubled the population of America in twenty, or five-and-twenty years, is every where in operation. But though the principle of increase be quite as strong in Yorkshire or Normandy as in Kentucky or Illinois, it is plainly impossible that the population of England or France can be doubled in so short a period. Owing to the greater sterility of the soils we are now cultivating, the quantity of produce to be divided between the undertakers of work in Great Britain and their labourers, is much less than in America; and both parties have, in consequence, less power to provide for the wants of a family. These circumstances have had a corresponding influence on the habits of our people, and have made them apply those checks to the progress of population, arising out of prudential considerations, to which allusion has been already made. They have felt that it would be equally ruinous to themselves and their offspring to enter into matrimonial connexions without having some reasonable prospect of being able to provide for the children which might be expected to spring from them. In consequence, marriages are here very generally deferred to a later period than in America, and a much larger proportion of the population find it expedient to pass their lives in a state of celibacy. And it is fortunate that these natural checks to an excessive increase, or, in other words, that the good sense of the people, and their laudable desire to preserve their place in society, have made them control the violence of their passions, and disregard the *dicta* of so many spurious advisers. Man cannot increase beyond the means of subsistence provided for his support: and hence, if the natural tendency of population to increase, in countries advanced in the career of civilisation, and where there is, in consequence, an increased difficulty of providing additional supplies of food, be not checked by the prevalence of moral restraint, or by prudence and forethought, it must be checked by the prevalence of vice, misery, and famine. There is no alternative. The population of every country has the power, supposing food to be adequately supplied, to go on doubling every five-and-twenty years. But as the limited extent and limited fertility of the soil render it impossible to go on producing food in this ratio, it is obvious, that unless the passions were moderated, and a check given to the increase of population, the standard of human subsistence would not only be reduced to the lowest assignable limit, but famine and pestilence would be perpetually at work to relieve the population of wretches born only to be starved.

The only criterion, then, of a real and beneficial increase in the population of a country, is an increase in the means of its subsistence. If these means be not increased, an increase in the number of births can be productive only of increased misery and mortality. "Other circumstances being the same," says Mr. Malthus, "it may be affirmed, that countries are *populous* according to the quantity of food they can produce or acquire; and *happy*, according to the liberality with which this food is divided, or the quantity which a day's labour will purchase. Corn countries are more populous than pasture countries, and rice countries more populous than corn countries. But, their happiness does not depend either upon their being more or less densely peopled, upon their poverty or their riches, their youth or their age, *but on the proportion which the population and the food bear to each other.*"*

It has been often said that, if the doctrines now laid down with respect to population were really well founded, they would go far to subvert all the best-established opinions with respect to the goodness of the Deity, and would effectually paralyse all attempts at improvement by shewing it to be in a great degree hopeless. There is not, however, any real ground for these statements. Not only are industry and forethought natural to man, but his advancement in the scale of being has been made to depend on their cultivation and improvement. We should infallibly die of hunger and cold, did we not exert ourselves to provide food and clothes. But could any thing be more ludicrously absurd than to object to those who simply state a fact of this sort, that they are impeaching the order of Providence? The powers and capacities implanted in man seem capable of an almost indefinite improvement; but instinct did not direct him in their use. The more remote the epoch to which we carry our researches, the more barbarous and uncomfortable do we find his condition. Pressed, on the one side, by the strong hand of necessity, and stimulated, on the other, by a desire to rise in the world, our powers have been gradually developed according as observation or accident taught us the best method of effecting our ends. *Want* and *ambition* are the powerful springs that gave the first impulse to industry and invention, and which continually prompt to new undertakings. It is idle to suppose that men will be industrious without a motive; and though the desire of bettering

* "Essay on Population," vol. ii. p. 214.

our condition be a very powerful one, it is less so than the pressure of want, or the fear of falling to an inferior station. Were this not the case, invention and industry would be exhibited in the same degree by the heirs of ample fortunes, as by those who have been educated in humbler circumstances and compelled to exert themselves. But every one knows that the fact is not so. The peerage cannot boast of having given birth to an Arkwright, a Watt, or a Wedgwood. Extraordinary exertions, whether of mind or body, are very rarely made by those who are enabled, without their assistance, to live comfortably. The principle of increase has, however, prevented this from ever becoming the condition of the great mass of mankind, and unceasingly applies the most powerful stimulus — the *duris urgens in rebus egestas*—to industry and invention. Much, indeed, of the effect usually ascribed to the desire of rising in the world, may be traced to the operation of this principle. It is not solely on the lower classes, nor by the actual pressure of necessity, that it exerts its beneficial influence. At that period of life when habits are formed, and man is best fitted for active pursuits, a prospect is presented to every one, whatever may be his rank or station, who is either married, or intends to marry, of an indefinite increase of his necessary expenses; and unless his fortune be very large indeed, he finds that economy and industry are virtues which he must not admire merely, but practise. With the lower classes the existence of present, and with the middle and upper classes the fear of future want, are the principal motives that stimulate intelligence and activity. The desire to maintain a family in respectability and comfort, or to advance their interests, makes the spring and summer of life be spent, even by the moderately wealthy, in laborious enterprises. And thus it is that either for ourselves, or for those with whose welfare our own is inseparably connected, the principle of increase is perpetually urging individuals to new efforts of skill and economy. Had this principle either not existed at all, or been comparatively feeble, activity would have been superseded by indolence, and men, from being enterprising and ambitious, would have sunk into a state of torpor; for in that case, every additional acquisition, whether of skill or wealth, would, by lessening the necessity for fresh acquisitions, have infallibly occasioned a decline in the spirit of improvement; so that, instead of proceeding, as it became older, with accelerated steps in the career of discovery, the fair inference is, that society would either have been entirely arrested in its progress, or its advance rendered next to imperceptible. But it has been so ordered that, whatever may at any time occasion a decline of the inventive powers, must be of an accidental and ephemeral character, and cannot originate in a diminution of the advantages resulting from their exercise. Even in the most improved societies, the principle of increase inspires by far the largest class—those who depend on their labour for the means of support — with all those powerful motives to contrive, produce, and accumulate, that actuated the whole community in more early ages. No people can rest satisfied with acquisitions already made. The constant pressure of population against the limits of subsistence renders the demand for fresh inventions and discoveries as great at one time as at another, and secures the forward progress of the species. A deficiency of subsistence at home leads to migrations to distant countries; and thus, not only provides for the gradual occupation of the earth, but carries the languages, arts, and sciences of those who have made the farthest advances in civilisation to those that are comparatively barbarous. It sometimes, no doubt, happens that, notwithstanding this resource, and the most strenuous efforts on the part of the industrious classes, population so far outruns production, that the condition of society is changed for the worse. But the evils thence arising bring with them a provision for their cure. They make all classes better acquainted with the circumstances which determine their situation in life; and while they call forth fresh displays of invention and economy, they at the same time dignify and exalt the character, by teaching us to exercise the prudential virtues, and to subject the passions to the control of reason.

It does, therefore, seem reasonable to conclude that the law of increase, as previously explained, is in every respect consistent with the beneficent arrangements of Providence, and that instead of being subversive of human happiness, it has increased it in no ordinary degree. Happiness is not to be found in apathy and idleness, but in zeal and activity. It depends far more on the intensity of the pursuit than on the attainment of the end. The "progressive state" is justly characterised by Dr. Smith, "as being in reality the *cheerful and hearty state to all the different orders of society;* the stationary is dull, the declining melancholy." But had the principle of increase been less strong, the progress of society would have been less rapid. While, however, its energy is, on the one hand, sufficient to bring every faculty of the mind and body into action, it is, on the other, so far subject to control that, speaking generally, its beneficial far outweighs its pernicious consequences.

That the tendency to increase is not inconsistent with the improvement of society, is a fact as to which there can be no dispute. Without going back to antiquity, let any one compare the state of Europe 500, or even 100 years ago, with its present state, and he will be satisfied that prodigious advances have been made. And to suppose, as some have done, that these advances would have been equal or greater, had the tendency to increase been less powerful, is, in truth, equivalent to supposing, that industry and invention would be promoted by lessening the motives to their exercise, and the advantages derivable from them. There might, perhaps, have been less squalid poverty amongst the very lowest class, had there been no principle of increase; but it is a contradiction to pretend, had such really been the case, that the powers and resources of industry would have been so astonishingly developed, that scientific investigations would have been prosecuted with equal perseverance and zeal, that so much wealth would have been accumulated by the upper and middle classes, or that the same circumstances which impelled society forward in its infancy, would have continued, in every subsequent age, to preserve their energy unimpaired; and it may well be doubted whether an exemption from the evils incident to poverty would not be dearly purchased, even by the lowest classes, by the sacrifice of the hopes and fears attached to their present condition, and the extraordinary gratification they now reap from successful industry.

If these conclusions be well founded, it follows that the schemes proposed for directly repressing population in the ancient and modern world, have not only been, for the most part, atrocious and disgusting, but have really been opposed to the ultimate objects their projectors had in view. Could we subject the rate of increase to any easily applied physical control, few comparatively, among the poorer classes, would be inclined to burden themselves with the task of providing for a family;* and the most effective stimulus to exertion being destroyed, society would gradually sink into apathy and languor. It is, therefore, to the principle of moral restraint, or to the exercise of the prudential virtues, that we should exclusively trust for the regulation of the principle of population. In an instructed society, where there are no institutions favourable to improvidence, this check is sufficiently powerful to confine the progress of population within due limits, at the same time that it is not so powerful as to hinder it from operating, in all cases, as the strongest incentive to industry and economy.

* The readiness with which the lower classes send their children to foundling hospitals seems a sufficient proof of this.

Those who wish to enter more at large upon the discussion of the very interesting topics now briefly touched upon, would do well to consult the second volume of the masterly work of Dr. Sumner, bishop of Chester, on the "Records of the Creation." This learned and excellent prelate has not endeavoured "to shew that the human race is in the best conceivable condition, or that no evils accompany the law which regulates their increase; but that this law makes, upon the whole, an effectual provision for their general welfare, and that the prospective wisdom of the Creator is distinguishable in the establishment of an ordinance which is no less beneficial in its collateral effects, than it is efficacious in accomplishing the first and principal design of its enactment."*

"If, then," says the bishop in another place, "the wisdom is to be estimated by the fitness of the design to its purpose, and the habitual exercise of the energies of mankind is allowed to be that purpose, enough has been said to confirm the original proposition. The Deity has provided, that by the operation of an instinctive principle in our nature, the human race should be uniformly brought into a state in which they are forced to exert and improve their powers: the lowest rank to obtain support; the one next in order to escape from the difficulties immediately beneath it; and all the classes upwards, either to keep their level, while they are pressed on each side by rival industry, or to raise themselves above the standard of their birth by useful exertions of their activity, or by successful cultivation of their natural powers. If, indeed, it were possible that the stimulus arising from this principle should be suddenly removed, it is not easy to determine what life would be except a dreary blank, or the world except an uncultivated waste. Every exertion to which civilisation can be traced proceeds, directly or indirectly, from its effects; either from the actual desire of having a

* "Records of the Creation," vol. ii. p. 160. 4th ed.

family, or the pressing obligation of providing for one, or from the necessity of rivalling the efforts produced by the operation of these motives in others."*

However inexplicable it may now seem, it is a fact no less true than melancholy, that the practice of infanticide has prevailed to a very great extent even in some highly civilized countries. It may, indeed, be said to have been general throughout the ancient world. The laws of Sparta ordered that every child that was either weakly or deformed should be put to death.† And this practice was not merely legalised by the savage enactments of a barbarous code, but was vindicated by the ablest Greek philosophers. Aristotle, in his work on government, does not so much as insinuate a doubt as to the propriety of destroying such children as are maimed or deformed, and carries still farther his "stern decisions," as they are gently termed by Dr. Gillies.‡ Even the "divine" Plato did not scruple to recommend the same monstrous practices. Thebes alone, of all the Grecian cities, seems to have been free from this infamy.§ The existence of infanticide in Athens is established beyond a doubt, by the allusions of the poets, and their descriptions of the prevailing manners.||

Every one is aware that a Roman citizen had the unrestrained power of life and death over his children, whatever might be their age. And there are abundant examples to prove that this right was not suffered to fall into disuse, but was frequently exercised with the most unrelenting severity.¶

* "Records of the Creation," vol. ii. p. 152.

† Cragius "de Republicâ Lacedæmoniorum," lib. iii. cap. 2.

‡ Aristotle's "Ethics and Politics," by Dr. Gillies, vol. ii. p. 287 3d edition.

§ "Travels of Anacharsis," vol. iii. p. 277. Eng. ed.

|| Gouroff, "Essai sur l'Histoire des Enfans Trouvés," p. 19.

¶ "Les Romains ne mirent point des bornes à l'empire des pères sur leurs enfans; quelque âge qu'ils eussent, et à quelque dignité qu'ils

At the birth of a child the father decided whether he would bring it up (*tollere*), or expose it. But it did not always happen that exposed children lost their lives. It was common to expose them in public places, where there was a chance of their attracting the notice of the benevolent, who might be incited to undertake the task of bringing them up. The greater number of these unhappy creatures were not, however, so fortunate as to fall into the hands of persons of this sort. They were declared by law to be the slaves, or absolute property, of those by whom they were reared. And several were saved from death, not from humane motives, but that their foster-fathers might, by mutilating their persons, and exhibiting them in the streets, derive an infamous livelihood from the alms given them by the passengers. This detestable practice seems to have been carried on pretty extensively; and if any thing could, more strikingly than the practice itself, display the sanguinary manners of the Romans, it would be the fact, that there is in Seneca a lengthened discussion upon the question, Whether the mutilation of exposed children can be deemed an offence against the state? which is conducted with the greatest imaginable coolness, and decided in the negative, upon the ground of their being slaves! *Gallio fecit illam questionem, An in expositis lædi possit respublica? Non potest, inquit. An lædi possit in aliquâ suâ parte? Hæc nulla reipublicæ pars est; non in censu illos invenies, non in testamentis.**

The period when the practice of infanticide was prohibited at Rome is not well ascertained; but the more probable opinion seems to be that it continued

fussent élevés, ils étoient toujours soumis à la correction de leurs pères. Ceux-ci avoient droit de les frapper, de les envoyer enchainés cultiver la terre, de les déshériter, de les vendre comme des esclaves, et même de leur donner la mort."—TERASSON, *Histoire de la Jurisprudence Romaine*, p. 54.

* "Senecæ Controvers." lib. v. cap. 33.

till the 374th year of the Christian era. The exposition of children was, however, practised long afterwards. Constantine made some ineffectual efforts to provide for these unfortunates; but their slavery continued till the year 530, when it was abolished by an edict of Justinian.

Infanticide has, most properly, been made a capital crime in all modern states; and to take away the motives to its perpetration, and at the same time to provide an asylum for such poor children as might be exposed through the inhumanity or poverty of their parents, foundling hospitals have been very generally established. But there are the best reasons for thinking that the influence of these establishments has been incomparably more pernicious than beneficial. That they have prevented a few cases of infanticide is, perhaps, true; but the facility of disposing of children which they have afforded has very much weakened the principle of moral restraint, while it has occasioned a prodigious sacrifice of infant life. The mortality in foundling hospitals is quite excessive. They open wide their doors for the reception of deserted and illegitimate children, but there are *pauca vestigia retrorsùm.* In the Foundling Hospital at Dublin, of 12,786 children admitted during the six years ending with 1797, there were no fewer than 12,561 deaths! It oppears, says M. de Chateauneuf, from the official reports, that the mortality amongst foundlings at Madrid, in 1817, was at the rate of 67 per cent; at Vienna, in 1811, it amounted to 92 per cent; at Brussels, at an average of the period from 1802 to 1817, it amounted to 79 per cent; but in consequence of improvements subsequently adopted, it had been reduced in 1824 to 56 per cent. And M. de Chateauneuf adds, that in France, at the present time, about *three-fifths*, or 60 per cent, of the foundlings perish in the course of the *first* year of their life!* In Moscow,

* "Considérations sur les Enfans Trouvés," p. 66.

of 37,607 children admitted in the course of twenty years, only 1,020 were sent out! *

Such is the appalling mortality in these establishments, the total suppression of which would be a signal benefit to society. It does not even appear that they lessen the practice of infanticide, a result which could not, indeed, be reasonably expected by any one who reflects upon their operation on the lower classes of females. Beckmann mentions, that subsequently to the establishment of an hospital for foundlings at Cassel, hardly a year elapsed without some children being found murdered, either in that city or its vicinity.†

The establishment of a foundling hospital in London was recommended, no doubt from the most benevolent motives, by Mr. Addison, in the reign of Queen Anne.‡ It was not, however, established till 1739. Experience was not long in developing its pernicious effects; and in 1760 a total change was effected in its constitution by authority of the legislature. It then ceased to be a receptacle for foundlings. No child whose mother does not personally appear, and who cannot satisfactorily answer the questions put to her, is received: if, however, the mother can shew that she had previously borne a good character, and that, owing to the desertion of the father, she is unable to maintain the child, it is admitted, but not otherwise. As now conducted, there does not seem to be much reason for thinking that this establishment is productive of any but beneficial effects.

In London, during the five years ending with 1823, there were 151 children exposed; and the number of illegitimate children received into the different workhouses in various parts of the city, during the same period, amounted to 4,668, about a fifth part of whom were maintained by their parents. But in Paris, whose population

* Beck's "Medical Jurisprudence," p. 193. Lond. ed.

† Beckmann "on Inventions," vol. iv. p. 456. Eng. ed.

‡ "Guardian," No. 105.

does not amount to two-thirds of that of London, there were, in the five years now referred to, no fewer than 25,277 children carried to the foundling hospitals! And even this profligacy, and consequent waste of human life, is not greater, in proportion to the population, than is found to prevail at Madrid, Vienna, and other large cities where such establishments are permitted to exist.

It is stated by M. Gouroff, that at Mentz, where there was no foundling hospital, 30 children were exposed in the interval between 1799 and 1811. Napoleon, who imagined that by multiplying these establishments he was increasing population, and providing for the future supply of his armies, ordered that one should be opened in Mentz, which was done accordingly in November 1811. It subsisted till the month of March 1815, when it was suppressed by the Grand Duke of Hesse-Darmstadt. During the three years and four months that it had been open, it received 516 children! But as time had not been given for the complete formation of the destructive habits which such institutions are certain to engender, as soon as the hospital had been suppressed, the previous order of things was restored,—only *seven* children being exposed in the nine following years!*

It is plain, therefore, that these establishments utterly fail of accomplishing their object. They do not preserve, but destroy myriads of children. Instead of preventing crime, they scatter its seeds and spread its roots on all sides. There is, however, reason to think that more correct opinions are now beginning to be entertained on the Continent with respect to their real operation. It is difficult, indeed, to suppose that they can be allowed to exist much longer. And, perhaps, no measure could be suggested that would do so much to improve the morals of those among whom they are established, and to lessen the frequency of crime and the destruction of infant life, as their abolition.

* "Essai sur l'Histoire des Enfans Trouvés," p. 153.

CHAPTER IX.

Object of Insurance—Calculation of Chances—Advantages of Insurance—Amount of Property Insured—Life Insurance, Objections to, and Advantages of.

It is the duty of government to assist by every means in its power, the efforts of individuals to protect their property. Losses do not always arise from accidental circumstances, but are frequently occasioned by the crimes and misconduct of individuals; and there are no means so effectual for their prevention, when they arise from this source, as the establishment of a vigilant system of police, and of such an administration of the law as may be calculated to afford those who are injured a ready and cheap method of obtaining every practicable redress; and, as far as possible, of insuring the punishment of culprits. But in despite of all that may be done by government, and of the utmost vigilance on the part of individuals, property must always be exposed to a variety of casualties from fire, shipwreck, and other unforeseen disasters. And hence the importance of inquiring how such unavoidable losses, when they do occur, may be rendered least injurious.

The loss of a ship, or the conflagration of a cotton mill, is a calamity that would press heavily even on the richest individual. But were it distributed among several individuals, each would feel it proportionally less; and provided the number of those among whom it was distributed were very considerable, it would hardly occasion any sensible inconvenience to any one in particular. Hence the advantage of combining to lessen the injury arising from the accidental destruction of property: and it is the diffusion of the risk of loss over a wide surface, and its valuation, that forms the employment of those engaged in insurance.

Though it is impossible to trace the circumstances which occasion those events that are, on that account, termed accidental, they are, notwithstanding, found to obey certain laws. The number of births, marriages, and deaths ; the proportions of male to female, and of legitimate to illegitimate births; the ships cast away ; the houses burned; and a vast variety of other apparently accidental events, are yet, when our experience embraces a sufficiently wide field, found to be nearly equal in equal periods of time; and it is easy, from observations made upon them, to estimate the sum which an individual should pay, either to guarantee his property from risk, or to secure a certain sum for his heirs at his death.

It must, however, be carefully observed, that no confidence can be placed in such estimates, unless they are deduced from a very wide induction. Suppose, for example, that it is found, that during the present year one house is accidentally burned, in a town containing a thousand houses ; this would afford very little ground for presuming that the *average* probability of fire in that town was as one to one thousand. For it might be found that not a single house had been burned during the previous ten years, or that ten were burned during each of these years. But supposing it were ascertained, that at an average of ten years one house had been annually burned, the presumption that one to one thousand was the real ratio of the probability of fire would be very much strengthened; and if it were found to obtain for twenty or thirty years together, it might be held, for all practical purposes at least, as indicating the precise degree of probability.

Besides its being necessary, in order to obtain the true measure of the probability of any event, that the series of events, of which it is one, should be observed for a rather lengthened period ; it is necessary also that the events should be numerous, or of pretty frequent occurrence. Suppose it were found, by observing the births and deaths of a million of individuals taken indiscriminately from among the whole population, that the mean duration of human life was forty years; we should have but very slender grounds for concluding that this ratio would hold in the case of the next ten, twenty, or fifty individuals that are born. Such a number is so small as hardly to admit of the operation of what is called the *law of average*. When a large number of lives is taken, those that exceed the medium term are balanced by those that fall short of it; but when the number is small, there is comparatively little room for the principle of compensation, and the result cannot, therefore, be depended upon.

It is found, by the experience of all countries in which censuses of the population have been taken with considerable accuracy, that the number of male children born is to that of female children in the proportion nearly of twenty-two to twenty-one. But unless the observations be made on a very large scale, this result will not be obtained. If we look at particular families, they sometimes consist wholly of boys, and sometimes wholly of girls; and it is not possible that the boys can be to the girls of a single family in the ratio of twenty-two to twenty-one. But when, instead of confining our observations to particular families, or even parishes, we extend them so as to embrace a population of half a million, these discrepancies disappear, and we find that there is invariably a small excess in the number of males born over the females.

The false inferences that have been drawn from the doctrine of chances, have uniformly almost proceeded from generalising too rapidly, or from deducing a rate of probability from such a number of instances as do not give a fair average. But when the instances on which we found our conclusions are sufficiently numerous, it is seen that the most anomalous events, such as suicides, deaths by accident, the number of letters put into the post-office without any address, &c. form pretty regular series, and consequently admit of being estimated *à priori*.

The business of insurance is founded upon the principles thus briefly stated. Suppose it has been remarked that of *forty* ships, of the ordinary degree of sea-worthiness, employed in a given trade, one is annually cast away, the probability of loss will plainly be equal to *one-fortieth*. And if an individual wish to insure a ship, or the cargo on board a ship engaged in this trade, he ought to pay a *premium* equal to the one-fortieth part of the sum he insures, exclusive of such an additional sum as may be required to indemnify the insurer for his trouble, and to leave him a fair profit. If the premium exceed this sum, the insurer is overpaid; and if it fall below it, he is underpaid.

Insurances are effected sometimes by societies and sometimes by individuals, the risk being in either case diffused amongst a number of persons. Companies formed for carrying on the business have generally a large subscribed capital, or such a number of proprietors as enables them to raise, without difficulty, whatever sums may at any time be required to make good losses. Societies of this sort do not limit their risks to small sums; that is, they do not often refuse to insure a large sum upon a ship, a house, a life, &c. The magnitude of their capitals affords them the means of easily defraying a heavy loss; and their premiums being proportioned to their risks, their profit is, at an average, independent of such contingencies.

Individuals, it is plain, could not act in this way unless they were possessed of very large capitals; and besides the taking of large risks would render the business so hazardous, that few would be disposed to engage in it. Instead, therefore, of insuring a large sum, as 20,000*l.* upon a single ship, a private under-writer or insurer may not probably, in ordinary cases, take a greater risk than 200*l.* or 500*l.*; so that, though his engagements may, when added together, amount to 20,000*l.*, they will be diffused over from forty to a hundred ships; and supposing one or two ships to be lost, the loss would not impair his capital, and would only lessen his profits. Hence it is, that while one transaction only may be required in getting a ship insured by a company, ten or twenty separate transactions may be required in getting the same thing done at Lloyd's, or by private individuals. When conducted in this cautious manner, the business of insurance is as safe a line of speculation as any in which individuals can engage.

To establish a policy of insurance on a fair foundation, or in such a way that the premiums paid by the insured shall exactly balance the risks incurred by the insurers, and the various necessary expenses to which they are put, including, of course, their profit, it is necessary, as previously remarked, that the experience of the risks should be pretty extensive. It is not, however, at all necessary, that either party should inquire into the circumstances that lead to those events that are most commonly made the subject of insurance. Such a research would indeed be entirely fruitless: we are, and must necessarily continue to be, wholly ignorant of the causes of their occurrence.

It appears, from the accounts given by Mr. Scoresby, in his valuable work on the Arctic Regions, that of 586 ships which sailed from the various ports of Great Britain for the northern whale fishery, during the four years ending with 1817, eight were lost,* being at the rate of about one ship out of every *seventy-three* of those employed. Now, supposing this to be about the average loss, it follows that the premium required to insure against it should be 1*l.* 7*s.* 4*d.* per cent, exclusive, as already observed, of the expenses and profits of the insurer. Both the insurer and the insured would gain by enter-

* Vol. ii. p. 131.

ing into a transaction founded on this fair principle. When the operations of the insurer are extensive, and his risks spread over a considerable number of ships, his profit does not depend upon chance, but is as steady, and may be as fairly calculated upon, as that of a manufacturer or a merchant; while, on the other hand, the individuals who have insured their property have exempted it from any chance of loss, and placed it, as it were, in a state of absolute security.

It is easy, from the brief statement now made, to perceive the immense advantages resulting to navigation and commerce from the practice of marine insurance. Without the aid that it affords, comparatively few individuals would be found disposed to expose their property to the risk of long and hazardous voyages; but by its means insecurity is changed for security, and the capital of the merchant whose ships are dispersed over every sea, and exposed to all the perils of the ocean, is as secure as that of the agriculturist. He can combine his measures and arrange his plans as if they could no longer be affected by accident. The chances of shipwreck, or of loss by unforeseen occurrences, enter not into his calculations. He has purchased an exemption from the effects of such casualties; and applies himself to the prosecution of his business with that confidence and energy which a feeling of security can only inspire.*

* "Les chances de la navigation entravaient le commerce. Le système des assurances a paru; il a consulté les saisons; il a porté ses regards sur la mer; il a interrogé ce terrible élément; il en a jugé l'inconstance; il en a pressenti les orages; il a épié la politique; il a reconnu les ports et les côtes des deux mondes; il a tout soumis à des calculs savans, à des théories approximatives; et il a dit au commerçant habile, au navigateur intrépide: certes, il y a des désastres sur lesquels l'humanité ne peut que gémir; mais quant à votre fortune, allez, franchissez les mers, déployez votre activité et votre industrie; je me charge de vos risques. Alors, Messieurs, s'il est permis de le dire, les quatre parties du monde se sont rapprochées."—*Code de Commerce, Exposé des Motifs*, liv. ii.

Besides insuring against the perils of the sea, and losses arising from accidents caused by the operation of natural causes, it is common to insure against enemies, pirates, thieves, and even the fraud, or, as it is technically termed, *barratry* of the master. The risk arising from these sources of casualty being extremely fluctuating and various, it is not easy to estimate it with any considerable degree of accuracy; and nothing more than a rough average can, in most cases, be looked for. In time of war, the fluctuations in the rates of insurance are particularly great; and the intelligence that an enemy's squadron, or even that a single privateer, is cruising in the course which the ships bound to, or returning from any given port, usually follow, causes an instantaneous rise in the premium. The appointment of convoys for the protection of trade during war, necessarily tends, by lessening the chances of capture, to lessen the premium on insurance. Still, however, the risk in such periods is, in most cases, very considerable; and as it is liable to change very suddenly, great caution is required on the part of the underwriters.

Provision may be made, by means of insurance, against almost all the casualties to which property on land is subject. Fire insurance has been carried, in this country, to a very great extent; and were it not for the heavy duty which is laid on the policy, or stamp, for executing the insurance, there can be no doubt it would be carried much farther. It appears, from the accounts printed by order of the House of Commons, that the nett duty received on policies of insurance against fire, amounted, for the United Kingdom, in the year 1828, to 745,710*l.*; which, as the duty is 3*s.* per cent, shews that the property insured amounted to the prodigious sum of 497,140,000*l.* It is supposed that about half the insurances are on common risks, being at the rate of only 1*s.* 6*d.* per cent exclusive of the duty. The premiums on what are called hazardous and doubly hazardous risks, amount to from 3*s.* to 5*s.* per cent; and there is besides a class of insurances that are effected only by special agreement with the insurers, the premium on which varies in each particular instance, according to the presumed nature of the risk. At present, most buildings are not insured up to their full value; even in towns, many are not insured at all; and in the country, it is far from being customary to insure farm-buildings or barn-yards. It is difficult to imagine that this can be owing to any thing else than the magnitude of the duty as compared with the premium; and there is, therefore, every reason to think, that were the duty reduced, the business of insurance would be very much extended; and as it could not be extended without an extension of security, and without lessening the injurious consequences arising from the casualties to which property is exposed, a reduction of the duty would be productive of the best consequences in a public point of view; while the increase of business would prevent the revenue from being diminished, and would, most probably, indeed, occasion its increase.

The tax upon policies of marine insurance varies according to the amount of the premium and the length of the voyage. But being far heavier than the corresponding tax in the Netherlands, it has occasioned the transfer of a considerable portion of the insurance business that would otherwise be transacted here to Holland. The total nett duty received from this source in 1814, in the United Kingdom, amounted to 458,067*l.*; but instead of increasing, it had sunk in 1828, from the cause now mentioned, to 243,360*l.*! This sufficiently evinces the necessity of reducing the duty.

But notwithstanding what has now been stated, it must be admitted, that the advantages derived from the practice of insuring against losses by sea and land are not altogether unmixed with evil. The security which it affords tends to relax that vigilant attention to the protection of property which the fear of its loss is sure otherwise to excite. This, however, is not its worst effect. The records of our courts, and the experience of all who are largely engaged in the business of insurance, too clearly prove that ships have been repeatedly sunk, and houses burned, in order to defraud the insurers. In despite, however, of the temptation to inattention and fraud which is thus afforded, there can be no doubt that, on the whole, the practice is, in a public as well as private point of view, decidedly beneficial. The frauds that are occasionally committed raise, in some degree, the rate of insurance. Still it is exceedingly moderate; and it is most probable, that the precautions adopted by the insurance offices for the prevention of fire, especially in great towns, where it is most destructive, outweigh the chances of increased conflagration arising from the greater tendency to carelessness and crime.

The business of life insurance has been carried to a far greater extent in Great Britain than in any other country, and has been productive of the most beneficial effects. Life insurances are of various kinds. Individuals without any very near connexions, and possessing only a limited fortune, are sometimes desirous, or are sometimes, from the necessity of their situation, obliged, annually to encroach on their capitals. But should the life of such persons be extended beyond the ordinary term of existence, they might be totally unprovided for in old age; and to secure themselves against this contingency, they pay to an insurance company the whole or a part of their capital, on condition of its guaranteeing them, as long as they live, a certain annuity, proportioned partly, of course, to the amount of the sum paid, and partly to their age when they buy the annuity. But though sometimes serviceable to individuals, it may be questioned whether insurances of this sort are, in a public point of view, really advantageous. So far as their influence extends, its obvious tendency is to weaken the principle of accumulation; to stimulate individuals to consume their capitals during their own life, without thinking or caring about the interest of their successors. Were such a practice to become general, it would be productive of the most extensively ruinous consequences. The interest which most men take in the welfare of their families and friends affords, indeed, a pretty strong security against its becoming injuriously prevalent. There can, however, be little doubt that this selfish practice may be strengthened by adventitious means; such, for example, as the opening of government loans in the shape of life annuities, or in the still more objectionable form of tontines. But when no extrinsic stimulus of this sort is given to it, there do not seem to be any very good grounds for thinking that the sale of annuities by private individuals or associations, can materially weaken the principle of accumulation.

Luckily, however, the species of insurance now referred to is but inconsiderable compared with that which has accumulation for its object. All professional persons, or persons living on salaries or wages, such as lawyers, physicians, military and naval officers, clerks in public and private offices, &c. whose incomes must, of course, terminate with their lives, and a host of others, who are either not possessed of capital, or cannot dispose of their capital at pleasure, must naturally be desirous of providing, so far as they may be able, for the comfortable subsistence of their families in the event of their death. Take, for example, a physician or lawyer, without fortune, but making, perhaps, 1,000*l*. or 2,000*l*. a year by his business; and suppose that he marries and has a family: if this individual attain to the average duration of human life, he may accumulate such a fortune as will provide for the adequate support of his family at his death. But who can presume to say that such will be the case?—that he will not be one of the many exceptions to the general rule? And suppose he were hurried into an untimely grave, his family would necessarily be destitute. Now, it is against such calamitous contingencies that life insurance is intended chiefly to provide. An individual possessed of an income terminating at his death, agrees to pay a certain sum annually to an insurance office; and this office binds itself to pay to his family, at his death, a sum equivalent, under deduction of the expenses of management and the profits of the insurers, to what these annual contributions, accumulated at compound interest, would amount to, supposing the insured to reach the common and average term of human life. Though he were to die the day after the insurance has been effected, his family would be as amply provided for as it is likely they would be by his accumulations were his life of the ordinary duration. In all cases, indeed, in which those insured die before attaining to an average age, their gain is obvious. But even in those cases in which their lives are prolonged beyond the ordinary term, they are not losers—they then merely pay for a security which they must otherwise have been without. During the whole period, from the time when they effect their insurances down to the time when they arrive at the mean duration of human life, they are protected against the risk of dying without leaving their families sufficiently provided for; and the sum which they pay after having passed this mean term is nothing more than a fair compensation for the security they previously enjoyed. Of those who insure houses against fire, a very small proportion only have occasion to claim an indemnity for losses actually sustained; but the possession of a security against loss in the event of accident, is a sufficient motive to induce every prudent individual to insure his property. The case of life insurance is in no respect different. When established on a proper footing, the extra sums which those pay whose lives exceed the estimated duration is but the value of the previous security.

In order so to adjust the terms of an insurance that the party insuring may neither pay too much nor too little, it is necessary that the probable duration of human life, at every different age, should be calculated with as much accuracy as possible.

This probable duration, or, as it is frequently termed, expectation of life, means the period when the chances that a person of a given age will be alive, are precisely equal to those that he will be dead. The results deduced from the observations made to determine this period, in different countries and places, have been published in the form of tables; and insurances are calculated by referring to them. Thus, in the table of the expectation of life at Carlisle, framed by Mr. Milne, of the Sun Life Office,* and which is believed to represent the average law of mortality in England with very considerable accuracy, the probable future life of a person of thirty years of age, is thirty-four years and four months; or, in other words, it has been found by observations carefully made at Carlisle, that at an average, *half* the individuals of *thirty* years of age attain to the age of sixty-four years and four months. If, therefore, an individual of thirty years of age were to insure a sum payable at his death, the insurers who adopt the Carlisle table would assume that he would live for thirty-four years and a third, and would make their calculations on that footing. If he did not live so long, the insurers would lose by the transaction; and if he lived longer, they would gain proportionally. But if their business be so extensive as to enable the law of average fully to apply, what they lose by premature death will be balanced by the payments received from those whose lives are prolonged beyond the ordinary degree of probability; so that the profits of the society will be wholly independent of chance.

Besides the vast advantage of that security against

* See his very valuable work on Annuities, vol. ii. p. 565.

disastrous contingencies afforded by the practice of life insurance, it has an obvious tendency to strengthen habits of accumulation. An individual who has insured a sum on his life, would forfeit all the advantages of the insurance were he not to continue regularly to make his annual payments. It is not, therefore, optional with him to save a sum from his ordinary expenditure adequate for this purpose. He is compelled, under a heavy penalty, to do so; and having thus been led to contract a habit of saving to a certain extent, it is most probable that the habit will acquire additional strength, and that he will either insure an additional sum or privately accumulate.

England is, perhaps, the only state in which the insurance of lives has never been prohibited. Notwithstanding the sagacity of the Dutch, insurances of this sort were not legalised in Holland till a comparatively recent period. In France they were long, and, it would appear, are still, deemed illegal.* They were expressly forbidden by the famous ordinance of 1681 (arts. 9 and 10), because, says its commentator, Valin, "it is an offence against public decency to set a price upon the life of a man, particularly

* It is said, in article 334 of the "Code de Commerce," that an insurance may be effected upon any thing *estimable à prix d'argent*. Count Corvetto, in his speech on laying this part of the "Code" before the legislative body, stated, that the above expressions had been introduced in order to make the article harmonise with the 9th and 10th articles of the ordinance of 1681, *qui permettent*, he says, *d'assurer la liberté des hommes, et qui défendent de faire des assurances sur leur vie. La liberté est estimable à prix d'argent; la vie de l'homme ne l'est pas.* It does not appear that this article has been modified by any new law. In the notes to the last edition of Pailliet's "Manuel de Droit," it is asked: "Peut on faire assurer la vie des personnes? Il faut distinguer celle des personnes libres. *Non:* elle n'est point estimable à prix d'argent." p. 1266.

It is not at all creditable to France that such an article should be found in her code; and its existence is the more singular, as the prohibition in the ordinance of 1681 had been virtually repealed by an *arrêt* of the Council of State, dated the 3d November, 1787, in which the advantages of life-insurance are ably pointed out.

the life of a freeman, which is above all valuation." There is reason, however, to think that the fear lest individuals might be tempted to destroy themselves, in order to enrich their families at the expense of those with whom they had insured their lives, has had the greatest influence in the prevention of this practice.* It is needless, however, to say, that this apprehension is the most futile imaginable. Attempts are, indeed, frequently made to get insurances effected upon lives by false representations as to the health of the parties; but it is doubtful whether the insurance offices have ever lost any thing from the cause previously alluded to. To prevent the possibility of its occurrence, most of the English offices stipulate that death by suicide or in a duel shall cancel the insurance.

* "Forbonnais, Elémens du Commerce," tom. ii. p. 51.

CHAPTER X.

Interference of Government with the Pursuits and Property of Individuals—Cases in, and Objects for which such Interference is necessary—Limits within which it should be confined.

THE discussions in which we have been engaged in the previous chapters, sufficiently evince the vast importance of the administration being powerful, and at the same time liberal and intelligent — that is, of its having power to carry its laws and regulations into effect, and wisdom to render them consistent with sound principles. Far more, indeed, of the prosperity of a country depends on the nature of its government than on any thing else. If it be feeble, and unable to enforce obedience to the laws, the insecurity thence arising cannot fail of being most pernicious; while, on the other hand, if its laws, though carried into effect, be founded on erroneous principles, their operation cannot be otherwise than injurious; and though they may not actually arrest, they must, at all events, retard the progress of the society. An idea seems, however, to have been recently gaining ground, that in so far as respects the production of wealth, the duty of government is almost entirely of a negative kind, and that it has merely to maintain the security of property and the freedom of industry. But its duty is by no means so simple and easily defined as those who advocate this opinion would have us to believe. It is, certainly, true, that its interference with the pursuits of individuals has been, in very many instances, carried to a ruinous excess. Still, however, it is easy to see that we should fall into the greatest imaginable error if we supposed that it might be entirely dispensed with. Freedom is not, as some appear to think, the end of government: the advancement of the public prosperity and happiness is its end; and freedom is valuable in so far only as it contributes to bring it about. In laying it down, for example, that individuals should be left at perfect liberty to engage in any business or profession they may think best for themselves, the condition that it is not injurious to others is always understood. No one can doubt the propriety of government interfering to suppress what might otherwise become a public nuisance; nor does any one doubt that it may advantageously interfere to give facilities to commerce by negotiating treaties with foreign powers, and removing such obstacles as cannot be removed by individuals. But the interference of government cannot be limited to cases of this sort. However disinclined, it cannot help interfering, in an infinite variety of ways, and for an infinite variety of purposes. It must, to notice only one or two of the *classes* of objects requiring its interference, decide as to the species of contracts to which it will lend its sanction, and the means to be adopted to enforce their performance; it must decide as to the distribution of the property of those who die intestate, and the effect to be given to the directions in wills and testaments; and it must frequently engage itself, or authorise individuals or associations to engage, in various sorts of undertakings deeply affecting the rights and interests of others. When, therefore, the subjects requiring the interference of government are so very numerous, and when we also take into view the necessity of accommodating the measures of administration to the changes that are perpetually occurring in the internal condition of nations, and in their external relations in respect of others, it is immediately seen that it is no easy matter to draw a distinct line of demarcation between what may be called the positive and negative duties of government, or to resolve what Mr. Burke has truly termed "one of the finest problems in legislation, namely, to determine what the state ought to take upon itself to direct by the public wisdom, and what it ought to leave, with as little interference as possible, to individual exertion."

It is, indeed, obvious, that no solution of this problem can be applicable at all times and under all circumstances. Although, however, it may not be possible previously to devise the measures proper to be adopted in particular emergencies, we may, notwithstanding, decide on pretty good grounds as to the description of objects with respect to which the interference of government is required upon ordinary occasions, and the extent to which it should be carried. Many difficult and delicate questions are involved in the discussion of this very interesting, though comparatively neglected department of the science; and to enter fully into their examination would require a lengthened treatise. I shall merely, therefore, endeavour to lay down a few leading principles, touching very briefly upon such topics only as seem most interesting.

The principles already established shew, that without the security of property, and the freedom of engaging in every employment not hurtful to others, no society can make any considerable advances. Government is, therefore, bound to take such measures as may be effectual to secure these objects. But we have just seen that it must not rest satisfied when this is accomplished. It will fail of its duty if it do not exert itself to prevent that confusion and disorder in the distribution of property, and in the prosecution of industrious employments, that could either not be prevented at all without its interference, or not so easily and completely prevented. It is also bound to give every due facility to individuals about to engage in such obviously useful undertakings as cannot be carried on without its sanction; and it should not only endeavour to protect its peaceable and industrious subjects from the machinations of those who are idle and profligate, but also against those accidents arising from the operation of natural causes to which their persons or properties might otherwise be exposed.

We have, therefore, *first*, to consider the means of obtaining security and protection.

Second, the species of contracts and of testamentary dispositions to which government ought to give a legal effect.

Third, the means of adjusting such disputes as may arise among the citizens, and of enforcing the observance of contracts.

Fourth, the means of obviating confusion and fraud in the dealings of individuals.

Fifth, the species of industrious undertakings in which government may engage, or to which it should lend some peculiar sanction.

Sixth, the means proper to be adopted to secure the property and persons of the citizens from such natural casualties as they would be subject to without the interference of government.

I. With respect to the first of these heads, or the provision of a force adequate to afford security and protection, its necessity is too obvious to require illustration. The best laws can be of little use if they may be insulted with impunity. All governments ought, therefore, to have a force at their command sufficient to carry their orders into effect at home, as well as to defend their territories from hostile attack. The question as to how this force may be most advantageously raised, is one of deep importance. Perhaps, however, its investigation belongs rather to the science of politics, properly so called, than to political economy; and, at any rate, my limits forbid me from engaging in it here. I may, however, remark, that in nothing, perhaps, has the beneficial influence of the division of labour been more perceptible than in the employment of a distinct class of individuals to maintain national tranquillity and security. To be a good soldier, or a good police-officer, a man must be nothing else. It is hardly possible for an individual taken from one of the ordinary employments of industry, to which after a short time he is to be restored, to serve as a militia-man, to acquire those habits of discipline, and of prompt and willing obedience to orders, so indispensable in a soldier. It is now very generally, if not universally, admitted, that when force must be employed to suppress any disturbance, it is always best to employ troops of the line, and to abstain as much as possible from the employment of yeomanry or local militia. The former have neither partialities nor antipathies; they do what they are ordered, and they do no more: but the latter are more than half citizens; and being so, are inflamed with all the passions and prejudices incident to the peculiar description of persons from among whom they are taken. When they act, they necessarily act under a strong bias, and can with difficulty be kept to the strict line of their duty.

II. The discussion of the *second* of the previously mentioned heads may be conveniently divided into two branches: the *first* having reference to the description of contracts between individuals to which government ought to give a legal sanction; and the *second*, how far it ought to give a legal effect to the instructions in wills and testaments.

1. It may be laid down in general, that every government is bound to assist in enforcing all contracts fairly entered into between individuals, unless they are made in opposition to some existing law; or unless they are clearly such as cannot fail of being prejudicial to the public interests.

Contracts or obligations arising out of purely gambling transactions, have been supposed to be of this latter description, and it has been customary to refuse to give them any legal effect. The wisdom of this custom seems abundantly obvious. No one can doubt, that the prevalence of gambling, by withdrawing the attention of those engaged in it from industrious pursuits, and making them trust to chance, and not to exertion and economy, for the means of rising in the world, must, both in a public and private point of view, be exceedingly pernicious. And I am not aware that any means have been suggested for checking the growth of this destructive habit, so easy of adoption, and, at the same time, so effectual, as the placing of all gambling engagements without the pale of the law, and depriving the parties of any guarantee other than their own honour. To interfere further than this, might perhaps be inexpedient; but there appears no good reason for thinking that the interference of government is not beneficially carried to this extent.

I shall afterwards endeavour to shew the impolicy of the restraints imposed on the rate of interest, and the injury which they occasion. And it is now pretty generally admitted, that the laws formerly enforced in this country, and still acted upon in various quarters, restricting the freedom of those engaged in the internal corn-trade, and for the prevention of the practices of forestalling, engrossing, and regrating, are in the last degree oppressive and inexpedient. It has been shewn, over and over again, that the interest of the corn-dealer is in all cases identical with that of the public, and that instead of any injury being occasioned by his speculations, they are uniformly productive of the greatest advantage.*

It is unnecessary, perhaps, to say any thing about the attempts that have occasionally been made to fix the price of commodities by law. Every one must see that it is not in the nature of things, that such attempts can have any but the most disastrous results. The price of

* For some illustrations of what is now stated, see the Chapter on the "Influence of Speculation on Prices."

commodities is continually varying, from innumerable causes, the operation of which can neither be foreseen nor prevented. If, therefore, an attempt were made to fix their prices, it would follow, that when their natural price sunk below their legal price, the buyers would have to pay so much more than their fair value; and, on the other hand, when their natural price happened to rise above their legal price, the producers, in order to avoid the loss they would incur by carrying on their business, would withdraw from it, so that the market would no longer be supplied. Nothing, consequently, can be more obvious than that the interference of government in the regulation of prices is productive only of unalloyed mischief. It will be shewn, in a subsequent chapter, that wherever industry is free, the competition of the producers uniformly causes commodities to be sold at their natural and proper price.

It was usual in this country, until very recently, to punish workmen for combining together to raise the rate of wages, or to diminish the hours of working. The oppressiveness of such a law is so very obvious as hardly to require being pointed out. An individual can be nothing but a slave if he be prevented from fixing, in concert with others, the conditions on which he will sell his labour. No bad consequences can result from the exercise of this power on the part of the workmen. If the price they demand for their labour be unreasonable, the masters may, and always *do*, refuse to employ them; and as they cannot afford to live for any considerable period without employment, it is plain that all combinations to obtain an undue rise of wages, or to effect an improper purpose, carry in their bosom a principle of dissolution, and must speedily fall to pieces. But when workmen have the power of refusing to work except upon such conditions as they may choose to prescribe, they have, in this respect, obtained *all* they can justly claim: and if they go one step farther, and attempt to carry their point by violence, by threatening the property of their employers, or obstructing such of their fellow-labourers as may have refused to join the combination, or seceded from it, they are guilty of an offence which deeply affects the security of property and freedom of industry, and which ought to be instantly repressed by prompt and suitable punishment.

2. Various questions, some of which are of the greatest interest, arise in deciding as to how far government ought to give effect to the instructions in wills and testaments. There is no question, indeed, as to the reasonableness and advantage of allowing individuals to bequeath their property to their children and nearest surviving relations. And, without stopping to make any observations on what is so very clear, I shall proceed to inquire, *first*, whether individuals ought to be authorised to leave their fortune to strangers, to the exclusion of their children and friends; *second*, whether, in distributing a fortune amongst children, it is expedient that the testator ought to be left to follow his own inclination, or be obliged to abide by any fixed rule; and *third*, whether an individual should be authorised to fix the conditions on which his property shall afterwards be enjoyed, or the purposes to which it is to be always applied.

(1.) It has been the practice in most countries, in a rude state of society, to confine the power of a testator within very narrow limits. A man's children, or next of kin, are then his only legal heirs, and he is not allowed to leave his fortune to any one else, to their exclusion. But, as society advances, this strict rule of succession is usually set aside; and individuals are permitted to bequeath a part, and sometimes the whole, of their property to strangers, in preference of the heirs of their own bodies, or their relations. A great diversity of opinion is, however, entertained with respect to the expediency of giving this power to the testator. It is contended, that, independently altogether of their merit or demerit, every one is under the most sacred obligations to the beings he has been the means of bringing into the world; and that no one who has any property ought to be permitted to throw his children destitute upon society, but should be obliged to make some provision for their support. But though the question is by no means free from difficulty, still it would appear that they are right who argue in favour of the uncontrolled power of bequeathing to strangers. It seems to be impossible to interfere to enforce a legal provision for children, without in so far weakening that parental authority which, though it may sometimes be abused, is yet, in the vast majority of instances, exerted in the best manner and with the best effect. The relations of private life should as seldom as possible be made the object of legislative enactments. If children be ordinarily well-behaved, we have, in the feeling of parental affection, a sufficient security that they will rarely be disinherited. The interference of the legislator in their behalf seems, therefore, to be quite unnecessary. In countries where the greatest extension is given to the power of the testator, nothing is more uncommon than to hear of the disinheritance of a really dutiful family: and it would surely be most inexpedient to attempt to remedy an evil of such rare occurrence, by exempting children from the influence of a salutary check on their vicious propensities, and forcing individuals to bestow that property on profligacy and idleness, which is the fruit, and ought to be the reward, of virtue and industry.

(2.) The same reasons which shew that it would be inexpedient to prevent individuals from leaving their fortunes to strangers, shew that it would be inexpedient to interfere to compel them to adopt any fixed rule in the division of their fortunes amongst their children.

It has long been customary in this, as well as in many other countries, when estates consist of land, to leave them either wholly or principally to the eldest son, and to give the younger sons and daughters smaller portions in money. Many objections have been made to this custom; but mostly, as it appears to me, without due consideration. That it has its inconveniences is, no doubt, true, but they seem to be trifling compared with the advantages which it exclusively possesses. It forces the younger sons to quit the home of their father, and makes them depend for success in life on the fair exercise of their talents; it helps to prevent the splitting of landed property into too small portions; and stimulates the holders of estates to endeavour to save a monied fortune adequate for the outfit of the younger children, without rendering them a burden on their senior. Its influence in these and other respects is equally powerful and salutary. The sense of inferiority as compared with others is, next to the pressure of want, one of the most powerful motives to exertion. It is not always because a man is absolutely poor, that he is perseveringly industrious, economical, and inventive; in many cases he is already wealthy, and is merely wishing to place himself in the same rank as others who have still larger fortunes. The younger sons of our great landed proprietors are particularly sensible to this stimulus. Their relative inferiority in point of wealth, and their desire to escape from this lower situation, and to attain to the same level as their elder brothers, inspires them with an energy and vigour they could not otherwise feel. But the advantage of preserving large estates from being frittered down by a scheme of equal division, is not limited to its effects on the younger children of their owners. It raises universally the standard of competence, and gives new force to the springs which set industry in motion. The manner of living among the great landlords is that in which every one is ambitious of being able to indulge; and their habits of expense, though sometimes injurious to themselves, act as powerful incentives to the ingenuity and enterprise of the other classes, who never think their fortunes sufficiently ample, unless they will enable them to emulate the splendour of the richest landlords; so that the custom of primogeniture seems to render all classes more industrious, and to augment, at the same time, the mass of wealth and the scale of enjoyment.

It is said, indeed, that this eager pursuit of wealth, and the engrossing interest which it inspires, occasion every thing to be undervalued that does not directly conspire to its advancement, and makes the possession of money be regarded as the only thing desirable. But this is plainly a very exaggerated and fallacious representation. It is not meant to say that a desire to outstrip our neighbours in the accumulation of wealth is the best motive to exertion, or that it might not be far preferable, could the same spirit of emulation be excited by a desire to excel in learning, benevolence, or integrity. After all, however, it rarely happens that the game itself is not of incomparably less value than the stimulus afforded by the chase. But though it were otherwise, there seems very little reason to think that the love of superiority in mental acquirements will ever be able to create that deep, lasting, and universal interest, that is created by a desire to mount in the scale of society, and to attain to the same elevation in point of fortune, that has been attained by others. It is false, however, to affirm that the prevalence of this spirit causes the virtues of industry and frugality to be cultivated, to the exclusion of all the rest. Every one, indeed, who is acquainted with what is going on around him, must know that the fact is not so. The business of those who inherit considerable fortunes is rather to spend than accumulate: and while, on the one hand, the desire to attain to an equality of riches with them is a powerful spur to industry; the manner of living, which they render fashionable, prevents, on the other, the growth of those sordid and miserly habits that are subversive of every generous impulse. Many holders of large fortunes, and many who are still striving to attain that distinction, influenced partly, no doubt, by vanity and ostentation, but in a far greater degree by worthier motives, are the liberal patrons of the arts, and are eminently distinguished by their benevolence. The example thus set by the higher ranks, re-acts on those below them ; being communicated from one class to another, until it pervades the whole society. And hence, though the spirit of emulation, industry, and invention, be stronger here, perhaps, than in any other country, it has not obliterated, but seems, on the contrary, rather to have strengthened, the social and generous sympathies.

But, to whatever cause it may be owing, we may safely affirm, that an interest in the welfare of others has never been more strongly manifested in any age or country than in our own. Those who contrast the benevolent institutions of England and the Netherlands (the country which has the nearest resemblance to England), and the efforts made by the middle and upper classes in them to relieve the distresses and improve the condition of those in inferior circumstances, with the institutions and the efforts of the same classes in France and Austria, will pause before affirming that the strong spirit of emulation, inspired by our peculiar laws and customs, has rendered us comparatively indifferent to the happiness of our fellow-men. In the United States, properties, whether consisting of land or movables, are almost invariably divided equally amongst the children. There are no very large estates, nor is there any thing approaching to that keen and eager competition in every department and line of business that exists in England. But, notwithstanding these apparently favourable circumstances, has any one ever pretended to say that generosity formed a prominent feature of the national character of the Americans? or that they are in this respect superior to the English?

In France, previously to the revolution, different provinces had different customs as to the division of landed property by will; but soon after the revolution one uniform system was established. According to this new system, an individual making a will, is obliged to divide his fortune, whether it consist of land or movables, in nearly equal portions amongst his children; and in the event of his dying intestate, it is distributed amongst the family in precisely equal portions, without respect of sex or seniority.

The principles already established shew that this law is radically bad. It necessarily weakens the desire to accumulate a fortune, over the disposal of which it allows so very little influence; it goes far to emancipate the children of persons possessed of property from any efficient control; it gives them the certainty of getting a provision, whatever be their conduct; and it cannot do this without paralysing their exertions and checking their enterprise. But its worst effect is the influence it has already had, and will, no doubt, continue to have, in occasioning the too great subdivision of landed property. In this respect its operation is most pernicious; and if it be not repealed, or some method of evading it discovered, it bids fair to reduce the agriculturists of France to something like the condition of those of Ireland.

In distributing the property of those who die intestate, the same rule should be adopted which has been seen to be most advantageous in the making of wills. When there is a landed estate, it should go to the eldest son; being, however, burdened with a reasonable provision for the other children. If the fortune consist of money or movables, it may be equally divided.

(3.) We have now to inquire whether an individual, in leaving a fortune by will, ought to be allowed to fix by whom, and under what conditions, it shall always be held, and the purposes to which it shall always be applied.

It is evident that those who decide these questions in the affirmative, really allow the presumption, folly, or ignorance of individuals to become a standard to all future ages. Every man should have such a reasonable degree of power over the disposal of his property as may be necessary to excite his industry, and to inspire him with the desire of accumulating. But if, in order to carry this principle to the farthest extent, individuals were allowed to chalk out an endless series of heirs, and to prescribe the conditions under which they shall successively hold the property, it would be taken entirely out of the market; it might be prevented from ever coming into the hands of those who would turn it to the best account; and it could neither be farmed nor managed in any way, however advantageous, that happened to be inconsistent with the directions in the will. To establish such a system, would evidently be most impolitic; and hence, in regulating the transfer of property by will, a term should be fixed beyond which the instructions of the testator should have no effect. It is of course impossible to lay down any general rule for determining this period. According to the law of England, a man is allowed to fix the destination of his property until the first unborn heir be twenty-one years of age, when his will ceases to have any further control over it. This is, perhaps, as judicious a term as could be devised. It gives every necessary inducement to accumulation, at the same time that it hinders the tying-up of property for too long a period.

In Scotland it is lawful to settle or entail estates upon an endless series of heirs, but repeated acts of parliament have been passed to obviate some of the defects incident to this system; and it is probable that it will, at no distant period, undergo still more essential modifications.

It appears pretty obvious that government should reserve to itself the power of controlling all bequests for the promotion of purposes of general utility. It is not certain that individuals will always leave their property for the advancement of objects believed, even at the time, to be worthy of support; and though such were the case, they might afterwards be deemed injurious. Institutions and establishments regarded at one period as of the highest utility, have been frequently ascertained, in some subsequent period, to be in no common degree prejudicial: and it is almost unnecessary to add, that this discovery is no sooner made than it becomes quite inconsistent with the duty of government to permit property to be any longer laid out upon them.*

III. The *third* duty of government is, to provide the means of adjusting such disputes as may arise among its subjects, and of enforcing the observance of contracts.

To do this it is necessary to establish convenient and proper tribunals, accessible at all times, at a moderate expense, to all who may have occasion to appeal to them.

Every practicable effort should also be made to simplify the law, and to render it as clear and precise as possible.

Nothing tends more to counteract the spirit of commercial enterprise than the existence of any doubt in the minds of the parties interested with respect to the nature and effect of the laws bearing on the transactions in which they happen to be engaged. "The property and daily negotiations of merchants ought not to depend upon subtleties and niceties, but upon rules easily learned and easily retained."† It is mentioned, in a report by a committee of the House of Commons on the foreign trade of the country, printed in 1820, that no fewer than TWO THOUSAND laws with respect to commerce had been passed at different periods; that many of these had originated in temporary circumstances; and that *eleven hundred* were actually in force in the year 1815, exclusive of the additions made in the subsequent five years! The committee justly and strongly condemn this excessive multiplication. They state, that the difficulty of deciding as to what transactions were or were not legal was so very

* For a further and more ample discussion of the subject of the disposal of property by will, see the fourth volume of my edition of the "Wealth of Nations," pp. 441—481.

† Speech of Lord Mansfield in an insurance case.

great, that the most experienced merchants could seldom venture to act without consulting a lawyer; and that it was quite impossible for them to proceed in their speculations with that promptitude and confidence so necessary to their success. And they declare that, in their opinion, no more valuable service could be rendered to the trade of the empire than an accurate revision of this vast and confused mass of legislation, and the establishment of some certain, simple, and constant principles, to which all commercial regulations might be referred, and under which all transactions might be conducted with facility, safety, and confidence.

Since this report was compiled, a good deal has been done in the way of simplifying and consolidating our commercial law. Much, however, still remains to be accomplished; and as it is an object of the highest importance, it is to be hoped that it may be kept steadily in view, and that nothing may be left undone to give precision, clearness, and simplicity, to every branch of the law, but especially to that affecting industrious undertakings.

No one can doubt that it is highly expedient that government should lend every reasonable facility towards enforcing the fulfilment of contracts. Were it to evince any backwardness in this respect, there would be an immediate diminution of confidence, and comparatively few engagements would be entered into. But when an individual is either unable or unwilling to abide by the stipulations into which he has entered, there is often great difficulty in determining the extent to which government ought to go in its attempts to enforce performance. The questions that occur with respect to bankruptcy exemplify this.

All classes of individuals, even those who have least to do with industrious undertakings, are exposed to vicissitudes and misfortunes, the occurrence of which may render them incapable of making good the engagements into which they have entered. Individuals in this situation are said to be bankrupt or insolvent. But though bankruptcy is most frequently, perhaps, produced by uncontrollable causes, it is frequently, also, produced by the thoughtlessness of individuals, or by their repugnance to make those retrenchments which the state of their affairs demands; and sometimes, also, by fraud or bad faith. Hence it is that the laws with respect to bankruptcy occupy a prominent place in the judicial system of every state in which commerce has made any progress, and credit been introduced. They differ exceedingly in different countries and stages of society; and it must be acknowledged that they present very many difficulties, and that it is not possible, perhaps, to suggest any system against which some pretty plausible objections may not be made.

The execrable atrocity of the early Roman laws with respect to bankruptcy is well known. According to the usual interpretation of the law of the twelve tables, which Cicero has so much eulogised,* the creditors of an insolvent debtor might, after some preliminary formalities, cut his body to pieces, each of them taking a share proportioned to the amount of his debt; and those who did not choose to resort to this horrible extremity, were authorised to subject the debtor to chains, stripes, and hard labour; or to sell him, his wife, and children, to perpetual foreign slavery, *trans Tyberim!* This law, and the law giving fathers the power of inflicting capital punishments on their children, strikingly illustrate the ferocious and sanguinary character of the early Romans.

There is reason to think, from the silence of historians on the subject, that no unfortunate debtor ever actually felt the utmost severity of this barbarous statute; but the history of the republic is full of accounts of popular com-

* Fremant omnes, licet! dicam quod sentio: bibliothecas, mehercule, omnium philosophorum unus mihi videtur duodecim tabularum libellus; si quis legum fontes et capita viderit, et authoritatis pondere et utilitatis ubertate superare.—*De Oratore*, lib. i.

motions, some of which led to very important changes, that were occasioned by the exercise of the power given to creditors of enslaving their debtors, and subjecting them to corporal punishments. The law, however, continued in this state till the year of Rome 427, 120 years after the promulgation of the twelve tables, when it was repealed. It was then enacted, that the persons of debtors should cease to be at the disposal of their creditors, and that the latter should merely be authorised to seize upon the debtor's goods, and sell them by auction in satisfaction of their claims. In the subsequent stages of Roman jurisprudence, further changes were made, which seem generally to have leaned to the side of the debtor; and it was ultimately ruled, that an individual who had become insolvent without having committed any fraud, should, upon making a *cessio bonorum*, or a surrender of his entire property to his creditors, be entitled to an exemption from all personal penalties.*

The law of England distinguishes between the insolvency of persons engaged in trade, and that of others. The former can alone be made bankrupts, and are dealt with in a comparatively lenient manner. "The law," says Blackstone, "is cautious of encouraging prodigality and extravagance by indulgence to debtors; and, therefore, it allows the benefit of the laws of bankruptcy to none but actual traders, since that set of men are, generally speaking, the only persons liable to accidental losses, and to an inability of paying their debts, without any fault of their own. If persons in other situations of life run in debt without the power of payment, they must take the consequences of their own indiscretion, even though they meet with sudden accidents that may reduce their fortunes; for the law holds it to be an unjustifiable practice for any person but a trader to encumber himself with debts of any considerable value. If a gentle-

* Terasson, "Histoire de la Jurisprudence Romaine," p. 117.

man, or one in a liberal profession, at the time of contracting his debts has a sufficient fund to pay them, the delay of payment is a species of dishonesty, and a temporary injustice to his creditor; and if at such time he has no sufficient fund, the dishonesty and injustice is the greater. He cannot, therefore, murmur if he suffer the punishment he has voluntarily drawn upon himself. But in mercantile transactions the case is far otherwise: trade cannot be carried on without mutual credit on both sides: the contracting of debts is here, therefore, not only justifiable, but necessary; and if, by accidental calamities, as by the loss of a ship in a tempest, the failure of brother traders, or by the non-payment of persons out of trade, a merchant or trader becomes incapable of discharging his own debts, it is his misfortune and not his fault.* To the misfortunes, therefore, of debtors, the law has given a compassionate remedy, but denied it to their faults; since, at the same time that it provides for the security of commerce, by enacting that every considerable trader may be declared a bankrupt, for the benefit of his creditors as well as himself, it has also, to discourage extravagance, declared that no one shall be capable of being made a bankrupt but only a trader, nor capable of receiving the full benefit of the statutes but only an *industrious* trader."†

* The opinion of Puffendorff upon this point is different from that of Blackstone; and being curious, I subjoin it:—" Il faut encore considerer ici la raison ou la nécessité qui a obligé un homme à s'endetter; car, selon qu'elle est plus ou moins grande, on doit avoir plus ou moins de support et de compassion pour un débiteur reduit à la pauvreté. Ainsi, ce n'est pas sans sujet que l'on traite les marchands avec plus de rigueur, lors même qu'un cas fortuit les a rendus insolvables, que d'autres qu'un besoin pressant a mis dans la nécessité d'emprunter; car il n'y a que le désir du gain qui porte les premiers à s'endetter: et comme ils font profession de l'art de s'enrichir, ils ne sont guères excusables lorsqu'ils n'ont pas bien pris leurs précautions même contre les accidens fortuits."—*Droit de la Nature et des Gens*, par Barbeyrac, liv. iii. cap. 7, § 3.

† Commentaries, book ii. cap. 31.

After the various proceedings with respect to bankruptcy have been gone through, if nothing be discovered to impeach the honesty of the debtor, he is allowed a certificate or discharge, provided that *three out of five* of his creditors, both in number and value, agree to sign it. The bankrupt is then entitled to a reasonable allowance out of his effects; which is, however, made to depend partly on his former good behaviour, and partly on the magnitude of his dividend. Thus, if his effects will not pay half his debts, or 10*s.* in the pound, he is left to the discretion of the commissioners and assignees, to have a competent sum allowed him, not exceeding 3 per cent upon his estate, or 300*l.* in all; but if his estate pay 10*s.* in the pound, he is to be allowed 5 per cent, provided such allowance do not exceed 400*l.*; if 12*s.* 6*d.*, then 7½ per cent, under a limitation, as before, of its not exceeding 500*l.*; and if 15*s.* in a pound, then the bankrupt shall be allowed 10 per cent upon his estate, provided it do not exceed 600*l.*

According to our present law, when a person not a trader becomes insolvent, he may, after being actually imprisoned, at the suit of some of his creditors, for fourteen days, present a petition to the court to be relieved; and upon his surrendering his entire property, he is, unless something fraudulent be established against him, entitled to a discharge. While, however, the certificate given to a bankrupt relieves him from all future claims on account of debts contracted previously to his bankruptcy, the discharge given to an insolvent only relieves him from imprisonment; in the event of his afterwards accumulating any property, it may be seized in payment of the debts contracted anterior to his insolvency. This principle was recognised in the *cessio bonorum* of the Romans, of which the insolvent act is nearly a copy.

It may be questioned, however, notwithstanding what Blackstone has stated, whether there be any good ground for making a distinction between the insolvency of traders and other individuals. There are very few trades so hazardous as that of a farmer, and yet, should he become insolvent, he is not entitled to the same privileges he would have enjoyed had he been the keeper of an inn or a commission agent! The injustice of this distinction is obvious; but, without dwelling upon it, it seems pretty clear, that certificates should be granted indiscriminately to all honest debtors. Being relieved from all concern as to his previous encumbrances, an insolvent who has obtained a certificate is prompted to exert himself vigorously in future, at the same time that his friends are not deterred from coming forward to his assistance. But when an insolvent continues liable for his previous debts, no one, however favourably disposed, can venture to aid him with a loan, and he is discouraged, even if he had means, from attempting to earn any thing more than a bare livelihood; so that, while the creditors do not in one case out of a hundred gain the smallest sum by this constant liability of the insolvent, his energies and usefulness are for ever paralysed.

The policy of imprisoning for debt seems also exceedingly questionable. Notwithstanding the deference due to the great authorities who have vindicated this practice, I confess I am unable to discover any thing very cogent in the reasonings advanced in its favour. Provided a person in insolvent circumstances intimate his situation to his creditors, and offer to make a voluntary surrender of his property to them, he has, as it appears to me, done all that should be required of him, and ought not to undergo any imprisonment. If he has deceived his creditors by false representations, or if he conceal or fraudulently convey away any part of his property, he should, of course, be subjected to the pains and penalties attached to swindling; but when such practices are not alleged, or cannot be proved, sound policy, I apprehend, would dictate that creditors ought to have no power over the persons of their debtors, and that they should be entitled only to their effects. The maxim *carcer non solvit*, is not more trite than true. It is said, indeed, that the fear of imprisonment operates as a check to prevent persons from getting into debt; and so, no doubt, it does. But then it must, on the other hand, be borne in mind, that the power to imprison tempts individuals to trust to its influence to enforce payment of their claims, and makes them less cautious in their inquiries as to the condition and circumstances of those to whom they give credit. The carelessness of tradesmen, and their extreme earnestness to obtain custom, are, more than any thing else, the great causes of insolvency; and the power of imprisoning merely tends to foster and encourage these habits. If a tradesman trust an individual with a loan of money or goods which he is unable to repay, he has made a bad speculation. But why ought he, because he has done so, to be allowed to arrest the debtor's person? If he wished to have perfect security, he either should not have dealt with him at all, or dealt with him only for ready money: such transactions are, on the part of tradesmen, perfectly voluntary; and if they place undue confidence in a debtor who has not misled them by erroneous representations of his affairs, they have themselves only to blame.

It would really, therefore, as it appears to me, be for the advantage of creditors, were all penal proceedings against the persons of honest debtors abolished. The dependence placed on their efficacy is deceitful. A tradesman ought rather to trust to his own prudence and sagacity to keep him out of scrapes than to the law for redress: he may deal upon credit with those whom he knows, but he should deal for ready money only with those of whose circumstances and characters he is either ignorant or suspicious. By bringing penal statutes to his aid, he is rendered remiss and negligent. He has the only effectual means of security in his own hand; and it seems highly inexpedient that he should be taught to neglect them and to put his trust in prisons.

It is pretty evident, too, that the efficacy of imprisonment in deterring individuals from running into debt, has been greatly overrated. Insolvents who are honest must have suffered from misfortune, or been disappointed in the hopes they entertained of being able, in one way or other, to discharge their debts. The fear of imprisonment does not greatly influence such persons; for when they contract debts they have no doubt of their ability to pay them. And, though the imprisonment of *bonâ fide* insolvents were abolished, it would give no encouragement to the practices of those who endeavour to raise money by false representations; for these are to be regarded as swindlers, and ought, as such, to be subjected to adequate punishment.

But the regulations with respect to bankruptcy and insolvency differ radically in other important respects. An individual cannot be subjected to the insolvent law except by *his own* act, that is, by his petitioning for relief from actual imprisonment for debt; and, on the other hand, an individual cannot be made a bankrupt, and subjected to the bankrupt law, except by the act of *another*, that is, of a petitioning creditor,* as he is called, swearing that the individual in question is indebted to him, and that he believes he has committed what is termed an act of bankruptcy. These differences, coupled with the refinements introduced into other branches of the law, give rise to some very extraordinary results.

While the law of England gives the creditor an unnecessary degree of power over the debtor's person, it does not give him sufficient power over his property. In this respect, indeed, it is so very defective, that one is

* One creditor whose debt is to the amount of upwards of 100*l.*, or two whose debts amount to 150*l.*, or three whose debts amount to 200*l.*

almost tempted to think it had been intended to promote the practices of fraudulent debtors. The property of persons subjected to the bankrupt laws, as well as of those who *choose to subject themselves* to the insolvent laws, is placed at the disposal of assignees or trustees, for the benefit of their creditors; but when a person possessed of property, but not subject to the bankrupt laws, contracts debt, if he go abroad, or live within the rules of the King's Bench or the Fleet, or remain in prison without petitioning for relief, (in neither of which cases can he be subjected to the insolvent laws), he may, most probably, continue to enjoy the income arising from that property without molestation.

It is true, the law says that the creditors shall be authorised to seize the debtor's *lands and goods*, a description which an unlearned person would be apt to conclude was abundantly comprehensive; but the law is so interpreted that neither funded property, money, nor securities for money, is considered goods: if the debtor have a copyhold estate, it cannot be touched in any way whatever; if his estate be freehold, the creditor may, after a tedious process, receive the rents and profits, but no more, during the lifetime of his debtor. Should the debtor die before judgment against him in a court has been obtained, then, unless the debt be on bond, the creditor has no recourse upon the land left by the debtor, whatever may be its tenure; "nay, though his money, borrowed on note or bill, has been laid out in buying land, the debtor's heir takes that land, wholly discharged of the debt!"*

In consequeuce of this preposterously absurd system, an individual known to have a large income, and enjoying a proportionally extensive credit, may, if he go to Paris or Brussels, or confine himself within the rules of the King's Bench or the Fleet, defraud his creditors of every farthing he owes them, without their being

* Brougham's "Speech on the State of the Law," p. 108.

entitled to touch any part of his fortune. All owners of funded, monied, and copyhold property, have a license given them to cheat with impunity; and the only wonder is, not that some do, but that a vast number more do not, avail themselves of this singular privilege.

In point of fact, therefore, the power of imprisonment is operative only on the really necessitous—on those from whom it can extract little or nothing. The rich debtor is seldom subjected to its operation; he resorts, before a writ can be executed against him, either to the Continent or the Rules, and then laughs at the impotent wrath of those he has defrauded, and perhaps ruined. That such a system of law should be suffered to exist in a commercial country, and so little outcry be raised against it, is truly astonishing, and strikingly exemplifies the power of habit in reconciling us to the most pernicious absurdities. Can any one wonder at the frequency of fraudulent bankruptcy, when it is thus fostered and encouraged?

A reform of the bankrupt law, on the principles already mentioned, seems, therefore, to be imperiously called for. Its evils were forcibly stated by Mr. Brougham in his masterly "Speech on the State of the Law."* He has also pointed out the remedial measures necessary to be adopted to render this important department of commercial jurisprudence consistent with the obvious principles of justice and common sense. "Let the whole," says he, "of every man's property, real and personal—his real, of what kind soever, copyhold, leasehold, freehold; his personal, of whatever nature, debts, money, stock, chattels—be taken for the payment of all his debts equally, and in case of insolvency let all be distributed rateably; let all he possesses be sifted, bolted from him unsparingly, until all his creditors are satisfied by payment or composition; but let his person only be taken when he conceals his goods, or has merited punishment by fraudulent conduct."—

* Pp. 106—110

Were these measures adopted, and a certificate given to every man who has been divested of his property for behoof of his creditors, and against whom no charge of fraud has been established, there would be little room for improvement in the law of bankruptcy.

IV. The fourth duty of government is to adopt such means as may be most effectual for the prevention of confusion and fraud in the dealings of individuals.

In furtherance of this object, the government of every civilised country has endeavoured to enforce the equality of all weights and measures of the same denomination. By its attention in this respect, great additional facilities are given to all sorts of commercial transactions; and that confusion and difficulty are obviated that could not fail to arise in the making of bargains and the adjustment of contracts, were the standards to which reference is usually made not legally and clearly defined.

For the same reasons, governments have every where reserved to themselves the privilege of issuing coined money; and it is obvious, that if individuals were allowed to exercise this privilege, the confusion that would be occasioned by the issue of coins of different denominations, and of the same denomination but of different degrees of purity and weight, would go far to deprive society of the advantage it has derived from the introduction and use of money. I do not, however, think that government ought to confine its attention wholly to the issue of coined money. It appears to me that it is equally bound to extend it to the issue of paper money.

Signal as are the advantages that may be derived from the substitution of a paper currency in the place of gold, they depend, in a very great degree, on the fact of such paper being issued by parties of unquestionable solvency, and of its being readily exchangeable for the gold it professes to represent. The permission, so long granted in this country, to all individuals to issue notes to be used as money in the ordinary transactions of life, without requiring any guarantee for their payment, has been productive of the most disastrous results; the destruction of country bank paper having, on three different occasions within the course of the last forty years—in 1793, in 1814, 1815, and 1816, and in 1826—overspread the whole empire with bankruptcy and ruin. That the recurrence of such calamities ought, if possible, to be prevented, is a proposition that will hardly be disputed: and the simple and effectual way of doing this is, for government to interpose to hinder the issue of all notes payable on demand, except by those who have previously given security for their payment. It is to no purpose to contend, in opposition to this proposal, that notes not being *legal tenders,* every one is at liberty to reject them. Whatever they may be in law, they are practically, in very many districts, legal tenders; and any one who should decline their acceptance would be exposed to the greatest inconvenience. Besides, it should be observed, that mechanics, labourers, women, and in short all individuals, how incapable soever of forming an estimate of the solvency of the issuers of paper, are dealers in money; and their protection from loss in cases where they cannot protect themselves, is certainly not one of the least obvious duties of government. There is hardly, indeed, a case in which the public interference seems to be so loudly called for. The circumstances which excite confidence in the stability of bankers are mostly of a very deceitful description; and instances have repeatedly occurred in which insolvent establishments have gone on for years before the imposture was discovered. That the obligation to give security would be some inconvenience to bankers, is admitted; though, as they would get the dividends payable on their security if it consisted of stock, or its rents if it consisted of land, the inconvenience would be far less than might, at first, be supposed; and would hardly, indeed, be felt by the richer and more respectable bankers. But it is surely needless to add, that their convenience, or even existence as a class, is to be attended to in so far only as it is not inconsistent with the public safety; the last is the paramount consideration: and it has not yet been shewn how the public can be protected from that fraud and misconduct on the part of bankers, which has already had such injurious consequences, except by compelling them to give security for their notes.*

The prevention of the sale of all articles of gold or silver not marked with a public stamp, seems a judicious regulation. It is very difficult to ascertain when these metals are really pure; and in order to prevent the frauds that might in consequence happen, government performs this difficult operation for its subjects, and gives them a guarantee on which they may rely.

The enactments against the adulteration of articles of food with deleterious ingredients, seem to be highly proper. Those who are detected in carrying on such nefarious practices, besides being exposed to the loss of employment, should be made to feel the vengeance of the law.

It was formerly customary to regulate the mode of preparing or manufacturing various articles; but such attempts at regulation are now admitted, by all competent judges, to be most injurious. Their only effect is to check invention and discovery, to render the arts stationary, and to occasion the decline of every branch of industry subjected to their operation.†

* For a more complete discussion of this important subject, see the note on Money in my edition of the "Wealth of Nations."

† The influence of corporations, statutory apprenticeships, regulations as to the mode of manufacturing articles, &c., has been investigated in the ablest and most instructive manner in a Report presented by M. Vital Roux to the Chamber of Commerce of Paris in 1805. It is well worthy of an attentive perusal. I subjoin the following extract:—"Il y a très peu d'objets manufacturés qui puissent être soumis à la censure ou à l'examen d'un inspecteur, par la grande raison que cette censure n'aurait aucun effet, et que l'inspecteur le plus sûr et le plus impartial, c'est le consommateur. Toutes vos inspections, toutes vos règles, toutes les précautions de vos syndics, ne pourront pas faire que j'em-

The registration of all deeds and contracts affecting fixed property, would give great additional facilities to its transfer, and to the negotiation of loans upon it.

Persons possessed of landed property, who wish to borrow, most commonly endeavour to attain their end by granting a bond for the sum, or a mortgage over their estates. When the title under which the granter of the bond holds the estate is perfectly clear, this forms a very unexceptionable species of security; and in Scotland money can be raised upon such bonds at a comparatively low rate of interest. But in this part of the island there are several circumstances which tend very much to limit the practice, and to render it less advantageous than it might be. The main defect lies in the want of any means of readily ascertaining what the estate, and the title to it, really are, upon which it is proposed to borrow. With the exception of York and Middlesex, there is no register established in England of the settlements, mortgages, conveyances, and bonds, by which property may be affected; so that it becomes impossible, as Mr. Justice Blackstone has observed, for either the purchaser or lender of money upon an estate to know the burdens that may attach to it. This is necessarily a very great obstacle to the lending

ploie de l'étoffe qui ne me conviendra pas, quand elle aurait les attestations les plus authentiques qui m'en garantiraient la bonté. Le consommateur est le juge souverain en ces matières; c'est le seul tribunal compétent, et dont il n'y a point d'appel. Il est donc inutile de créer moyens de conciliation; car on ne peut faire changer la volonté de celui qui consomme, on ne peut être plus habile que son expérience. C'est au manufacturier à la rendre profitable à ses intérêts, s'il veut avoir du débit. Nous croyons donc, que l'intérêt même du manufacturier est le meilleur moyen de police pour les manufactures, et que les inspecteurs, les surveillans les plus sûrs, ce sont les consommateurs. Il ne faut pas chercher des chemins détournés, quand la route est connue de tout le monde: laissons donc aller les choses, puisqu'elles marchent sans secours, qu'elles arrivent par la force même de leurs courans au but que chacun se propose, et ne donnons pas des guides à ceux qui savent se conduire."

of money upon land, as well as to the conveyance of estates from one individual to another. Blackstone has stated that in the previously mentioned counties, where registers are kept, as many disputes arise from the inattention and omissions of parties as would most probably have arisen had they wanted registers.* But this must be from some defect in the plan of registration, which no doubt might be easily repaired. Were it, for example, declared that no deed or bond, affecting landed property, should be good against a third party unless it were entered in a public register, the rights of those who either purchased an estate, or advanced money upon it, would cease to be influenced by the circumstance of any previous but unregistered bond or conveyance being subsequently brought to light. A regulation of this sort would speedily teach parties the necessity of registering every deed or instrument affecting landed property, and would give that security to its purchasers, and to the lenders upon it, that is in all respects so desirable.

This system was adopted at a very early period in Scotland, and has been found to be productive of the best effects. All deeds touching landed property are regularly registered; and there is a special register kept, in which all deeds of entail are entered. These registers are open to the inspection of the public; and the first thing that is done by the bidder for an estate, or by a lender of money on bond upon it, is to desire his agent to inspect the register, to ascertain whether there are any burdens affecting it, and their nature and extent. In this way every man is made exactly aware of what he is doing; and if he either buy an estate with a vitiated title, or lend money upon one that is already encumbered up to its value, he has himself only to blame. A degree of security is thus given, both to purchasers and lenders, that is at once highly advantageous, and is not otherwise attainable.

* "Commentaries," book ii. chap. 20.

V. We have, in the *fifth* place, to consider the species of industrious undertakings which government may engage in or control, or to which it may lend some peculiar sanction.

Perhaps, with the single exception of the conveyance of letters, there is no branch of industry which government had not better leave to be conducted by individuals. It does not, however, appear that the post-office could be so well conducted by any one else as by government:—the latter alone can enforce perfect regularity in all its subordinate departments; can carry it to the smallest villages, and even beyond the frontier; and can combine all its separate parts into one uniform system, on which the public may confidently rely both for security and despatch. Besides providing for the speedy and safe communication of intelligence, the post-office has every where almost been rendered subservient to fiscal purposes, and made a source of revenue: and provided that the duty laid on letters be not so heavy as to oppose any very serious obstacle to the frequency and facility of correspondence, it seems to be a very unobjectionable tax, and one that is paid and collected with comparatively little trouble and inconvenience.

The construction and police of roads, harbours, &c. are among the most important objects to which the attention of government should be directed. In some countries, as France, the administration of roads is placed in the hands of government; while in others, as England, it is placed in the hands of the gentry of the different counties, who act under authority given them by the legislature. Each plan has its peculiar advantages and defects; but the balance on the side of advantage seems, on the whole, to preponderate very decidedly in favour of the English system. The French system is perhaps preferable, were it applied only to the great lines of road; but these bear a very small proportion to the cross and other roads with which every extensive kingdom either is or ought to be intersected. And it seems reasonable to suppose that, when the gentry and those most directly interested in having good roads, and on whom the expense of their construction and maintenance principally falls, have to superintend their execution and repair, they will be made and maintained better and cheaper than if their management were left wholly to the care of engineers employed by government, and responsible only to it.

It is the duty of government to take care that the tolls be not oppressive; and to assist, by making grants, in enabling roads to be carried through districts, and bridges to be constructed, where the necessary funds could not otherwise be raised. The money advanced on account of the Menaï bridge is of this description; and has been judiciously and profitably expended.

As a general rule, however, government ought to be exceedingly shy about advancing funds for the prosecution of undertakings that have failed in the hands of private individuals, or that will not be engaged in by them. The money expended on the Caledonian Canal, and on several canals in Ireland, executed by government, has been little better than thrown away.

There are some branches of industry which must be carried on in some degree in common, but with respect to the prosecution of which the views and interests of individuals are so very various, that government is obliged to interfere to regulate their respective pretensions. The salmon fishery is an instance of this sort. Government has not only to fix when the fishery shall begin and terminate, but it has also to decide as to how far the proprietors, near the mouths of rivers, shall be entitled to carry their weirs and other fishing machinery into the channel.

Undertakings in which the hazard is considerable, or that require, in order to their successful prosecution, a larger amount of capital than can be conveniently furnished by private individuals, are usually carried on by companies, which frequently require the sanction of the legislature to their formation. When these bodies claim no peculiar privileges, but are formed on the principle of coming into fair and open competition with each other and with individuals, there does not seem, in ordinary cases, to be any good reason for opposing their incorporation. But in the event of their claiming any peculiar privileges, or if the purpose for which they seek to be incorporated would give them such privileges, the fair presumption being that they will employ them to promote their own private interests, in opposition to those of the public, they should not be incorporated without the maturest deliberation. Still, however, there are cases in which it is for the public advantage that companies with such privileges should be established, under proper modifications. A city is ill supplied with water; there is a copious spring ten or twenty miles distant, and a company offer to undertake the task of bringing this water into the city, on their getting an act authorising them to appropriate the spring, and to lay pipes or construct an aqueduct for the conveyance of the water. In this case the object in view is most desirable: but it is plain that, were the authority they require given unconditionally to the company, it would be in their power to raise the price of water to the highest level, and to make an enormous profit, to the great injury of the inhabitants. To prevent such an abuse, the dividend on the company's stock ought to be limited; and it should be enacted, that all that a moderate water-duty produced over and above this limited dividend, should be applied to buy up the stock of the company; so that ultimately the entire charge on account of water might be got rid of.

It is sometimes necessary, in order to encourage the formation of a company for some desirable object, such as the lighting of a middling-sized town with gas, that it should get an exclusive privilege for a given number of years. But this ought in no case to be ceded without due examination, and without the insertion of conditions, to protect the public from any extortion on the part of the company.

No exclusive company ought ever to be established for carrying on any sort of manufacture, or for conducting any branch either of internal or external commerce. No such institution, formed for such an object, has ever been any thing else than a public nuisance. If it be necessary that those engaged in any particular trade should contribute to defray some public expenses required for its prosecution, they may be formed into a *regulated* company; that is, a company into which every one may enter on paying a moderate fine, or annual premium, being then at liberty to trade on his own account, and to act in all respects according to his own judgment and discretion. The necessity of providing for the expense of the armaments, without which it was alleged the trade with India could not be conducted, formed, during a lengthened period, the only circumstance urged in defence of the exclusive and oppressive privileges granted to the East India Company. But admitting that these armaments were necessary, and that government declined to provide them out of the ordinary revenue at its disposal, it is obvious that their cost might have been defrayed either by a peculiar duty on Indian exports and imports appropriated to that object, or by forming the traders into a *regulated* company. The latter, indeed, was the mode in which the Levant and Russia trades were long conducted, and the expenses of a public nature attached to them provided for. And had either of these plans been adopted in conducting the East India trade, it is abundantly certain that it would have been rendered infinitely more extensive and beneficial than it has been.

The businesses of insurance and banking are those which are most commonly prosecuted in this country by companies. With the exception of the Bank of England, none of these companies enjoys any peculiar privilege. But I have elsewhere endeavoured to shew, that the monopoly granted to the Bank is one which ought, under certain regulations, to be continued to that establishment.*

No authority ought ever to be granted to companies or individuals to undertake any work, however useful, by which the private property of others may be affected, without providing for their full indemnity. To act on any other principle would be to shake the security of property; it would be injuring one set of individuals for the benefit of some other set.

The law with respect to patents for new inventions and discoveries in the arts, is encumbered with several difficulties. The expediency of granting patents has been disputed, though, as it would seem, without any sufficient reason. Were they refused, the inducement to make discoveries would, in many cases, be very much weakened; at the same time that it would plainly be for the interest of every one who had made a discovery to endeavour, if possible, to conceal it. And, notwithstanding the difficulties in the way of concealment, they are not insuperable; and it is believed that several important inventions have been lost, from the secret dying with their authors. On the other hand, it is not easy to decide as to the term for which the patent or exclusive privilege should be granted. Some have proposed that it should be made perpetual; but this would be a very great obstacle to the progress of improvements, and would lead to the most injurious results. Perhaps the term of fourteen years, to which the duration of a patent is limited in England, is as proper a one as could be suggested. It may be too short for some inventions, and too long for others, but, on the whole, it seems a pretty fair average.

Previously to the reign of Queen Anne, it was common to grant patents without any condition except that they should be for really new inventions. But it was then ordered, that those who obtained patents should deliver a

* "Wealth of Nations," vol. iv. p. 313.

minute and accurate description or *specification* of the invention for which the patent is granted, into the Court of Chancery. This was a very judicious regulation. It secures the invention from being lost, and the moment the patent expires every one is in a condition to profit by it.*

VI. We have now, in the *sixth* and last place, to consider the means proper to be adopted for securing the property and persons of the citizens from such natural casualties as they might be subject to without the interference of government.

The measures of a public character devised for the protection of property from natural casualties, are principally confined to those intended to give security to navigation. Without the co-operation or sanction of government, light-houses could not be erected, nor safe and convenient harbours constructed. To defray the expense of such works, a revenue of some sort or other must be provided; and as it belongs to the legislature to say how this revenue shall be raised, or to find the funds for their construction and maintenance, it must also belong to it to decide as to the propriety of undertaking them. No doubt can be entertained as to the great additional facility and security given to navigation by the erection of so many light-houses, and the formation and improvement of so many docks and harbours, during the last half century. At the same time, however, it is highly expedient, with a view to the encouragement of commerce, that the charges laid on shipping, on account of these works, should be kept as low as possible. Where they are heavy, the navigator is too often tempted to resort to less secure but less expensive channels.

* For farther information on this subject the reader is referred to Godson's work on the "Law of Copyrights and Patents;" and to the "Report of the Committee of the House of Commons on Patents," particularly the valuable evidence of Mr. Farey.

Except in so far as they may be obviated by the establishment of a good system of police, government can do but little to protect property on land from the casualties to which it is subject. It may, indeed, enact regulations, in order to guard against fire, as to the thickness of party-walls in cities, and the materials to be used in roofing, &c.; but farther than this it had better not interfere, but leave the care of property to the vigilance of its owners.

The measures of a public character intended to protect the persons of the citizens against casualties, have principally for their object to prevent the spread of contagious diseases, and to secure the proper education of medical men.

From a belief that the plague is contagious, and that the infection may be conveyed to a great distance, it has long been usual, in all civilised countries, to adopt precautions to hinder its importation. For this purpose, all ships coming from places where the plague is a prevalent disease, are obliged to anchor for forty days in some particular port or road; and the individuals coming from them are obliged to resort, for the same period, to a public building prepared for their reception, denominated a *lazaretto,* where they are placed under surveillance, and are not allowed to have any intercourse with any one except the officers of health. The ships and individuals so confined are said to be performing *quarantine.* If at the end of forty days no symptoms of disease appear, they are set at liberty.

It should, however, be stated, that the fact of the plague being contagious has been denied, and that the precautions referred to have been said to be useless, and to have no other effect than the imposition of some very vexatious and burdensome restraints on commerce. Perhaps, indeed, these precautions may, in some instances, have been carried too far; but in a matter of this sort, innovations should not be rashly adopted: and far better evidence than any hitherto laid before the public would be necessary to warrant the total abolition of all restraints on the intercourse with infected countries.

When a virulent contagious disease breaks out in any particular district, it is the duty of government, by surrounding it with a cordon of troops, to prevent, if possible, its further progress. Such a measure may, indeed, occasion a greater intensity of mortality within the infected district; but the safety of a few individuals is not to be purchased by seriously endangering the lives of many more.

Much difference of opinion has existed as to the extent to which government ought to interfere in recommending or enforcing the adoption of any efficient remedy against a mortal disease; such, for example, as vaccination. In such cases it had better, perhaps, confine its attention to the institution of experiments and examinations as to the facts, laying the result before the public, and leaving to individuals to use their own discretion with respect to them.

It has been argued, that government is only imposing on itself a needless task when it interferes to regulate and ascertain the qualifications of those engaged in the medical profession; for that the desire of promoting their own interest will, in that as in all other businesses, insure proficiency. But there is a very wide difference between the employment of those who exercise their art on the bodies of men, and those who exercise it on some sort of raw or manufactured produce. If an individual employ a tailor to make him a coat, he will not employ him again unless it be made to his mind; nor, though the cloth were spoiled, would the loss be considerable: but if an individual employ a physician, surgeon, or apothecary, to prescribe for him, he may, in the event of the person so employed being ignorant of his art, lose his life; while, owing to the difficulty of ascertaining when death is occasioned by the natural progress of disease, or by the unskilfulness of the practitioner, the business of the latter may not be materially diminished; and he may continue, for an indefinite period, to prosecute his destructive career. It does, therefore, seem to be quite clear, that government is bound to take such measures as may be effectual to secure the proper education of medical men; and that no one should be permitted to practise who has not been properly educated, and has not been examined and obtained a certificate of his capacity from some public board constituted for that purpose. All individuals, though very many are nowise fitted to judge as to their qualifications, must occasionally resort to medical men; and it is the duty of government to provide that the lives of its subjects be not sacrificed to ignorance, cupidity, or quackery.

In some countries it is usual to prohibit the sale of poisons, except under certain regulations; and the many crimes that are perpetrated here by means of arsenic, seem to evince the propriety of making its sale illegal, except when the buyer brings a note from a physician, specifying the quantity required, and the purpose to which it is meant to be applied.

It has been usual, in order to guard against accidents, to limit the number of passengers to be carried by stage-coaches, and to subject packet-boats and other public conveyances to examination.

I shall briefly touch, in another part of this work, on the interference of government with respect to public education, and the organisation of a provision for the support of the poor. It belongs to the politician and moral philosopher to discuss how far, and in what way, it should interfere to strengthen and promote moral and religious habits.

The previous observations may, perhaps, suffice to give a general idea of the sort of objects with respect to which the interference of government is required, in conducting the ordinary business of society, and the extent to which it should be carried. It cannot, however, be too strongly or too often impressed upon those in authority, that non-interference ought to be the leading principle of their policy, and interference the exception only; that in all ordinary cases individuals should be left to shape their conduct according to their own judgment and discretion; and that no interference should ever be made on any speculative or doubtful grounds, but only when its necessity is apparent, or when it can be clearly made out that it will be productive of *public* advantage. The maxim *pas trop gouverner* should never be absent from the recollection of legislators and ministers. Whenever they set about regulating, they are treading a path encompassed with difficulties; and while they advance with extreme caution, they should be ready to stop the moment they do not see the way clearly before them, and are not urgently impelled, by a sense of public duty, to go forward.

PRINCIPLES

OF

POLITICAL ECONOMY.

PART II.

VALUE AND PRICE.

THE various methods by which labour may be rendered most productive, and the relation and dependence of the different kinds of industry, being previously traced and exhibited, we now proceed to the *second division* of our subject, or to an investigation of the laws regulating the value and price of the products of industry.

In treating of the production of wealth, it was not necessary to examine whether the labour required to appropriate and produce commodities, and without the expenditure of which they would be wholly destitute of value, was the sole limiting principle and mèasure of that value; or whether it was not partly derived from other causes, and partly only from labour. But an acquaintance with the circumstances which determine the value of commodities, in all the different stages of society, is necessary to enable us to ascertain, with due precision, the principles which regulate their distribution.

CHAPTER I.

Value of two Sorts—Exchangeable Value—How it is determined—Conditions required to render a Commodity invariable in its Exchangeable Value—Real Value—How it is determined—Conditions required to render a Commodity invariable in its Real Value—Quantity of Labour required to produce a Commodity different from the Quantity of Labour for which it will exchange—Corn not invariable in its Value—Changes in the Value of Money.

I ENDEAVOURED to shew, at the commencement of this work, that the value of commodities, and their utility, were totally distinct qualities, and could not be confounded, or regarded in the same point of view, without leading to the most erroneous conclusions. An article is useful, or possessed of utility, when it has the power or capacity of exciting, satisfying, or gratifying one or more of the various wants and desires of man. But an article is not valuable, or possessed of value, unless it may be exchanged for a certain quantity of labour, or of some other article or species of produce, obtainable only through the exertion of labour.

Without the possession of utility of some sort or other, no article will ever be desired. But the most useful article, if it be a spontaneous production of nature, and may be freely enjoyed by every individual, is wholly destitute of value; for no one will either labour, or give the produce of labour, to obtain that with which Providence has gratuitously supplied him. It is indispensable, in order that an article may have value, that it should require some expenditure of labour, or, which is the same thing, some sacrifice of sweat and toil, in its acquisition. The maximum of utility, if it be obtained independently of this sacrifice, can give no value to any thing. What can be more useful than atmospheric air and the rays of the sun? and what can be more completely destitute of value?

An article or product possessed of utility and value must derive the latter from one of two sources, or from both. Labour must have been required for the production or appropriation of a valuable article, or it must exist in a limited quantity, or under such circumstances that the supply is inferior to the demand. All those articles and products of which the supply may be indefinitely increased, and which are not subjected to any artificial restraints, derive their value either wholly from the labour expended upon them, or partly from that cause, and partly from the accidental circumstance of their supply being inferior to the demand; but the value of such articles and products as exist only in limited quantities, and the supply of which does not admit of an indefinite extension, or is subjected to a natural or an artificial monopoly, is altogether independent of the labour required to produce them; and is derived partly, as in the case of waterfalls, from the labour they are fitted to save, and partly, as in the case of antique gems, statues, &c. from the mere competition of those who wish to obtain them.

We must, therefore, carefully distinguish between the exchangeable value of an article, or the quantity of produce or labour for which it will exchange, and its *cost*, or, as it is more commonly termed, its real value; meaning, by cost or real value, the quantity of labour originally required to produce or acquire an article.

I. Exchangeable Value.—The capacity of exchanging for or buying other things is inherent in all commodities which, at the same time that they are in demand, are not spontaneous productions; but it can neither be manifested nor appreciated except when they are compared with each other, or with labour. It is, indeed, quite impossible to speak of the value of a commodity without referring either to some other commodity, or to labour, as a standard. No article or product can have any exchangeable value, except in relation to something else that is or may be exchanged for it. We might as well talk about absolute height or absolute depth, as about absolute value. A is said to possess value, *because* it has the power of exchanging for some quantity of B or C; and it is evident, that the quantity of B or C for which A exchanges, forms the only attainable measure of, or expression for, the value of A; just as the quantity of A forms the only attainable measure of, or expression for the value of, B or C.

It follows, from the circumstance of exchangeable value being the power which a commodity has of exchanging for other commodities, or for labour, that the exchangeable value of no single commodity can vary without occasioning a simultaneous variation in the exchangeable value of those with which it is compared. Suppose that a bushel of wheat exchanged, in 1700, for an ounce of silver, and that it now exchanges for two ounces: on this hypothesis, it is evident that wheat has doubled in value as compared with silver; or, which is the same thing, that silver has lost half its value as compared with wheat. This case is, *mutatis mutandis,* the identical case of all commodities or products exchanged for each other. If A rise, it must be in relation to something else, as B; and if B fall, it must be in relation to something else, as A; so that it is obviously impossible to change the relation of A to B, without, at the same time, changing that of B to A.

It appears, therefore, that no commodity can be constant or invariable in its exchangeable value, unless it will at all times exchange for, or purchase, the same quantity of all other commodities and of labour. Suppose A exchanges for one B, two C, three D, &c. its exchangeable value will be constant, provided it always preserves its present relation to them, but not otherwise. And it is obvious, that to communicate this constancy of value to A, it would be indispensable that those circumstances, whatever they may be, that now determine its relation to, or its power of exchanging for or purchasing the commodities, B, C, D, &c. should, in all time to come, continue to exert precisely the same influence over it and them.* Experience, by exhibiting the exchangeable value of commodities in a state of constant fluctuation, sufficiently proves that the circumstances under which they are actually produced are widely different from those now supposed. Perhaps, however, it may be worth while to observe, that had commodities been really produced under such circumstances, not A only, but every other commodity, would have been an invariable standard; as any given commodity in a market may be used as a standard to which to refer the value of all the rest. It is evident, too, that the possession of such an invariable standard would be of no use whatever: all that it would teach us would be, that the causes which first made A exchange for B, C, &c. continued equally to affect them all; but of the nature of those causes, and the intensity of their operation, it would leave us wholly in the dark.

II. Real Value.—Having thus ascertained that the exchangeable value of any one commodity must always be expressed by the relation it bears to some other commodity or to labour, the next subject claiming our attention is, the investigation of the circumstances which determine this relation, or of the regulating principle of value.

A person destitute of an article, and wishing to acquire it, has only two ways of effecting his object; he must set about producing the article, or he must exchange a

* The conditions essential to an invariable measure of exchangeable value were first clearly pointed out in the "Dissertation on the Nature, Measures, and Causes of Value," p. 17.

quantity of labour, or the produce or equivalent of a quantity of labour, for it. In either case, the *cost* of the article is to be estimated by the quantity of labour, directly or indirectly expended in its acquisition. Demand may, therefore, be considered as the ultimate source or origin of both exchangeable and real value; for it is the desire of individuals to possess themselves of articles that is the sole cause of their being produced or appropriated; but it is the quantity of labour, or of sweat and toil, required to render a demand effectual, or to produce or obtain articles or products, that forms the single principle by which their cost or real value is, in all cases, regulated and determined.

It has been already stated, that some commodities exist only in limited quantities, and are, consequently, subjected to a natural monopoly; while the production of others, the supply of which might be indefinitely increased, is sometimes subjected to artificial restraints. The exchangeable value of these commodities bears no definite proportion to their real value, but varies in every different degree, according to the closeness of the monopoly, and the competition for them. They may, however, be always readily discriminated from those that are freely produced in unlimited quantities; and are but few and unimportant, when compared with the latter.

If the demand and supply of freely produced commodities were always exactly proportioned to each other—that is, if the supply brought to market were uniformly such as could be taken off by those who were desirous of obtaining them, and willing to pay the cost of their production, their exchangeable value would always bear the same proportion to their real value, or cost. That this would be so is obvious; for under the circumstances supposed, there is nothing that could determine, or indeed affect the exchangeable value of commodities, except the labour expended upon them.

Practically speaking, the supply of commodities is, owing to an infinity of causes, such as changes of fashion, of seasons, and of the usual channels of commercial intercourse, the speculations of merchants, &c. seldom or never adjusted precisely in proportion to the effectual demand, or the demand of those who are able and willing to pay them. But it will be shewn in the next chapter, that fluctuations of value, arising from these causes, are confined within certain limits; that the producers always exert themselves to reduce the value of those that yield more than the fair average rate of profit, and to elevate those that do not; and that the *common* level of value and price which is thus attained, may be considered as identical with the cost of production, being, generally speaking, determined by the quantity of labour required to produce commodities. But as my present object is only to establish the leading or constant principles with respect to value, I shall suppose that these accidental causes of variation do not exist, or that allowance has been made for them, confining myself to an investigation of the circumstances which determine the value of freely produced commodities, the supply of which is about commensurate with the demand.

Suppose that a commodity, A, the supply of which is neither in excess nor defect, varies in relation to some other commodity, B, supplied in a similar way; the cause of this variation will be found in the circumstance of the labour required to produce them having varied in the same proportion. Thus, suppose A and B are now equal: if, twelve months hence, A should be worth two B, this change must be occasioned by the quantity of labour required to produce A having doubled, while that required to produce B has remained stationary; or by that required to produce B having diminished a half, while that required to produce A has been constant; or the labour required to produce them both may have varied in the same or in opposite directions, but so that the quantity required to produce A has doubled as compared with the quantity required to produce B. There cannot, however, be, in most cases, much practical difficulty in deciding in which of these modes the variation has been really brought about. An improvement is made in the manufacture of cotton, for example, and its value immediately declines as compared with other things in which no improvement has been made, or in which the improvement has been less; and it would obviously do this, not because these others have increased in real value, but because it has sunk. Thus, if we suppose that a still greater improvement had been, at the same time, made in the woollen manufacture, cottons would rise as compared with woollens, not because they had risen in real value, but because they had not fallen so much as woollens.*

The produce obtained by equal quantities of toil and trouble is not always equal: but *real* value depends on the quantity of labour expended, and not on the mode in which it is expended, or on the degree of its productiveness. The inventions and discoveries which augment the

* The acute and ingenious author of the "Templars' Dialogues," ("London Magazine," May 1824, p. 551,) has stated, that "It is possible for A continually to increase in value— in *real* value observe—and yet command a continually decreasing quantity of B." This passage has been controverted by the author of the "Critical Dissertation on the Nature, Measures, and Causes of Value." Nothing, however, can be more perfectly correct than the statement in the "Dialogues."—A and B have been produced by certain quantities of labour; but more labour is now required to produce A, and a still greater proportional quantity to produce B: under these circumstances, A must obviously have increased in real value, or in the estimation of its producers, for it has cost them a greater sacrifice of toil and trouble; but as A has not increased so fast in real value as B, it is plain it will now exchange for, or purchase a less quantity of B. Had the author of the "Dissertation" perceived this distinction, he would, most probably, have spared not a few of his remarks on the statements advanced by Mr. Ricardo, as well as by the author of the "Dialogues."—*Dissertation on the Nature, &c.* p. 41.

productiveness of labour, add nothing either to its real value, or to that of the commodities produced by its means. A day's labour in a rude state of society, when the arts are in their infancy, and the machines used by the labourer comparatively inefficient, yields a very different quantity of produce from a day's labour in an advanced and civilised period, when the arts are highly improved, and the most powerful machinery universally introduced. Nothing, however, can be more obvious than that the sacrifice made by the labourer is as great in the former case as in the latter. The variation is not in the amount of physical force, or of labour, exerted by the agent that produces, but merely in the mode in which that force is applied. But however the same quantity of labour may be laid out, and whatever may be its produce, it unavoidably occasions the *same sacrifice* to those by whom it is performed; and hence it is plain, that the products of equal quantities of labour, or of toil and trouble, must, how much soever they may differ in magnitude, always be of precisely the same real value. Nothing that is valuable can be obtained except by the exertion of labour, or physical force. This is the price that man must pay for all things with which he is not spontaneously furnished; and it is by the magnitude of the price so paid, and not by the magnitude of the things themselves, that their real value is to be estimated.

A given quantity of labour is not, therefore, to be considered in the same light as a given quantity of its produce, or of commodities: for, whether the quantity of commodities produced by a fixed quantity of labour does or does not vary, the value of that quantity, in the estimation of the producer, is necessarily constant; and he will always be disposed to exchange it for an equal quantity, or the produce of an equal quantity of other men's labour. Suppose an individual could produce *two* pecks of wheat by a day's labour in 1820, and that he can now produce only *one* peck by the same expenditure of labour; this single peck will be deemed by him, and every one else, of exactly the same real value that the two pecks were before; for it has cost the same amount of sweat and toil to raise it; and it will, consequently, exchange for, or buy the same quantity of such commodities as continue to be produced by equal outlays of labour as in 1820, that the two pecks did then.

When it is said that a given quantity, or the produce of a given quantity of labour, is always of equal *real* value, it is not meant to affirm that it always fetches the same *real* price, or that it always exchanges for the produce of an unvarying quantity of labour. What is meant is, that in a free and open market, when the supply of commodities is nearly proportioned to the effectual demand, the quantities of labour required for their production determine the proportions in which they exchange for each other, and for labour. It is material, however, to observe, that, speaking generally, commodities uniformly exchange for or buy more labour, or the produce of more labour, than was required for their production. And unless such were the case, a capitalist could have no motive to lay out stock on the employment of labour; for his profit depends on his getting back the produce of a greater quantity of labour than he advances. When he buys labour he gives the produce of that which has been performed for that which is *to be* performed. It is obvious, too, inasmuch as there is no fund except capital, or the commodities already produced and actually existing in a country, to feed and support labourers, that the quantity of produce they receive in exchange for their labour, or their wages, must vary according to the variations in the amount of that capital, and in their number. At one period, they may be so numerous, compared with capital, that a labourer may be willing to offer a future day's work for the produce of five or six hours' work already performed; while, at another period, their number, as compared with capital, may be so much reduced, that they may be able to obtain the produce of *ten* hours' performed labour for *twelve* hours' future labour. But the real, and, most commonly, also, the exchangeable value of those commodities, on which *equal quantities* of labour have been laid out, is not in any degree affected by these variations. The change is not in the principle that regulates and determines value—the physical exertion, or sweat and toil of the labourer—but in what he obtains for it. What he produces, or acquires by equal quantities of labour, always costs him the same sacrifice, and has, therefore, the same real value, whether it be large or small. He gives a constant, but receives a variable quantity in its stead.

This distinction must be kept constantly in view. Dr. Smith seems to have considered the quantity of labour required to produce a commodity as an equivalent expression for the quantity of labour for which it will exchange; and that, consequently, it might either be said that the real value of A is to the real value of B as the quantity of labour required to produce A is to the quantity required to produce B, or that the real value of A is to the real value of B as the quantity of labour for which A will exchange is to the quantity for which B will exchange. But the difference between these two propositions is, in most cases, nothing less than the difference between what is true and what is false. And it is to Mr. Ricardo's sagacity, in distinguishing between them, and in shewing that while the first is undeniably correct, the second, instead of being an equivalent proposition, is frequently opposed to the first, and, consequently, quite inaccurate, that the theory of the science is indebted for a very considerable improvement.

In stating that the quantity of labour required to produce commodities is at once the only determining principle and measure of their real, and, generally speaking, also of their exchangeable value, it is taken for granted, of course, that all sorts of labour are reduced to the same common standard of intensity. The inequalities in the physical force of those individuals who have attained to their full growth, and who are perfectly formed, are in themselves immaterial, and entirely disappear when considered in a general point of view. Suppose the work performed by the generality of full-grown men, in a given time, to amount to any certain quantity (a): if, on the one hand, the labour of a few individuals should amount to a little more than this common quantity (to $a + \frac{a}{10}$, or $a + \frac{a}{15}$, &c.), it is abundantly certain, that the labour of as many will, on the other hand, fall as much short of it, (to $a - \frac{a}{10}$, or $a - \frac{a}{15}$, &c.) So that, whatever excess may obtain among one set of labourers being fully balanced by a corresponding deficiency among another set, the common and average real value of all sorts of commodities will be proportioned to, or coincident with, the common and average quantities of labour required for their production.

It will be shewn, in a subsequent chapter, that the circumstance of certain sorts of labour being of the description which is called skilled, and of their being paid at a higher rate than those common sorts that all may perform, depends on principles which do not in any degree affect the correctness of the principle we have been endeavouring to establish with respect to the real value of commodities.

The result of these investigations may be thus briefly recapitulated:—

1*st*, That nothing can possess either real or exchangeable value, unless it be in demand, and unless some portion of voluntary human labour be required for its production or appropriation.

2d, That a commodity possessed of *real* must also be possessed of *exchangeable* value, and conversely.

3d, That the real value, or cost, of a commodity is dependent on, and exactly proportioned to, the quantity of labour required for its production or appropriation.

4th, That the exchangeable value of a commodity is dependent partly and principally on its cost, and partly on accidental variations of supply and demand; and is measured by the quantity of any other commodity, or of labour, for which it will exchange.

Assuming, then, that the amount of labour expended on the production of commodities is the sole determining principle of their *real* value, it follows, that, if any commodity required at all times the same quantity of labour for its production, its real value would be *invariable.* It is obvious, however, that there can be no such commodity. The varying fertility of the soils to which recourse must successively be had, and the improvements that are every now and then occurring in the application of labour, occasion perpetual variations in the quantities of labour required to produce all sorts of commodities. And therefore it is not to any one commodity, or set of commodities, but to some given quantity of labour, that we must refer for an unvarying standard of *real* value.

But though a commodity did exist requiring at all times the same quantity of labour for its production, it could not be used, without certain precautions, as a standard by which to measure variations in the exchangeable value of other commodities, or of labour; for its value in exchange might vary, from the influence of variations in its demand and supply, or from causes extrinsic to, and independent on, the quantity of labour required for its production; or it might vary from similar causes operating on the commodity with which it was to be compared. If A were always produced by the same quantity of labour, and if B and C were produced by varying quantities of labour, then, if value in exchange depended on nothing but quantities of labour, or if it always bore the same proportion to these quantities, we should be able, by comparing B and C with A, to say at once whether their value had remained constant, or to point out the precise extent to which it had varied. But when there are other causes which may affect the value of A itself, as well as the values of B and C, it is obvious we should not be able, without referring to periods of average duration, or previously inquiring whether the supply of each article was exactly adjusted according to the effective demand, to say, if a variation took place in the relation that had formerly obtained amongst them, whether it had been occasioned by causes exclusively affecting A, or exclusively affecting B and C, or whether they had all been affected, though in different degrees.

But notwithstanding what has now been stated, Dr. Smith, and, more recently, M. Say, the Marquis Garnier, and others, have contended that corn may be assumed as an invariable standard of value; and that, taking the prices of corn for a few years together, to get rid of the disturbing effects of variable harvests, whatever fluctuation may take place in them must be in the value of the money or commodity in which the price of corn is estimated, and not in the value of corn itself, which they regard as constant. Founding upon this hypothesis, attempts have been made, by comparing the prices of corn with the prices of other things mentioned in history, to determine the fluctuations of their value. It is, however, to be regretted, that the learning and ingenuity displayed in this research have not been more profitably employed. It is hardly necessary, after what has been previously stated, to make any observations to shew that the hypothesis referred to is altogether visionary. Dr. Smith says, that the value of corn is invariable, because the demand is always proportioned to the supply; — increasing when it increases, and diminishing when it diminishes. Now, admitting that such is the case, what has this constancy of demand to do with the value of corn? It will not, it is true, be produced if it be not demanded; but its value, when produced, depends, not on the demand, but on the quantity of labour required for its production. The producers of corn in Kentucky, Poland, Holland, and England, have all an effectual demand for what they produce; but owing to the varying fertility of the soils which they cultivate, or to the varying quantities of labour required to produce an equal quantity of corn, its real, and, consequently, also its exchangeable value and price, is not half so great in some of those countries as in others.

If we knew the quantity of labour that had been, at an average, required to produce a bushel of wheat in Italy, in the reign of Augustus, and what is now required for the production of the same quantity in England, we should be able readily to determine their value with respect to each other, and the value of all other things the relation of which to corn was known at both periods. It is plain, however, that if we knew the quantity of labour required to produce any other commodity at the periods in question, it would serve for a standard quite as well as corn. There is nothing about the latter to render it invariable more than there is about most other things. M. Say, indeed, *supposes* that the effect of improvements in agriculture in reducing the price of corn, is about equal to the effect which the necessity of resorting to poorer soils has in raising it!* But if this were really the case, agricultural industry would be always equally productive; and capital, and consequently population, would increase with equal rapidity, whatever might be the quality of the soils under tillage. I shall afterwards endeavour to trace and exhibit the real effects of improvements: at present it is enough to remark, that the supposition that they are in

* "Cours d'Economie Politique," tom. iii. p. 7.

all cases capable of neutralising the influence of increasing sterility, is inconsistent with the best-established principles, and contradicted by the experience of every nation.

Although, however, the mere comparison of corn and silver is incapable of communicating any information with respect to the variations that have taken place in the real value of either or both of them, still it is, on several accounts, desirable to know the proportion which the one has borne to the other. According to M. Say,* or rather to M. Garnier,† the hectolitre of wheat exchanged, at an average, in antiquity, for 289 grains of pure silver; and for

245 grains, under Charlemagne;
219 „ under Charles VII., of France, towards 1450;
333 „ in 1514;—(America was discovered in 1492.)
731 „ in 1536;
1130 „ in 1610;
1280 „ in 1640;
1342 „ in 1789;
1610 „ in 1820.

There is, however, reason to think that M. Garnier has undervalued the price of wheat in antiquity. The learned M. Létronne‡ has endeavoured to shew, that the price of the hectolitre of wheat in Greece, in the age of Socrates, should not be reckoned at less than 468 grains of pure silver; and that its price at Rome, in the reign of Augustus, was about 550 grains. The statements of M. Létronne seem to be fully established; and if so, it will

* "Cours d'Economie Politique," vol. iii. p. 24.

† "Richesse des Nations," vol. v. pp. 152—184.

‡ "Considérations Générales sur l'Evaluation des Monnoies Grecques et Romaines," pp. 113—124.

follow, that the value of silver, as compared with corn, instead of having, as M. Say supposes, fallen to *one-sixth* of its value in antiquity, has not fallen to quite *one-fourth* of its value in Greece, about 400 years before the Christian era, and to about *one-third* only of its value in Rome, at its commencement.

CHAPTER II.

Cost of Production or real Value the regulating Principle of exchangeable Value and Price—Influence of Variations in the Demand for and Supply of Commodities on their Price — Influence of Monopolies—Average Price always coincident with Cost of Production.

I ENDEAVOURED, in the foregoing chapter, to elucidate the leading and fundamental principles with respect to value, by investigating the circumstances which determine the value of commodities, when the supply is adjusted according to the effective demand. In the present chapter I shall endeavour to appreciate the influence of variations in the demand and supply of commodities on their value and price, whatever may be the source of these variations.

To render what has to be stated on these subjects, and those that will be discussed in the following chapter, perfectly intelligible, I shall anticipate so far on what will hereafter be more fully proved, as to assume that the wages earned by those who are engaged as labourers in the different branches of industry, are, all things considered, either equal, or differ only by so small a quantity as may be neglected without occasioning any material error; and that the profits realised by those who undertake different businesses are in the same predicament. It is obvious, indeed, that such must be the case: if, on the one hand, the profits or wages of those who undertake or employ themselves in difficult, hazardous, dirty, unhealthy, or disagreeable businesses, were to exceed what was necessary to afford them a reasonable compensation for the greater skill required, or the peculiar inconveniences to which they are exposed, they would be in a better situation than others; and there would, consequently, be an influx of capital and labourers into those businesses, until that natural equilibrium that must always subsist amongst the different branches of industry had been restored: and if, on the other hand, the inconveniences attending any particular business are not sufficiently compensated to those engaged in it, they gradually withdraw from it, till, by the diminution of the supply, the price of the article is raised, so as to yield the necessary indemnification. The law of competition, or the attention paid by every individual to his own interest, will not allow this principle to be infringed upon for any considerable period; and, speaking generally, will insure the equality, all things taken into account, of wages, and also of profits, in different occupations.

The cost, or real value, of commodities,—denominated by Dr. Smith and the Marquis Garnier *natural* or *necessary* price—has been shewn to be identical with the quantity of labour required to produce them and bring them to market. Now, it is quite obvious that it is this cost that is the permanent and ultimate regulator of the exchangeable value or price of every commodity which is not subjected to a monopoly, and which may be indefinitely increased in quantity by the application of fresh capital and labour to its production. That the market price of such commodities and their cost do not always coincide, is certain; but they cannot, for any considerable period, be far separated, and have a constant tendency to equality. If, owing to any one circumstance or combination of circumstances, a commodity were brought to market and exchanged for a greater amount, either of other commodities or of money, than was required to defray the cost of its production, including the common and average rate of nett profit at the time, its producers would, obviously, be placed in a relatively advantageous situation; and there would, in consequence, be an influx of capital into that particular department, until competition had sunk the value, or price, of the article, to the level that would yield only the customary rate of profit on the capital employed in its production. And, on the other hand, were a commodity brought to market which did not exchange for so great an amount of other commodities, or of money, as was required to cover the cost of its production, its producers would be placed in a relatively disadvantageous situation; and would, consequently, withdraw their capital from the production of the commodity, until its value or price had risen so as to place them in the same situation as their neighbours, or to yield them the same rate of profit. It is plain, that no man will continue to produce commodities if they sell for *less* than they cost; that is, for less than will indemnify him for his outlay, including the common and average rate of profit on his capital. This is a limit below which, it is obvious, prices cannot be permanently reduced; and if they were, for any considerable period, to rise above it, additional capital would be attracted to the advantageous business; and the competition of the producers would lower prices.

A demand, to be effectual, must be such as will cover the expense of production. If it be not sufficient to do this, it can never be a means of causing commodities to be produced and brought to market. The demand of those who have both the *power* and the *will* to purchase, may become ten or ten thousand times more extensive, or it may decline in the same proportion; but if the cost of producing the commodities demanded continue the same, no permanent variation will be occasioned in their price. Were the demand for hats suddenly doubled, their price would be very greatly increased, and the hatters would, of course, make large profits; but these would immediately attract additional capital to the hat manufacture; an increased supply of hats would, consequently, be brought to market, and if no variation took place in the cost of their production, their price would infallibly sink, in a very short time, to its former level. Suppose, on the other hand, that the demand for hats is increased tenfold, and the cost of their production diminished in the same proportion: we should, notwithstanding the increased demand, be able, before any very lengthened period had elapsed, to buy a hat for a tenth part of what it now costs. Again, suppose the demand for hats to decline, and the cost of producing them to increase: the price would, notwithstanding the diminished demand, gradually rise, till it had reached the point at which it would yield the hatters the customary rate of profit on the capital employed in their business. It is admitted that variations of demand and supply occasion variations of price; but it is essential to remark, that they are only temporary. The *cost of production* is the grand regulator of price—the centre of all those transitory and evanescent oscillations on the one side and the other. Wherever industry is free, the competition of the producers will always elevate or sink prices to this level.

In certain branches of industry, such, for example, as agriculture, which are liable to be seriously affected by variations in the seasons, and from which capital cannot be easily withdrawn, there is a somewhat longer interval than in others, before the market price of produce and the cost of producing it are equalised; but that such an equalisation must take place in the end, is sufficiently plain. Neither farmers, nor any other class of producers, will continue to bring products to market, unless they sell for such a price as will remunerate them for the expense of their production, including therein the average rate of profit on the capital they employ. *Nemo enim sanus debet velle impensam ac sumptum facere in culturam, si videt non posse refici.** The cost of production is a limit below which prices cannot permanently sink, and above which they cannot permanently rise. When, on the one hand,

* Varro "de Re Rusticâ," lib. i. § 2.

an excess of supply depresses the price of corn below this limit, the occupiers of poor land are involved in the greatest difficulties; a number of them are, in consequence, driven from their employments, and a smaller supply of corn being brought to market, prices are again elevated so as to yield the customary rate of profit to the cultivators of the poorest soils that are still continued under tillage. And when, on the other hand, prices rise above this natural limit, the cultivators gain more than the average rate of profit; the effect of which is, to attract new entrants and additional capital to agriculture, until the supply has been so far increased, and the price so far depressed, that the cultivators obtain no more than ordinary profits. This is the point at which *average* prices continue stationary, and about which market prices oscillate. If any great discovery were made in agriculture — such a discovery, for instance, as would reduce the cost of cultivation one half — the price of agricultural produce would fall in the same proportion, and would continue to sell at that reduced rate until the increase of population forced recourse to soils of a decreasing degree of fertility. Whenever this took place, prices would again rise. Why is the price of corn almost invariably higher in this country than in Poland? Is it because we have a greater demand for it, or because of the greater cost of production in this country?

A pound weight of gold is at present worth about fifteen pounds of silver. It cannot, however, be said, that this is a consequence of the demand for gold being greater than the demand for silver; for the reverse is the fact. Neither can it be said to be occasioned by an absolute scarcity of gold; for those who choose to pay a sufficient price for it may obtain it in any quantity they please. The cause of the difference in the price of the two metals consists entirely in the circumstance of its costing about fifteen times as much to produce a pound of gold as to produce a pound of silver. That this is really the case, is plain from the admitted fact, that the producers of gold do not gain any greater profit than the producers of silver, iron, lead, or any other metal. They have no monopoly of its production. Every individual is at liberty to send capital to Brazil, and become a producer of gold; and wherever this is the case, the principle of competition never fails of forcing the product to be sold at such a price as will merely pay the expenses of its production. Were a gold mine discovered of equal productiveness with the silver mines, the production of gold would immediately become the most advantageous of all businesses; an immense supply of that metal would be thrown upon the market, and its price would, in a very short period, be reduced to the same level as silver.

If a set of men were brought together from various countries, ignorant of each other's wants, and of the labour and expense required to produce the commodities which we may suppose each of them to possess, these commodities would be bought and sold according to the wants and fancies of the parties. Under such circumstances, a pound of gold might be given for a pound of iron, and a gallon of wine for a gallon of small beer. As soon, however, as a system of commercial intercourse has been established, and as the wants of society and the powers of production come to be well and generally known, an end is put to this arbitrary method of bartering. Thousands of sellers then enter the market. But when such is the case, it is no longer possible to sell a pound of iron for a pound of gold; and why?—because the producers of iron will undersell each other until, by their competition, they reduce its exchangeable value, or price, to the level of the cost of its production. This is, in every civilised society, the pivot on which exchangeable value always turns. It is usual for voyagers who touch at countries occupied by savages, to obtain commodities in exchange for toys or trinkets, which it cost infinitely less to produce; but in all civilised and commercial countries, the proportion in which, generally speaking, commodities exchange for each other, depends on the comparative cost of their production.

Thus, then, it appears, that no variation in the demand for commodities, unaccompanied by a variation in their cost, or real value, can have any lasting influence on price. If their cost be diminished, price will be equally diminished, though the demand should be increased to any conceivable extent; while, if their cost be increased, price will be equally increased, though the demand should sink to the lowest possible limit.

It must always be remembered, that this reasoning applies to those commodities only which may be freely produced, and the quantity of which may, at the same time, be increased to any extent by fresh outlays of capital and labour. But there are circumstances under which the supply of commodities is strictly limited; and when such is the case, their price is no longer determined by their cost, but by the degree of their real or supposed *utility*, compared with the means and necessities of the buyers. In a desert, or a besieged city, a barrel of water or a pound of bread may be more valuable than a pipe of burgundy or a pound of gold.* And though artificial monopolies are rarely carried to so very oppressive a height, the same principle holds with respect to the value of all commodities produced under them. When a particular individual, or class of individuals, obtains the exclusive privilege of manufacturing certain species of goods, the operation of the principle of

* Pliny (" Hist. Nat." lib. viii. cap. 57) and Valerius Maximus (lib. vii. cap. 6) relate that, during the siege of Casilinum by Hannibal, the scarcity of provisions became so extreme, that a rat was sold for 200 denarii! They add, that the seller had the worst of the bargain, having died of hunger, while the rat was the means of preserving the life of the buyer. " Avaro enim," says Valerius, " fame consumpto, manubiis sordium suarum frui non licuit; æqui animi vir, ad salutarem impensam faciendam; carè quidem, verùm necessariè, comparato cibo vixit."

competition is suspended with respect to them, and their price must, therefore, entirely depend on the proportion in which they are brought to market, compared with the demand. If monopolists supplied the market liberally, or kept it always as fully stocked with commodities as it would be were there no monopoly, the commodities would sell at their natural price, and the monopoly would have no disadvantage farther than the exclusion of the public from an employment which every one ought to have leave to carry on. In point of fact, however, the market is seldom or never fully supplied with commodities produced under a monopoly. All classes of producers endeavour to procure the highest possible price for their commodities; and those who are protected by a monopoly against the risk of being undersold by others, uniformly keep the market understocked, or supply it with inferior articles, or both. Under such circumstances, the price of commodities, if they cannot be easily smuggled from abroad, or clandestinely produced at home, may be elevated to the highest point to which the competition of the *buyers* can raise it; and may, consequently, amount to five, ten, or twenty times the sum it would amount to, were competition permitted to operate on their production and sale. The *power* of the purchasers to offer a high price forms the only limit to the rapacity of monopolists.

Besides the commodities produced under artificial monopolies, there is another class, the supply of which cannot be increased by the operation of human industry, and whose price is not, therefore, dependent on the cost of their production. Ancient statues, vases, and gems, the pictures of the great masters, some species of wines which can be produced in limited quantities only from soils of a particular quality and exposure, and a few other commodities, belong to this class. As their supply cannot be increased, their price varies as the demand, and is totally unaffected by any other circumstance.

But with these exceptions, which, when compared

to the mass of commodities, are of small importance, wherever industry is unrestricted, and competition allowed to operate, the *average* price of the various products of art and industry always coincides with the cost of their production. When a fall takes place in the market price of any commodity, we cannot say whether that fall be really advantageous, or whether a part of the wealth of the producers be not gratuitously transferred to the consumers, until we learn whether the cost of production has been equally diminished. If this be the case, the fall of price will not have been disadvantageous to the producers, and will be permanent; but if this has not been the case—if the cost of production continue the same, the fall must have been injurious to the producers, and prices will, in consequence, speedily regain their former level. In like manner, no rise of prices can be permanent, except when the cost of production has been proportionally increased. If that cost has remained stationary, or has not increased in a corresponding ratio, prices will decline as soon as the ephemeral causes of enhancement have disappeared.

CHAPTER III.

Influence of Mercantile Speculations on Price—Difference between Speculation and Gambling—Speculations in Corn beneficial to the Public, but dangerous to the Dealers—Imitative Speculations—Influence of Knowledge on Speculation.

THE proposition so universally assented to, that market prices depend upon the proportion which the supply of commodities bears to the demand, would be more accurate were it expressed with some modifications. It very rarely happens that either the actual supply of any species of produce in extensive demand, or the intensity of that demand, can be exactly measured. Every transaction in which an individual buys produce in order to sell it again, is, in fact, a speculation. The buyer anticipates that the demand for the article he has purchased will be such, at some future period, either more or less distant, that he will be able to dispose of it with a profit; and the success of the speculation depends, it is evident, on the skill with which he has estimated the circumstances that must determine the future price of the commodity. It follows, therefore, that in all highly commercial countries, where merchants are possessed of large capitals, and where they are left to be guided in the use of them by their own discretion and foresight, the prices of commodities will frequently be very much influenced, not merely by the actual occurrence of changes in the accustomed relation of the supply and demand, but by the anticipation of such changes. It is the business of the merchant to acquaint himself with every circumstance affecting the particular description of commodities in which he deals. He endeavours to obtain, by means of an extensive correspondence, the earliest and most authentic information with respect to every thing that may affect their supply or demand, or the cost of their production: and if he learned that the supply of an article had failed, or that, owing to changes of fashion, or to the opening of new channels of commerce, the demand for it had been increased, he would most likely be disposed to become a buyer, in anticipation of profiting by the rise of price, which, under the circumstances of the case, could hardly fail of taking place; or if he were a holder of the article, he would refuse to part with it unless for a higher price than he would previously have accepted. If the intelligence received by the merchant had been of a contrary description—if, for example, he had learned that the article was now produced with greater facility, or that there was a falling off in the demand for it, caused by a change of fashion, or by the shutting up of some of the markets to which it had previously been admitted—he would have acted differently: in this case he would have anticipated a fall of prices, and would either have declined purchasing the article, except at a reduced rate, or have endeavoured to get rid of it, supposing him to be a holder, by offering it at a lower price. In consequence of these operations, the prices of commodities, in different places and periods, are brought comparatively near to equality. All abrupt transitions, from scarcity to abundance, and from abundance to scarcity, are avoided: an excess in one case is made to balance a deficiency in another, and the supply is distributed with a degree of steadiness and regularity that could hardly have been deemed attainable.

It is obvious, from what has now been stated, that those who indiscriminately condemn all sorts of speculative engagements, have never reflected on the circumstances incident to the prosecution of every undertaking. In truth and reality, they are all speculations. Their undertakers must look forward to periods more or less distant, and their success depends entirely on the sagacity with which they have estimated the probability of certain events occurring, and the influence which they have ascribed to them. Speculation is, therefore, really only another name for foresight; and though fortunes have sometimes been made by a lucky hit, the character of a successful speculator is, in the vast majority of instances, due to him only who has skilfully devised the means of effecting the end he had in view, and who has outstripped his competitors in the judgment with which he has looked into futurity, and appreciated the operation of causes producing distant effects. Even in those businesses, such as agriculture and manufactures, that are apparently the most secure, there is, and must be, a great deal of speculation. Those engaged in the former have to encounter the variations of seasons, while those engaged in the latter have to encounter the variations of fashion; and each is, besides, liable to be affected by legislative enactments, by new discoveries in the arts, and by an endless variety of circumstances which it is always very difficult, and sometimes quite impossible, to foresee. On the whole, indeed, the gains of the undertakers are so adjusted, that those who carry them on obtain, at an average, the common and ordinary rate of profit. But the inequality in the gains of individuals is most commonly very great; and while the superior tact, industry, or good fortune of some enable them to realise large fortunes, the want of discernment, the less vigilant attention, or the bad fortune of others, frequently reduces them from the situation of capitalists to that of labourers.*

* The necessity of speculation in the ordinary affairs of life has been well illustrated by Seneca: "Huic respondebimus, nunquam expectare nos certissimam rerum comprehensionem: quoniam in arduo est veri exploratio; sed eâ ire quà ducit veri similitudo. Omne hâc viâ procedit officium. Sic serimus, sic navigamus, sic militamus, sic uxores ducimus, sic liberos tollimus; quanquam omnium horum incertus sit eventus. Ad ea accedimus, de quibus benè sperandum esse credimus. Quis enim pollicetur serenti proventum, naviganti portum, militanti victoriam, marito pudicam uxorem, patri pios liberos? Sequimur quà ratio, non quà veritas trahit. Expecta, ut nisi benè cessurâ non facias, et nisi com-

It is by no means an easy task to draw a distinct line of demarcation between speculation and gambling. The truth is, that they run into one another by almost imperceptible degrees. Practically, however, that may be termed a safe, and therefore a legitimate speculation, in which, on a fair and careful estimate of the favourable and unfavourable contingencies, the former preponderate; while that may be termed a gambling adventure in which the contingencies are unknown, or in which they are nearly equal, or incline to the unfavourable side. Suppose a race-horse and a dray-horse were matched to run against each other; an individual who bet that the race-horse would win, could not fairly be deemed a gambler; for he would, it is plain, encounter no risk. But if two race-horses were to be matched against each other, the risk would then become very great; and the success of either of them would depend on so many accidental and almost inappreciable circumstances, that those who betted on the event might fairly be denominated gamblers.

Among the various speculations carried on by merchants, there are few that have exposed them more to the public odium, while, at the same time, there are few more really beneficial, than those of the dealers in corn. Not only do they distribute the produce of the harvest equally throughout the country, according to the wants of different districts, but they manage their operations so as to reserve a portion of the surplus produce of plentiful years as a resource against future emergencies; and when a scarcity occurs, they distribute its pressure equally throughout the year, and prevent the society from ever actually feeling the extremity of want.

pertâ veritate nihil moveris, relicto omni actu, vita consistit. Dum verisimilia me in hoc aut illud impellant, non verebor beneficium, dare ei, quem verisimile erit gratum esse."—*De Benefic.* lib. iv. cap. 33.

I shall briefly endeavour to shew how speculation produces these effects.

Were the harvests always equally productive, nothing would be gained by storing up supplies of corn; and all that would be necessary would be to distribute the crop equally throughout the country, and throughout the year. But such is not the order of nature. The variations in the aggregate produce of a country in different seasons, though not, perhaps, so great as are commonly supposed, are still very considerable; and experience has shewn, that two or three unusually luxuriant harvests seldom take place in succession; or that when they do they are invariably followed by those that are deficient. The speculators in corn anticipate this result. Whenever prices begin to give way, in consequence of an unusually luxuriant harvest, speculation is at work. The more opulent farmers withhold either the whole, or a part of their produce from market; and the more opulent dealers purchase largely of the corn brought to market, and store it up in expectation of a future advance. And thus, without intending to promote any one's interest but their own, the speculators in corn become the great benefactors of the public. They provide a reserve stock against those years of scarcity which are sure, at no distant period, to recur: while, by withdrawing a portion of the redundant supply from immediate consumption, prices are prevented from falling so low as to be injurious to the farmers, or at least are maintained at a higher level than they would otherwise have reached; provident habits are maintained amongst the people; and that waste and extravagance are checked which always take place in plentiful years, but which would be carried to a much greater extent if the whole produce of an abundant crop were to be consumed within the season.

It is, however, in scarce years that the speculations of the corn merchants are principally advantageous. Even in the richest counties, a very large proportion of the individuals engaged in the business of agriculture are comparatively poor, and are totally without the means of withholding their produce from market, in order to speculate upon any future advance. In consequence, the markets are always most abundantly supplied with produce immediately after harvest; and in countries where the merchants engaged in the corn trade are not possessed of large capitals, or where their proceedings are fettered and restricted, there is then, almost invariably, a heavy fall of prices. But as the vast majority of the people buy their food in small quantities, or from day to day as they want it, their consumption is necessarily extended or contracted according to its price at the time. Their views do not extend to the future; they have no means of judging whether the crop is or is not deficient; they live, as the phrase is, from hand to mouth, and are satisfied if, in the meantime, they obtain abundant supplies at a cheap rate. But it is obvious, that were there nothing to control or counteract this improvidence, the consequence would, very often, be fatal in the extreme. The crop of one harvest must support the population till the crop of the succeeding harvest has been gathered in; and if that crop should be deficient—if, for instance, it should only be adequate to afford, at the usual rate of consumption, a supply of nine or ten months' provisions instead of twelve—it is plain, that unless the price were so raised immediately after harvest as to enforce economy, and put, as it were, the whole nation upon short allowance, the most dreadful famine would be experienced previously to the ensuing harvest. Those who examine the accounts of the prices of wheat and other grain in England, from the conquest downwards, collected by Bishop Fleetwood, Sir F. M. Eden, and others, will meet with abundant proofs of the accuracy of what has now been stated. In those remote periods, when the farmers were generally without the means of withholding their crops from market, and when the trade of a corn dealer was proscribed, the utmost improvidence was exhibited in the consumption of grain. There were then, indeed, very few years in which a considerable scarcity was not experienced immediately before harvest, and many in which there was an absolute famine. The fluctuations of price exceeded every thing of which we can now form an idea; the price of wheat and other grain being often four and five times as high in June and July as in September and October. Thanks, however, to the increase of capital in the hands of the large farmers and dealers, and to the freedom given to the operations of the corn merchants, we are no longer exposed to such ruinous vicissitudes. Whenever the dealers, who, in consequence of their superior means of information, are better acquainted with the real state of the crops than any other class of persons, find the harvest likely to be deficient, they raise the price of the corn they have warehoused, and bid against each other for the corn which the farmers are bringing to market. In consequence of this rise of prices, all ranks and orders, but especially the lower, who are the great consumers of corn, find it indispensable to use greater economy, and to check all improvident and wasteful consumption. Every class being thus immediately put upon short allowance, the pressure of the scarcity is distributed equally throughout the year; and instead of indulging, as was formerly the case, in the same scale of consumption as in seasons of plenty, until the supply became altogether deficient, and then being exposed without resource to the attacks of famine and pestilence, the speculations of the corn merchants warn us of our danger, and compel us to provide against it.

It is not easy to suppose that these proceedings of the corn merchants should ever be injurious to the public. It has been said, that in scarce years they are not disposed to bring the corn they have purchased to market until it has attained an exorbitant price, and that the pressure of the scarcity is thus, often, very much aggravated: but there is no real ground for any such statement. The immense amount of capital required to store up any considerable quantity of corn, and the waste to which it is liable, render most holders disposed to sell as soon as they can realise a fair profit. In every extensive country in which the corn trade is free, there are infinitely too many persons engaged in it to enable any sort of combination or concert to be formed amongst them; and though it were formed, it could not be maintained for an instant. A large proportion of the farmers and other small holders of corn are always in straitened circumstances, more particularly if a scarce year has not occurred so soon as they expected; and they are, consequently, anxious to relieve themselves, as soon as prices rise, of a portion of the stock on their hands. Occasionally, indeed, individuals are found who retain their stocks for too long a period, or until a re-action takes place, and prices begin to decline. But, instead of joining in the popular cry against such persons, every one who takes a dispassionate view of the matter will immediately perceive that, inasmuch as their miscalculation must, under the circumstances supposed, be exceedingly injurious to themselves, we have the best security against its being carried to such an extent as to be productive of any material injury, or even inconvenience, to the public. It ought also to be borne in mind, that it is rarely, if ever, possible to determine beforehand when a scarcity is to abate in consequence of new supplies being brought to market; and had it continued a little longer, there would have been no miscalculation on the part of the holders. At all events, it is plain, that by declining to bring their corn to market, they preserved a resource on which, in the event of the harvest being longer delayed than usual, or of any unfavourable contingency taking place, the public could have fallen back; so that, instead of deserving abuse, these speculators are most justly entitled to every fair encouragement and protection. A country in which there is no considerable stock of grain in the barn-yards of the farmers, or the warehouses of the merchants, is in one of the most perilous situations that can easily be imagined, and may be exposed to the severest privations, or even famine. But so long as the sagacity, the miscalculation, or the avarice, of merchants and dealers, retain a stock of grain in the warehouses, this last extremity cannot take place. By refusing to sell till it has reached a very high price, they put an effectual stop to all sorts of waste, and husband for the public those supplies which they could not have so frugally husbanded for themselves.

The advantage of the speculative purchases of corn made by the merchants in plentiful years, and of the immediate rise of price which their operations occasion in years when a scarcity is apprehended, have been very clearly stated in a Report by the Lords of the Privy Council, in 1790, on the Corn Laws.—" In other countries," say their lordships, " magazines of corn are formed by their respective governments, or by the principal magistrates of great cities, as a resource in times of scarcity. This country has no such institution. The stores of corn are here deposited in the barns and stacks of wealthy farmers, and in magazines of merchants and dealers in corn, who ought by no means to be restrained, but rather encouraged in laying up stores of this nature; as, after a deficient crop, they are thereby enabled to divide the inconvenience arising from it as equally as possible, through every part of the year; and by checking improvident consumption in the beginning of scarcity, prevent famine, which might otherwise happen before the next harvest. The inland trade of corn ought, therefore, to be perfectly free. This freedom can never be abused. To suppose that there can be a monopoly of so bulky and perishable an article, dispersed through so many hands, over every part of the country, is an idle and vain apprehension."

The regulations once so prevalent with respect to the

assize of bread, were originally devised and intended as measures of security, lest, owing to the small number of bakers in most towns, they should combine together, and artificially raise the price of bread. According, however, as sounder notions upon these subjects were diffused throughout the country, these regulations fell gradually into disuse; and I am not aware that any ill effects have, in any instance, been found to result from their neglect. The assize of bread in London was abolished by an act of the legislature in 1815; and it is well known, that no such thing as a combination amongst the bakers has ever since been thought of, and that the public have always had an ample supply of bread, at the lowest prices that the state of the corn market would admit. And when such has been the case,—when no combination has ever been even so much as attempted amongst the bakers of a single town, can any thing be more perfectly visionary, than to suppose that it should ever be attempted among the innumerable multitude of farmers and corn dealers dispersed throughout an extensive country? "The unlimited, unrestrained freedom of the corn trade," says Dr. Smith, "as it is the only effectual preventive of the miseries of a famine, so it is the best palliative of the inconveniences of a dearth. No trade deserves more the full protection of the law, and none requires it so much, because none is so much exposed to undeserved popular odium."*

But though the speculations of the corn merchants be in every case beneficial to the public, they are very often injurious to themselves. The corn trade is, indeed, one of the most hazardous businesses in which it is possible to engage. This arises partly and principally from the extreme difficulty of procuring correct information, with respect to the productiveness of the harvest in particular countries and districts, and of the supplies of corn that

* "Wealth of Nations," vol. ii. p. 399.

may be made available in case of deficiency; partly from the difficulty of estimating the effect of weather on the crops; and partly from the difficulty of estimating how much any given rise of price may affect consumption. When the elements of speculation are so very uncertain, or when, at least, they are so difficult to disentangle and appreciate, it requires no ordinary prudence for a merchant to avoid very heavy losses; and how cautious soever, he can never be secure against unfavourable chances. A few days' rain, immediately before or during harvest, have often, by exciting what were apparently the best-founded apprehensions with respect to the safety of the crop, occasioned a sudden rise of prices, which have again as suddenly fallen back to their former level when the weather improved. It is idle to suppose that these causes of risk and uncertainty will ever be completely obviated; but it is pretty evident that nothing would tend so much to weaken their frequency and force, as the establishment of a free corn trade with other countries. Such is the wise arrangement of Providence, that the seasons that are most unfavourable to the crops in one country or district, are generally the most favourable to those in countries or districts having a different soil or climate. There is no reason, indeed, for supposing that the crops throughout the world, or throughout those countries which have an extensive intercourse together, differ materially in different years; and if the foreign corn trade were not subjected to restrictions, the facility of importing additional supplies from foreign countries when the home supply happened to be unusually deficient, or of exporting to them in unusually abundant years, would give infinitely greater steadiness to prices, and would, in consequence, proportionally lessen the hazard to which the dealers are now exposed.*

* The admirable paragraph which follows is from the "Commercio di Grani" of the Count di Verri:—"La terra che abitiamo riproduce ogni anno una quantità corrispondente alla universale consumazione; il com-

The great risk to which all classes of merchants are exposed, who offer an unusually high price for any description of commodities, in anticipation of a future advance of price, is a consequence, principally, of the difficulty of ascertaining the true state of the fact, with respect to the grounds on which a deficient supply or an increased demand is expected.* This, however, is entirely a practical question, for the solution of the merchant, whose success depends on the skill and sagacity which he evinces in conducting his speculations under such circumstances. The great cotton speculation of 1825 took its rise partly and chiefly from a supposed deficiency in the supply of cotton, partly from an idea that there was a greatly increased demand for raw cotton in this country and the

mercio supplisce col superfluo di una terra al bisogno dell' altra e colla legge de continuità si equilibrano, dopo alcune oscillazioni, periodicamente bisogno ed abbondanza. Quei che suggeriscono i vincoli risguardono gli uomini sulla terra come ridotti a gettar il dado a chi debba morir di fame; risguardiamoli con occhio tranquillo e riceveremo idee più consolanti o vere, conosendoci fratelli di una vasta famiglia sparza sul globo, spinti a darci vicendevolmente soccorso, e provveduti largamente dal gran motore della vegetazione a quanto fà d' uopo per sostenere i bisogni della vita. I soli vincoli artificiali, immaginati dalla timida ignoranza o dall' astuta ambizione, hanno ridotti gli stati ai timori della fame ed a soffrirla."—p. 33, ed. 1818.

* The famous philosopher Thales, of Miletus, who flourished about 550 years before the Christian era, is reported to have engaged in at least one successful speculation. "His poverty," says Aristotle, "was thought to upbraid his studies as serving no gainful, and therefore no useful purpose. But Thales, by his skill in meteorology, contrived to wipe off the reproach; for as his science enabled him to foresee that next season there would be an extraordinary crop of olives, he hired in the winter all the oil-presses in Chios and Miletus, employing his little fortune in giving earnest to their respective proprietors. When the gathering season approached, and the olives were seen loading the branches, all men wished to provide oil-presses at the same time, and suddenly: but Thales being master of the whole number, let them separately at a high price; and thereby accumulating vast wealth, proved that philosophers might be rich if they pleased, but that riches were not the object of their pursuit."—GILLIES' *Aristotle*, vol. ii. p. 54.

continent, and partly from a belief that the stocks on hand were unusually low. Now it is obvious, that the success of those who embarked in this speculation depended entirely on two circumstances; viz. *first*, that they were right in the fundamental supposition on which the whole speculation rested, that the supply of cotton was no longer commensurate with the demand; and *second*, that their competition did not raise the price so high as to diminish the consumption by the manufacturers in too great a degree to enable them to take off the quantity to be actually brought to market. If the merchants had been well founded in their suppositions, and if their competition had not raised the price of cotton too high, the speculation would certainly have been successful. But, instead of being well founded, the hypothesis on which the whole thing rested was perfectly visionary. There was no deficiency in the supply of cotton, but, on the contrary, a great superabundance; and though there had been such a deficiency, the excess to which the price was carried must have checked consumption so much as to occasion a serious decline.*

When a few leading merchants purchase, in anticipation of an advance, or sell, in anticipation of a fall, the speculation is often pushed beyond all reasonable limits,

* Several extremely well-informed merchants embarked in this speculation, and suffered by it. The falling off in the imports of cotton from America, in 1824, seems to have been the source of the delusion. It was supposed that this falling off was not accidental, but that it was a consequence of the price of cotton having been for a series of years so low as to be inadequate to defray the expenses of its cultivation. The result shewed that this calculation was most erroneous. And besides, in entering on the speculation no attention was paid to Egypt and Italy, countries from which only about 1,400,000 lbs. of cotton were obtained in 1824, but from which no less than 23,800,000 lbs. were obtained in 1825! This unlooked-for importation was of itself almost enough to overturn the combinations of the speculators; and, coupled with the increased importation from America and other countries, actually occasioned a heavy glut of the market.

by the operations of those who are influenced by imitation only, and who have never, perhaps, reflected for a moment on the grounds on which a variation of price is anticipated. In speculation, as in most other things, one individual derives confidence from another. Such a one purchases or sells, not because he has any really accurate information as to the state of the demand and supply, but because some one else has done so before him. The original impulse is thus rapidly extended; and even those who are satisfied that a speculation, in anticipation of a rise of prices, is unsafe, and that there will be a recoil, not unfrequently adventure, in the expectation that they will be able to withdraw before the recoil has begun.

The only guarantee against the spread of imitative speculations, if I may so term them, must be sought for in the diffusion of sounder information, and, consequently, of a more searching spirit of analysis, amongst the mercantile class. The crowd who engage in speculative adventures, once set on foot, consist partly of determined gamblers, who having, for the most part, nothing of their own to lose, are at all times ready to embark in any adventure, however hazardous, by which they imagine they have a chance of rapidly making a fortune; but the far greater number of those who quit their ordinary employments to enter into such speculations, though partly, no doubt, actuated by a spirit of gambling, are mainly influenced by the principle of imitation: and it is difficult to see how this dangerous tendency can be lessened otherwise than by the better education of merchants, and by impressing on every one who may be tempted to speculate either on a rise or fall of prices, the necessity, if he would secure himself against the most extreme risk, of carefully investigating the causes of any anticipated variation, and estimating for himself the probability of success in the adventure, instead of embarking in it in imitation of others.

It may, I believe, speaking generally, be laid down as

a sound practical rule, to avoid having any thing to do with a speculation in which many have already engaged. The competition of the speculators seldom fails speedily to render an adventure that might have been originally safe, extremely hazardous. If a commodity happen to be at an unusually reduced price in any particular market, it will rise the moment that different buyers appear in the field; and supposing, on the other hand, that it is fetching an unusually high price, it will fall, perhaps far below the cost of production, as soon as supplies begin to be poured in by different merchants. Whatever, therefore, may be the success of those who originate a speculation, those who enter into it at an advanced period are almost sure to lose. To have been preceded by others ought not, in such matters, to inspire confidence; on the contrary, it ought, unless there be something special in the case, to induce every considerate person to decline interfering with it.

The pernicious effects of miscalculation and ignorance are strikingly exhibited in the overstocking of such new markets as are occasionally opened, and in filling them with articles totally unsuited to the wants and habits of the people. When the continental markets were opened in 1814 and 1815, the first shippers of colonial and other produce made large profits; but in consequence of the crowding of fresh speculators, many of whom were strangers to commercial affairs, into the field, the markets were quite overloaded; and such a recoil took place, that it is doubtful whether Leith, and some other towns, have even now recovered from the effect of the bankruptcy and ruin of which it was productive. But the exportations consequent to the first opening of the trade to Buenos Ayres, Brazil, and the Caraccas, were, in this respect, still more extraordinary. Speculation was then carried beyond the boundaries within which even gambling is usually confined; and was pushed to an extent and into channels that could hardly have been deemed practicable.

We are informed by Mr. Mawe, an intelligent traveller, resident at Rio Janeiro, at the period in question, that more Manchester goods were sent out in the course of a few weeks than had been consumed in the twenty years preceding; and the quantity of English goods of all sorts poured into the city was so very great, that warehouses could not be provided sufficient to contain them, and that the most valuable merchandise was actually exposed for weeks, on the beach, to the weather, and to every sort of depredation! But the folly and ignorance of those who had crowded into this speculation was still more strikingly evinced in the selection of the articles sent to South America. Elegant services of cut-glass and china were offered to persons whose most splendid drinking-vessels consisted of a horn or the shell of a cocoa nut; tools were sent out having a hammer on the one side and a hatchet on the other, as if the inhabitants had had nothing more to do than to break the first stone they met with, and then cut the gold and diamonds from it; and some speculators actually went so far as to send out *skates* to Rio Janeiro!*

The wide-spread distress and ruin which followed these exportations is plainly to be ascribed to the almost inconceivable folly of those by whom they were made. If there be one species of knowledge more essential to those who embark in mercantile speculations than another, it is that they should be acquainted with the various productions of the different commercial countries of the world, and of those which are in demand in them. And when ships are freighted and commodities sent abroad by those who are so entirely destitute of this elementary instruction as to send skates to Rio Janeiro, the wonder is, not that they should sometimes calculate wrong, but that they ever calculate right.

But, as has been before observed, the maintenance of

* Mawe's "Travels in Brazil," new ed. pp. 453—458.

the freedom of intercourse between different countries, and the more general diffusion of sound instruction, seem to be the only means by which such miscalculations can be either obviated or mitigated. The effects consequent to such improvident speculations being always far more injurious to the parties engaged in them than to any other class, the presumption is, that they will diminish both in frequency and force, according as the true principles of commerce come to be better understood. But whatever inconvenience may occasionally flow from them, it is abundantly plain, that instead of being lessened, it would be very much increased, were any restraints imposed on the freedom of adventure. When the attention of many individuals is directed to the same line of speculation; when they prosecute it as a business, and are responsible in their own private fortunes for any errors they may commit, they acquire a knowledge of the various circumstances influencing prices, and give by their combinations a steadiness to them, which it is easy to see could not be attained by any other means. It is material, too, to bear in mind, as was previously stated, that many, perhaps it might be said *most*, of those who press so eagerly into the market, when any new channel of commerce is opened, or when any considerable rise of price is anticipated, are not merchants, but persons engaged in other businesses, or living, perhaps, on fixed incomes, who speculate in the hope of suddenly increasing their fortune. This tendency to gambling seldom fails to break out upon such occasions; but fortunately, these are only of comparatively rare occurrence; and in the ordinary course of affairs, mercantile speculations are left to be conducted by those who are familiar with business, and who, in exerting themselves to equalise the variations of price, caused by variations of climate and of seasons, and to distribute the supply of produce proportionally to the effective demand, and with so much providence that it may not at any time be wholly exhausted, perform functions that are in the highest degree important and beneficial. They are, it is true, actuated only by a desire to advance their own interests; but the results of their operations are not less advantageous than those of the agriculturist who gives greater fertility to the soil, or of the mechanist who invents new and more powerful machines.*

In the first chapter of this Part, I endeavoured to shew that the quantity of labour required for the production of commodities forms the grand principle which determines their exhangeable worth, or the proportion in which any one commodity exchanges for others; and in the second chapter, and the present, I have endeavoured to trace the influence of variations of demand and supply, and of speculation, on prices. These seem to exhaust all the really important practical questions involved in this part of the science. But as it is necessary, in order fully to understand the various questions involved in the *theory* of value, that the precise influence of variations in the rates of wages and profits, and in the species of capitals employed, should be appreciated, I shall devote the following chapter to an investigation of these matters. Being principally, however, intended for the use of the student or scientific reader, it may, with propriety, be passed over by others.

* The reader will find a great deal of valuable information with respect to most of the points touched upon in this and the previous chapter, as well as many others, in Mr. Tooke's excellent work "On High and Low Prices."

CHAPTER IV.

Effect of the Employment of Capital in Production, and of Variations in the Rates of Wages and Profits on Value—(1) *When the Capitals employed in Production are of the same Degree of Durability; and* (2) *when they are of different Degrees of Durability—A High Rate of Wages does not lay the Commerce of a Country under any Disadvantage.*

It is admitted on all hands, that in the early stages of society, before capital is accumulated, the quantity of labour required to produce a commodity and bring it to market, forms the only principle by which its value is regulated. But capital is only another name for all those commodities or articles produced by human industry, that may be made directly available to the support of man or the facilitating of production. It is, in fact, nothing but the accumulated produce of *anterior labour;* and when it is employed in the production of commodities, their value must plainly be regulated, not by the quantity of immediate labour only, but by the total quantity, as well of immediate as of accumulated labour, or capital, necessarily laid out on their production. Suppose that an individual can, by a day's labour, without the assistance of capital, kill a deer; but that it requires a day's labour to construct weapons necessary to enable him to kill a beaver, and another day's labour to kill it: it is evident, supposing the weapons to be rendered useless in killing the beaver, that one beaver would really take as much labour to kill it as was required to kill two deer, and would, therefore, be worth twice as much. The durability of the weapons, or of the capital employed by the beaver-hunter, is obviously an element of the greatest importance in estimating the value of the animals killed by him.

Had the weapons been more durable than has been supposed—had they served, for example, to kill twenty beavers instead of one—then the quantity of labour required to kill a beaver would only have been one-twentieth more than the labour required to kill a deer, and the animals would, of course, have been exchanged for each other in that proportion; and it is plain that, with every extension of the durability of the weapons, the value of deer and beavers would be brought still nearer to equality.

It appears, therefore, inasmuch as capital is nothing but the accumulated produce of anterior labour, that its employment cannot affect the principle which makes the exchangeable value of commodities depend on the quantities of labour required for their production. A commodity may be altogether produced by capital, without the co-operation of any immediate labour whatever; but, inasmuch as the value of this capital is regulated and determined by the labour required for its production, it is obvious, that the value of the commodities produced by its means must, at bottom, be determined by this same labour: or a commodity may be partly produced by capital, and partly by immediate labour, and then its exchangeable value will be proportioned to the *sum of the two*, or, which is still the same thing, to the total quantity of labour bestowed upon it. These principles are almost self-evident, and it is not easy to see how they can be made the subject of dispute or controversy; but a considerable difference of opinion is entertained respecting the effects on value, of the employment of workmen by capitalists, and of fluctuations in the rate of wages.

It does not, however, seem that there is really much room for these differences. Suppose that a certain quantity of goods, a pair of stockings for example, manufactured by weavers working on their own account, freely exchanges for a pair of gloves, also manufactured by independent workmen, they would continue to exchange in this proportion, provided the quantities of labour required for their production continue invariable, though the workmen were employed by some master manufacturer. In the first case, it is true, as Dr. Smith has observed that the whole goods produced by the workmen belong to themselves, and that, in the second case, they have to share them with their employers. But it must be recollected, that in the first case the capital, or accumulated produce of labour, made use of in the production of the commodities, belongs also to the workmen, and that, in the latter case, it is furnished to them by others. The question then comes to be, Does the circumstance of labourers voluntarily agreeing to relinquish a portion of the commodities they produce, as an equivalent or compensation for the use of the capital that has been lent to them, afford any ground for raising the value of these commodities? It is evident it does not. The profits of capital are only another name for the wages of accumulated labour. They make a part of the price of every commodity in the production of which any portion of capital has been wasted. But whether this capital belong to the labourer himself, or is supplied by another, is obviously of no consequence. When the capital does not belong to the labourer, the commodities which he produces are divided into two specific portions, whereof one is the produce of the immediate labour, and the other of the capital, or accumulated labour, laid out upon them. But so long as the same quantity of labour is required for the production of commodities, their value will continue constant, whether that labour be supplied by one or by fifty individuals. A shoemaker who manufactures shoes on his own account, obtains the same rate of profit on their sale that would accrue to a master shoemaker were he employed by him as a workman; for he must not only possess a capital adequate to maintain himself and his family until his shoes can be disposed of, but he must also be able to furnish himself with a workshop and tools, to advance money to the tanner for leather, and to provide for various other outgoings. If, then, he did not, exclusive of the ordinary wages of labour, realise a profit, or compensation for the employment of his capital, equal to the profit obtained by the master shoemaker, it would obviously be for his advantage to lend it to him, and to work on his account; and it is plain, inasmuch as his shoes would not sell for a higher price than those of the capitalist, that he could not realise a greater profit.

Hence it follows, that the circumstance of the accumlated labour or capital, and the manual labour, required in production, being furnished by different persons, cannot affect the value of commodities. That depends on the total *quantity* of every sort of labour laid out, and not on those by whom it is laid out. It now only remains to trace the effects of fluctuations in the rates of wages and profits on the value of commodities. When this has been done, this subject will be exhausted.

To simplify this inquiry, I shall divide it into two branches: I shall inquire, *first*, whether fluctuations in the rate of wages have any, and if any, what, effects on the value of commodities produced by the aid of capitals of equal degrees of durability, or returnable in equal periods; and, *second*, whether these fluctuations have any, and if any, what, effects when the capitals employed are of unequal degrees of durability, or are returnable in unequal periods.

The better to understand what follows, it may be necessary to premise that the term durability is applied to those capitals that are denominated fixed, or that consist of machines, houses, &c. It means the period required for their consumption, or during which they may be expected to last; and this, of course, varies according to the nature of the article. One machine may be capable of lasting fifty years, another forty, a third ten, and so on; while a granite dock or a bridge may last for five hundred or a thousand years.

Circulating capital, or capital employed in the payment of wages, is said to be returnable in given periods, which are estimated from the time when the wages are advanced by the capitalist, to the time when he disposes of the produce.

When it is said that capitalists are placed under the same circumstances, it is understood that they employ fixed capitals of the same degree of durability, or circulating capitals returnable in equal periods.

Supposing, now, that they are in this situation, they would be equally affected by a rise or fall of wages. This proposition is self-evident, and must be assented to by every one. But were such the case, it is plainly impossible that a rise or fall of wages could occasion any variation in the value, or price of commodities. Suppose, for example, that a hat, produced when wages are 2*s*. a-day, freely exchanges for a pair of boots; and let us suppose that, from some cause or other, wages rise to 3*s*., the question is, will this rise of wages affect the value or price of hats and boots? It is obvious that it will not. The relation of A to B cannot vary, unless one of them be operated upon by some cause which does not extend its influence, or the same degree of influence, to the other. But fluctuations in the rate of wages are not of this description. They cannot be confined to one department. Competition never fails to elevate or depress their rate in any one trade to what is really, when all things are taken into account, the common level. If wages really rise 1*s*. a day in the hat trade, they must, and they certainly will, unless restrictive and injurious regulations interpose, rise 1*s*. in every other business. It is plain, then, that the hatter could not urge the circumstance of his being obliged to pay a greater amount of wages to his workmen, as a reason why the boot-maker should give him a greater number of boots in exchange for the same number of his hats; for the boot-maker would have it in his power to reply, that the same rise of wages affected him to precisely the same extent.

If, therefore, a hat was previously worth, or exchanged for a pair of boots, they would continue to preserve this relation to each other, until some variation took place in the quantities of labour required to produce them and bring them to market. So long as these quantities continue the same, wages may rise to a guinea, or they may fall to a penny a day, without its being possible for either the rise or the fall to have the slightest effect on their value.

But it may perhaps be thought, that though the relation which commodities produced by the aid of capitals of equal degrees of durability bear to each other, may not be affected by fluctuations in the rate of wages, these fluctuations may, notwithstanding, affect their *price*, or their value estimated in money. But if the variation in the rate of wages affect their *cost*,—that is, if the labourer get either a greater or less proportion of the produce of his industry, or a greater or less quantity of money of the same value,— this will not happen. Money is itself a commodity, whose value depends on the same circumstances that determine the value of all other commodities. If the mine which supplies the gold and silver, of which money is made, be situated in the country, then it is clear, that the rise of wages that affects other producers, will equally affect those engaged in the production of gold and silver; and if gold and silver be imported from abroad, it is clear, that no more of them will be obtained in exchange for commodities produced by the dearer labour than was previously obtained for the commodities produced by the cheaper labour; for, if those who export commodities to foreign countries, and exchange them for the precious metals, were to obtain more of such metals after wages rose than previously, they would be gaining so much more than the average rate of profit gained by their neighbours at home, whose competition would speedily compel them to give the same quantity of goods produced by the dear labour, for the same quantity of the precious metals that they had obtained previously to the rise in the rate of wages.

In this statement it is taken for granted that the value of money has been all the while invariable; that is, that the same quantity of labour continues necessary to produce the same quantity of it. If the value of money fluctuate, if it become either more or less difficult of production, then, undoubtedly, both the rate of wages and the price of commodities will vary. But they will do so, not because the labourer gets a greater or less amount of wages, but because the value of the commodity, or standard in which wages and prices are estimated, has varied. Wages, though most commonly paid in money, really consist of a portion of the produce of the industry of the labourer; consequently, they bear a high *proportional*, or *cost* value, when the labourer gets a comparatively large share of the produce of his industry, and a low *proportional* value when he gets a comparatively small share of that produce. Instead of being identical with wages estimated in money or commodities, proportional wages are often lowest when money wages are highest, and they are often rising at the moment that money wages are falling, and *vice versâ*. And hence, in order to avoid falling into endless mistakes, it is best, in all theoretical investigations with respect to value, to consider wages in the light of a certain proportion of the produce of industry—as being really invariable, so long as this proportion continues unchanged—as having really risen when it is increased, and really fallen when it is diminished.

The mistaking of fluctuations in the rate of money wages for fluctuations in the rate of proportional wages, has been the source of much error and misapprehension. A man whose wages are 1*s*. a day, must get 2*s*. to keep them at the same level, should the value of money decline a half; and the hat which now sells for 10*s*. must then, for the same reason, sell for 20*s*. It is obviously false to call this a real rise, either of wages or prices: this, however, is what is generally done. The manufacturer who gives sixpence a day more to his men, and who sells his goods at a proportionally higher price because of a fall in the real value of money, rarely suspects that there has been any such fall, and almost invariably concludes that the rise of wages has been the cause of the rise of prices, overlooking entirely the real cause of the rise of both—the decline in the value of the money or commodity in which wages and prices are estimated.

Even if it were true, which most certainly it is not, that when money is constant in its value a rise of wages occasioned an equal rise in the money price of commodities, it would be no advantage to the producers. Commodities are always bought either by other commodities or by labour, and it is almost superfluous to add, that it is quite impossible they can ever be bought by any thing else. Of what benefit, then, would it be to a capitalist, a cotton-manufacturer for example, to sell his cottons for ten per cent advance when wages rise ten per cent, he being at the same time obliged to give so much more for every commodity for which he has a demand? When wages really rise, it is absolutely indifferent to the producers whether they sell the commodities they have to spare, and purchase those they have occasion for at their former price, or whether they are all raised proportionally to the rise of wages.

This principle may be still farther illustrated by supposing the quantities of labour required for the production of all sorts of commodities to be increased in exactly the same proportion: under such circumstances, it is quite clear that their exchangeable values would remain unaltered. A bushel of corn would not then exchange for a greater quantity of muslin or of broad cloth than it did before the increased expense of its production; but each would have a greater *real* value, because each would be the produce of a greater quantity of labour. Under these circumstances, the prices of commodities would remain stationary, while the wealth and comforts of the society would be materially diminished. Every person would have to make greater exertions to obtain a given quantity of any one commodity; but as the expense of producing *all* commodities is, by the supposition, equally increased, it would not be necessary to make any greater exertions to obtain one than another, and their values as compared with each other would be totally unaffected.

But if a general and equal increase of the quantities of labour required for the production of commodities cannot alter their relation to one another, it is quite obvious that this relation cannot be altered by a general and equal increase of the wages paid for that labour. Fluctuations in the rate of cost wages affect the *proportion* in which the produce of industry, under deduction of rent, is divided between capitalists and labourers—diminishing the proportion belonging to the capitalists when they rise, and increasing it when they fall. But as these changes in the distribution of commodities neither add to nor take from the quantity of labour required to produce them and bring them to market, they do not affect either their real or exchangeable value.

II. The arguments now brought forward, to shew that fluctuations in the rate of wages do not affect the exchangeable value of commodities produced by capitals of the same durability, were first advanced by Mr. Ricardo. He, too, was the first who endeavoured to analyse and discover the effects of fluctuations in the rate of wages on the value of commodities, when the capitals employed in their production were *not* of the same degree of durability. The results of his researches in this more difficult inquiry were still more important, and more completely at variance with the universally received opinions: for Mr. Ricardo has not only shewn that it is impossible for any rise of wages to raise the price of *all* commodities, but he has also shewn that in most cases a rise of wages necessarily leads to a *fall* in the price of some descriptions of commodities, and a fall of wages to a *rise* in the price of others.

It must be admitted, that this proposition appears, when first stated, not a little paradoxical. The paradox, however, is only in appearance. On adverting to the means by which certain classes of commodities are produced, it is immediately seen that no proposition can, apparently, be more reasonable, or consistent with probability; and it may be very easily shewn that there is none more certain.

Some commodities are almost exclusively the produce of accumulated labour, or capital, and others of the immediate labour of man. Nearly the whole of the first class will, consequently, belong to the capitalist, and the latter to the labourer. Suppose a manufacturer has a machine worth 20,000*l.* endued with a high degree of durability, and which can manufacture commodities without the assistance of any, or with but very little, manual labour. In this case, it is quite clear that the goods produced by the machine really form the profits of the capital vested in it; and their value in exchange, or their price rated in money, must, therefore, vary with every variation in the rate of profit. If profits were at ten per cent, the goods annually produced by the machine must sell for 2,000*l.*, with a small additional sum to cover the wear and tear of the engine: should profits rise to fifteen per cent, the price of the goods produced by the machine must rise to 3,000*l.*, for otherwise the manufacturer would not obtain the common and average rate of profit; and if, on the other hand, profits should fall to five per cent, the price of the goods must, for the same reason, fall to 1,000*l.* If, therefore, it can be shewn that a rise of wages reduces the rate of profits, it necessarily follows that it must also reduce the exchangeable value and price of all such commodities as are chiefly produced by machinery, or fixed capital of a considerable degree of durability, or by circulating capitals returnable at distant periods, and *vice versâ*.

Now it is easy to shew that, so long as no variation takes place in the quantity of labour required for the production of commodities,* every rise of wages must reduce profits, and must, therefore, reduce the exchangeable value of those commodities which have been chiefly produced by the aid of fixed capital or machinery. It is plain, from what has been previously stated, that to whatever extent wages rise, no set of producers, whether the capitals employed by them be returnable in a day, a week, a year, or a hundred years, can obtain a larger share of the commodities produced by others of the *same class*,—that is, of those whose capitals are returnable in equal periods with their own. This is evidently as impossible as it is to change the relation of numbers by multiplying or dividing them all by the *same* number; and therefore it is certain, that a rise of wages cannot raise the value of any one commodity as compared with all other commodities. But if it cannot do this, it must universally lower profits. Suppose wages rise ten per cent: assuredly that rise will not enable those manufacturers who employ the fewest labourers in proportion to their capital, to obtain any larger share of the products belonging to those who are placed under similar circumstances,—that is, who employ equal quantities of machinery and labour, and still less of those who expend a larger portion of their capital in the payment of wages. It is clear, therefore, that the profits of the manufacturers in question, and, consequently, the profits of all other producers whatever, must be reduced by this rise of wages; and whenever this reduction takes place, the exchangeable value of the commodities, produced chiefly by the aid of fixed capital or machinery, will be diminished as compared with those produced chiefly by the hand.

Suppose that the numbers 1, 2, 3, 4, 5, 6, 7, 8, 9, 10, 11, &c. represent the various descriptions of capitals,

* The reason for this limitation will be subsequently explained.

classed according to the respective degrees of their average durability; that No. 1 represents that class of capitals which are wholly employed in the payment of wages, and which are most speedily consumed and reproduced; No. 2, that class which is next in durability; and so on until we come to No. 11, which represents that class of capitals which chiefly consist of highly durable machinery, and which are longest in being consumed and reproduced. Let us farther suppose that the commodities produced by the agency of these capitals are all yielding the same common and average rate of profit to their proprietors; and let us endeavour to discover what would, under these circumstances, be the effect of fluctuations in the rate of cost wages on the value of commodities. If wages rise, it is plain that the holders of the least durable capitals (No. 1), who may be supposed to use no machinery, will be more affected by the rise than the holders of the second class (No. 2), who may be supposed to employ some little machinery; and these again more than the holders of the third class (No. 3); and so on till we come to the holders of the capital of the highest degree of durability (No. 11), which may be supposed to consist almost wholly of very durable machinery; and who will, on that account, be comparatively little affected by the rise. Suppose, now, to illustrate the principle, that wages have so risen that the increased rate paid by the proprietors of the most durable capitals to the few labourers they employ—for they cannot possibly avoid employing a few to superintend their machinery—has had the effect of reducing their profits *one* per cent: there is obviously no mode in which these capitalists can indemnify themselves for this fall of profits; for, as they employ the fewest labourers, they are least of all affected by the rise of wages, the profits of all other capitalists being more reduced than theirs in proportion to the greater number of labourers they employ. Thus, supposing the proprietors of the most durable capitals, or of No. 11, to employ a certain number of labourers; the proprietors of the next class, or of No. 10, to employ twice that number; and those of No. 9, three times that number, and so on; then, on the hypothesis that the rise of wages has reduced the profits of the most durable capitals, or No. 11, *one* per cent, it will have reduced those of No. 10 *two* per cent, those of No. 9 *three* per cent, and so on till we come to the least durable class, No. 1, whose profits will be reduced *eleven* per cent. It is plain, however, that this discrepancy in the rate of profit must be of very temporary duration. For the undertakers of those businesses in which either the whole or the greater portion of the capital is employed in paying the wages of labour, observing that their neighbours, who have laid out the greater portion of their capital on machinery, are less affected by the rise of wages, will immediately begin to withdraw from their own businesses, and to engage in those that are more lucrative. The commodities produced by the most durable capitals, Nos. 7, 8, 9, 10, &c. will, therefore, become redundant, as compared with those produced by the least durable capitals, Nos. 1, 2, 3, 4, &c.; and this increase on the one hand, and diminution on the other, will sink the value of the former, compared with the latter, till they all yield the same rate of profit.

The value of the commodities produced by capital of the *medium* degree of durability, or by No. 6, would not be affected by the rise; for, whatever they lost in exchangeable value as compared with the commodities produced by the less durable capitals, they would gain as compared with those produced by the more durable capitals.

It has, however, been contended, that though the equalisation in the rate of profit now alluded to might be effected by the destruction of a portion of the less durable capital, or by the comparatively great accumulations that would henceforth be made by the holders of the more durable capitals, who were but little affected by the rise of wages, it could not be effected by such a transference of capital from the one class of businesses to the other as has been supposed; for it is said, that the fixed stock, or machinery, belonging to the holders of the capitals of the greatest degree of durability, being itself the produce of labour, it would not be possible to obtain this machinery at its former price after wages rose, so that the profits of the existing holders of Nos. 7, 8, 9, &c. could not be beaten down to a common level with those of the holders of the less durable capitals, by an influx of new competitors. But it is easy to see that this view of the matter is not correct. Suppose, which is the strongest case for the argument I am combating, that the machines belonging to the capitalists of the class No. 11, are the produce of the labourers employed by the capitalists of the class No. 1: when wages rise, it is evident the machines and other commodities produced by No. 1 cannot rise in value, as compared with money, or any other commodity produced under different circumstances, until they are diminished, or the others increased in quantity. And hence there are two very sufficient reasons why the producers of the machines should not be disposed to sell them after wages rise; for, in the *first* place, if they sell them they will get no more for them than they got before the rise; and, in the *second* place, as the more lucrative businesses, or those that are least affected by the rise of wages, can only be carried on by means of machinery, they could not, if they sold the machines, transfer circulating capital to them, but would be compelled to continue in those businesses that had become relatively disadvantageous. Instead, therefore, of selling the machines, it may be fairly presumed that a large proportion of their producers would be induced to employ them in the businesses for which they were intended, and would thus come into competition with the existing holders of the capitals Nos. 7, 8, 9, 10, &c. exactly on the same footing that they stand, or with machines that have cost exactly the same price as theirs;

nor would this transference of capital cease until the quantity of the commodities produced on the least durable side of the scale had been so much diminished, and their value so much increased, as compared with those produced on the more durable side, that they were all brought to yield the same common and average rate of profit.

If wages, instead of rising, had fallen, the opposite effects would have been produced. The holders of the capitals Nos. 1, 2, 3, &c., who employ a comparatively large proportion of labourers, deriving a greater advantage from the fall of wages than the holders of the capitals Nos. 7, 8, 9, &c., their profits would be raised above the level of the latter. In consequence, capital would begin to move from those businesses that employ the fewest to those that employ the greatest number of labourers; and the average equilibrium of profit would be restored by an increase of the exchangeable value of the commodities produced by the most durable, as compared with those produced by the least durable capitals.

It is abundantly certain, therefore, that no rise of wages can ever occasion a general rise of prices, and no fall of wages a general fall of prices; but, supposing the productiveness of industry, or the quantity of labour required to produce commodities, to remain the same, a rise of wages, instead of occasioning a general rise of prices, will have the effect to occasion a general fall of profits; and a fall of wages, instead of reducing prices, will occasion a general rise of profits. Owing, however, to the different and ever-varying degrees of the durability of the machinery, or fixed capital, employed in the production of commodities, and the varying relation which the portion of capital employed as wages, or in the payment of immediate labour, bears to the whole capital employed, it is very difficult to determine, *à priori,* the extent to which any given fluctuation in the rate of wages will affect the rate of profit, and the exchangeable value of commodities. But, when due pains are taken, this may be approximated with sufficient accuracy for practical purposes; and the following three cases will briefly, and, I hope, satisfactorily elucidate the manner in which fluctuations in the rate of wages always operate, and the method to be followed in estimating their influence on profits and prices.

1. If all commodities were produced by immediate labour, or by capital employed in the payment of wages, it is obvious, supposing the productiveness of industry not to vary, that every rise of wages would cause an equal fall of profits. A capitalist who employed 1,000*l.* in the payment of wages, must, if profits were at 10 per cent, sell the commodities for 1,100*l.* But when wages rise 5 per cent, or to 1,050*l.*, he would not be able to sell his commodities for more than 1,100*l.*; for money is itself a commodity; and as, by the supposition, all commodities are produced by immediate labour, the rise of wages would affect the producers of money in the same way that it affected all other producers. In this case, therefore, it is plain that every rise of wages will equally sink profits, and every fall of wages will equally raise them.

2. If all commodities were produced, *one-half* by immediate labour, and the *other half* by capital, profits would only fall to half the extent that wages rose. Suppose a capitalist employs 500*l.* in the payment of wages, and 500*l.* as a fixed capital, when profits are at 10 per cent, the commodities produced must, as before, sell for 1,100*l.* If wages rose 5 per cent, the capitalist would have to pay 525*l.* as wages, and would, consequently, only retain 75*l.* as profits. In this case, therefore, a rise of wages to the extent of 5 per cent would, because of the employment of equal quantities of capital and immediate labour in the production of commodities, only sink profits 2½ per cent.

3. If all commodities were produced by capital of a high degree of durability, the capitalists, it is obvious, would not be at all affected by a rise of wages, and profits would, of course, continue as before.

Now, suppose that commodities, instead of being wholly produced either by immediate labour, as in the first case; or wholly by equal quantities of immediate labour and of capital, as in the second; or wholly by fixed capital, as in the third,—are partly produced in the one mode and partly in the other, and let us see what effect this increase of 5 per cent in the rate of wages would have on their relative values, supposing, as before, that the productiveness of industry continues constant. To facilitate this inquiry, let us distinguish these three descriptions of commodities by the Nos. 1, 2, and 3. Now it is quite evident that the rise of wages has affected No. 1, 2½ per cent more than it has affected No. 2, and 5 per cent more than it has affected No. 3. No. 1 must, therefore, as compared with No. 2, have risen 2½ per cent in exchangeable value, and, as compared with No. 3, it must have risen 5 per cent; No. 2 must have fallen 2½ per cent as compared with No. 1, and risen 2½ per cent as compared with No. 3; and No. 3 must have fallen 5 per cent as compared with No. 1, and 2½ per cent as compared with No. 2. If wages, instead of rising, had fallen, the same effects would obviously have been produced, but in a reversed order. The proprietors of the commodities of the class No. 1 would gain 5 per cent by the fall; those of No. 2 would gain 2½ per cent; and those of No. 3 nothing; and the relative values of these commodities would be adjusted accordingly.*

Thus, then, it appears, inasmuch as any commodity taken for a standard by which to estimate the relative values of other commodities, must itself be produced by capital returnable in a certain period, that when wages rise all commodities produced by *less* durable capitals than those which produce the commodity taken for a standard, will rise in exchangeable value, and all those produced

* These examples are substantially the same with those given by Mr. Mill. "Elements of Political Economy," 2d edit. p. 103.

by *more* durable capitals will fall; and conversely when wages are reduced. Suppose, as before, that the Nos. 1, 2, 3, 4, 5, 6, 7, 8, 9, 10, and 11, represent capitals of corresponding degrees of durability. If a commodity produced by the least durable capital, No. 1, and which may be supposed to be wholly employed in the payment of wages, be taken for a standard, all commodities whatever produced by the other and more durable capitals would *fall* in value when wages rose; and if we suppose those produced by No. 2 to decline 1 per cent, those produced by No. 3 would decline 2 per cent, those produced by No. 4, 3 per cent, and so on until we arrive at No. 11, which will have fallen 10 per cent. If, on the other hand, a commodity, produced by the most durable capital, No. 11, and which may be supposed to consist wholly of highly durable machinery, be made the standard, when wages rise, all the commodities produced by the other less durable capitals would also rise; and if those produced by No. 10 rose 1 per cent, those produced by No. 9 would rise 2 per cent, and those produced by No. 1 10 per cent. If a commodity, produced by a capital of the *medium* degree of durability, as No. 6, and which may be supposed to consist half of circulating capital employed in the payment of wages, and half of fixed capital or machinery, be taken as a standard, the commodities produced by the less durable capitals, Nos. 5, 4, 3, 2, and 1, will *rise* with a rise of wages, on the former hypothesis, the first, or No. 5, 1 per cent, the second, or No. 4, 2 per cent, &c.; while those produced by the more durable capitals, Nos. 7, 8, 9, 10, and 11, will *fall*, the first, or No. 7, 1 per cent, the second, or No. 8, 2 per cent, &c. exactly the reverse of the other.

Hence it is obvious, that the effect which variations in the rate of wages have on the *price* of commodities must principally depend on the nature of the capital employed in the production of gold or silver. Whatever may be the proportions of circulating capital appropriated to the payment of wages, and of fixed capital employed in the production of the material of which money is made, all those commodities which are produced by the agency of a greater quantity of circulating capital, and with less fixed capital or machinery, will rise when wages rise, and fall when wages fall; but those that are produced by the agency of a less quantity of circulating capital, and with more fixed capital or machinery, will fall when wages rise, and rise when wages fall; while those that are produced under nearly the same circumstances, or by the agency of the same quantities of circulating and fixed capital as money, will not be affected by these fluctuations.

It should be observed, however, that the variations in the exchangeable value of most commodities, caused by variations in the rate of proportional wages, are confined within comparatively narrow limits. We have already seen that, if all commodities were either produced wholly by immediate labour, or wholly by capital, or wholly by equal quantities of both, no variation in the rate of wages would have any effect on the value of commodities. But, in point of fact, a very large class of commodities are produced by means of nearly equal portions of fixed and circulating capital; and as every rise of proportional wages that may take place must, under such circumstances, be balanced either by a fall in the rate of profit or by a proportional increase in the productiveness of industry, it is evident that the value of the commodities in question, as compared with each other, would remain nearly stationary. Although, therefore, a rise of wages has a necessary tendency to raise the exchangeable value of one class of commodities, and consequently to lower that of another class, the fall of profits, which must inevitably follow every rise of wages that is not accompanied by an increased productiveness of industry, has a contrary effect, and tends to sink the value of the commodities which the increased rate of wages would raise, and to elevate the value of those which the same increased rate would sink. And it is only in the extreme cases, or in the case of the commodities produced almost wholly by direct manual labour, on the one hand, or in that of those produced almost wholly by the aid of fixed capital or machinery, on the other, that a variation in the rate of proportional wages occasions a considerable variation in their relative values.

It must also be observed, that though fluctuations in the rate of wages occasion some variation in the exchangeable value of particular commodities, they neither add to nor take from the *total value* of the entire mass of commodities. If they increase the value of those produced by the least durable capitals, they equally diminish the value of those produced by the more durable capitals. Their aggregate value continues, therefore, always the same. And though it may not be strictly true of a particular commodity, that its exchangeable value is directly as its *real* value, or as the quantity of labour required to produce it and bring it to market, it is most true to affirm this of the mass of commodities taken together.

In thus endeavouring to trace the real value of all descriptions of non-monopolised commodities to the quantity of labour required for their production, it is not meant to deny that a very large portion of the useful or desirable qualities of such commodities may be the result of the action or labour of natural agents. But it is, as I formerly stated, the peculiar and distinguishing feature of natural agents, or powers, that they render their services gratuitously. Whatever is done by them is done without fee or reward. And thence, though their assistance and co-operation be necessary to the production of every species of useful and desirable articles, they add nothing to its value. This is a quality that can be communicated only by the labour of man, or by the instrumentality of that capital that has been appropriated or accumulated by his labour. In estimating the value of a quantity of corn, for example, we include only the labour of the individuals employed, as ploughmen, reapers, thrashers, &c. the value of the corn used as seed, and the value of the services rendered by the horses and instruments made use of in the different operations. Nothing whatever is set down on account of the aid derived from the vegetative powers of nature, and the action of the sun and showers; for though without them the crop could not be obtained, and our utmost exertions would be altogether fruitless, yet, as they are the free gift of Providence, they add nothing to the value of the produce, that is, they add nothing to its power of exchanging for or buying labour, or other things produced by the intervention of labour.

It may be thought, perhaps, that this principle is at variance with what is observed to take place in the production of certain descriptions of commodities. Thus, if a cask of new wine be kept for a definite period, or till it arrives at maturity, it will acquire a higher value: now, as the change produced on the wine is entirely brought about by the operation of natural agents, and as, without the change, the wine would have no higher value, it has been contended that this is a case in which the labour of natural agents is plainly productive of an increased value. But it is easy to see that this is a mistake. The cask of wine is a capital, or is the result of the labour employed in cultivating, gathering, pressing, and otherwise preparing, the grapes from which it was made. But it is necessary, in order to give time for the processes of fermentation, decomposition, &c. to effect the desired changes in the wine, that it should be laid aside until they are completed. The producer of wine would not, however, employ his capital in this way, unless it were to yield him the same return that is derived from the capital employed in other businesses. And hence it follows, that though the processes carried on by nature render the wine more desirable, or bestow on it a greater degree of utility, they add nothing to its value; the additional value which it acquires being a consequence of the profit accruing on the capital required to enable the processes to be carried on.

Besides the objection now stated, it has been contended by Colonel Torrens, in his valuable work, "On the Production of Wealth," in opposition to the theory I have been endeavouring to establish, that, after capital has been accumulated, the exchangeable value of commodities is no longer, as in the early stages of society, determined by the total quantities of labour required to bring them to market, but by the *quantities of capital* required for that purpose. At bottom, however, this theory is precisely the same as that just explained. Capital is nothing but the accumulated produce of anterior labour; and its value, like the value of every thing else, is to be estimated by the quantity of labour required to procure it. In this respect, too, there is no difference, as has been already shewn, between labourers and any other species of machines. A labourer is himself a portion of the national capital, and may, without impropriety, be considered, in theoretical investigations of this sort, in the light of a machine which it has required a certain outlay of labour to construct: the wages which he earns are no more than a fair remuneration for the services performed by him, or, if I may so speak, they yield him only the common and ordinary rate of profit on his capital, exclusive of a sum to replace its wear and tear, or, which is the same thing, to supply the place of the old and decayed labourers with new ones. Whether, therefore, a commodity has been produced by the expenditure of a capital which it cost a certain quantity of labour to provide, or whether it has been immediately produced by the expenditure of that quantity of labour directly upon it, is of no moment. In either case it is produced by exactly the same amount of labour, or, if it should be deemed a better phrase, of capital. There is, in truth, no substantial difference between the mere manual labour of man and the labour of machinery. Men are themselves, in so far as their purely physical powers are concerned, and it is such only that are now in question, to be looked upon as capital, or are to be considered in the same point of view as the tools or engines with which they perform their tasks: and to say that the exchangeable value of commodities depends on the quantities of capital expended on their production, is not to contradict, but is, in fact, only another way of expressing the identical proposition I have been endeavouring to illustrate.

Many practical conclusions of great interest and importance may be deduced from the principles developed in this chapter. It had, for example, been long and universally supposed, that a country where wages are comparatively low would be able, provided it possessed the same facilities for the production of commodities, to undersell all other countries in markets equally accessible to all parties. But the principles now laid down shew the fallacy of this opinion. Suppose, to exemplify the mode in which variations in the rate of wages really affect foreign commerce, that England and France have *equal* facilities for producing all sorts of commodities, and that the rate of wages is equal in both countries; and let the following numbers represent the different classes of capital, ranged according to the different degrees of their durability, employed in production in England and France, viz.

Nos. 1, 2, 3, 4, 5, 6, 7, 8, 9, 10, 11, &c. England.

Nos. 1′, 2′, 3′, 4′, 5′, 6′, 7′, 8′, 9′, 10′, 11′, &c. France.

Now, as the two countries are supposed to have equal facilities of production, and as the rate of wages in them both is also supposed to be the same, the commodities produced by each will sell equally well in any third market, as in that of the United States, equally open to both: but suppose, that while wages continue stationary in France they rise in England, and mark the result. All those commodities produced in England by the capitals Nos. 7, 8, 9, 10, &c., which are above the *medium* degree of durability, and may be supposed to consist chiefly of machinery, will fall, while those produced by the less durable capitals, Nos. 1, 2, 3, 4, &c., will rise. The former will not, however, fall only in relation to the commodities produced in England by less durable capitals, but they will also fall in relation to the commodities produced in France by the corresponding and equally durable capitals, Nos. 7′, 8′, 9′, 10′, &c.; while the latter, or the commodities produced in England by the capitals Nos. 1, 2, 3, 4, &c. will rise in value as compared with the commodities produced in France by the corresponding capitals, Nos. 1′, 2′, 3′, 4′, &c. The merchants of England and France will, therefore, no longer come into the American market on the same terms as formerly; for England will henceforth have a decided advantage over France in the production and sale of those commodities that are produced chiefly by machinery; while France will, on her part, have an equally decided advantage over England in the production and sale of those commodities that are chiefly the direct produce of the hand. And such, in point of fact, is actually the case. The bulk of our exports consists of cotton goods and other products of machinery; whereas the bulk of the exports of France consists of the productions of her soil, and of jewellery and fancy articles, principally the product of manual labour. It is, therefore, quite idle to suppose that a rise of wages can ever be fatal to the foreign commerce of a country. It may, indeed, turn it into new channels, but that is all it can do. If, on the one hand, it raises the value of certain descriptions of commodities and checks their exportation, on the other, it proportionally lowers the value of other descriptions, and fits them the better for the foreign market.

It appears, therefore, that instead of our high wages laying our cotton manufacturers under any comparative disadvantage in the sale of their goods, their effect is distinctly the reverse. The high wages we pay to our workmen, and the other burdens laid on the manufacturers, cause *low* profits; and as the principal part of the value of cottons and other commodities chiefly produced by the agency of machinery, consists of profits, it must be comparatively low where profits are low. Suppose, for example, that two highly durable machines, of equal power and goodness, and which can be used with but little manual labour, are erected, the one in France and the other in England: if the machines cost 20,000*l.* each, and if the rate of profit in France were six and in England five per cent, the work done by the French machine would be worth 1,200*l.*, whereas that done by the English machine would only be worth 1,000*l.* It should also be observed, inasmuch as one description of machinery is for the most part largely employed in the production of another, that it is most probable, in the event of one of the machines being made in England and the other in France, that the English one would not cost so much as 20,000*l.* and that its produce might on that account be sold under 1,000*l.* Independently, however, of this circumstance, the advantage that our manufacturers who are large employers of machinery must have over those of France, in consequence of our lower profits, is obvious and decided. This principle shews how unnecessary it is to restrict the exportation of machinery. It is quite evident, that although France were possessed of all those facilities for manufacturing cottons we now enjoy, though Normandy were a second Lancashire, and Rouen a fac-simile of Manchester, her manufacturers would not be able to enter into a successful competition with those of England. The possession of better machinery would not lower profits in France; and, till this is done, we must, supposing we continue to possess *equal facilities* of production, always have an ascendancy over the French in the sale of such articles as are mainly produced by means of machinery.

The statement now made is not meant to convey the impression that low profits are really advantageous. On the contrary, the tendency of a low rate of profit is not only to occasion all countries in which it obtains to advance slowly as compared with those in which it is higher, but it also forms a strong temptation to convey capital from them. A reduction of taxation, or a reduction of wages, following a corresponding reduction in the price of corn, or any of the principal necessaries that enter into the consumption of the labourer, would raise the rate of profit, and would, consequently, by raising their price, narrow the demand for cottons. But a diminution in our exports to foreign countries, arising from this cause, instead of being injurious would be most beneficial. It would be the effect of industry having become more productive; and any capital that had previously been employed in the production of goods for the foreign market, that could not, under the supposed change of circumstances, be advantageously sent abroad, would be certain to meet with a more profitable employment in other branches. In so far, however, as the cotton manufacture is concerned, there can be no manner of doubt that the depression in the rate of profit has powerfully contributed to its extraordinary extension. And, however paradoxical it may seem, it is nevertheless true, that were wages to rise and profits to sustain a further decline, additional capital would be attracted to the manufacture, and the price of cottons would experience a further reduction; whereas, were wages to fall and profits to rise, capital would be drawn from the manufacture to those businesses that employ less machinery, and the price of cottons would rise.*

* Sir William Petty seems to have been the first economist who has distinctly stated the principle, that the value of commodities depends on the quantities of labour required for their production. "If," says he, "a man bring to London an ounce of silver out of the earth in Peru, in the same time that he can produce a bushel of corn, the one is the natural price of the other: now if, by reason of new and more easie mines, a man can get two ounces of silver as easily as formerly he did one, then corn will be as cheap at ten shillings the bushel as it was before at five shillings, *cæteris paribus*."—*Treatise of Taxes and Contributions*, ed. 1679, p. 31. At page 24 he says, "Let a hundred men work ten years upon corn, and the same number of men the same time upon silver; I say that the neat proceed of the silver is the price of the whole neat proceed of the corn, and like parts of the one the price of like parts of the other:" and at page 67 he says, "Corn will be twice as dear when there are two hundred husbandmen to do the same work which a hundred could perform." These passages are curious and interesting, as exhibiting the first germs of the theory which Mr. Ricardo did so much to perfect.

PRINCIPLES

OF

POLITICAL ECONOMY.

PART III.

DISTRIBUTION OF WEALTH.

THE inhabitants of such countries as have made any considerable progress in civilisation and the arts, may be divided into the *three* classes of labourers, landlords, and capitalists; and whatever be the condition of any society—whether rude or refined, rich or poor—every person belonging to it, who is not a pauper, or who does not subsist on the bounty of others, may be reckoned in one or other of these classes. They divide amongst them all the wealth of the community. Public functionaries of all sorts, and the various individuals engaged in what are called liberal or learned professions, exchange their services for valuable considerations. The whole subsistence of such persons, in so far as they depend upon their employments, is derived from wages; and they are as evidently labourers as if they handled a spade or a plough. "Every man," says Dr. Paley, "has his work. The kind of work varies, and that is all the difference there is. A great deal of labour exists besides that of the hands; many species of industry beside bodily operation; equally necessary, requiring equal assiduity, more attention, more anxiety. It is not true, therefore, that men of elevated stations are exempted from work; it is only true that there is assigned to them work of a different kind: whether more easy or more pleasant may be questioned; but certainly not less wanted, nor less essential to the common good."* Hence it is that the inquiry into the distribution of wealth among the different orders of the society, resolves itself into an investigation of the laws which regulate wages, rent, and profit, and of the best methods of providing for the exigencies of the poor, or of those who are unable to provide for themselves. I shall begin by endeavouring to lay before the reader a view of the circumstances which determine the wages of labour in different employments.

* "Assize Sermon," 29th July, 1795.

CHAPTER I.

Wages in the different Departments of Industry—Really approach very near to Equality.

THE wages paid to the labourers engaged in different employments, differ so very widely, that, at first sight, it may seem to be impossible to lay down any principles that should be generally applicable to them all. Such however, is not the case. The differences in question are rather apparent than real; and when the various circumstances, exclusive of wages, connected with different employments, are taken into account, it will be found, that the remuneration of those engaged in them is very nearly the same at any given period.

If all employments were equally agreeable and healthy, if the labour to be performed in each was of the same intensity, and if each required the same degree of dexterity and skill on the part of those employed, it is evident, supposing industry to be quite free, that there could be no permanent or considerable difference in the wages of labour. For if those employed in a particular business were to earn either *more* or *less* than their neighbours, labourers would, in the former case, leave other businesses to engage in it, and in the latter they would leave it to engage in others, until the increase or diminution of their numbers had lowered or elevated wages to the common level. In point of fact, however, the intensity of the labour to be performed in different employments, the degree of skill required to carry them on, their healthiness, and the estimation in which they are held, differ exceedingly; and these varying circumstances necessarily occasion proportional differences in the wages of different classes of workmen. Wages are a compensation paid to the labourer for the exertion of his physical powers, or of his skill or ingenuity. They therefore necessarily vary according to the severity of the labour to be performed, and the degree of skill and ingenuity required. A jeweller or engraver, for example, must be paid a higher rate of wages than a common servant or a scavenger. A long course of training is necessary to instruct a man in the business of jewelling and engraving; and were he not indemnified for the cost of this training by a higher rate of wages, he would, instead of learning so difficult an art, addict himself, in preference, to such employments as hardly require any instruction. Hence, the discrepancies that actually obtain in the rate of wages are all confined within certain limits—increasing or diminishing it only so far as may be necessary fully to equalise the unfavourable or favourable peculiarities attending any employment.

The following have been stated by Dr. Smith as the principal circumstances which occasion the rate of wages in some employments to fall below or rise above the *general average* rate of wages:—

1st, The agreeableness and disagreeableness of the employments:

2d, The easiness or cheapness, or the difficulty and expense, of learning them:

3d, The constancy or inconstancy of the employments:

4th, The small or great trust that must be reposed in those who carry them on:

5th, The probability or improbability of succeeding in them.

First, The agreeableness of an employment may arise either from physical or moral causes—from the lightness of the labour, its healthiness or cleanliness, the degree of estimation in which it is held, &c.; and its disagreeableness will arise from the opposite circumstances—from the severity of the labour, its unhealthiness or dirtiness, the degree of odium attached to it, &c. The rate of wages must obviously vary proportionally to the variations in circumstances which exert so powerful an influence over the labourer. It is indeed quite out of the question to suppose, that any individual should ever be so blind to his own interest, as to engage in an occupation considered as mean and disreputable, or where the labour is severe, if he obtain only the same rate of wages that is obtained by those engaged in employments in higher estimation, and where the labour to be performed is comparatively light. The labour of the ploughman is not unhealthy, nor is it either irksome or disagreeable; but being more severe than that of the shepherd, it is uniformly better rewarded. The same principle holds universally. Miners, gilders, type-founders, smiths, distillers, and all who carry on unhealthy, disagreeable, and dangerous businesses, invariably obtain higher wages than those who have equal skill, but who are engaged in more desirable employments. The unfavourable opinion entertained respecting some businesses has a similar effect on wages as if the labour to be performed in them were unusually unhealthy or severe. The trade of a butcher, for example, is generally looked upon as rather low and discreditable; and this feeling occasions such a disinclination on the part of young men to enter it, as can only be overcome by the high wages that butchers are said to earn, notwithstanding the lightness of their labour: this also is the reason that the keeper of a small inn or tavern, who is never master of his own house, and who is exposed to the brutality of every drunkard, exercises one of the most profitable of the common trades. The contrary circumstances have contrary effects. Hunting and fishing form, in an advanced state of society, among the most agreeable amusements of the rich; but from their being held in this degree of estimation, and from the lightness of their labour, those who practise them as a trade generally receive very small wages, and are proverbially poor: and the agreeableness and healthiness of the employments, rather than the lightness of their labour or the little skill which they require, seem to be the principal cause of the redundant numbers, and consequent low wages, of common farm-servants, and generally of all workmen employed in ordinary field labour.

The severe discipline and various hardships to which common soldiers are exposed, and the little chance they have of arriving at a higher station, are unfavourable circumstances, which, it might have been supposed, would have required a very high rate of wages to counterbalance. It is found, however, that there are really very few common trades in which labourers can be procured for such low wages as those for which recruits are willing to enlist in the army. Nor is it difficult to discover the causes of this apparent anomaly. Except when actually engaged in warlike operations, a soldier is comparatively idle; while his free, dissipated, and generally adventurous life, the splendour of his uniform, the imposing spectacle of military parades and evolutions, and the martial music by which they are accompanied, exert a most seductive influence over the young and inconsiderate. The dangers and privations of campaigns are undervalued, while the chances of advancement are proportionally exaggerated in their sanguine and heated imaginations. "Without regarding the danger," says Dr. Smith, "soldiers are never obtained so easily as at the beginning of a new war; and though they have scarce any chance of preferment, they figure to themselves, in their youthful fancies, a thousand occasions of acquiring honour and distinction which never occur. These romantic hopes make the whole price of their blood. Their pay is less than that of common labourers, and in actual service their fatigues are much greater."*

It is observed by Dr. Smith, that the chances of suc-

* Vol. i. p. 180.

ceeding in the sea service are greater than in the army. "The son of a creditable labourer or artificer may frequently go to sea with his father's consent; but if he enlists as a soldier, it is always without it. Other people see some chance of his making something by the one trade: nobody but himself sees any of his making any thing by the other." But, the allurements to enlist in the army are, notwithstanding, found to be much greater than those which prompt young men to enter the navy. The life of a sailor is perhaps more adventurous than that of a soldier, but he has no regular uniform, his employment is comparatively dirty and disagreeable, his labour more severe, and while at sea he suffers a species of imprisonment, and cannot, like the soldier, excite either the envy or admiration of his countrymen. In consequence, the wages of seamen almost invariably exceed those of soldiers, and there is a greater difficulty of obtaining recruits at the breaking out of a war.

In England, the disadvantages and drawbacks naturally incident to a seafaring life have been considerably increased by the practice of impressment. The violence and injustice to which this practice exposes sailors have a powerful influence in preventing young men from entering on board ship, and consequently tend, by artificially lessening the supply of sailors, to raise their wages above their natural level, to the extreme injury both of the king's and the merchant service. "The custom of impressment," says Sir Matthew Decker, "puts a freeborn British sailor on the same footing as a Turkish slave. The Grand Seignior cannot do a more absolute act than to order a man to be dragged away from his family, and against his will run his head against the mouth of a cannon; and if such acts should be frequent in Turkey, upon any one set of useful men, would it not drive them away to other countries, and thin their numbers yearly? and would not the remaining few double or treble their wages? which is the case with our sailors, in time of war, to the great detriment of our commerce." *

In corroboration of what has now been stated, it may be mentioned, that while the wages of all other sorts of labourers and artisans are uniformly higher in the United States than in England, those of sailors are most commonly *lower*. The reason is, that the navy of the United States is manned by means of voluntary enlistment only. The Americans are desirous of becoming a great naval power, and they have wisely relinquished a practice which would have driven their best sailors from their service, and have forced them to man their fleet with the sweepings of their jails.

It has been estimated, that there were above 16,000 British sailors on board American ships at the close of last war; and the wages of our seamen, which in time of peace rarely exceed 40*s*. or 50*s*. a month, had then risen to 100*s*. and 120*s*.! This extraordinary influx of British seamen into the American service, and no less extraordinary rise in their wages, can be accounted for only by our continuing the practice of impressment after its abandonment by the United States. Formerly, our seamen were in the habit, on the breaking out of a war, of deserting to Holland; but the difference of language was an insuperable obstacle to this being done to any very injurious extent. With the United States, however, the case is altogether different. In them our sailors may expect to find a safe asylum among their kindred and friends—among those whose language, religion, customs, and habits, are all identical with their own—and who will naturally be disposed to hold out every temptation to draw them to their service. Nothing but the abolition of impressment can counteract such overpowering inducements to desertion, and effectually reduce the wages of our seamen.

* "Essay on the Causes of the Decline of Foreign Trade." Ed. 1756. p 24.

And as it has been shewn, that impressment is in no respect, nor under any circumstances, necessary to the manning of the fleet,* it is to be hoped that it may speedily be abolished; and that the efforts of the Americans to increase their naval power may not be assisted by our obstinately clinging to a system fraught with injustice and oppression.

The officers of the army and navy, and many of those functionaries who fill situations of great trust and responsibility, receive only a comparatively small pecuniary remuneration. The consideration attached to such offices, and the influence they confer on their possessors, form a principal part of their salary.

Secondly, The wages of labour, in particular businesses, vary according to the comparative facility with which they may be learned.

There are several sorts of labour which a man may perform without any, or with but very little, previous instruction; and in which he will, consequently, gain a certain rate of wages from the moment he is employed. But, in all civilised societies, there is a great variety of employments which can be carried on by those only who have been regularly instructed in them. And it is evident, that the wages of such skilled labour should so far exceed the wages of that which is comparatively rude, as to afford the workmen a sufficient compensation for the time they have lost, and the expense they have incurred in their education. Suppose that the education of a skilled labourer—a jeweller or engraver, for example—and his maintenance down to the period when he begins to support himself, cost 300*l*. more than is required for the maintenance of an unskilled labourer, down to the same period; it is plain, that to place these two individuals in the same situation, the skilled labourer should earn as much wages over and above those earned by the one that

* See my edition of the "Wealth of Nations," vol. iv. pp. 397—406.

is unskilled, as may be sufficient, not only to yield him the usual rate of profit on the extra capital of 300*l*. expended on his education, but also to replace the capital itself previously to the probable termination of his life. If he obtain less than this he will be underpaid; and if he obtain more he will be overpaid, and there will be an influx of new entrants, until their competition has reduced wages to their proper level.

The policy of most European nations has added to the natural and necessary cost of breeding up skilled labourers, by forcing them to serve as apprentices for a longer period than is commonly required to obtain a knowledge of the trades they mean to exercise. But, as the wages of labour must always be proportioned, not only to the skill and dexterity of the labourer, but also to the time he has spent, and the difficulties and expense he has had to encounter, in learning his business, it is plain, that if an individual be compelled to serve an apprenticeship of *seven* years to a business which he might have learned in two or three years, he must obtain a proportionally higher rate of wages after the expiration of his apprenticeship. The institution of unnecessarily long apprenticeships is, therefore, productive of a double injury: in the *first* place, it is injurious to the employers of workmen, by artificially raising the wages of their journeymen; and, in the *second* place, it is injurious to the workmen, from its tendency to generate idle and dissipated habits, by making them pass so large a portion of their youth without any sufficient motive to be industrious.

By the common law of England, every man has a right to employ himself at pleasure in every lawful trade. But this sound principle was almost entirely subverted by a statute passed, in compliance with the solicitations of the corporate bodies, in the 5th year of the reign of Queen Elizabeth, commonly called the statute of apprenticeship. It enacted that no person should, for the future, exercise any trade, craft, or mystery, at that time exercised in England or Wales, unless he had previously served to it an apprenticeship of *seven* years at least; so that what had before been a by-law of a few corporations, became the general and statute law of the kingdom. Fortunately, however, the courts were always singularly disinclined to enforce the provisions of this statute. Though the words of the act plainly include the whole kingdom of England and Wales, it was interpreted to refer to *market towns* only, and to those trades which had been practised in England when the statute was passed, without any reference to such as had been subsequently introduced. This interpretation gave occasion to several very absurd and even ludicrous distinctions. It was adjudged, for example, that a coachmaker could neither himself make, nor employ a journeyman to make his coach wheels, but must buy them of a master wheelwright, this latter trade having been exercised in England before the 5th of Elizabeth. But a wheelwright, though he had never served an apprenticeship to a coachmaker, might either make himself, or employ journeymen to make coaches, the trade of a coachmaker not being within the statute, because not exercised in England at the time when it was passed. The contradiction and absurdity of these regulations, and the impolicy and injurious operation of the statute, had long been obvious; but so slow is the progress of sound legislation, and so powerful the opposition to every change affecting private interests, that its repeal did not take place until 1814. The act for this purpose did not, however, interfere with any of the existing rights, privileges, or by-laws of the different corporations; but wherever these do not interpose, the formation of apprenticeships and their duration is now left to be wholly adjusted by the parties themselves.

Thirdly, The wages of labour, in different employments, vary with the constancy and inconstancy of employment.

Employment is much more constant in some trades than in others. Many trades can only be carried on in particular states of the weather and seasons of the year; and if the workmen who are engaged in such trades cannot easily find employment in others during the time they are thrown out of them, their wages must be proportionally augmented. A journeyman jeweller, weaver, shoemaker, or tailor, for example, may, under ordinary circumstances, reckon upon obtaining constant employment; but masons, bricklayers, paviors, and, in general, all those workmen who carry on their business in the open air, are liable to perpetual interruptions. Their wages must, however, not only suffice for their maintenance while they are employed, but also during the time they are necessarily idle; and they ought also to afford them, as Dr. Smith has remarked, some compensation for those anxious and desponding moments which the thought of so precarious a situation must sometimes occasion.

This principle shews the fallacy of the opinion so generally entertained respecting the great earnings of porters, hackney-coachmen, watermen, and generally of all workmen employed only for short periods, and on particular occasions. Such persons frequently make as much in an hour or two as a regularly employed workman makes in a day; but this greater hire, during the time they are employed, is found to be only a bare compensation for the labour they perform, and for the time they are necessarily idle; instead of making money, such persons are almost invariably poorer than those who are engaged in more constant occupations.

The interruption to employments occasioned by the celebration of holydays, has a similar effect on wages. There are countries in which the holydays, including Sundays, make a full half of the year; and the *necessary* wages of labour must there be about double of what they would be were these holydays abolished.

Fourthly, The wages of labour vary according to the

small or great trust which must be reposed in the workmen.

"The wages of goldsmiths and jewellers are every where superior to those of many other workmen, not only of equal, but of much superior ingenuity; on account of the precious materials with which they are intrusted.

"We trust our health to the physician; our fortune, and sometimes our life and reputation, to the lawyer and attorney. Such confidence could not safely be reposed in people of a very mean or low condition. Their reward must be such, therefore, as may give them that rank in society which so important a trust requires. The long time and the great expense which must be laid out in their education, when combined with this circumstance, necessarily enhance still further the price of their labour."*

Fifthly, The wages of labour in different employments vary according to the probability or improbability of success in them.

This cause of variation chiefly affects the wages of the higher class of labourers, or of those who practise what are usually denominated liberal professions.

If a young man is bound apprentice to a shoemaker or a tailor, there is hardly any doubt but he will attain to an ordinary degree of proficiency and expertness in his business, and that he will be able to live by it. But if he is bound apprentice to a lawyer, a painter, a sculptor, or a player, there are five chances to one against his ever attaining to such a degree of proficiency in any of these callings as will enable him to subsist on his earnings. But in professions where many fail for one who succeeds, the fortunate one ought not only to gain such a rate of wages as will indemnify him for all the expenses incurred in his education, but also for all that has been expended on the education of his unsuccessful competitors. It is

* "Wealth of Nations," vol. i. p. 173.

abundantly certain, however, that the wages of lawyers, players, sculptors, &c. taken in the aggregate, never amount to so large a sum. The lottery of the law and other liberal professions has many great prizes, but there is, notwithstanding, a large excess of blanks. "Compute," says Dr. Smith, "in any particular place, what is likely to be annually gained, and what is likely to be annually spent, by all the different workmen in any common trade, such as that of shoemakers or weavers, and you will find that the former sum will generally exceed the latter. But make the same computation with regard to all the counsellors and students of law, in all the different inns of court, and you will find that their annual gains bear but a very small proportion to their annual expense, even though you rate the former as high, and the latter as low as can well be done. The lottery of the law, therefore, is very far from being a perfectly fair lottery; and that, as well as many other liberal and honourable professions, is, in point of pecuniary gains, evidently under recompensed."

But the love of that wealth, power, and consideration, that most commonly attend superior excellence in any of the liberal professions, and the overweening confidence placed by each individual in his own good fortune, are sufficient to overbalance all the disadvantages and drawbacks that attend them; and never fail of crowding their ranks with all the most generous and aspiring spirits.

The pecuniary wages or earnings of scientific and literary men are, with a few rare exceptions, very inconsiderable. This arises from a variety of causes; but principally, perhaps, from the indestructibility, if I may so term it, and rapid circulation of their works and inventions. The cloth of the manufacturer, and the corn of the agriculturist, are speedily consumed, and there is a continued demand for fresh supplies of the same articles. Such, however, is not the case with new inventions, new theories, or new literary works. They may be universally made use of, but they cannot be consumed. The moment that the invention of logarithms, the mode of spinning by rollers, and the discovery of the cow-pox, had been published, they were rendered imperishable, and every one was in a condition to profit by them. It was no longer necessary to resort to their authors. The results of their researches had become public property, had conferred new powers on every individual, and might be applied by any one. The institution of patents does not materially affect what is now stated. In order not to check the progress of the arts, it is indispensable to limit the duration of the patent to a comparatively short period. And as the invention is known in other countries to which the patent does not extend, if the discoverer were to exact a high price for the produce of his invention, it would be clandestinely imported from abroad.

The condition of purely literary men, in a pecuniary point of view, is still less to be envied. However profound and learned, if a work be not at the same time popular and pleasing, its sale will be comparatively limited. And as principles and theories may be developed in an endless variety of ways, whatever is new and original may be appropriated by others, and served up in what may probably prove a more desirable form.

Hence, though a work should have the greatest influence on the legislation of the country, or the state of the arts, it may redound but little to the advantage of the author. A scientific work is seldom very attractive in point of style; and unless it has this recommendation, it will be read only by a few. It may have a great reputation among those capable of appreciating its merits, but it will not have a great sale. It will be bought, or rather, perhaps, borrowed and consulted, by those who are anxious to profit by its statements and discussions; but the generality of readers will know it only by report. It is not, therefore, so much on the depth, originality, and importance of its views, as on the circumstance of its being agreeable to the public taste, that the success, and consequently the productiveness, of a book to the author must depend. The value of the work of a man's hands is generally proportioned to the quantity of labour expended upon it; but in works of the mind no such correspondence can be traced between the toil and the recompense. Many a middling novel has produced more money than the "Principia," or the "Wealth of Nations;" and in this respect, the "Decline and Fall of the Roman Empire" has been far inferior to the "Arabian Nights"! Works of fancy are at once the most popular and the least easily superseded by others. Success in them is not, however, common; and except when it is very decided, it rarely confers much celebrity. It is fortunate, therefore, that a few individuals should be at all times captivated by the delights of study, and eager in the pursuit of learned and scientific researches for the gratification resulting from them. Had the taste for study depended only on the pecuniary emoluments which it brings along with it, it may well be doubted whether it would ever have found a single votary; and we should have been deprived, not only of very many of our most valuable and important discoveries in the arts, as well as in philosophy and legislation, but of much that refines and exalts the character, and supplies the best species of amusement.

It is unnecessary to enter upon any farther details with respect to this part of our subject. It has been sufficiently proved, that the permanent differences that actually obtain in the wages paid to those who are engaged in different employments in countries where industry is free and unfettered, are rarely more than sufficient to balance the favourable or unfavourable circumstances attending them. When the cost of their education, the chances of their success, and the various disadvantages incident to their professions, are taken into account, those who receive the highest wages are not really better paid than those who receive the lowest. The wages earned by the different classes of workmen are equal, not when each individual earns the same number of shillings, or of pence, in a given space of time, but when each is paid in proportion to the severity of the labour he has to perform, to the degree of previous education and skill that it requires, and to the other causes of variation already specified. So long, indeed, as the principle of competition is allowed to operate without restraint, or so long as each individual is allowed to employ himself as he pleases, we may be assured, that the higgling of the market will adjust the rate of wages in different employments on the principle now stated, and that they will be, all things considered, very nearly equal. If wages in one employment be depressed below the common level, labourers will leave it to go to others; and if they be raised above that level, labourers will be attracted to it from those departments where wages are lower, until their increased competition has sunk them to the average standard. A period of greater or less duration, according to the peculiar circumstances affecting each particular employment, is always required to bring about this equalisation. But all inquiries that have the establishment of general principles for their object, either are, or ought to be, founded on periods of average duration; and whenever such is the case, we may always, without occasioning any material error, assume that the wages earned in different employments are, all things taken into account, about equal.

CHAPTER II.

Circumstances which determine the Rate of Wages—(1) *Market, or Real Wages; depend on the Proportion between Capital and Population*—(2) *Natural or Necessary Wages; depend on the Species and Quantity of Food and other Articles required for the Consumption of the Labourer; different in different Countries and Periods— Effect of Fluctuations in the Rate of Wages on the Condition of the Labouring Classes—Advantage of a High Rate of Wages—Disadvantage of having the Labourers dependent for Support on the cheapest Species of Food—High Wages not a Cause of Idleness*—(3) *Proportional Wages; depend partly on the Amount and Species of the Articles consumed by the Labourers, and partly on the Productiveness of Industry.*

It has just been seen that the wages earned by the labourers engaged in different employments may, when all things are taken into account, be considered as about equal; and therefore, without regarding the differences that actually exist in the amount of money, or of commodities, earned by different sets of workmen, I shall suppose the wages of all sorts of labour to be reduced to the same common standard, and shall endeavour to discover the principle which regulates this common or average rate.

This inquiry will be facilitated by dividing it into three branches; the object in the *first* being to discover the circumstances which determine the *market* or *actual* rate of wages at any given moment; in the *second*, to discover the circumstances which determine the *natural or necessary* rate of wages, or the wages required to enable the labourer to subsist and continue his race; and in the *third*, to discover the circumstances which determine *proportional* wages, or the share of the produce of his industry falling to the labourer.

I. Circumstances which determine the Market or actual Rate of Wages.—The capacity of a country to support and employ labourers is in no degree dependent on advantageousness of situation, richness of soil, or extent of territory. These, undoubtedly, are circumstances of very great importance, and have a powerful influence in determining the rate at which a people advances in the career of wealth and civilisation. But it is obviously not on them, but on the actual amount of the accumulated produce of previous labour, or of capital, applicable to the payment of wages, in the possession of a country, that its power of supporting and employing labourers must depend. A fertile soil affords the means of rapidly increasing capital; but that is all. Before this soil can be cultivated, capital must be provided for the support of the labourers employed upon it, as it must be provided for the support of those engaged in manufactures, or in any other department of industry.

It is a necessary consequence of this principle, that the amount of subsistence falling to each labourer, or the rate of wages, must depend on the proportion which the whole capital bears to the whole labouring population. If the amount of capital were increased, without a corresponding increase taking place in the population, each individual would get a larger share, or the rate of wages would be augmented. And if, on the other hand, population were increased faster than capital, a less share would be apportioned to each individual, or the rate of wages would be reduced.

To illustrate this, let us suppose that the capital of a country appropriated to the payment of wages, would, if reduced to the standard of wheat, form a mass of 10,000,000 quarters: if the number of labourers in that country were *two* millions, it is evident that the wages of each, reducing them all to the same common standard, would be *five* quarters; and it is further evident, that this rate of wages could not be increased otherwise than by increasing the quantity of capital in a greater proportion than the number of labourers, or by diminishing the number of labourers in a greater proportion than the quantity of capital. So long as capital and population continue to march abreast, or to increase or diminish in the same proportion, so long will the rate of wages, and consequently the condition of the labourers, continue unaffected; and it is only when the proportion of capital to population varies,—when it is either increased or diminished, that the rate of wages sustains a corresponding advance or diminution. The well-being and comfort of the labouring classes are, therefore, especially dependent on the relation which their increase bears to the increase of the capital that is to feed and employ them. If they increase faster than capital, their wages will be reduced; and if they increase slower, they will be augmented. In fact, there are no means whatever by which the command of the labouring class over the necessaries and conveniences of life can be enlarged, other than by accelerating the increase of capital as compared with population, or by retarding the increase of population as compared with capital; and every scheme for improving the condition of the labourer which is not bottomed on this principle, or which has not an increase of the ratio of capital to population for its object, must be completely nugatory and ineffectual.

The wages of labour are most commonly either paid or estimated in money; and it may perhaps be thought that they will, in consequence, depend more on the quantity of money in circulation than on the quantity of capital. It is really, however, quite the same to the labourer whether the amount of money received by him as wages be great or small. He will always receive such a sum as will suffice to put him in possession of the portion of capital falling to his share. Men cannot subsist on coin or paper. Where wages are paid in money, the labourers immediately exchange it for necessaries and conveniences; and it is not the quantity of money they receive, but the quantity of necessaries and conveniences for which that money will exchange, that is to be considered as really forming their wages. If the quantity of money in Great Britain were reduced a half, the rate of wages, estimated in money, would decline in the same proportion; but, unless some change had, at the same time, taken place in the magnitude of that portion of the capital of the country which consists of the food, clothes, and other articles that enter into the consumption of the labourer, he would continue in precisely the same situation. He would carry a smaller quantity of pieces of gold and silver to market, but he would obtain the same quantity of commodities in exchange for them.

Whatever, therefore, may be the rate of money wages in a country—whether they amount to 1*s*. or 5*s*. a day—it is still certain, that if capital and population continue the same, or increase or diminish in the same proportion, no real variation will take place in the rate of wages. Wages never really rise except when the proportion of capital to population is enlarged, and they never really fall except when that proportion is diminished.

The influence of the different rates at which capital and population advance in different countries on the condition of the inhabitants, may be exemplified in a very striking manner by comparing the rate of increase and the actual state of the people of Great Britain with the rate of increase and the actual state of the people of Ireland. It is certainly true, that there has been a considerable increase in the capital of Ireland during the last hundred years; though no one, in the least acquainted with the progress of the different parts of the empire, has ever pretended that this increase has amounted to a *third* or even a *fourth* of the proportional increase of capital in England and Scotland during the same period. But the population of Ireland has, notwithstanding, increased more than *twice* as fast as that of Great Britain. According to the tables given in the Parliamentary Reports, the population of this part of the empire amounted, in 1720, to

6,955,000, and, in 1821, it amounted to 14,391,000, having a little more than doubled in the course of the century; while it appears, from the same Reports, that the population of Ireland, whose capital had increased so very slowly, amounted to little more than *two* millions in 1731, and to near *seven* millions in 1821; having nearly *quadrupled* in less time than the population of Britain took to *double.*

Without entering upon any lengthened inquiries respecting the causes of this difference, it may be observed, that, on the first introduction of the potato into Ireland, in 1610, the peasantry, then very much degraded, and without any elevated notions of what was necessary for their comfortable subsistence, eagerly resorted to so cheap a species of food; and, owing to the unfortunate circumstances under which they have ever since been placed, they have never endeavoured to attain to any thing higher. Provided they have sufficient supplies of potatoes, they are content to vegetate, for they cannot be said to live, in rags and wretchedness. But whatever may have been the causes which have led to the disparity previously stated in the increase of population in Great Britain and Ireland, as compared with the increase of their capitals, there cannot be the shadow of a doubt, that its excessive augmentation in Ireland is the immediate cause of the want of demand for labour in that country, and of the misery and extreme poverty of the people. The number of persons soliciting employment, compared with the means of rewarding their exertions, is so very great, that wages have been reduced to the lowest pittance that can afford the smallest necessary supply of the coarsest and cheapest species of food capable of supporting human life. All the witnesses examined by the Committee of the House of Commons, on "*The Employment of the Poor of Ireland,*" in 1823, concur in representing their numbers as excessive, and their condition as wretched in the extreme. Their cabins, which are of the most miserable description, are utterly unprovided with any thing that can be called furniture; in many families there are no such things as bed-clothes; the children, in extensive districts of Munster and the other provinces, have not a single rag to cover their nakedness; and whenever the potato crop becomes even in a slight degree deficient, the scourge of famine and disease is felt in every corner of the country. Mr. Maurice Fitzgerald, M.P., mentions, that "he had known the peasantry of Kerry quit their houses in search of employment, offering to work for the merest subsistence that could be obtained—for twopence a-day; in short, for any thing that would purchase food enough to keep them alive for the ensuing twenty-four hours."* Mr. Tighe mentions, that "the number of persons in Ireland supported by charity is quite inconceivable; they must be supported either by charity, or by pillage and plunder: to the want of employment I attribute every thing that afflicts and disgraces that country."† And Dr. Rogan, who had been employed by Government to report on the state of disease in the north of Ireland, states, in his valuable work on the Fever in Ulster, published in 1819, that "throughout the extensive counties of Tyrone, Donegal, and Derry, the population is only limited by the difficulty of procuring food. Owing to the universal adoption of the cottier system, and to the custom of dividing farms among the sons, on the death of the father, the labouring classes are infinitely more numerous than are required for the purposes of industry. Under these circumstances, they are engaged in a constant struggle for the bare necessaries of life, and never enjoy its comforts."‡

These statements, which might, were it necessary, and did my space permit, be multiplied a thousand fold, conclusively shew that a vast increase has taken place in the population of Ireland, and that it is now both superabundant and miserable in the extreme. And hence the obvious and undeniable inference, that, in the event of the popu-

* Report, p. 158. † Ib. p. 108. ‡ Ib. p. 8.

lation having increased less rapidly than it has done, there would have been fewer individuals soliciting employment, and that, consequently, the rate of wages would have been proportionally higher, and the condition of the poor so far improved. No proposition, then, can be more true, than that the unexampled misery of the Irish people is directly owing to the excessive augmentation of their numbers; and nothing can be more perfectly futile, than to expect any real or lasting amendment in their situation until an effectual check has been given to the progress of population. It is obvious, too, that the low and degraded condition into which the people of Ireland are now sunk, is the condition to which every people must be reduced whose numbers continue, for any considerable period, to increase faster than the means of providing for their comfortable and decent subsistence; and such will, most assuredly, be the case in every old settled country in which the principle of increase is not powerfully countervailed by the operation of moral restraint, or by the exercise of a proper degree of prudence and forethought in the formation of matrimonial connexions.

II. Circumstances which determine the Natural or Necessary Rate of Wages.—There are obviously limits, however difficult it may be to specify them, to the extent to which a reduction of wages can be carried. *The cost of producing labour,* like that of all other articles brought to market, must be paid by the purchasers. The race of labourers would become altogether extinct were they not to obtain sufficient quantities of food and other articles required for their support and that of their families. This is the lowest amount to which the rate of wages can be permanently reduced; and it is for this reason that it has been defined to be the *natural or necessary rate of wages.* The market, or actual rate of wages, may sink to the level of this rate; but it is plainly impossible it can continue below it. It is not, as has been already shewn, on the quantity of money received by the labourer, but on the quantity of food and other articles for which that money will exchange, that his ability to maintain himself, and to rear children to keep up the supply of labourers, must depend. Hence the natural or necessary rate of wages is determined by the cost of producing the food, clothes, fuel, &c. required for the use and accommodation of the labourers.* And though a rise in the market or current rate of wages be seldom exactly coincident with a rise in the price of necessaries, they can never, except in the rare case when the market rate of wages greatly exceeds the natural or necessary rate, be very far separated. However high the price of commodities may rise, the labourers must always receive a supply equivalent for their support: if they did not obtain this much, they would be left destitute; and disease and death would continue to thin the population, until the reduced numbers bore such a proportion to the national capital as would enable them to obtain the means of subsistence.

The opinion of those who contend that the rate of wages is in no degree influenced by the cost of producing the articles consumed by the labourers, has obviously originated in their confounding the principles which determine the market rate of wages at any given period, with those which determine their natural or necessary rate. No proposition can be better established than that the market rate of wages, when reference is made only to a given moment, is exclusively determined by the proportion be-

* "L'ouvrier mineur en Saxe reçoit 18 sols par jour de salaire, tandis que l'ouvrier employé au même genre de travail dans là province de Choco au Perou reçoit en argent six à sept fois plus. Mais ce dernier paie aussi six à sept plus cher le pain dont il se nourrit, parceque la farine des Etats-Unis y est transportée à dos de mulet à une longue distance des côtes, par des routes montueuses et difficiles. Ce que le maître doit fournir à l'ouvrier c'est la subsistance, et l'argent donné ne peut jamais être que la representation de cette subsistance."—Garnier, *Richesse des Nations*, tom. v. p. 351.

tween capital and population. But in every inquiry of this nature, we ought not only to refer to particular points of time, but also to periods of *average* duration; and if we do this, we shall immediately perceive that the average rate of wages does not depend wholly on this proportion. The price of shoes, at any given instant, to take a parallel case, is plainly dependent on the extent of their supply compared with the demand of those who have the means of purchasing them; but it is quite obvious, that if this price were to sink below the sum necessary to pay the cost of producing shoes and bringing them to market, they would no longer be supplied:—and such is precisely the case with labourers. They neither will, nor in fact can, be brought to market, unless the rate of wages be such as will, at an average, suffice to bring them up and maintain them. From whatever point of the political compass we may set out at first, we shall find that the cost of production is the grand principle to which we must always come at last. It is this cost that determines the natural or necessary rate of wages, just as it determines the average price of commodities. However low the demand for labour may be reduced, still if the price of the articles necessary for the maintenance of the labourer be increased, the natural or necessary rate of wages must be increased also. Let it be supposed that, owing to a scarcity, the price of the quartern loaf rises to 5*s*. In this case it is plain, inasmuch as the same number of labourers would be seeking for employment after the rise as before, and as a rise in the price of bread, occasioned by a scarcity, could not increase the demand for labour, that wages would not be increased. The labourers would, in consequence, be forced to economise, and the rise of price would have the beneficial effect of lessening the consumption of food, and of distributing the pressure equally throughout the year. But suppose that the rise, instead of being occasioned by the accidental occurrence of a scarcity, has been occasioned by an increased difficulty of production, and that it will be permanent, the question to be determined is, will the money wages paid the labourer continue at their former elevation, or will they rise? Now, in this case it may be easily shewn that they must rise: for it is abundantly obvious, that the comforts of all classes of labourers would be greatly impaired by the rise in the price of bread; and those who, previously to its taking place, had only enough to subsist upon, would now be reduced to a state of extreme destitution, or rather of absolute famine. Under such circumstances, an increase of mortality could not fail of taking place; while the greater difficulty of providing subsistence would interpose a powerful check to the formation of matrimonial connexions, and the increase of population. By these means, therefore, the actual amount of the population, or the ratio of its increase, or both, would be diminished; and this diminution, by lessening the number of labourers, would increase the proportion of capital to population, and enable them to obtain higher wages.

The statements now made are not advanced on any arbitrary or supposed grounds, but have been deduced from and are consistent with the widest experience. Those who examine the registers of births, marriages, and deaths, kept in all large and populous cities, will find that there is invariably a diminution of the former, and an increase of the latter, whenever the price of corn, or of the principal necessaries of life, sustains any material advance. "It will be observed," says Mr. Milne, in his "Treatise on Annuities," in reference to the prices of wheat in England, "that any material reduction in the price of wheat is almost always accompanied by an increase both of the marriages and births, and by a decrease in the number of burials; consequently, by an increase in the excess of the births above the deaths. Also that any material rise in the price is generally attended by a corresponding decrease in the marriages and births, and by an increase in the burials; therefore, by a decrease in the excess of the births above the deaths. Thus it appears that an increase in the quantity of food, or in the facility with which the labouring classes can obtain it, accelerates the progress of the population, both by augmenting the number of births and diminishing the rate of mortality; and that a scarcity of food retards the increase of the people, by producing in both ways opposite effects." And in proof of the correctness of this statement, Mr. Milne gives, among many others to the same effect, the following account of the number of births and deaths within the London bills of mortality, in 1798, 1800, and 1802:—

	Births.		Deaths.		Price of Wheat.
1798 .	19,581	—	20,755	—	£.2 10 3 per Qr.
1802	21,308	—	20,260	—	3 7 5
Medium of these two years. .	20,445	—	20,508	—	2 18 10
1800	18,275	—	25,670	—	5 13 7
Differences. .	2,170	—	5,162	—	2 14 9
	Decrease.		Increase.		Increase.*

M. Messance, the author of a valuable work on the population of France,† has collected a great deal of important information on the same subject. "It has been established," says he, "by the various investigations that have been made, that those years in which corn has sold at the highest price, have also been those in which mortality was greatest and disease most prevalent; and that those, on the contrary, in which corn has been cheapest, have been the healthiest and least mortal." The tables published by M. Messance of the number of deaths and the price of wheat, for a considerable number of years, at Paris, Lyons, Rouen, and some other cities of France, bear the most unequivocal testimony to the truth of this doctrine. In 1744, for example, when the price of wheat

* Milne on Annuities, vol. ii. p. 402.

† "Recherches sur la Population," p. 291.

at Paris was 11 livres 15 sols the septier, the number of deaths amounted to 16,205; and in 1753, when the price of wheat was 20 livres 3 sols, the deaths amounted to 21,716. In the *four* years of the *greatest* mortality at Paris, in the interval between 1743 and 1763, the average price of the septier of wheat was 19 livres 1 sol, and the average annual number of deaths 20,895; and in the *four* years of the *least* mortality during the same interval, the average price of the septier was 14 livres 18 sols, and the average annual number of deaths 16,859.*

It may here, perhaps, be proper to mention, that it has been long observed that the tendency of wages is not to rise, but rather to fall, in unusually dear years; and several of the witnesses examined before the committees of the Houses of Lords and Commons, on the state of agriculture in 1814, endeavoured to prove, by comparing wages with the prices of corn and other necessaries, that there was really no such connexion between the two as has been supposed; and that, so far from their varying in the same way, wages were generally *lowest* in years when the price of corn was highest. But it is not difficult to explain the causes of this apparent anomaly. The truth is, that the number of labourers, which is in no case immediately reduced, is, in most cases, immediately increased by a rise of prices. In dear years, an increased number of females, and of such poor children of both sexes as are fit to work, are obliged to quit their homes, or to engage in some species of employment; while those labourers who work by the piece, endeavour, by increasing the quantity of their work, to obtain the means of purchasing a greater quantity of food. It is natural, therefore, that the *immediate* effect of a rise of prices should be to lower, not to raise the rate of wages. But we should fall into the greatest imaginable error, if we supposed that because this is the immediate, it is also the lasting and constant effect of such a rise!

* "Recherches sur la Population," p. 311.

It is obvious, indeed, that this immediate fall of wages, and the greater exertions the rise of prices forces the labourers to make, must have a powerful tendency, as well by lessening their supplies of food, as by adding to the severity of their labour, to increase the rate of mortality, and consequently, by diminishing their number, to hasten that rise of wages that will certainly take place if prices continue high.

But, in endeavouring to shew that the market rate of wages cannot be permanently reduced below their natural or necessary rate, it is not meant to represent the latter as fixed and unvarying. If any given quantity of certain articles were absolutely necessary to enable the labourer to subsist and continue his race, no lasting reduction could be effected in its amount. But such is not the case. By the natural or necessary rate of wages, is meant only, in the words of Dr. Smith, such a rate as will enable the labourer to obtain "not only the commodities that are indispensably necessary for the support of life, but whatever the custom of the country renders it indecent for creditable people, even of the lowest order, to be without." Now it is plain, from this definition, that there can be no absolute standard of natural or necessary wages. It is impossible to say what commodities are indispensable for the support of life; for these, as well as the other articles required for the use of the lower orders, depend essentially on the physical circumstances under which every people is placed, and on custom and habit. The differences of climate, for example, by giving rise to very different physical wants in the inhabitants of different countries, necessarily occasion very considerable variations in the natural or necessary rate of wages. The labourer in cold climates, who must be warmly clad, and whose cottage must be built of solid materials and heated with a fire, could not possibly subsist on the same rate of wages that would suffice to supply all the wants of the labourer inhabiting more genial climates, where clothing, lodging, and fire, were of very inferior importance. Humboldt mentions, that there is a difference of nearly a *third* in the cost of maintaining, and consequently in the necessary wages of a labourer in the hot and temperate districts of Mexico; and there is a still greater difference in the rates of necessary wages in different and distant countries. The food, too, of the labourers in different countries varies extremely. In some it is both expensive and abundant, compared to what it is in others. In England, for example, the labourers principally subsist on wheaten bread and beef, in Ireland on potatoes, and in China and Hindostan on rice. In many provinces of France and Spain, an allowance of wine is considered indispensable to existence; and in England, the labouring class entertain nearly the same opinion with respect to beer; whereas the drink of the Chinese and Hindoos consists of nothing but water. In Ireland the peasantry live in miserable mud cabins, no better than the wig-wams of the American Indians, without either a window or a chimney; while in England the cottages of the peasantry have all glass windows and chimneys, are well furnished, and are as much distinguished for their neatness, cleanliness, and comfort, as those of the Irish for their filth and misery. In consequence of these different habits, there is an extreme difference, not in the rate of necessary wages merely, but in their actual or market rate in these countries; so much so, that while the average market price of a day's labour in England may be taken at from 20*d.* to 2*s.*, it cannot be taken at more than 5*d.* in Ireland, and 3*d.* in Hindostan! Nor have the habits of the people of the same countries, and the standard by which the natural rate of wages has been regulated at different periods, been less fluctuating and various. The habits of the English and Scotch labourers of the present day are as widely different from those of their ancestors in the reigns of Elizabeth, James I., and Charles I., as they now are from the habits of the labourers of France and Spain. The standard by which the natural rate of wages was formerly regulated has been raised; there has been a greater prevalence of moral restraint; the proportion of capital to population has been increased; and the poor have been most fortunately taught to form far more elevated opinions respecting the amount of necessaries and conveniences required for their subsistence.

The natural or necessary rate of wages is not, therefore, a fixed and unvarying quantity; and though it be true that the market rate of wages can never sink permanently below its contemporary natural rate, it is no less true that this natural rate has a tendency to rise when the market rate rises, and to fall when it falls. The reason is, that the number of labourers in the market is a given quantity, which can neither be speedily increased when wages rise, nor speedily diminished when they fall. When wages rise, a period of eighteen or twenty years must plainly elapse before the effect of the increased stimulus that the rise gives to the principle of population can be felt in the market. During all this period, therefore, the labourers have an increased command over the necessaries and conveniences of life: in consequence, their habits are improved; and as they learn to form more exalted notions with respect to what is required for their comfortable and decent support, the natural or necessary rate of wages is proportionally augmented. But, on the other hand, when the rate of wages declines, either in consequence of an actual diminution of the capital of the country, or of a disproportionate increase of population, no corresponding immediate diminution can take place in the number of labourers, unless they have previously been subsisting on the smallest possible quantity of the cheapest species of food required to support mere animal existence. If the labourers have not been placed so very near the extreme limit of subsistence, their numbers will not be immediately reduced when wages fall, by an increase of mortality; but they will be gradually reduced, partly, as has been already shewn, in that way, and partly by a diminished number of marriages and births: and in most countries, unless the fall were both sudden and extensive, it would require some years to render the effects of increased mortality, in diminishing the supply of labour in the market, very sensibly; while the force of habit, and the universal ignorance of the people with respect to the circumstances which determine the rate of wages, would prevent any effectual check from being given to the formation of matrimonial connexions, and consequently to the rate at which fresh labourers had previously been coming into market, until the misery occasioned by the restricted demand on the one hand, and the undiminished supply on the other, had been very generally and widely felt.

It is this circumstance—the impossibility which usually obtains of speedily adjusting the supply of labour proportionally to the variations which occur in the rate of wages—that gives to these variations the peculiar and extraordinary influence they exert over the condition of the labouring classes. Were the supply of labour suddenly increased when wages rise, that rise would be of no advantage to the existing labourers. It would increase their number, but it would not enable them to mount in the scale of society, or to acquire a greater command over the necessaries and conveniencies of human life: and, on the other hand, were the supply of labourers suddenly diminished when wages fall, that fall would merely lessen their number, without having any tendency to degrade their habits, or to lower the condition of those that survived. But, in the vast majority of instances, before a rise of wages can be counteracted by the increased number of labourers it may be supposed to be the means of bringing into the market, time is afforded for the formation of those new and improved tastes and habits which are not the hasty product of a day, a month, or a year, but the late result of a long series of continuous impressions. After the labourers have once acquired these tastes, population will advance in a slower ratio, as compared with capital, than formerly; and the labourers will be disposed rather to defer the period of marriage, than by entering on it prematurely to depress their own condition and that of their children. But if the number of labourers cannot be suddenly increased when wages rise, neither can it be suddenly diminished when they fall; a fall of wages has, therefore, a precisely opposite effect, and is, in most cases, as injurious to the labourer as their rise is beneficial. In whatever way wages may be restored to their former level after they have fallen, whether it be by a decrease in the number of marriages, or an increase in the number of deaths, or both, it is never, except in the exceedingly rare case already mentioned, suddenly effected. It must, generally speaking, require a considerable time before it can be brought about; and an extreme risk arises in consequence, lest the tastes and habits of the labourers, and their opinion respecting what is necessary for their comfortable subsistence, should be degraded in the interim. When wages are considerably reduced, the poor are obliged to economise, or to submit to live on a smaller quantity of necessaries and conveniences, and those too of an inferior species; and the danger is, that the coarse and scanty fare which has thus been, in the first instance, forced on them by necessity, should in time become congenial from habit. Should this, unfortunately, be the case, the condition of the poor would be permanently depressed, and no principle would be left in operation that could raise wages to their former level; for the labourers would no longer have a motive to lessen the increase of population as compared with that of capital, and unless they do this, it is quite impossible they should ever emerge from their depressed condition. Under the circumstances supposed, the cost of raising and supporting labourers would be reduced; and it is by this cost that the natural or necessary rate of wages, to which the market rate must generally be proportioned, is always regulated. This lowering of the opinions of the labouring class with respect to the mode in which they ought to live, is perhaps the most serious of all the evils that can befall them. Let them once become contented with a lower species of food, and an inferior standard of comfort, and they may bid a long adieu to any thing better. And every reduction in the rate of real wages, which is not of a very transient description, will certainly have this effect, if its debasing influence be not counteracted by the intelligence, forethought, and consideration of the people, producing an increased prevalence of moral restraint, and a diminished supply of labourers. An increase in the proportion of capital to population, is the only means by which a rise of wages can ever be effected; and unless the labourers, who have been reduced from a higher to a lower rate of wages, defer the period of marriage, and thus retard the progress of population, the chances are five to one that they will never again attain to the elevation from which they have fallen.

The example of such individuals, or bodies of individuals, as submit quietly to have their wages reduced, and who are content if they get only the mere necessaries of life, ought never to be held up for public imitation. On the contrary, every thing should be done to make such apathy be esteemed disgraceful. The best interests of society require that the rate of wages should be elevated as high as possible — that a taste for the comforts, luxuries, and enjoyments of human life, should be widely diffused, and, if possible, interwoven with national habits and prejudices. Very low wages, by rendering it impossible for increased exertions to obtain any considerable increase of comforts and enjoyments, effectually hinders them from being made, and is of all others the most powerful cause of that idleness and apathy that contents itself with what can barely continue animal existence.

The state of the peasantry of Ireland furnishes a

striking example of the disastrous effects resulting from the natural or necessary rate of wages being determined by a very low standard. Having no taste for conveniences or luxuries, they are satisfied if they obtain a sufficient supply of potatoes. But as the potato is raised at less expense than any other species of food hitherto cultivated in Europe, and as the wages of labour, where it forms the main article of subsistence, are, of course, chiefly determined by the cost of its production, it is easy to see that the labourers must be reduced to a state of extreme and indeed almost irremediable distress, whenever that root happens to be deficient. When the standard of natural or necessary wages is high — when wheat and beef, for example, form the principal part of the food of the labourer, and porter and beer the principal part of his drink—he can bear to retrench in a period of scarcity. Such a man has room to fall; he can resort to cheaper sorts of food — to barley, oats, rice, and potatoes. But he who is habitually fed on the cheapest food has nothing to resort to when deprived of it. Labourers placed in this situation are absolutely cut off from every resource. You may take from an Englishman, but you cannot take from an Irishman. The latter is already so low, he can fall no lower: he is placed on the very verge of existence: his wages, being regulated by the price of potatoes, will not buy him wheat, or barley, or oats; and whenever, therefore, the supply of potatoes fails, it is next to impossible he can escape falling a sacrifice to famine!

The history of the late scarcity in Ireland affords a melancholy illustration of the accuracy of the statement now made. Owing to the failure of the potato crop of 1821, a very large proportion of the peasantry of Clare, Limerick, and other counties bordering on the Shannon, was reduced to a state of almost absolute destitution, and had nothing but a miserable mixture, consisting of a little oatmeal, nettles, and water-cresses, to subsist upon.

In some instances the potatoes, after being planted, were again dug from the ground and eaten; and in consequence of the insufficiency and bad quality of the food, disease became exceedingly prevalent; and *typhus* fever, in its worst and most malignant form, carried its destructive ravages into every corner of the country. But there was, notwithstanding, a continued exportation of oats and other grain from Ireland to this country, down to the very moment when the contributions of government and the public were applied to purchase corn for the peasantry. The price of potatoes rose in Limerick, in the course of a few weeks, from 1½*d.* to 6*d.* and 7*d.* a stone, being a rise of from 400 to 500 per cent, while the price of corn sustained no material elevation, none at least to prevent its being sent to the then overloaded markets of England! And it is obvious, that to whatever extremity the peasantry might have been reduced, they could not have relieved themselves by purchasing corn; whereas, had wheat formed the principal part of their subsistence, grain would have been poured into Ireland from every quarter of the world, as soon as it was known that the crop was materially deficient. But a people, habitually dependent on the potato, cannot become purchasers of corn; nor can they even become purchasers of foreign potatoes, inasmuch as the freight of so bulky a commodity would raise its price far above their limited means. In a period of scarcity, men cannot go from a low to a high level; they must always go from a higher to a lower. But to the Irish this is impossible; they have already reached the lowest point in the descending scale, and dearth is to them attended with all the horrors of famine.

It is, therefore, quite essential to the protection of the people from famine, in seasons when the crops happen to be deficient, that they should not subsist principally on the cheapest species of food. They may advantageously use it in limited quantities, and as a subsidiary and subordinate article; but if they once adopt it for the principal part of their diet, their wages will be regulated accordingly; and whenever a period of deficient supply occurs, they will be absolutely without resource.

It has sometimes, indeed, been contended, by many very intelligent persons, of whose benevolence no doubt can be entertained, and to whose opinions on most subjects the greatest deference is due, that high wages, instead of encouraging industry, uniformly become a fruitful source of idleness and dissipation. Nothing, however, can be more entirely incorrect than these representations—more completely opposed both to principle and experience. It is true, indeed, that, in every country and situation of life, individuals will be found who are careless of the future, and intent only on present enjoyment; but these always form a very small and even inconsiderable minority of each particular class. Whatever may be the case with a few individuals, the principle of accumulation always predominates in aggregate bodies over the passion for expense. Wherever the wages of labour are so low as to render it impossible for an ordinary increase of exertion to make any material and visible addition to their comforts and conveniences, the labourers are invariably sunk in idleness, and seem indifferent to their situation. But the desire to rise in the world and to improve our condition, is too deeply seated in the human breast ever to be wholly eradicated. And as soon as labour is rendered more productive, as soon as an increase of industry brings a visible increase of comforts and enjoyments along with it, indolence uniformly gives place to exertion; a taste for the conveniences and enjoyments of life is gradually diffused; increased exertions are made to obtain them; and ultimately the workman considers it discreditable to be without them. Have the *low* wages of the Irish, Poles, and Hindoos, made them industrious? or the *high* wages of the Americans, English, and Hollanders made them lazy, riotous, and profligate? —Just the contrary. The former are as notoriously and proverbially indolent, as the latter are laborious, active, and enterprising. This is not a point as to which there is any room for doubt. The experience of all ages and nations proves that high wages are at once the most powerful stimulus to unremitting and assiduous exertion, and the best means of attaching the people to the institutions under which they live. It was said of old, "*nihil lætius est populo Romano saturo;*" and the same thing may be said of the English, the French, and, indeed, of every people. It is not when wages are high and provisions abundant, but when wages are low and the harvest less productive than usual, that the manufacturing and thickly peopled districts are disturbed by popular clamour and commotions. It is, in fact, quite visionary to suppose that security and tranquillity should ever exist in any considerable degree, in countries where wages are very much depressed, and the mass of the people sunk in poverty and destitution. Those who have no property of their own to protect, and no prospect of acquiring any, will never entertain any real respect for that of others; nor can any country be so ripe for revolution as that where the mass of the people may hope to gain something, at the same time that they feel they can lose nothing, by subverting the existing institutions. Nothing, therefore, can be so signally disastrous as a permanent depression in the rate of wages. It is destructive alike of the industry of the people, and of that security which is the most indispensable requisite to the advancement of society.

III. Circumstances which determine the rate of proportional wages.—Proportional wages, or the share of the produce of his industry falling to the workman, depend partly on the magnitude of the market, or actual rate of wages at the time, and partly on the difficulty of producing the commodities which enter into and really form this market-rate. Suppose, to illustrate this, that the wages actually paid to the labourers in England and the United States are, when reduced to the standard of wheat, precisely equal: Under these circumstances, the condition of the labourer, or his power over the necessaries and luxuries of life, will be about equal in both countries; but the rate of proportional wages will, at the same time, be higher in England than in the United States; for, owing to the greater fertility of the soil under cultivation in America, the same quantity of labour that would there produce 100 quarters of wheat, will not probably produce more than 60 or 70 quarters in England; and as the labourers in both countries are supposed to get the same actual quantity of produce in return for a given quantity of work, they are obviously getting a greater proportion of the produce of their labour, and consequently a greater real value, in England than in the United States.

Hence it is plain, that proportional wages may, as was previously remarked, be increased at the same time that wages, if estimated in silver, corn, or any other commodity, are reduced; and such, in point of fact, is almost uniformly found to be the case when tillage is extended over inferior soils. Wherever the best lands only are cultivated, the proportion, or share of the produce falling to the labourer, is, generally speaking, small; but as labour is, under such circumstances, comparatively productive, a small share of its total produce gives a large absolute quantity of necessaries and conveniences: while in the advanced stages of society, and where cultivation is widely extended over lands of very inferior fertility, proportional wages are almost invariably high; but owing to the increased difficulty that then obtains of producing supplies of food, these high proportional wages rarely afford a large supply of necessaries and conveniences.

CHAPTER III.

Impotent Poor ought to be provided for by a Poor's Rate—Question as to the best Means of providing for the Able-bodied Poor—Arguments in favour of a Poor's Rate—Objections to it—May be so administered as to obviate most of these Objections—Operation of the English Poor Laws—Ought to be reformed, not abolished.

How prosperous soever the condition of the bulk of the inhabitants, still it is found, even in the most favoured countries, that poverty and destitution are the lot of a considerable number of persons; and the questions whether, and to what extent, the public ought to interfere to relieve those in this unfortunate condition, are among the most important that the legislature has to resolve.

The poor and destitute may be divided into two great classes: the *first* consisting of maimed and impotent persons, or of those whom natural or accidental infirmities disable from working; and the *second* of those who, though able and willing to work, are unable to find employment, or do not receive wages adequate for their support and that of their families. There is a very wide difference between the situation of these classes; and the same means of relief that may be advantageously afforded to the one, may not, in various respects, be suitable for the other.

I. With respect, however, to the first class, or the impotent poor, there does not seem to be much room for doubt as to the policy, as well as humanity, of giving them a legal claim to relief. It has sometimes, indeed, been contended, that by affording relief to those who are unable, from age or the gradual decay of their bodily powers, to provide for themselves, the motives that induce individuals, while in health, to make a provision against future contingencies, are weakened; so that, in attempting to protect a few from the effects of their own improvidence, an injury is done to the whole community. This statement is, probably, true to a certain extent; though it is difficult to imagine that any considerable portion of a moderately intelligent population will ever be tempted to relax in their efforts to save and accumulate, when they have the means of doing so, from a knowledge that the workhouse will receive them in old age!* But whatever may have been the faults of individuals, it would be abhorrent to all the feelings of humanity to allow them to suffer the extremity of want. An individual is unfortunate, perhaps, or he may not have been as thrifty or as prudent as he ought; but is he, therefore, to be allowed to die in the streets? It is proper, certainly, to do nothing that can really weaken the spirit of industry; but if, in order to strengthen it, all relief were refused to the maimed and impotent poor, the habits and feelings of the people would be degraded and brutalised by familiarity with the most abject wretchedness; at the same time that, by driving the victims of poverty to despair, a foundation would be laid for the most dreadful crimes, and such a shock given to the security of property as would very much overbalance whatever additional spur the refusal of support might give to industry and economy. It does, therefore, appear sufficiently clear, that this class of poor should be supported in one way or other; and that, when the parties are either without relations or friends, or when they do not come voluntarily forward to discharge this indispensable duty, the necessary funds should be provided by a tax or rate, made equally to affect all classes; for, if they are not so raised, the poor will either not be provided for at all, or the burden of providing for them will fall wholly on the benevolent, who ought not, in such a case, to be called upon to contribute more than their fair share.

* Mr. Howlett has some very forcible observations on this point in his tract on the Poor Laws, p. 6.

II. The only question, then, about which there seems to be any real ground for doubt or difference of opinion is, whether any legal claim for relief should be given to the able-bodied poor, or to those who are able and ready to work, but who cannot find employment, or cannot earn wages adequate for their support? Now this, it must be confessed, is a very difficult question, and one which does not, perhaps, admit of any very satisfactory solution. On the whole, however, it appears to me, for the reasons which I shall now state, that it ought, under certain restrictions, to be decided in the affirmative.

In the first place, it may be observed, that owing to changes of fashion, to the miscalculation of producers and merchants, and to political events, those engaged in manufacturing employments are necessarily exposed to many vicissitudes. And when their number is so very great as in this country, it is quite essential that a resource should be provided for their support in periods of adversity. In the event of no such provision being made, and of the distress being at the same time extensive and severe, the public tranquillity would most likely be seriously endangered. Lord Bacon has observed, that "of all rebellions, those of the belly are the worst." It would be visionary indeed to imagine that those who have nothing should quietly submit to suffer the extremity of want without attacking the property of others. And hence, if we would preserve unimpaired the peace, and consequently the prosperity of the country, we must beware of allowing any considerable portion of the population to fall into a state of destitution. But without the establishment of a compulsory provision for the support of the unemployed poor, it is difficult to see how they could avoid occasionally falling into this state. Through its instrumentality, however, they are sustained in periods of adversity, without being driven by necessity to commit crimes. It must, indeed, be admitted that a provision of this sort is very liable to abuse. Means have, however, been devised for checking this tendency; and whatever imperfections may, after all, attach to it, it has not yet been shewn how security and good order could be maintained in periods when either employment or food was deficient, were it abolished.

In the second place, supposing it were possible to maintain tranquillity without making a legal provision for the support of the unemployed poor, the privations to which, under such circumstances, they would be forced to submit, would, in all probability, lower their notions as to what was necessary for their comfortable subsistence, and exert a most pernicious influence over their conduct and character. It is perhaps unnecessary, after what has been advanced in the preceding chapter, to enter into any further statements to shew the importance of endeavouring to guard against any such results. But Mr. Barton has made some observations on this point which are so striking and conclusive, that I cannot forbear laying them before the reader. "It is to be remembered," says he, "that even those who most strongly assert the impolicy and injurious tendency of our poor laws, admit that causes wholly unconnected with these laws do, at times, depress the condition of the labourer. Poor families are often thrown into a state of severe necessity by long-continued illness or unavoidable misfortunes, from which it would be impossible for them to return to the enjoyment of decent competence, if not supported by extraneous means. It is well known, too, that a general rise in the price of commodities is seldom immediately followed by a rise in the wages of country labour. In the mean time, great suffering must be endured by the whole class of peasantry, if no legislative provision existed for their relief; and when such a rise of prices goes on gradually increasing for a series of years, as sometimes happens, the suffering resulting from it must be proportionally prolonged. The question at issue is simply this: whether that suffering be calculated to cherish habits of sober and self-denying prudence, or to generate a spirit of careless desperation?

"During these periods of extraordinary privation, the labourer, if not effectually relieved, would imperceptibly lose that taste for order, decency, and cleanliness, which had been gradually formed and accumulated, in better times, by the insensible operation of habit and example. And no strength of argument, no force of authority, could again instil into the minds of a new generation, growing up under more prosperous circumstances, the sentiments and tastes thus blighted and destroyed by the cold breath of penury. Every return of temporary distress would, therefore, vitiate the feelings and lower the sensibilities of the labouring classes. The little progress of improvement made in happier times would be lost and forgotten. If we ward off a few of the bitterest blasts of calamity, the sacred flame may be kept alive till the tempest be past; but if once extinguished, how hard is the task of re-kindling it in minds long inured to degradation and wretchedness!"*

In the third place, it will, I suppose, be admitted, that when a considerable number of destitute poor persons are thrown out of employment, a provision of some sort or other should be made for their support. Suppose now, that it is made, not by a compulsory rate, but by the charitable contributions of the benevolent: it is contended that such a mode of relieving their distress tends to nourish the better feelings of the poor, and that many would rather choose to undergo the greatest privations than submit to solicit a share of this charitable contribution, who yet would make no scruple of claiming it, had the state given them a legal right to look to it for support. But, admitting the truth of this statement, it has been already seen that it is not for the advantage of society that the poor should be forced to submit to such extraordinary privations. It is, besides, abundantly certain, that many would not be influenced by the motives alluded to;

* "Inquiry into the Causes of the Depreciation of Agricultural Labour," p. 32.

and in the event of the distress being either very severe or long continued, even those most disinclined to become a burden on others might be forced to beg a pittance. And it is pretty obvious, notwithstanding all that has been said to the contrary, that the necessary result of such a state of things would be far more prejudicial to the character of the poor, that it would do more to prostrate their pride and independence, and to sink them in their own estimation, than the acceptance of relief from a poor's rate. It is idle, indeed, to talk about the independence of a man who is receiving charity; but an individual supported by the poor's rate cannot fairly be regarded in such a point of view. He is merely sharing in a public provision made by the state; and as all property has been acquired with the knowledge that it was responsible to this claim on the part of the poor, it cannot justly be considered as entailing any burden on any particular individual. It may, therefore, one should think, be fairly presumed, that the pride and independence of the poor will be more likely to be supported under a system of this sort, than if they were obliged to depend, in periods of distress, on the bounty of others. Wherever the poor have not, either *de jure* or *de facto*, a claim for support, they must, unavoidably, in such periods, be allowed to beg. But of all the scourges that afflict and disgrace humanity, there is, perhaps, none more destructive than the prevalence of mendicity. A common beggar is the most degraded of beings; and the experience of Ireland, France,* Italy,

* A committee of the National Assembly, appointed to inquire into the state of the poor of France, described our poor laws as *la plaie politique la plus dévorante de l'Angleterre*—an expression that has been often quoted on this side the channel. There are, however, pretty good grounds for thinking that the condition of all classes in France would have been decidedly improved had she been subjected to the operation of a similar code. Very large sums have been expended by government, and by individuals, in efforts to relieve the distresses of the poor; but as the burden of their support was thus removed from those who could, by their interference, have prevented the misapplication of the funds, and the undue

Spain, and, in short, of every country where there is no established provision for the support of the poor, shews that wherever the people are compelled to depend on so precarious a resource as charity, we shall look in vain for that manliness and independence of character which distin-

increase of the poor, the efforts in question have been of very little use. In despite of the repeated enactment of laws of the most extreme severity, mendicity has been at all times the scourge and disgrace of France. It is stated, in a valuable communication addressed by one of the ministers of Orleans to Mr. Howlett, immediately before the Revolution, that "no season of uncommon scarcity occurs but vast numbers of entire families, especially in the country, perish for want, being literally starved and frozen to death!"—(Mr. Howlett's *Tract*, p. 18.) At the Revolution the property of the hospitals, and other establishments for the support of the poor, was confiscated; and the seductive, but dangerous and inapplicable principle laid down, that the care and support of the poor was the duty of government, and not of municipalities. Practically, indeed, owing to the confusion of the times, this declaration had no effect. When, however, order was again restored, the attention of government was forcibly drawn to the wretched condition of the poor, who had for some years been wholly neglected. In consequence, *dépôts de mendicité*, and *bureaux de bienfaisance*, were established; the prefects being at present authorised, in the event of the funds derived from charitable contributions being inadequate for their support, to levy *octrois municipaux*, or duties on some of the principal articles conveyed into the towns where they are established. This is plainly a species of poor's rate; but it is a most objectionable one, inasmuch as it does not lay the burden upon those who alone have power to prevent the multiplication of the poor. But this new system has only been introduced into the more considerable towns; so that in the country, pauperism and mendicity are still as prevalent as ever, licenses to beg being frequently granted even by the public authorities. It is affirmed by the Baron Dupin ("Secours Publics," p. 460), that "in the country, in the dead season, want and misery abound, and *there are no means of relief*." Whenever, therefore, there is a deficient crop, famine and disease prevail to a frightful extent. Farther information as to the state of the French poor will be found in the work just quoted of M. Dupin, entitled, "Histoire de l'Administration des Secours Publics," in the "Visiteur du Pauvre," of M. Degerando, and particularly in Dr. Johnston's elaborate and excellent work on "Public Charity in France." There are some valuable details with respect to pauperism in France, and other continental states, in Mr. Page's able pamphlet, "The Principle of the English Poor Laws defended."

guish the poor of England, and find in their stead all those degrading vices which beggary is sure to produce.

At the same time, however, it must be confessed, that these statements, even supposing their accuracy were admitted, are not enough to determine this question. Whatever may be the disadvantages incident to charitable contributions for the support of the able-bodied poor, it is, notwithstanding, contended, by those who admit them fully, that they are the only device that can be resorted to without leading to consequences far more destructive than any that have been previously pointed out. A regard for their own interest, were there no other motives to be depended upon, will, it is affirmed, teach those who possess property the advantage of providing for the wants of those who are really necessitous, and will consequently prevent those outrages to which allusion has already been made. This contribution will, however, cease with the stern necessity which gave it birth. When the pressure has passed away, it will not remain to induce the idle and dissipated to linger on in their vicious courses. The whole labouring class would, under such circumstances, feel that they had nothing real to depend upon but their own efforts; and no one would be tempted to hesitate about saving a little stock when it was in his power, by trusting to so precarious and humiliating a resource as that of mendicancy. But such, it is alleged, is not the case with a legally established, compulsory provision; and granting all that has been urged in its defence, still, it is contended, that the evils inseparable from it far outweigh its advantages. It is acknowledged by all parties to be in most cases quite impossible to discriminate between that poverty and misery that has been produced by accidental and uncontrollable causes, and that which has originated in folly or ill conduct. And it appears obvious, that unless this can be done, the establishment of a provision on which every pauper shall have a legal claim, must, by placing the industrious and the idle, the frugal and the dissipated, on the same footing, have a powerful tendency to weaken all the motives to good conduct in the virtuous part of the community, and to strengthen the vicious propensities in those that are bad.

Supposing, however, that it were possible to organise such a system as would prevent all poor persons except those that were really deserving from being admitted to participate in the parish funds, still its operation would, it is affirmed, be most objectionable. No man, it must be remembered, loves exertion and industry for their own sakes. Every one has some end in view, some purpose which is to be served, and the accomplishment of which is to repay the toils and privations to which he may at present submit. But the desire to provide immediate subsistence, and to amass a little capital for the support of age and infirmity, must, with the great body of mankind, be the principal motive impelling them to industry and economy; and whatever tends, like the establishment of a poor's rate, to weaken or rather destroy this motive—whatever tends to make a man trust to others instead of himself, must, in so far, paralyse his exertions, and render him less industrious and economical. "*Languescet industria, intendetur socordia, si nullus ex se metus aut spes, et securi omnes aliena subsidia expectabunt, sibi ignavi, nobis graves.*"*

I have endeavoured to set the objections to a compulsory provision in the strongest point of view; and it is not to be denied that they are very formidable. I acknowledge that at one time they appeared to me to be quite unanswerable; and that, great as the evils incident to the scheme of leaving the poor to be supported by voluntary contributions certainly are, they seemed to be less than those attached to the compulsory system. But a closer examination of the subject, and especially of the history of the poor laws, has led me to doubt the correctness of this

* Taciti "Annal." lib. ii. cap. 38.

opinion; and I am now satisfied that the evils incident to a poor's rate may be, and in fact have been, so far repressed by regulations as to its management, as to render them comparatively innocuous, and that its advantages may be secured without any material alloy.

A statutory provision has been established in this country for about two hundred and thirty years, for all who cannot support themselves; and we are bound to avail ourselves of this experience, and to decide with respect to its effects, not upon theoretical grounds, or conclusions drawn from *imagining* what the conduct of the labouring class must be when they have a recognised claim to public support in all seasons of difficulty, but by looking to what that conduct really has been during this long period of probation. It is affirmed, and truly, that there was no considerable increase of population in England from the period when the poor laws were established down to the middle of last century; and it is alleged, that its recent increase has been wholly owing to the prodigious extension of manufactures and commerce, and has not exceeded its increase in Scotland, where the system of compulsory provision has made but very little progress. It is farther affirmed, that it is false to say that the labouring population of England have, at any time, discovered a want of forethought and consideration; that they were formerly eminently distinguished for these virtues; and that, notwithstanding the unfavourable change made in their condition, by the rise of prices, and the revulsions of industry, since the commencement of the late war, they will still bear an advantageous comparison in these respects with the people of any other country: and, in proof of this, we are referred to the returns obtained under authority of the House of Commons, which shew that in 1815 there were no fewer than 925,439 individuals in England and Wales, being about *one-eleventh* of the then existing population, members of friendly societies, formed for the express purpose of affording protection to the members during sickness and old age, and enabling them to subsist without resorting to the parish funds, and that the deposits in the savings' banks amount at present to about *fourteen millions* sterling! It is alleged, that no such unquestionable proofs of the prevalence of a spirit of providence and independence can be exhibited in any other European country. If the poor have, in some districts, become degraded, it is affirmed, that this degradation has not been owing to the poor laws, but to extrinsic and adventitious causes; and, in particular, to the excessive influx of paupers from Ireland, a country where there are no poor laws; and the condition of the population of which affords, it is said, a decisive proof of the fallacy of all the complaints that have been made as to their injurious operation.

Such, in a few words, is the substance of the statements that are occasionally put forth by the apologists of the poor laws: and it is impossible to deny that they are well-founded. From the period (1601) when the act of the 43d of Elizabeth, the foundation of the existing code of poor laws, was promulgated, to the commencement of the late war, there was scarcely any increase of pauperism; and few or none of those pernicious consequences had actually resulted from their operation which we are naturally led, looking only to some of the principles they involve, to suppose they must produce. This apparent anomaly may, however, be satisfactorily explained. A compulsory provision for the support of the poor would, undoubtedly, have the effects commonly ascribed to it, *unless it were accompanied by some very powerful counteracting checks*. But a very little consideration will shew that the establishment of such a provision could hardly fail of speedily producing these checks. The error into which the opponents of the poor laws have universally fallen, does not consist so much in their having made any false estimate of their operation on the labouring classes, as in having fixed their attention exclusively on it, without having adverted to their operation on others. It is plain, however, that the rates affect the *payers* as well as the *receivers;* and that no sound conclusion can be drawn as to their real operation, without looking carefully at the circumstances under which both parties are placed, and at the conduct which they respectively follow.* If the object of the one party be, speaking generally, to increase the rates to the highest limit, that of the other is to sink them to the lowest; and it not unfrequently happens that the latter is the more powerful of the two. The act of the 43d of Elizabeth laid the burden of providing for the poor on the landlords and tenants of the country; but it left them to administer that relief in the way they thought best; and it stimulated them to take measures to prevent the growth of a pauper population, which have not only prevented it from increasing in an unnatural proportion, but which, there are good grounds for thinking, have confined it within far narrower limits than it would have attained had the poor laws not been in existence.

The truth is, that the act of the 43d of Elizabeth has not been *bonâ fide* carried into execution. The act says, that employment and subsistence shall be found for all who are unable to find them for themselves. But those who have had the interpretation of the act were long in the habit of denying all relief, except to those who resorted to public workhouses; and there are very many needy persons who would be eager to claim assistance from the public, if it could be obtained without any extraordinary sacrifice, who would yet reject it when coupled with the condition of submitting to imprisonment in a workhouse, and subjecting themselves to the vexatious tyranny of overseers.

It is, indeed, distinctly mentioned by Sir F. M. Eden, that when workhouses began to be generally erected, after the act of 1723, a number of persons who had previously received a pension from the parish, preferred depending

* Public attention was, I believe, first directed to this view of the subject by Mr. Black, the learned and able editor of the "Morning Chronicle."

on their own exertions, rather than take up their abode in them: and the aversion of the poor to these establishments was so great, that we are told by Sir F. M. Eden of some whose humanity seems to have exceeded their good sense, proposing, by way of weakening this aversion, "*to call workhouses by some softer and more inoffensive name.*"*

But of all the circumstances which contributed to render the growth of pauperism in England so much slower than might have been expected under the system of compulsory provision, the most powerful, undoubtedly, has been, that that very system made it the obvious interest of the landlords and occupiers of land to oppose themselves to the too rapid increase of the labouring population. They saw that if, either by the erection of cottages, the splitting of farms, or otherwise, the population upon their estates or occupancies were augmented, they would, through the operation of the poor laws, be burdened with the support of all who, from old age, sickness, want of employment, or any other cause, might become, at any future period, unable to provide for themselves. The wish to avoid incurring such an indefinite responsibility, not only rendered landlords and farmers exceedingly cautious about admitting new settlers upon their estates and farms, but stimulated them to take vigorous measures for the diminution of the population, wherever the demand for labour was not pretty brisk and constant. It is to the operation of this principle that the complicated system of laws with respect to settlements owes its origin; and until it was relaxed, it is admitted to have opposed a formidable barrier to the increase of the agricultural population. There is, indeed, very great reason to doubt whether the purely agricultural population of England was not rather diminished than increased in the interval between the Revolution and 1770. And it is to the operation of the poor laws, more, perhaps, than to any thing else, that we find so few small occu-

* "State of the Poor," vol. i. p. 285.

pancies in England; and that this country has been saved from that excessive subdivision of the land, that has been and is the bane and curse of Ireland. If, indeed, we reflect upon the high rents that cottagers will offer for slips of land, and the circumstance that the law of England has, by granting the elective franchise to all persons possessed of a cottage and a piece of land valued at 40*s.* a-year, given a very strong stimulus to the increase of cottages, we must be satisfied that some powerful principle has been at work to render their multiplication so inconsiderable. Political influence is as dear to an English as to an Irish gentleman; but as the former would, had he manufactured voters by the hundred or the thousand, have made himself directly responsible for their maintenance, he has been deterred by a motive, which had no influence in the case of the latter, to abstain from so ruinous a practice. Most landlords early saw the consequences that would infallibly result from their being bound to provide for all who, either through misfortune, misconduct, or profligacy, could not provide for themselves; and since they could not subvert the principle of the system, they naturally exerted themselves to counteract it in practice, by adopting every possible device for checking the undue increase of population, and by administering relief in such a mode as might prevent any but the really indigent from having recourse to it.

The truth is, that down to 1795 the universal complaint was, not that the poor laws had increased population and lowered wages, but *that they had diminished it and raised wages.* A host of authorities, some of which are referred to below,* might be quoted in proof of this

* "Britannia Languens, or a Discourse of Trade," &c. p. 155. Lond. 1680. Alcock's "Observations on the Effects of the Poor Laws," pp. 19, 20. Lond. 1752. Dr. Burn's "History of the Poor Laws," p. 211. Lond. 1764. Mr. Young's work, quoted in the text. Brown's "Agricultural Survey of the West Riding of Yorkshire," p. 13. Lond. 1793, &c. Debates in the House of Commons, 28th April, 1773.

statement, and explanatory of the means by which so singular a result was brought about; but the following passage from Mr. Young's "Farmer's Letters" will probably be deemed sufficient.

"The law of *settlement*," says Mr. Young, "is attended with nearly as many ill consequences as that of *maintenance*. I have said enough to prove of how great importance our labouring poor are to the public welfare; the strength of the state lies in their numbers, but the prodigious restrictions thrown on their settlements *tend strongly to prevent an increase.* One great inducement to marriage is the finding, without difficulty, a comfortable habitation; and another, nearly as material, when such requisite is found, to be able to exercise in it whatever business a man has been educated to or brought up in. The first of these points is no easy matter to be accomplished; for it is too much the interest of a parish, both landlords and tenants, to decrease the cottages in it, and, above all, to prevent their increase, so that, in process of time, habitations are extremely difficult to be procured. There is no parish but had much rather that its young labourers would continue single: in that state they are not in danger of becoming chargeable, but when married the case alters; *all obstructions are, therefore, thrown in the way of their marrying;* and none more immediately than that of rendering it as difficult as possible for the men, when married, to procure a house to live in; and *this conduct is found so conducive to easing the rates, that it universally gives rise to an open war against cottages.* How often do gentlemen who have possessions in a parish, when cottages come to sale, purchase them, and immediately rase them to the foundation, that they may never become the *nests,* as they are called, of *beggars' brats!* by which means their tenants are not so burdened in their rates, and their farms let better; for the rates are considered as much by tenants as the rent. In this manner cottages are the perpetual objects of jealousy, the young inhabitants are prevented from marrying, and population is obstructed."*

It may perhaps be said, that, had the poor laws never existed, had the poor not been tempted to place a deceitful trust in parish assistance, their natural sagacity would have led them to act with prudence and consideration, and prevented them from multiplying their numbers beyond the demand for them. That this would have been, in some measure, the case, is true; but considering the state of depression in which the poor have usually been involved, and their total ignorance of the most efficient causes of poverty, there are but slender grounds for thinking that this influence would have been very sensibly felt. A man must be in tolerably comfortable circumstances before he is at all likely to be much influenced by prospective considerations. It is the pressure of actual, not the fear of future want, that is the great incentive to the industry of the poor. Those who have speculated with respect to the operation of the poor laws on the prudential virtues, have usually belonged to the upper classes, and have supposed the lower classes to be actuated by the same motives as those with whom they associate. But the circumstances under which these classes are placed are so very different, as to render it exceedingly difficult to draw any accurate conclusion as to the conduct of the one, in respect of such matters, from observations made upon the conduct of the other. A man who is comfortable in his circumstances, must, in order not to lose *caste*, and to secure a continuance of the advantages which he enjoys, exercise a certain degree of prudence; but those who possess few comforts, who are near the verge of human society, and have but little to lose, do not act under any such serious responsibility. A want of caution, and a recklessness of consequences, are in their case productive of comparatively little in-

* "Farmer's Letters to the People of England," 3d edit. vol. i. pp. 300—302.

jury, and are less guarded against. The most comprehensive experience proves that this is the case. The lower we descend in the scale of society, the less consideration and forethought do we find to prevail. When we either compare the different classes of the same country, or of different countries, we invariably find, that poverty is never so little dreaded as by those who are most likely to become its victims. The nearer they approach to it, the less is it feared by them. And that generally numerous class who are already so low that they can fall no lower, scruple not to plunge into excesses that would be shunned by others, and often indulge in gratifications productive of the most injurious consequences.

On the whole, therefore, there seems to be but little reason for thinking that the fear of being left destitute in old age, had the poor laws not existed, would have operated so powerfully in the way of deterring those who were already poor and uninstructed, as the labouring classes have generally been, from entering into improvident unions, as the formidable restraints that grew out of the poor laws. " A labouring man in his youth," it has been justly observed, " is not disposed to look forward to the decline of life, but listens to the impulses of passion. He sees the picture through the deceitful mirror which his inclinations hold up to him. Hence those restraints which persons of property, interested in keeping down poor-rates, will infallibly impose upon him, are far more likely to be efficacious than those which he will impose on himself."

It may be inferred, from the statements of contemporary writers, that the poor's rates amounted to about a million at the commencement of last century.* In 1776, they amounted, according to the official returns, to 1,720,316*l.*; and at an average of the years 1783, 4, and 5, being those immediately subsequent to the American war, they amounted to 2,167,748*l.* This, when we consider

* Sir F. M. Eden on the State of the Poor, vol. i. p. 408.

the rise in the price of food, the great increase of population, and the distressed situation of the country at the termination of a disastrous contest, if it be really an increase, is certainly a very small one, and shews that the checks that had grown out of the system had been sufficient effectually to hinder the growth of pauperism.[a]

[a] *Account of the Sums assessed and levied under the name of Poor's Rates; of the Sums annually expended for the support of the Poor; of the Sums expended in Law, Removals, &c.; and of the Prices of Wheat in England and Wales in the under-mentioned years.—From Parliamentary Papers.*

YEARS.	Total Sum Assessed and Levied.	Payments thereout for other Purposes than the Relief of the Poor.	Sums Expended in Law, Removals, &c.	Sums Expended for the Relief of the Poor.	Total Sums Expended.	Average Price of Wheat.
	£.	£.	£.	£.	£.	s. d.
Average of 1748–49–50*	730,135	40,164	† ...	689,971	‡ ...	...
1776	1,720,316	137,655	35,071	1,521,732	1,694,458	...
Average of 1783–4–5	2,167,748	163,511	91,996	1,912,241	2,167,148	...
1803	5,348,204	1,034,105	190,072	4,077,891	5,302,070	63 2
1812–13	8,640,842	1,861,073	325,107	6,656,105	8,865,838	128 8
1813–14	8,388,974	1,881,565	332,966	6,294,584	8,511,863	98 0
1814–15	7,457,676	1,763,020	324,664	5,418,845	7,508,853	70 6
1815–16	6,937,425	1,212,918	† ...	5,724,506	‡ ...	61 10
1816–17	8,128,418	1,210,200	...	6,918,217	‡ ...	87 4
1817–18	9,320,440	1,430,292	...	7,890,148	‡ ...	90 7
1818–19	8,932,185	1,300,534	...	7,531,650	‡ ...	82 9
1819–20	8,719,655	1,342,658	...	7,329,594	8,672,252	69 5
‖ 1820–21	8,411,893	1,375,868	...	6,958,445	8,334,313	62 5
1821–22	7,761,441	1,336,533	...	6,358,703	7,695,235	53 0
1822–23	6,898,153	1,148,230	...	5,772,958	6,921,187	41 11
1823–24	6,833,630	1,137,405	...	5,734,216	6,871,621	56 8
1824–25	..	...	...	5,786,991	...	62 9
1825–26	6,965,051	1,246,145	...	5,928,501	7,174,647	56 11
1826–27	7,784,351	1,362,377	...	6,441,088	7,803,465	56 7½
1827–28	7,715,055	1,372,433	...	6,298,000	7,670,433	

* No great dependence can be placed upon the returns for these years.

† For this and the years so marked there is no particular account of the Sums expended in Law, or in Removals.

‡ For these periods there is no account of the Sums expended, as distinguished from those assessed and levied.

‖ For this and the subsequent years the Orders required Returns, not of the Sums assessed and levied, but of the Sum levied.

During the period between the termination of the American war and the commencement of the late French war, the rates were again considerably reduced; but in 1795 a total change was unhappily made in the system which had been productive of such beneficial results. The price of corn, which had, upon an average of the three preceding years, averaged 54*s.*, rose, in 1795, to 74*s.* As wages continued stationary at their former elevation, the distress of the poor was very great; and many able-bodied labourers, who had rarely before applied for parish assistance, became claimants for relief. But, instead of meeting this emergency as it ought to have been met, by temporary expedients, and by grants of relief proportioned to the exigency of every given case, one uniform system was adopted. The magistrates of Berks, and some other southern counties, issued tables, shewing the wages which, as they affirmed, every labouring man *ought* to receive, according to the variations in the number of his family, and the price of bread; and they accompanied these tables with an order, directing the parish officers to make up the deficit to the labourer, in the event of the wages paid him by his employers falling short of the tabular allowance. An act was at the same time passed to allow the justices to administer relief *out* of the workhouse, and also to relieve such poor persons as had property of their own! As might have been expected, this system did not cease with the temporary circumstances which gave it birth, but has ever since been acted upon. It is now almost universally established in the southern half of England, and has been productive of an extent of mischief that could hardly have been conceived possible.

It is needless to dwell on the folly of attempting to make the wages of labour vary directly and immediately with every change in the price of bread. Every one must see, that if this system were *bonâ fide* acted upon,— if the poor were always supplied with the power of purchasing an equal quantity of corn, whether it happened to be abundant and cheap, or scarce and dear, they could have no motive to lessen their consumption in seasons when the supply is deficient; so that the whole pressure of the scarcity would, in such cases, be removed from them and thrown entirely upon the other, and chiefly the middle, classes. But not to insist on this point, let us look at the practical operation of this system as it affects the labourer and his employers. The allowance scales now issued from time to time by the magistrates are usually framed on the principle that every labourer should have a gallon loaf of standard wheaten bread weekly for every member of his family, and one over; that is, four loaves for three persons, five for four, six for five, and so on. Suppose, now, that the gallon loaf costs 1*s.* 6*d.*, and that the average rate of wages in any particular district is 8*s.* a week: A, an industrious unmarried labourer, will get 8*s.*; but B has a wife and four children; hence he claims *seven* gallon loaves, or 10*s.* 6*d.* a week: and as wages are only 8*s.*, he gets 2*s.* 6*d.* a week from the parish. C, again, has a wife and six children; he consequently requires *nine* gallon loaves, or 13*s.* 6*d.* a week, and gets, of course, a pension, over and above his wages, of 5*s.* 6*d.* D is so idle and disorderly that no one will employ him; but he has a wife and five children, and is in consequence entitled to *eight* gallon loaves for their support; so that he must have a pension of 12*s.* a week to support him in his dissolute mode of life.

It is clear that this system, by making the parish allowance to labourers increase with every increase in the number of their children, acts as a bounty on marriage, and that, by increasing the supply of labourers beyond the demand, it must necessarily depress the rate of wages. And it is farther clear, that by giving the *same* allowance to the idle and disorderly as to the industrious and well-behaved workman, it must operate as a premium on idleness and profligacy, and takes away some of the most powerful motives to industry and good conduct. These, however, are not the only effects of this system. Under its operation a labourer dares not venture to earn beyond a certain amount; for if he did, his allowance from the parish would either be withheld altogether, or proportionally reduced. In consequence, working by the piece is now comparatively unknown in the southern counties of England; and the whole labouring population are reduced to the condition of paupers, deprived of the means and almost of the desire to emerge from the state of helotism in which they are sunk.

It must be obvious to every one that, if we would avert the plague of universal poverty from the land, a vigorous effort must be made to counteract this system; and we have experience to teach us how this may be done. All, in fact, that is necessary is to revert to the regulations established previously to 1795, to abolish every vestige of the allowance system, and to enact that henceforth no able-bodied labourer shall have a legal claim for relief, unless he consents to accept it in a workhouse. This condition would go far to prevent relief from being claimed by any except those who are really necessitous; for there is nothing of which the idle and disorderly are so much afraid as of the strict discipline, scanty fare, and hard labour, that ought to be enforced in every workhouse. It is not, however, meant to recommend that relief should, in all cases, be refused except to the inmates of such establishments. In the great majority of instances, that temporary assistance which the able-bodied poor alone require, may be far more advantageously afforded at their own houses. But to prevent its being abused, it is indispensable that authority to refuse it, except under condition of residence in a workhouse, and of unconditional submission to all its regulations, should be vested in the administrators of the law. The maimed and impotent poor may, in all cases, be more cheaply and better provided for in their own houses than in workhouses.

Were the change now proposed effected, most of the

inconveniences attached to the poor laws would be removed, and their salutary and sustaining influence would alone remain.

It has been said that the poor's rate, as now assessed, imposes a heavy burden on land and other fixed property, from which all sorts of movable property and professional incomes are exempted. Inasmuch, however, as all fixed property has been acquired by its present owners since the poor laws were enacted, this regulation cannot truly be said to be unjust; neither does there seem to be any good ground for impeaching its expediency. The proprietors and occupiers of land and houses are those only who have any power over the increase of population; and by laying the burden of providing for the poor wholly upon them, they are prompted to take the most effectual measures for preventing the too rapid increase of the labouring class. This, indeed, is one of the principal recommendations of the poor laws. So long as the poor are left to trust to the unconstrained bounty of the benevolent, the landlords and occupiers of land take comparatively little interest in their situation, in the administration of the provision made for them, or in the increase of their numbers. But the moment that they acquire a legal claim to relief, it becomes the obvious interest of every one who has property to see that the funds for their relief are properly administered, and to exert himself to oppose their too rapid increase. To suppose that it should not be so, would be to suppose what is contradictory and absurd; it would be equivalent to supposing that the protection of their property had ceased powerfully to interest its possessors.

Independently, too, of these considerations, the circumstance of a legal provision existing for their support, by giving the poor an interest in the state, or, as it has been termed, a *stake in the hedge*, interests them in the preservation of the public tranquillity, and inspires them with an attachment to their country and its institutions that they could not otherwise feel. In densely peopled manufacturing districts, where the poor have nothing but their wages to depend upon, and where hardly one in a hundred can reasonably hope to attain to a more elevated situation, the poor laws are their only security against falling a sacrifice to absolute want. They are, in fact, a bulwark raised by the state to protect its subjects from famine and despair; and while they support them in seasons of calamity, and prevent them from being driven to excesses ruinous alike to themselves and others, they do not degrade them by making them depend on what is often the grudging and stunted charity of others. A wise statesman will pause before attempting to pull down so venerable and so useful an institution; and will prefer exerting himself to repair the defects that have been discovered in its structure, and to make it effectual to its truly benevolent object of affording an asylum to the really necessitous, without at the same time becoming an incentive to sloth and improvidence.

CHAPTER IV.

Education of the Poor — Influence of Friendly Societies and Savings' Banks.

Of all the means for providing for the permanent improvement of the poor hitherto suggested, there does not seem to be any that promises to be so effectual as the establishment of a really useful system of public education. It is no exaggeration to affirm, that nine-tenths of the misery and crime which afflict and disgrace society have their source in ignorance. Those who have laboured to promote the education of the poor, seem, generally speaking, to be satisfied, provided they succeed in making them able to read and write. But the education that stops at this point omits those parts that are really the most important. A knowledge of the arts of reading, writing, and arithmetic, may, and indeed very often does, exist in company with the grossest ignorance of all those principles with respect to which it is most for the interest of the poor themselves, as well as of the other classes, that they should be well informed. To render education productive of all the utility that may be derived from it, the poor ought, in addition to the elementary instruction now communicated to them, to be made acquainted with the duties enjoined by religion and morality, and with the circumstances which occasion that gradation of ranks and inequality of fortunes that usually exist; and they should, above all, be impressed, from their earliest years, with a conviction of the important and undoubted truth, that they are really the arbiters of their own fortune, that what others can do for them is but as the dust of the balance compared with what they can do for themselves, and that the most tolerant and liberal government, and the best institutions, cannot shield them from poverty and degradation, without the exercise of a reasonable degree of forethought, frugality, and good conduct, on their part. That the ultimate effect of such a system of education would be most advantageous, is abundantly obvious. Neither the errors nor the vices of the poor are incurable: they investigate all those plain practical questions which affect their own immediate interest, with the greatest sagacity and penetration, and do not fail to trace their remote consequences; and if education were made to embrace objects of real utility—if it were made a means of instructing the poor with respect to the circumstances which elevate and depress the rate of wages, and which, consequently, exert the most powerful influence over their condition, there can be no doubt that the great majority would endeavour to profit by it. It would be unreasonable, indeed, to expect, that it should produce any very immediate effect on the habits of the multitude. Although, however, there may be but little room for the formation of sanguine hopes of early improvement, there is none for despondency. The harvest of sound instruction may be late, but in the end it will be most luxuriant; and will amply reward the efforts of those who are not discouraged in their attempts to make it a means of improving the condition of the poor, by the difficulties they may expect to encounter at the commencement and during the progress of their labours.

It has been excellently observed, in reference to the diffusion of education, that—"Of all obstacles to improvement, ignorance is the most formidable, because the only true secret of assisting the poor is to make them agents in bettering their own condition, and to supply them, not with a temporary stimulus, but with a permanent energy. As fast as the standard of intelligence is raised, the poor become more and more able to co-operate in any plan proposed for their advantage, more likely to listen to any reasonable suggestion, more able to understand, and therefore more willing to pursue it. Hence it follows, that when gross ignorance is once removed, and right principles are introduced, a great advantage has been already gained against squalid poverty. Many avenues to an improved condition are opened to one whose faculties are enlarged and exercised; he sees his own interest more clearly, he pursues it more steadily, he does not study immediate gratification at the expense of bitter and late repentance, or mortgage the labour of his future life without an adequate return. Indigence, therefore, will rarely be found in company with good education."*

The formation of benefit clubs or friendly societies seems to be one of the best devices for enabling the poor to provide for themselves, without depending on the charity of their more opulent neighbours. Friendly societies are formed on a principle of mutual insurance. Each member contributes a certain sum by weekly, monthly, or annual subscriptions, while he is in health, and receives from the society a corresponding pension or allowance when he is incapacitated for work by accident, sickness, or old age. Nothing, it is obvious, can be more unexceptionable than the principle of these associations. Owing to the general exemption from sickness till a comparatively late period of life, if a number of individuals under thirty or thirty-five years of age, form themselves into a society, and subscribe each a small sum from their surplus earnings, they are able to secure a comfortable provision in the event of their becoming unfit for labour. But it is plain that any single individual who should trust to his own unassisted efforts for support, would be placed in a very different situation from those who are members of such a society; for, however industrious and parsimonious, he might not be able to accomplish his object, inasmuch as the occurrence of any accident, or an obstinate fit of sick-

* Sumner's "Records of the Creation," vol. ii. p. 298.

ness, might, by throwing him out of employment, and forcing him to consume the savings he had accumulated against old age, reduce him to a state of indigence, and oblige him to become dependent on others. It may, therefore, be regarded as an exceedingly favourable circumstance, that the number of persons in England enrolled in friendly societies is supposed at this moment to exceed a *million*. But though great, the progress of these societies has hitherto been very much counteracted by the ignorance and mismanagement of their officers, and by the real difficulty of establishing them on a solid foundation. The principal error has consisted in their fixing their allowance-scales too high. When instituted, they consist, for the most part, of members in the prime of life; and there is comparatively little sickness and mortality amongst them: in consequence, their funds rapidly accumulate, and they are naturally tempted, from the apparently flourishing state of their affairs, to deal liberally by those members who are occasionally incapacitated. But the circumstances under which the society is placed at an advanced period are materially different: sickness and mortality are then comparatively prevalent; the contributions to the fund decline at the same time that the outgoings increase; and it has not unfrequently happened that the society has become altogether bankrupt, and that the oldest members have been left, at the close of their lives, destitute of all support from a fund on which they had relied, and to which they had largely contributed.

But the defects in the constitution of friendly societies have been, in a considerable degree, amended; various efforts, many of which have been productive of the best effects, having been made by private individuals and associations, as well as by the legislature, to obviate the chances of their failure, and to encourage their foundation on sound principles. Two reports by a committee of the House of Commons, "On the Laws respecting Friendly Societies," printed in 1825 and 1827, contain a great deal of authentic information as to their constitution; and the "Report and Tables," published by the Highland Society, are also valuable.

The recent institution of savings' banks deserves also the warmest support of all who are friendly to the improvement and independence of the poor. The want of a safe place of deposit for their savings, where they would yield them a reasonable interest, and whence they could withdraw them at pleasure without loss, has formed one of the most serious obstacles to the formation of a habit of accumulation among labourers. The difficulty of investment has led many to neglect opportunities of saving of which they might have availed themselves; and it has frequently happened that those who, in despite of every discouragement, had accumulated a little capital, have been tempted, by the offer of a high rate of interest, to lend it to persons of doubtful characters and desperate fortunes, whose bankruptcy has involved them in irremediable ruin. But the poor man has now the means of readily depositing his smallest savings, where he is assured they will be faithfully preserved, as well as the interest accruing upon them, to assist his future wants; and as there are very few who are insensible of the blessings of independence, there is no reason to suppose that they will be slow to avail themselves of the means of accumulation when in their power.

Still, however, it must be admitted, that savings' banks by no means fully obviate the difficulty that has always existed in England of profitably investing small sums. They are, in fact, applicable only to the exigencies of the labourers, and not to those of little tradesmen, farmers, &c. No one can deposit more than 50*l.* the first year, in a savings' bank, and 30*l.* in every subsequent year, until he has deposited 200*l.*, when no more will be received. But it is exceedingly desirable that this system should be extended as widely as possible. In Scotland, it has long been customary for the public banks to receive deposits of such small sums as 10*l.*, or even 5*l.*, and to allow interest upon them at about one per cent less than the interest obtained by investing in the funds. And, perhaps, no single circumstance could be specified that has done more to generate and diffuse those habits of foresight and economy by which the Scotch peasantry and small tradesmen are so honourably distinguished. Such facilities of accumulation have not been at any time afforded in England. Neither the Bank of England, nor any of the London private banks, allow interest upon deposits, and the practice is far from being general in the country. Hence it is that tradesmen in London and other places who wish to invest a small sum so as to make it profitable, must either lend it to a private individual, which is in most cases attended with risk, or buy funded property with it. This latter mode of investment, however, though extensively practised, has several drawbacks; it renders the sum invested liable to be affected by the fluctuations of the funds; the investment cannot be made without the assistance of third parties; the money cannot be drawn out at once without any sort of trouble, and some little acquaintance with the nature of stocks and the business of stock-jobbing is required. It would, therefore, as it appears to me, be a great public good were the plan of giving interest on deposits adopted by the Bank of England and her branches; and it is to be hoped that this very important subject may not be lost sight of when the question as to the renewal of the bank charter comes before parliament.

CHAPTER V.

Conflicting Opinions with respect to the Origin of Rent — Theory of Dr. Anderson — Nature and Progress of Rent — Not a Cause but a Consequence of the High Value of Raw Produce — Does not enter into Price— Distinction between Agriculture and Manufactures — Money Rents depend partly on the Extent to which Tillage has been carried, and partly on Situation — Inequality and Mischievous Operation of Taxes on Rent—Real Value of Commodities not affected by the Payment of Rent.

M. QUESNAY and Dr. Smith supposed, as has been already seen, that rent formed the recompense of nature in assisting the operations of the husbandman after all that part of the produce had been deducted which could be considered as the recompense of the work of man.* Others supposed that rent originated in the circumstance of the landlords enjoying a monopoly of the soil, and being, in consequence, enabled to obtain an artificially enhanced price for its produce. The latter contended, of course, that rent entered as an important element into the cost of corn and other agricultural products. But in the system of the *Economists*, rent being looked upon as a free gift of nature, was not supposed to affect prices. Dr. Smith, though he adopted the opinions of the *Economists* as to the origin of rent, is not very consistent in his statement as to its operation on prices; on the whole, however, it would seem that he considered it as directly influencing them.†

The fallacy of these contradictory statements is sufficiently obvious. Were rent really the recompense of the work of nature, it would always exist, wherever cultivation

* Ante, p. 48; and "Wealth of Nations," vol. ii. p. 149.

† "Wealth of Nations," vol. i. p. 86.

is practised, and would be equal at all times, neither of which is the case. To suppose that it is the result of a monopoly, in the ordinary sense of the term, on the part of the landlords, is still more visionary. No combination of any sort exists among them; and at the very moment that some are receiving high rents, the rents of others amount to little or nothing — a sufficient proof that they depend on something else than monopoly.

The true theory of rent was, for the first time, satisfactorily unfolded, very soon after the publication of the "Wealth of Nations," by Dr. James Anderson. He shewed, by an original and able analysis, that rent was not the recompense of the work of nature, nor a consequence of land being made private property; but that it was owing to its being of various degrees of fertility, and to the circumstance of its being impossible to apply capital indefinitely to any quality of land without, generally speaking, obtaining from it a constantly diminishing return. He further shewed, that corn was always sold at its natural price, or at the price necessary to obtain the required supply; and that this price was totally unaffected by the payment of rent; and he deduced from this doctrine many important practical conclusions, particularly with reference to the effect of tithes and other taxes on raw produce. These doctrines have since been illustrated aud enforced by others. But the subject is not yet exhausted; and I shall endeavour to place it in a somewhat novel point of view, and to obviate some of the more specious objections that have been made to the theory.*

* Dr. Anderson was born at Hermandston, in Midlothian, in 1740. He was long extensively engaged in the business of farming in the neighbourhood of Aberdeen. In 1777, he published a quarto volume, entitled "Observations on the Means of exciting a Spirit of National Industry," which contains (pp. 375–377) the earliest developement of the theory of rent. In the course of the same year he published a pamphlet on the Corn Laws, "An Inquiry into the Corn Laws," in which (pp. 45–50) he has expounded the theory with a sagacity and discrimina-

1. Corn or Produce Rents.—Rent is properly that portion of the produce of the earth which is paid by the farmer to the landlord for the use of the *natural and inherent* powers of the soil. If buildings have been erected on a farm, or if it has been enclosed, drained, or in any way improved, the sum which a farmer will pay to the landlord for its use will be composed, not only of what is properly rent, but also of a remuneration for the use of the capital laid out on its improvement. In common language, these two sums are always confounded together under the name of rent; but in an inquiry of this nature, it is necessary to regard them as perfectly distinct. The laws by which rent and profits are regulated are totally different; nor can those which govern the one be ascertained if they be not considered separately from those which govern the other.

On the first settling of any country abounding in large tracts of unappropriated land, no rent is ever paid; and for this obvious reason, that no person will pay rent for what may be procured in unlimited quantities for nothing. Thus in New Holland, where there is an ample supply of fertile and *unappropriated* land, rent will not be heard

tion that has never been surpassed. Having left Aberdeenshire, Dr. Anderson resided for some time in the neighbourhood of Edinburgh, where he projected and edited the "Bee," a respectable weekly publication. In 1797, he removed to the vicinity of London, where he edited, "Recreations in Agriculture, Natural History, Arts," &c. In this work, (vol. v. pp. 401–405) he gave a new and able exposition of the nature, origin, and progress of rent, (see my edition of the "Wealth of Nations," vol. iv. pp. 574–578); but, notwithstanding these repeated publications, it does not appear that his profound and important disquisitions attracted any attention. And so completely were they forgotten, that when Mr. Malthus and Sir Edward West published their tracts on rent, in 1815, they were universally regarded as the real authors of the theory! There is no question, indeed, as to their originality; but it may be doubted whether they have succeeded in explaining the theory as well as it had been explained about forty years before. Dr. Anderson died in 1808.

of until the best lands are occupied. Suppose, however, that tillage has been carried to this point, and that the increasing demand for raw produce can, in the actual state of agriculture, be no longer supplied by the culture of the best lands; under these circumstances it is plain that population must become stationary, or the inhabitants must consent to pay such an additional price for raw produce as may enable the *second* quality of land to be cultivated. No advance short of this will procure them another bushel of corn; and competition will not, as will be immediately shewn, allow them to pay more for it. They have, therefore, but one alternative. If they choose to pay a price sufficient to cover the expense of cultivating land of the second quality, they will obtain additional supplies; if they do not, they must be without them.

Suppose, now, that such a price is offered as will pay the expense of producing corn on soils which, in return for the same expenditure that would have produced 100 quarters on lands of the *first quality*, will only yield 90 quarters; it is plain it will then be indifferent to a farmer whether he pays a rent of ten quarters for the first quality of land, or farms the second quality, which is unappropriated and open to him, without paying any rent. If the population went on increasing, lands which would yield only 80, 70, 60, 50, &c. quarters in return for the same expenditure that had raised 100 quarters on the best lands, might be successively brought under cultivation. And when recourse has been had to these inferior lands, the corn rent of those that are superior would plainly be equal to the difference between the quantity of produce obtained from them and the quantity obtained from the worst quality under tillage. Suppose, for example, that the worst quality cultivated yields 60 quarters, then the rent of the *first* quality will be 40 quarters, or 100—60; the rent of the *second* quality will, in like manner, be equal to the difference between 90 and 60, or

30 quarters; the rent of the third quality will be equal to 80—60, or 20 quarters, and so on. The produce raised on the land last cultivated, or by means of the capital last applied to the soil, being all the while sold at its *necessary price*, or at that price which is merely sufficient to yield the cultivators the common and average rate of profit, or, which is the same thing, to cover the cost of its production. If the price were above this level, agriculture would be the best of all businesses, and tillage would be immediately extended; if, on the other hand, the price fell below this level, capital would be withdrawn from the soil, and the poorer lands thrown out of cultivation. Under such circumstances, it is quite clear that rent could not enter into the price of that portion of produce raised by means of the capital last applied to the soil. Its price is exclusively made up of wages and profits. The proprietors of the superior lands obtain rent; but this is the necessary result of their greater fertility. The demand cannot be supplied without cultivating inferior soils; and to enable them to be cultivated, their produce must sell for such a price as will afford the ordinary rate of profit to *their* cultivators. This price will, however, yield a surplus over and above the ordinary rate of profit to the cultivators of the more fertile lands; and it is this surplus that forms rent.

"In every country," says Dr. Anderson, in the earliest exposition of this doctrine, "there are various soils which are endued with different degrees of fertility; and hence it must happen, that the farmer who cultivates the most fertile of these can afford to bring his corn to market at a lower price than others who cultivate poorer fields. But if the corn that grows on these fertile spots be not sufficient fully to supply the market, the price will naturally be raised to such a height as to indemnify others for the expense of cultivating poorer soils. The farmer, however, who cultivates the rich spots, will be able to sell his corn at the same rate with those who occupy poorer fields; he will, consequently, receive more than the intrinsic value for the corn he raises. Many persons will, therefore, be desirous of obtaining possession of these fertile fields; being content to give a certain premium for an exclusive privilege to cultivate them, varying, of course, according to the more or less fertility of the soil. It is this premium which constitutes what we now call *rent;* a medium by which the expense of cultivating soils of very different degrees of fertility is reduced to a perfect equality."*

Rent, therefore, in so far as it is not a return for the capital laid out on improvements, results entirely from the necessity of resorting, as population increases, to soils of a *decreasing* degree of fertility, or of applying capital to the old land with a less return. It varies inversely as the produce obtained by means of the capital and labour employed in cultivation; that is, it increases when the profits of agricultural labour diminish, and diminishes when they increase. Profits are at their maximum in countries like New Holland, Indiana, and Illinois, and generally in all situations in which no rent is paid, and the best of the good lands only cultivated; but it cannot be said that rents have attained their maximum so long as capital yields any surplus in the shape of profit.

A quarter of wheat may be raised in Essex, or in the Carse of Gowrie, at a *fourth* or a *fifth* part, perhaps, of the expense necessary to raise it on the worst soils in cultivation in other parts of the country. The same article cannot, however, have two or more prices at the same time and in the same market. Hence, if the price be not such as will indemnify the producers of the wheat raised on the worst soils, they will cease bringing it to market, and the required supplies will no longer be obtained; while, if the price exceed this sum, fresh capital

* "Observations on the Means of exciting a Spirit of Industry," p. 376.

will be applied to its production, and competition will soon sink prices to their natural level—that is, to such a sum as will afford the common and ordinary rate of profit to the raisers of that portion of the required supply which is produced under the most unfavourable circumstances, and at the greatest expense. It is by the cost of producing this portion that the price of the whole crop must be regulated. And, therefore, it is plainly the same thing to the consumers whether, in an advanced stage of society, the excess of return over the cost of production on lands of the first quality belong to a non-resident landlord or an occupier. It *must* belong to the one or the other. Corn is not high because a rent is paid, but a rent is paid because corn is high—because the demand is such, that it cannot be supplied without cultivating soils of a diminished degree of fertility as compared with the best. Suppose there is in any country an effectual demand for ten millions of quarters of corn; that nine millions may be raised upon lands that yield a high rent, but that it is necessary to raise the other million on lands which yield nothing but the common and average rate of profit to their cultivators: Under these circumstances it is clear that the relinquishing of the rents payable on the superior lands would be no boon to the cultivators of those that are inferior. It would not lessen their expenses; that is, it would not lessen the capital and labour necessary to enable them to produce that portion of the required supply which is raised in the least favourable situation; and if it did not do this, it is obviously impossible, supposing the demand not to decline, that it could lower prices. But the case is entirely different when the cost of production varies. If it diminish, the competition of the producers will infallibly sink prices in an equal proportion. If it increase, no supplies will be brought to market, unless the price rise to a corresponding level. In no case, therefore, whether the demand be great or small

—whether for one or one million of quarters, can the price of raw produce ever permanently exceed or fall below the sum necessary to pay the cost of producing that portion of the supply that is raised on the worst land, or by means of the last capital laid out on the soil.

Two objections have been made to this theory. In the *first* place, it has been said that, though it may apply in unappropriated countries like New Holland, it will not apply in countries like England, where land is universally appropriated, and where, it is alleged, the worst qualities always yield some small rent to the proprietor.

Mr. Mill has justly observed of this objection, that even if it were well-founded, it would not practically affect any of the conclusions previously established. There are in England and Scotland vast tracts of land which do not let for 6*d*. an acre; but to cultivate them would require an outlay of many thousands of pounds; and the rent would consequently bear so small a proportion to the expenses of production, as to become altogether evanescent and inappreciable.*

There can be no doubt, however, that there is in this, and most other extensive countries, a great deal of land which yields no rent.† In the United States and Russia, such is unquestionably the case; and yet no one presumes to say, that the laws which regulate rent in them, are different from those which regulate it in England and France. The poorest lands are always let in immense tracts. If it were attempted to let particular

* "Elements of Political Economy," 1st edit. p. 19.

† A noble earl is the owner of a farm in Ayrshire, consisting of about 10,000 English acres, which he lets for 70*l*. a-year! There is a house upon the farm, and some further capital has been laid out upon it. Perhaps, taking these circumstances into account, it might be truly said that this vast tract fetches no rent properly so called. Several similar instances might be mentioned.

portions of these tracts separately, no one would offer for them; but they appear to yield rent, because, though they really fetch nothing, the more fertile spots with which they are intermixed, may, in most cases, be let for a larger or smaller rent. But although every rood of land in Britain paid a high rent, it might still be truly affirmed, that such rent did not enter into the price of raw produce. The rent of a country consists of the difference, or the value of the difference, between the produce obtained through the agency of the capital first applied to the land, and that which is last applied to it. It would, as has been already shewn, be exactly the same thing to a cultivator, whether he paid a rent of ten quarters to a landlord for land yielding, with a certain outlay, 100 quarters of corn, or employed the same capital in cultivating inferior land yielding only 90 quarters, for which he paid no rent. Were it possible always to obtain 100 quarters for every equal additional capital applied to the superior soils, no person, it is obvious, would ever resort to those of inferior fertility. But the fact, that in the progress of society new and less fertile land is invariably brought under cultivation, demonstrates that additional capital and labour cannot be indefinitely applied with the same advantage to the old land. The state of a country may be such, the demand for agricultural produce may be so great, that every quality of land actually yields rent; but it is the same thing, in respect of this theory, if there be any capital employed on land which yields only the return of stock, with its ordinary profits, whether it be employed on old or new land. And that there is every where a very large amount of capital employed in such a manner, is a fact of which there cannot be any doubt whatever. The owners and occupiers of land are influenced by the same principles in the employment of their capital and labour that influence other men. Like them, they endeavour, in prosecuting their own interest, so to adjust the capital they employ, that the last quantity laid out may yield the common and ordinary rate of profit, neither more nor less. Suppose, for example, that a landlord occupies a farm which he might let for 200*l*. a year, producing, with a certain outlay of capital, 300 quarters of wheat. If the farm be managed with the requisite skill and attention, the wheat should, at an average, sell for so much money as is equivalent to the rent, the expense of labour, and the profit on the capital employed. Suppose, now, that the landlord finds that by laying out additional capital on the farm it may be made to yield 10, 20, 50, or 100 quarters more, he will make the outlay; provided the additional produce yield the ordinary rate of profit. He will not wait, before commencing the improvement, until prices rise to a still higher elevation. It will be quite enough to induce him immediately to set about it, that they are such as to afford a fair prospect of realising the usual return to the capital to be expended. He will, in fact, act exactly as the merchant or manufacturer acts who sends another ship to sea, or builds another cotton-mill, whenever he supposes that the capital so embarked will yield customary profits. And supposing that the farm had been let to a tenant, he, it is obvious, would have done the very same thing as the proprietor, in the event of his having been able to obtain so much profit as would, over and above the usual return, suffice to replace the capital itself previously to the termination of the lease. Whether he will employ this additional capital depends entirely on the circumstance of prices being such as will repay his expenses and profits; for he knows he will have no additional rent to pay. Even at the expiration of his lease, the fact of an additional capital being employed would not occasion any rise of rent; for if his landlord should require more rent because more capital had been laid out, he would cease to lay it out;

since, by employing it in agriculture, he gets only the same profits he might get by employing it in any other department of industry.

If we reverse the previous suppositions, and suppose that the owner of the farm finds that, owing to a fall in the price of corn, the capital employed in its cultivation does not yield the common and ordinary rate of profit, he will then, acting on the very same principle that led him in the other case to increase the capital on the farm, immediately withdraw a part of it; and, supposing it to be let, the rent would be reduced at the end of the lease, or sooner, and less capital would henceforth be employed upon it by the tenant.

Generally, therefore, the last portion of capital laid out on the soil yields only the common and average rate of profit: if, on the one hand, it were to yield *more*, fresh capital would be drawn to agriculture, and competition would sink prices to such a level that they would merely yield this rate. If, on the other hand, the capital last applied to the soil should yield *less* than this common and average rate, it would be withdrawn, until, by the rise of price, the last remaining portion of capital left this rate to its owners; and hence it follows, that whether the last quality of land taken into cultivation yield rent or not, the last capital applied to the land yields only the common and average rate of profit; and, consequently, the price of the produce which it yields, and which regulates the price of all the rest, is totally unaffected by rent.

It has, in the *second* place, been objected to this account of the nature and causes of rent, that it takes for granted that, in all extensive countries, landlords permit the farmers of the worst lands to occupy them without paying any rent. But it is easy to see that this is a mistake. Raw produce is kept down to its necessary price by the competition of landlords, and not of farmers. Though there must necessarily be a very wide difference, in all countries of considerable extent, between the best and worst soils, still the gradation from the one extreme to the other is gradual and almost imperceptible. The best differ but little from those which are immediately inferior to them, and the worst from those immediately above them. It is about as impossible to point out the precise point where the first quality ends and the second begins, or where the second ends and the third begins, as it is to point out the precise point where the contiguous colours of the rainbow differ. Suppose that the letters A, B, C, D, E, F, G, &c. designate the different qualities of soil in an extensive country, and suppose that the effectual demand for raw produce is such as will afford the common and average rate of profit, and no more, to those who cultivate land of the *fifth* degree of fertility, or that represented by E: when such is the case, there can be no doubt that land of this quality will be cultivated; for, besides the peculiar attractions which agriculture possesses, it will be quite as advantageous to cultivate it as to engage in any other business. It will not, however, be more advantageous, for its produce will yield no surplus in the shape of rent. But suppose that a combination is entered into among the proprietors of A, B, C, D, and E, to withhold a portion of their produce from market, and that, in consequence of this or any other cause, the price of corn is raised ever so little above the expense of its production on land of the fifth degree of fertility, or that represented by E; in this case it is obvious, that soils of the *very next* degree of fertility, or that that portion of the class represented by F, which, in point of productive power, differs extremely little from E, would be immediately brought under cultivation; and the increased supply of corn that would, in consequence, be thrown upon the market, would infallibly sink prices to the level that would barely afford the average rate of profit to the cultivators of E, or of the poorest soil, which the supply of the effectual demand renders it necessary to cultivate. It is quite the same thing, therefore, in so far as price is concerned, whether a country be appropriated or not. When it is appropriated, prices are kept down to their lowest limit by the competition of the landlords. And it is by the self-same principle—the cost of producing that portion of the necessary supply raised under the most unfavourable circumstances—that the price of corn is determined in England and France, as well as in New Holland and Illinois.

But then it is said that this reasoning involves a contradiction,—that it accounts for both a rise and a fall of price in the same way, or by an extension of cultivation. In point of fact, however, it does no such thing. The market price of corn will always be low where it is cheaply produced, as in Poland; and it will occasionally be low where it costs a great deal to produce it, as in England, when a redundant supply is brought to market. Suppose, as before, that the effectual demand for corn in Great Britain is such as will enable lands of the class E, or of the *fifth* degree of fertility, to be cultivated with the customary return to the cultivators; but that, owing to variable harvests, to injudicious encouragement held out by the legislature, the ardour of speculation, the miscalculation of farmers, or any other cause, lands of the class F, or of the *sixth* degree of fertility, have been cultivated; the increased quantity of produce that will thus be brought to market will plainly depress prices to such an extent, that, instead of yielding average profits to the cultivators of the class F, they will not yield them to the cultivators of the class E. But they will yield *more* to the cultivators of E than to those of F; the latter, therefore, will be first driven from their business; and when they have retired, prices will rise, not indeed to such a height as to enable F to be cultivated, but so high as to enable the cultivators of E to continue their business; that is, as has been already shewn, to the precise sum that will enable the raisers of the last portion of the produce required to supply the effectual demand to obtain the common and average rate of profit. Should the demand, instead of continuing stationary, increase so that it could not be supplied without cultivating F and G, the price of corn would rise in proportion to the increased expense of their cultivation. But to whatever extent the demand might increase, still, if such an improvement were made in agriculture, or in the art of raising corn, as would enable the supply to be obtained from A only, the price would necessarily fall to the precise sum that paid the expenses of its cultivators, and rent would entirely disappear.

It is farther said, by those who have cavilled at this theory, that it represents the cultivation of bad land as the cause of rent; whereas it is, they affirm, the growing demand of the population for food that is its cause, it being the rise of price consequent to this increased demand that occasions the cultivation of bad lands, and the payment of a rent for those that are superior. This, however, is at best mere verbal trifling. The demand of the population for corn elevates its price to such a height as is necessary to obtain the required supply, and may, therefore, be truly said to be the cause of its being produced. But rent *originates in the peculiar circumstances under which supplies of corn are produced.* Were it not that it is most frequently necessary, in order to obtain an increased supply of corn, to resort to soils of different degrees of fertility, or to apply capital, with a less return, to the old land, rent would be altogether unknown; nor, though the demand for corn were increased in a tenfold proportion, would prices be permanently elevated. It does, therefore, seem to be logically as well as substantially correct to affirm, that the decreasing fertility of the soil is the immediate cause of rent; and that its amount is determined by the extent to which bad land is cultivated or good land forced.

This analysis of the nature and causes of rent discovers an important and fundamental distinction between agricultural and commercial and manufacturing industry. In manufactures, the worst machinery is first set in motion, and every day its powers are improved by new inventions, and it is rendered capable of yielding a greater amount of produce with the same expense; and as no limits can be assigned to the quantity of improved machinery that may be introduced—as a million of steam-engines may be constructed for the same, or rather for a less, proportional expense than would be required for the construction of one,—competition never fails of reducing the price of manufactured commodities to the sum for which they may be produced according to the least expensive method.

In agriculture, on the contrary, the best machines, that is, the *best soils*, are brought first into use, and recourse is afterwards had to inferior soils, which require a greater expenditure to make them yield the same supplies. It is true that improvements in farming implements, and the occasionally occurring meliorations in agricultural management, reduce the price of raw produce; but a fall of price, though permanent in manufactures, is only temporary in agriculture. When the price of corn is reduced, all classes being enabled to obtain greater quantities than before in exchange for their products or their labour, the rate of profit, and consequently the rate of accumulation, are increased; and this increase, by causing a greater demand for labour, and higher wages, leads immediately to an increased population, and ultimately to a further demand for raw produce and an extended cultivation. Agricultural improvements obviate, for a while, the necessity of having recourse to inferior soils; but the check can only be temporary. The stimulus which they at the same time give to population, and the natural tendency of mankind to increase up to the means of subsistence, is sure, in the end, to raise prices, and, by forcing recourse to poor lands, rents also.

In illustrating this important distinction between agricultural and manufacturing industry, Mr. Malthus has set the theory of rent in a clear and striking point of view. "The earth," he observes, "has been sometimes compared to a vast machine, presented by nature to man for the production of food and raw materials; but to make the resemblance more just, as far as they admit of comparison, we should consider the soil as a present to man of a great number of machines, all susceptible of continued improvement by the application of capital to them, but yet of very different original qualities and powers.

"This great inequality in the powers of the machinery employed in procuring raw produce, forms one of the most remarkable features which distinguishes the machinery of the land from the machinery employed in manufactures.

"When a machine in manufactures is invented which will produce more finished work with less labour and capital than before, if there be no patent, or as soon as the patent is over, a sufficient number of such machines may be made to supply the whole demand, and to supersede entirely the use of all the old machinery. The natural consequence is, that the price is reduced to the price of production from the best machinery; and if the price were to be depressed lower, the whole of the commodity would be withdrawn from the market.

"The machines which produce corn and raw materials, on the contrary, are the gifts of nature, not the works of man; and we find by experience that these gifts have very different qualities and powers. The most fertile lands of a country, those which, like the best machinery in manufactures, yield the greatest products with the least labour and capital, are never found sufficient to supply the effective demand of an increasing population. The price of raw produce, therefore, naturally rises till it becomes sufficiently high to pay the cost of raising it with inferior machines, and by a more expensive process; and, as there cannot be two prices for corn of the same quality, all the other machines, the working of which requires less capital compared with the produce, must *yield rents in proportion to their goodness.*

"Every extensive country may thus be considered as possessing a gradation of machines for the production of corn and raw materials, including in this gradation not only all the various qualities of poor land, of which every large territory has generally an abundance, but the inferior machinery which may be said to be employed when good land is further and further forced for additional produce. As the price of raw produce continues to rise, these inferior machines are successively called into action; and as the price of raw produce continues to fall, they are successively thrown out of action. The illustration here used serves to shew at once the necessity of the actual price of corn to the actual produce, and the different effect which would attend a great reduction in the price of any particular manufacture, and a great reduction in the price of raw produce." *

It appears, therefore, that, in the earlier stages of society, and when only the best lands are cultivated, rent is unknown. The landlords, as such, do not begin to share in the produce of the soil until it becomes necessary to cultivate lands of an inferior degree of fertility, or to apply capital to the superior lands with a diminishing return. Whenever this is the case, rent begins to be paid; and it continues to increase according as cultivation is extended over poorer soils, and diminishes according as these poorer soils are thrown out of cultivation. Rent, therefore, depends exclusively on the extension of tillage. It is high where tillage is widely extended over inferior lands, and low where it is confined to the superior descriptions only. But in no case does rent enter into price; for the produce raised on the poorest lands, or by means of the capital last applied to the cul-

* "Inquiry into the Nature and Progress of Rent," p. 37.

tivation of the soil, regulates the price of all the rest; and this produce yields no surplus above the common and average rate of profit.*

II. Money Rents.—We have now seen that the corn, or produce rent of a farm, depends wholly on the extent to which bad lands are under tillage, or to which good lands are forced; but the money rent of a farm depends partly on situation, and partly only on the extent to which tillage has been carried. If all lands were equally well situated, or were equally contiguous to markets, the corn rents and the money rents of those of equal fertility would be every where equal. But differences of situation occasion very great differences in the money rents paid for lands of equal fertility. Thus, suppose two farmers employ equal *quantities* of capital, as 5,000 quarters each, in the cultivation of farms of the same goodness, the one situated in the immediate vicinity of London, and the other in Yorkshire; and suppose, farther, that London is the market to which the produce of both farms is sent, and that the cost of conveying corn from Yorkshire to London is 5*s.* a quarter: under these circumstances, if the gross produce of

* The rise in the price of raw produce, occasioned by the decreasing fertility of the soils to which every advancing society must resort, was, I believe, first distinctly shewn in a work in which there are many just and ingenious, intermixed with many fanciful and erroneous views, entitled, "Principes de tout Gouvernement," in two vols. 12mo, published in 1766. The author has, on one occasion, hit upon the real origin of rent:—"Quand les cultivateurs, devenus nombreux," says he, "auront défriché toutes les bonnes terres, par leur augmentation successive, et par la continuité du défrichement, il se trouvera un point où il sera plus avantageux à un nouveau colon de prendre à ferme des terres fecondes, que d'en défricher de nouvelles beaucoup moins bonnes." Tom. i. p. 126. It is plain, however, from his not reverting to the subject, that he was not at all aware of the importance of the principle he had stated; and it is apparent, indeed, from other passages of the work, that he supposed rent entered into price.

each farm was 1,000 quarters, of which the landlord received *one-fifth* part, or 200 quarters, as rent, the farm near London would fetch 50*l.* a-year more than the farm in Yorkshire. For, as the corn raised in the districts adjacent to London is not adequate for its supply, its price in the city must suffice to pay those who bring any portion of the necessary supplies from the greatest distance, as well for the expenses of carriage as for those of production: and the farmer in the immediate vicinity, who gets this increased price for his produce, will have to pay a proportional increase of money rent, just as the occupier of good land has to pay an increase of corn or produce rent, as soon as inferior lands are taken into cultivation.

It has been said, however, that the Middlesex farmer must not only pay a higher money rent, but that he must also pay a higher corn rent; for, if he do not, it is contended that a quantity of corn will remain to him as profit equal to that which remains to the Yorkshire farmer; and as the value of corn in Middlesex is greater than in Yorkshire, his profits will also be proportionally greater, which cannot be the case. But the circumstance of their paying equal corn rents would not really cause any sensible discrepancy in their profits. I have supposed that both farmers employ *equal quantities* of capital; but it must be kept in view that, generally speaking, to whatever extent the value of raw produce in Middlesex may exceed its value in Yorkshire, the *value* of by far the largest portion of the capital belonging to the Middlesex farmer will be increased in about the same degree: and hence it follows, that the increased value or price of the produce belonging to the last as profits, is no more than equal to the additional value of the capital he has employed, and that he is not, consequently, in any respect, in a better situation than the other.

It would be, on many accounts, desirable to be able

readily to distinguish between that portion of the *gross* rental of a country, which is to be considered as rent properly so called, or as the remuneration paid to the landlords for the use of the natural powers of the soil, and that portion which is the return to, or the interest upon, the capital laid out upon houses, fences, drains, roads, and other improvements. But how desirable soever, it is admitted by all practical men that it is quite impossible to make such a distinction with any thing approaching to accuracy. No two of the most expert agriculturists, supposing them to be desired to resolve the gross rental of a single improved farm into its constituent parts, would arrive at the same result. Improvements become so much blended with the natural powers of the soil, that the influence of the one cannot be separated from that of the other; and it is merely the joint value of the two that can be estimated. No doubt can, however, be entertained by any one who reflects for a moment on the vast sums—the hundreds, if not thousands of millions—that have been laid out upon the soil of England, that the rent paid to the landlords for the use of its natural powers is but inconsiderable compared with what is paid to them on account of improvements. And hence the inequality and mischievous operation of taxes on rent. Two landlords receive equal rents from their estates; but the rent of one is principally a consequence of natural fertility, while that of the other is derived principally from outlays of capital. What then could be more unfair than to subject them both to the same equal tax? And yet the amount of their rents is the only criterion to which recourse could be had in fixing the amount of the tax — for all the tax-collectors in the world could not separate between what was really rent, in the scientific sense of the term, and what was interest on capital. Such a tax would oppose the most effectual obstacle to improvements. Instead of carrying capital from other employments to the land, it would henceforth be carried from the land to them. The object would not then be to have an estate look well, but to have it look ill. And it may be said of estates as of individuals,

"Pauper videri vult Cinna, et est pauper."

The effects that were formerly produced by the *taille*, and that are now produced by the *contribution foncière* in France, and the fluctuating land taxes imposed in other countries, abundantly confirm the truth of this statement. Their influence has been most disastrous.

Before closing this chapter, I may observe, that the author of the "Critical Dissertation on Value,"* contends, that because the value of that corn which is raised on lands paying rent, is not, after inferior lands are taken into cultivation, proportioned to the cost of its production, it is incorrect to represent the value of the aggregate quantity of produce raised in a country where cultivation has been extended over inferior lands, as depending on that principle. But those who maintain that the value of raw products, and other commodities the quantities of which admit of an indefinite increase, is determined by the cost of their production, invariably refer to the quantity of labour required to produce that portion of raw produce, or of any required commodity which is raised under the most unfavourable circumstances. "The exchangeable value of all commodities," says Mr. Ricardo, "whether they be manufactured, or the produce of the mines, or the produce of land, is always regulated, not by the less quantity of labour that will suffice for their production under circumstances highly favourable, and exclusively enjoyed by those who have peculiar facilities of production, but by the greater quantity of labour necessarily bestowed on their production by those who have no such facilities; by those who continue to produce them under

* P. 194.

the most unfavourable circumstances — meaning, by the most unfavourable circumstances, the most unfavourable under which the quantity of produce required renders it necessary to carry on the production." *

This is the sense in which we are always to understand the proposition that the value of commodities depends on the cost of their production, or on the quantity of labour required to produce them and bring them to market. It is not meant to affirm, that the value of every particular hat or bushel of corn offered for sale is determined by the quantity of labour actually expended on *its* production. What is really meant is, that the value of all the hats, as of all the corn brought to market, is determined by a certain standard; and that this standard is the quantity of labour required to produce that hat, or that bushel of corn, which has been produced with the greatest difficulty.

It is obvious that no error can arise in estimating the value of raw produce, from supposing it to have been wholly raised under the same circumstances as that portion which is raised by means of the capital last applied to the soil; for though portions of it may have been raised under very different circumstances, it is certain that their value must, notwithstanding, be exclusively determined by, and identical with, the value of that which is raised by this last applied capital. And hence, when a quantity of corn is employed as capital in any industrious undertaking, we are to consider it as being, in fact, either the actual product, or the *full equivalent* of the product, of a given quantity of the labour of those who raise corn on the worst lands cultivated; and the quantity of labour so wrought up in this capital, or represented by it, must plainly determine the *real* value of the commodities produced by its agency. This principle holds in the case of all commodities whose quantity admits of being inde-

* "Principles of Political Economy," 3d edit. p. 60.

finitely extended. On tracing the exchangeable value of any article of this description, we shall find that it is determined, in all ordinary states of the market, by the quantity of labour actually expended on its production, if it be produced under the most unfavourable circumstances, or that is actually expended on a similar article produced under these circumstances.

CHAPTER VI.

Influence of Improvements—Slowness with which they spread—Beneficial to all Classes—Different Methods of Letting Lands—Remarks upon those Methods—Reduction of Rents—Regulations as to Management—Size of Farms—Profits of Farmers.

A GOOD deal of misconception has been entertained with respect to the effect of improvements on rent. It has been already shewn that rent depends on the extent to which tillage has been carried; but the most common effect of improvements being to enable the same quantity of produce to be obtained from a less extent of land, it would seem, on a superficial view, that they are injurious to the landlord. But there is no such opposition between his interests and those of the rest of the community; and it will be found, when rightly examined, that improvements are no less advantageous to the owners and occupiers of land than to others.

1. To have a distinct idea of the operation and effect of improvements, it may be proper to consider them both as applying generally to all sorts of land, and to some particular sorts only. In the first case, then, let it be supposed, to illustrate the principle, that the following quantities of produce are obtained from the different qualities of land cultivated, and the following rents paid, viz.

A	B	C	D	E	Qualities of land.
100	90	80	70	60	Quantities of produce obtained with equal capitals.
40	30	20	10	0	Rent.

Now, suppose an improvement is made which enables ten per cent more produce to be obtained with the same outlay, and that this improvement extends to all qualities of land, the quantities produced, and the rent, would then be—

110	99	88	77	66	Quantities of produce.
44	33	22	11	0	Rent.

In this case it is plain, that if the demand for corn were increased so as to take off the greater quantity brought to market, the landlord would not sustain any inconvenience whatever from the improvement, but would be immediately as well as permanently benefited by it. He would obtain a greater quantity of corn as rent; and notwithstanding the reduction of its price, that greater quantity would exchange for the same quantity of other things that the smaller quantity did before. If, however, there were no increase of demand, ten per cent of the capital at present employed in agriculture would be withdrawn from that business, so that the quantity of produce would be the same as before the improvements: the corn rent would also be the same; though as corn would, under the circumstances supposed, be ten per cent cheaper, money rents would fall in that proportion. But it is abundantly obvious, that though the demand might not be immediately increased, so as to take off the whole additional quantity brought to market in consequence of the improvement, it would not remain constant. It is impossible, indeed, that such should be the case. The consumption of the lower classes, and the quantity of corn given to the horses employed in industrious undertakings, or kept for pleasure, is invariably increased when prices fall; at the same time that the stimulus which the fall gives to population, would of itself speedily increase the demand, so as to absorb not only the increased quantity of corn, but to occasion the cultivation of fresh soils.

2. Let it now be supposed that the improvement is partial; that it affects the *superior* qualities of land only;

and that the quantities produced after it has been carried into effect are as follow, viz.

A	B	C	D	E	Qualities of land.
110	95	82½	70	60	Quantities of produce after improvement.
50	35	22½	10	0	Rent after ditto.

Now it is evident, that if the improvement in the productiveness of the qualities A, B, C, increased the produce brought to market, so as merely to lessen the extent of land of the class E under tillage, without causing its cultivation to be entirely relinquished, it would not affect prices; and the money rents, as well as the corn rents of the proprietors of A, B, C, would rise so as to enable them to gain the whole advantage resulting from the improvement.

If the whole of the class E were thrown out of tillage, corn rents would be as follow:—

A	B	C	D	Qualities of land.
40	25	12½	0	Rent.

But in this case, as in the former, the contraction of cultivation would be but of very short duration; for, owing to the increased cheapness, the demand would very speedily rise so as to require the renewed cultivation of E; so that any inconvenience that might by possibility arise to the proprietors in the first instance would at most be only trifling and transitory, while the advantage would be great and permanent.

3. In the third and last case, let it be supposed that the improvement is greatest on the *worst* lands, and that it decreases as their fertility improves. Thus suppose

A	B	C	D	E	Qualities of land.
100	90	80	70	60	Quantities before improvement.
40	30	20	10	0	Rent before ditto.
100	90	82½	75	70	Quantities after improvement.
30	20	12½	5	0	Rent after ditto.

If the improvement were so great as to throw E out of cultivation, rents would be 25, 16, 7½, 0. But as in this case the fall of price, and consequent rise of profits, would be very great, a proportionally powerful stimulus would be given to population; and the increased demand that would, at no distant period, be experienced, would be such as inevitably to bring the next qualities of land, or F, G., &c. under cultivation; so that in this, as in all other cases, both corn and money rents would be, in the end, very greatly increased by the improvement.

These statements sufficiently shew that, supposing an improvement were introduced so rapidly and widely as to occasion an immediate fall of price, and consequently of money rents, these effects would be of very limited duration; for the greater cheapness of raw produce, by increasing the demand for it on the part of the existing population, as well as by stimulating the increase of that population, could not fail speedily to raise prices to their old level, and even to carry them beyond it.

But it is material to observe, that these suppositions have been made merely to illustrate the principle, and that, in point of fact, they are never realised in practice. In the vast majority of cases improvements apply nearly equally to all sorts of soil. They take place principally in machinery, in the rotation of crops, in the breeds of stock, the composition and application of manures, &c., which are generally applicable not to one or a few only, but to almost every description of land. Improvements, too, rarely if ever precede, but almost always follow, a rise of prices, occasioned either by an increased demand for raw produce, or by some previous scarcity. Neither do they ever rapidly spread over any considerable extent of country; they make their way only by slow and, indeed, almost imperceptible degrees; and tend not so much to occasion any actual reduction of prices as to prevent their rising to an oppressive height. Improvements are at first adopted by a few of the more intelligent proprietors and farmers in different districts, and are thence gradually diffused throughout the country. This progress is, however, much more tedious than one not acquainted with the obstacles by which it is opposed might be inclined to believe. Improvements which effect material changes in long-established customs have always been slowly and reluctantly admitted. But the agricultural class is the least of all disposed to innovation, and the most peculiarly attached to ancient customs and routine. "The farmer is not so much within reach of information as the merchant and manufacturer; he has not, like those who reside in towns, the means of ready intercourse and constant communication with others engaged in the same occupation. He lives retired; his acquaintance is limited and but little varied; and unless he is accustomed to read, he is little likely to acquire any other knowledge of his art than what is traditionary—what is transmitted from father to son, and limited in its application to his own immediate neighbourhood."*

So powerful has been the influence of these circumstances, that notwithstanding the advances in agricultural science during the last century, and the efforts made to diffuse it, there is but a comparatively small portion of England and Scotland where the most improved system of husbandry is introduced, while in Ireland it cannot be said to be introduced at all. Even in some of the counties adjoining to the metropolis, practices are persevered in that are utterly inconsistent with all the rules of good agriculture. In the rich soil of Essex, the wretched system of fleet ploughing and whole year fallows, is still pretty generally followed; the agriculture of Sussex is said to be at least a century behind that of East Lothian or Norfolk; and in some of the midland counties, it is

* Preface to Dr. Rigby's "Translation of Chateauvieux on the Agriculture of Italy."

customary to yoke four or five horses to a plough for the tillage of light land! "Those improvements that are well known and systematically practised in one county, are frequently unknown or utterly disregarded in the adjacent district; and what is to every unprejudiced observer evidently erroneous and injurious to the land, is, in some quarters, persisted in most pertinaciously, though a journey of not many miles would open to view the beneficial effects of a contrary practice."*

Practically, therefore, nothing can be more futile and visionary than to suppose that there is the least chance of improvements ever becoming, even for the shortest period, injurious to the landlords, in consequence of their introduction causing a fall of prices. There is not the shadow of a ground for supposing that they can ever be so rapidly diffused as to produce this effect. And the most extensive and successful improver may prosecute his patriotic labours, without any apprehension that either his efforts or example will be sufficiently powerful to occasion any glut of the market, or fall of price.

It is unnecessary, perhaps, to say more in illustration of the importance and advantage of improvements. I may, however, observe, that were it not for their influence, it is most probable that the progress of society would have been long since arrested. The nearer that the quantity of produce necessarily consumed in carrying on industrious undertakings approaches to that which is obtained from them, the smaller is the rate of profit, and the slower the advance of the society; and were the two quantities to become nearly equal, or to balance each other, society would be at a stand; and if, under such circumstances, population increased, it would be at the expense of the existing inhabitants. But the inventions and discoveries that are every now and then occurring, prevent the progress of society from being arrested in the way now

* Kennedy and Grainger "On the Tenancy of Land." Introd. p. 8.

mentioned. No limits can be set to the inventive powers; and the very moment when cultivation seems improved to the utmost may be distinguished by discoveries sufficient to give a new aspect to the whole business of husbandry, and to carry the society forward for many generations.

For reasons similar to those now stated, I believe it will be found that the landlords do not really gain any thing by the restrictions laid on the importation of foreign corn; and that their interests would be best promoted by throwing the ports open to importation from abroad, under such a duty as might be sufficient fully to countervail any excess of taxation to which they may be subjected above what is borne by the manufacturing and commercial classes. I have elsewhere stated, at considerable length, the reasons which induce me to look upon this conclusion as one that is no longer susceptible of doubt or controversy.* Here, therefore, it is enough to mention, that to whatever extent restrictions on the importation of corn into a comparatively populous and highly manufacturing country like Great Britain, raise the price of food above its natural level, they must, exclusively of their other ill effects, proportionally depress the rate of profit, and act as a premium on the transfer of capital to other countries. But it would be the extreme of folly to imagine that a system productive of such results can be really beneficial to those who have so deep an interest in the public prosperity as the landlords. Numerous and affluent consumers, or, which is substantially the same thing, flourishing manufactures and commerce, are indispensable to a flourishing agriculture; and any nation which imposes an oppressive burden on the former in order to promote the interests of the latter, is, in fact, contradicting and defeating the very purpose she is anxious to forward. Perseverance in such short-

* My edition of the "Wealth of Nations," vol. iv. pp. 350—362.

sighted policy can hardly fail, by injuring or ruining those on whom the agriculturist must depend for a market, or driving them and their capital to other countries, seriously to injure if it do not ultimately ruin agriculture itself.

This is a point on which Colonel Torrens has made some very pertinent observations: "The landed proprietors of England," says he, "possess the important advantage of immediate vicinity to the largest and most flourishing manufacturing towns in the world; and the consequence is, that in proportion to its fertility, land in England pays a higher rent, whether estimated in produce or in money, than in any other country. Let not short-sighted avarice destroy the sources of the golden eggs: let not the proprietors of England, by restricting the importation of foreign agricultural produce, artificially raise the value of such produce in our markets, and thus depress the rate of profit, until the seats of manufacture are transferred to France, or Holland, or Germany. No proposition, we believe, admits of a more rigid demonstration, than that the highest rents will be paid in countries in which manufacturing industry is carried to the greatest height. But it is obviously impossible that manufactures should continue to flourish in a country where restrictions on the importation of corn raise the value of raw produce in relation to wrought goods, and thereby depress manufacturing profits below the rate prevailing in the neighbouring countries. If we do not freely import foreign produce, our manufacturing superiority cannot be maintained, and, by necessity, our high comparative rents cannot continue to be paid."*

It would lead us too far from the proper object of this work, were I to attempt to enter, at any considerable length, on an examination of the more interesting questions con-

* "Treatise on the External Corn Trade," 4th edit. p. 168.

nected with the letting of land. Perhaps, however, there is no single circumstance that has so much influence on the prosperity of agriculture and the condition of the agricultural class as the terms of leases, or the stipulations that are usually entered into between the landlords and those to whom they let or assign the power of cultivating their estates.

The most important of these stipulations are those which respect the duration of the lease, the payment of the rent, and the mode of management.

Though there may be various opinions as to what ought to be the duration of a lease, and though it may differ in different cases, there is no room for doubt as to the superiority of the plan of letting lands for a number of years certain. When a tenant is secured in the possession of his farm for a fixed and reasonable period, he has every inducement to exert himself, and to apply whatever capital and skill he may possess to its improvement. But a tenant at will, or a tenant who may be turned out of his farm at any time, without having any good grounds for affirming that he has been ill treated, dares not venture upon any outlay. Such a tenant is really, in so far at least as the business of farming is concerned, deprived of the advantages resulting from the security of property. And as he has no guarantee that he will be allowed to continue in the occupation of his farm for such a period as would give him the means of reaping the advantage of improvements, he never once thinks of undertaking any. He continues to move on in the accustomed routine of the district to which he belongs; and if he should be so fortunate as to accumulate a little capital, which is but seldom the case, he either employs it in some other business, or in taking a greater extent of land: but he scrupulously abstains from laying out any thing on improvements, unless they happen to be such as promise an almost immediate return. There can, therefore, be no question, that the granting of leases for a fixed and reasonable number of years has been of the utmost consequence to agriculture; and those best acquainted with the business affirm, that it has done more for its improvement than all the other encouragements that have been given to it.

The term "tenants at will" is sometimes rather improperly applied to tenants who have no leases, but who, notwithstanding, either from the custom of the estate or district, or the promises of the landlord, have a tolerable security that they will not be capriciously ejected, and that their rents will not be raised immediately upon their making an improvement. Still, however, the security afforded by such a tenure is very far short of what is afforded by a lease. Where the rights of both parties are not clearly defined, disputes may unintentionally arise; the tenant is in such cases kept in a state of degrading dependency upon his landlord; and however well he may be treated by the individual now in possession of the estate, he cannot foretell what may be the views and objects of his successor. And hence, as Mr. Loudon has justly observed, "no prudent man will ever invest his fortune in the improvement of another person's property, unless, from the length of his lease, he has a reasonable prospect of being reimbursed with profit; and the servility which a holding at will necessarily exacts, is altogether incompatible with that spirit of enterprise which belongs to an enlightened and independent mind."*

The rent of a farm is sometimes fixed in money, sometimes in a given quantity of produce, sometimes in a proportional quantity of its produce, and sometimes in services.

With respect to money rents it may be observed, that when the lease is only for a few years, during which no great change in the value of money or in the price of corn can reasonably be anticipated, they are, perhaps,

* "Encyclopædia of Agriculture," p. 699.

the best of any; but when the lease embraces a period of nineteen or twenty-one years, which is believed to be the most proper for leases of ordinary tillage farms, the safer plan will be to fix the rent at a certain quantity of produce, making it convertible into money at the current prices of the day. By this means the disturbing effects of changes in the value of money are averted, at the same time that the effect of those which occur in the cost of producing corn are mitigated. This plan is, however, defective, inasmuch as it obliges the tenant to pay more than the fair value of his farm in scarce years; while, on the other hand, it has the effect of improperly reducing the landlord's rents in years of unusual plenty. A simple device has, however, been fallen upon which has gone far to remove these defects. This consists in fixing a *muximum* and a *minimum* price; it being declared in the lease that the produce to be paid to the landlord shall be converted into money according to the current prices of the year; but that to whatever extent prices may rise above the maximum price fixed in the lease, the landlord shall have no claim for such excess of price. By means of this check, the tenant is prevented from paying any great excess of rent in scarce years. And to prevent, on the other hand, the rent from being improperly reduced in very plentiful years, a minimum price is agreed upon by the parties; and it is stipulated that, to whatever extent prices may sink below this limit, the landlord shall be entitled to receive this minimum price for the fixed quantity of produce payable to him. This plan has been introduced into some of the best-cultivated districts of the empire, particularly East Lothian and Berwickshire. And the experience of the estates in which it has been adopted shews, that it is as effectual as can well be desired for the protection of the just rights of both parties, and for securing the progress of agriculture.

The mode of letting lands for proportional rents, that

is, for a half, a third, a fourth, or a fifth, &c. of the produce, whatever it may be, is the most objectionable of any. The widest experience shews that tenants never make any real or considerable improvements unless when they have a firm conviction that they will be allowed to reap the whole advantage arising from them. It is in vain to contend that, as the tenant knows beforehand the proportion of the increased produce going to the landlord, if the remainder be a due return on his capital, he will lay it out. Not one tenant out of a hundred would so act. There are always very considerable hazards to be run by those who embark capital in agricultural improvements; and if to these were added the obligation to pay a half, a third, or a fourth of the *gross* produce arising from an improvement, to the landlord, either none would ever be attempted by a tenant, or none that required any considerable outlay, or where the prospect of a return was not very immediate. A flourishing and improving system of agriculture cannot be carried on except by enterprising tenants, ready to avail themselves of new discoveries; and such are only found where they have leases, or are secured in the possession of their farms, for adequate periods, and allowed to reap, during their continuance, the entire benefit arising from whatever improvements they may execute. If either of these principles be encroached upon, the spirit of industry will be paralysed. Those who insist upon immediately sharing the benefit resulting from ameliorations effected by the capital or labour of their tenants, will effectually prevent them from being undertaken; and if they do not occasion agriculture to retrograde, will, at least, hinder it from making the smallest advance.

Unluckily, however, it is not necessary to argue this question speculatively. The practice of letting lands by proportional rents, or, as it is there termed, on the *métayer* principle, is very general upon the continent; and wherever it has been adopted, it has put a stop to all improvement, and has reduced the cultivators of the land to the most abject poverty.*

The method of paying rent by services,—the last of those previously alluded to,—is also very objectionable. This method grew out of the feudal system: it was at one time spread over almost all Europe, and is still maintained in many countries; but wherever civilisation has made considerable progress, and manufactures and commerce been extensively introduced, it has been superseded by money or produce rents. It is needless to dwell on its inexpediency. The labour performed by tenants on the grounds, or for the behoof of their landlords, is sure to be very slovenly performed. Men do not exert themselves with spirit and effect, unless they are working on their own account, and are themselves reaping all the advantages of superior industry and enterprise. In Great Britain these sort of services are now almost wholly abolished; or if any vestiges of them still exist, they are only to be found in a few of the Highland counties. Their abolition has been of the greatest service to agriculture, and has redounded, in a very high degree, to the advantage of the landlords. The tenants, relieved from

* For an account of the métayer system, see "Young's Travels in France," &c., second edition, vol. i. p. 404, and vol. ii. p. 216; and the article "On the Métayer System," in the eighth number of the "Foreign Quarterly Review," where the latest information on the subject is collected.

Most part of India is occupied by métayers, or tenants paying from two-thirds to one-third of the produce to government as rent; no wonder, therefore, that the occupiers are in the most abject state of poverty. This, however, is a subject which I cannot now enter upon; but those who wish to inform themselves with respect to it, would do well to consult Mr. Rickards' very valuable work on India. Mr. R. has discussed all the difficult and important questions with respect to the state of landed property in India, the revenue systems adopted by its successive rulers, and the condition and capacity of the natives, with extraordinary sagacity and intelligence, and has set them in the most luminous point of view.

every sort of service, secured in the possession of their farms by leases of a reasonable length, and left to pursue their own interest in their own way, subject only to restrictions preventing them from exhausting the land, have exerted themselves with a degree of energy and success, and have carried agriculture to a pitch of improvement, that could not previously have been supposed possible.

When it has been ascertained that a farm is let at too high a rent—that is, when the utmost exertions of industry and economy on the part of a skilful tenant cannot enable him to pay his rent and gain a fair return for his outlay and trouble—the landlord, if he consult his own interest, ought to make an adequate reduction. If he attempt to hold the farmer to the letter of his agreement, he will most likely occasion his ruin; but in the efforts of the farmer to save himself and his family, the farm is sure to suffer. It will not be properly manured or tilled scourging crops will be resorted to; so that, though the landlord should succeed in squeezing the stipulated rent out of the occupier during the currency of the lease, the bad state of the farm at its close, and the bad character the landlord will have justly acquired in the vicinity, will cause a far greater reduction of rent than would have taken place had it been made at the proper period. It appears, also, that when a reduction of rent is necessary, it should be made unconditionally, and for the whole course of the lease, or at least for a reasonable and definite period. Some landlords are in the habit, when their tenants state that they are unable to pay their entire rents, of taking from them what they can afford, and giving them a receipt for so much on account; but this is a most pernicious practice, and is not more injurious to the tenant than to the landlord. The fear of being called upon, at some future period, for payment of bygone arrears, induces the tenant to counterfeit poverty, even though he be not really poor, at the same time that his liability to such claims prevents him from getting any assistance from those who might otherwise have been disposed to support him. The same effects, though not quite in the same degree, are experienced when the landlord grants an unconditional abatement for one year only. The consciousness that the farm is too dear, and that he may be called upon, at the pleasure of the landlord, to pay the full rent, paralyses all the energies of the tenant. In this, as in the former case, his credit is at an end; for no one, how much soever he might otherwise feel disposed, would ever think of accommodating so dependent an individual with a loan. A tenant in this unhappy situation invariably becomes dispirited: instead of zealously exerting himself, as he would do were his rent permanently reduced to the real value of the farm, he strives only to take unfair advantages, to defeat the stipulations in his lease as to management, and is, through poverty and inability to pay, protected from an increase of rent.

As soon, therefore, as it is discovered that a farm is really too dear, and that neither skill nor industry can make it pay, the rent ought to be unconditionally abated, if not at once for the whole lease, at least for a period of not fewer than five or seven years, with a stipulation that it shall not even then be raised unless prices have advanced. The estates of those landlords who act on this sound principle are always in the best order, and at an average their rents are decidedly higher than the rents of those who refuse to make any abatements, or make them only from year to year. The policy of the latter is quite destructive of the independence, the credit, and industry of their tenants; and where these are wanting, agriculture must be comparatively degraded, and rents, though nominally high, really low and ill paid.

Much difference of opinion has existed as to the expediency of inserting conditions in leases with respect to management. Those who are adverse to such conditions argue, that being in general framed by the landlord, whose knowledge of the practical business of farming is seldom very accurate or extensive, they are exceedingly apt to proceed on mistaken views, and are for the most part either vexatious or impossible; that the strict observance of conditions can rarely be enforced; that if it were, it would reduce the occupiers to the condition of mere machines; that it would prevent them from taking advantage of such discoveries as might be made during the currency of their leases; and that, having no means of escaping from the prescribed mode of management, they would cease to interest themselves in the progress of agriculture, and would become indifferent to every sort of improvement. Dr. Smith has given the sanction of his authority to these objections. He proposes, in the event of a tax being laid upon rent, that it should be made somewhat heavier on all those farms the tenants of which are bound by their leases to a prescribed mode of management. Such conditions are, he says, the effect of the ill-founded conceit entertained by the landlord of his own superior knowledge, and uniformly tend to the prejudice of agriculture.*

But notwithstanding the plausible nature of some of these objections, and the high authority by which they are supported, they seem to be, generally speaking, without foundation; and the best practical farmers concur in the opinion, that conditions, when judiciously devised, may be of great service to agriculture, and that they ought never to be dispensed with.

This, it must be observed, is not a question that can be decided on the principle of leaving every one to be regulated by his own sense of what is most advantageous; for here we have two parties, the landlord and tenant, each with separate and often conflicting interests. It is for the landlord's interest that his farm should always be

* "Wealth of Nations," vol. iii. p. 377.

in good order, and more especially that it should be in good order when the lease is about to expire, inasmuch as the rent that it will then bring will depend very much upon this circumstance. But the tenant is in a very different situation; his interest in the farm being limited to the period for which his lease endures, his object naturally is to make the most of it during that period, without caring about the state in which he leaves it. Although, therefore, restrictions as to the mode of cultivation in the early part of a lease of considerable duration may perhaps be fairly objected to, I do not think that any landlord who has a proper sense of his own interest, or who wishes to get his estate restored to him in good order, ought ever to let a farm without prescribing certain conditions as to its management, which it should be imperative on the tenant to follow during the six or seven years immediately preceding the termination of his lease. It is true that these conditions may not always be the best that might be devised, but they can hardly be so defective as to be insufficient to preserve the farm from being over-cropped and exhausted previously to the tenant's leaving it; and if they do this, they must, both in a private and public point of view, be decidedly beneficial.

Much discussion has taken place as to the proper size of farms. This, however, is not a point as to which it is possible to come to any very precise conclusions. A great deal must obviously depend on the purposes to which the farm is to be applied. Farms that are to be wholly employed in pasture may be very much larger than those that are to be employed partly only in that way, and partly in tillage; and the latter, again, than those that are to be wholly employed in tillage. And in regard to tillage farms, it is plain that their size must depend on various circumstances, but principally, perhaps, on the amount of the tenant's capital. But supposing that the tenants offering for farms have sufficient capital, their size ought, as it appears to me, to be determined by considering what extent of land an individual may be able to manage in the best and most approved manner. Most practical farmers, in this country at least, seem to think that this size might run from 400 to 600 acres, or 500 at a medium. This conclusion has, however, been strongly denied; and it has been contended that the public interests are best consulted by letting land in small farms, or in farms of from 15 to 30 or 40 acres. To enter fully into an examination of this question would encroach too much on my limits: it may, however, be observed, that the opinions of the great majority of those who, from their acquaintance with agriculture, are best entitled to decide as to such matters, are exceedingly hostile to the small farming system; and that their statements as to its inexpediency seem to be founded on the soundest principles, and to be consistent with a very extensive experience. It is plain that that system of occupation must, in all ordinary cases, be the best which gives the greatest scope to improvement, which allows of the division of labour being carried to the farthest extent, and which puts it into the power of the occupier to avail himself of every new improvement and increased facility of production. But it is almost superfluous to say that these objects can only be attained when the lands of a country are occupied by large and opulent farmers. The produce of a small farm of 15, 20, or even 50 acres, cannot, after paying a rent to the landlord, do more than furnish the barest subsistence to its occupiers. To suppose that such persons should accumulate capital, or that they should be in a condition to undertake any considerable improvement, is really quite visionary. "In England," says Mr. Young, "there are no persons who work so hard and fare so ill as the small farmers."* And Mr. Oliver tells us that "in Scotland it is the rarest thing imaginable to find a small farm,

* "Travels in France," vol. i. p. 415.

say from 20 to 50 acres, that would not be a disgrace to the cultivators of a century ago."*

Perhaps it may be thought that it is superfluous to enforce the propriety of letting land in preference in large farms; that the occupiers of such farms are able to pay a higher rent than those who occupy small ones; and that according as capital is accumulated in a country, the size of farms is sure to be augmented. But these statements are by no means so well-founded as we might at first be disposed to conclude. Nothing is so much coveted by a poor man as the possession of a small piece of ground. It secures him so long as he possesses it against falling a sacrifice to absolute want; it renders him, in some measure, his own master, and relieves him from the necessity of unremitting labour. In consequence, there is often a very extensive competition for cottages and slips of land. An individual possessed of capital will not engage in farming unless he expect to realise, over and above a remuneration for his trouble in superintending the business, the common and average rate of profit on his capital. But the offerer for a small piece of ground is not influenced by such considerations: he is anxious to get it, not that he may make profits and wages by it, but that he may live. He is willing, indeed, to pay the proprietor all that it can be made to yield over and above his subsistence and that of his family, and this not unfrequently amounts to more than would be offered by a tenant possessed of capital, and capable of farming the land in the best manner. But any advantage that a landlord may occasionally gain, in the first instance, by the adoption of such a system as this, is sure to be far more than counterbalanced in the end. The small farmer having no means of disposing of

* My edition of the "Wealth of Nations," vol. iv. p. 487. Mr. Oliver's authority is the greater, from his uniting to an intimate practical acquaintance with the most improved systems of modern husbandry, the most extensive and profound knowledge of the history and principles of the art.

his children when they grow up, they naturally look to the land for support; and if his little possession be not divided during his life, it can hardly escape being divided at his death. In this way the country is overspread with a redundant and wretched population; so that in the end rents are not paid, and the whole produce of the land becomes barely sufficient for the support of its occupiers. The splitting of farms, in the way now described, has been carried to a very great extent in Ireland, and has been productive of the most injurious consequences. Instead of increasing, the size of Irish farms has rapidly diminished during the last half century; so that large tracts are now parcelled out into patches of the size of potato-gardens, occupied by the merest beggars. Nothing, therefore, ought to be more cautiously gone about by landlords than a reduction in the size of their farms. If they ever allow them to be frittered down into minute portions, they will find that the improvement of their estates is at an end; that they have no security that their rents will continue to be paid; and that very formidable obstacles will stand in the way of the ejectment of the tenants, and of a return to a better system.

There can be no doubt, taking every thing into account, that the profits of farmers are upon a level with those of the undertakers of other businesses. It is generally believed, however, that when estimated in money, they are about the lowest of any. This arises from a variety of circumstances. The healthy and agreeable nature of the business, the independence which it gives, and the prevalence among the other classes of the unfounded notion that every man may become a farmer without any previous learning or education, occasion a very keen competition for land; while the uncertainty of the seasons, the multiplicity of operations and details to which the farmer has to attend, and the difficulty of giving that attention to each which is so very essential, conspire powerfully to increase the hazard, and to lessen the profit of farming. In many places, indeed, the business is carried on according to a system of routine. But wherever an improved plan of agriculture is practised, or where it is carried on by persons of considerable capital, farming for a profit, skill and attention are alike indispensable. The farmer has to decide upon the rotation of crops, and the species of stock best fitted for the soil and situation which he occupies; he has to fix the number of horses and labourers that he will employ, so that they may neither be too many nor too few; he has to seize upon the proper moment for performing the various operations of the farm, and to arrange them in such a manner that none may be neglected or cause the neglect of others; and he has to make himself acquainted with the state of the markets, and decide as well upon the most advantageous period for selling his produce, as upon the quantities he ought to sell. No business, in short, requires greater sagacity or more constant application. The best-laid combinations and plans of the farmer are always liable to be overturned by changes of weather or by prices proving different from what he had anticipated; and he should be able to act with decision and energy in the altered circumstances under which he may, on such occasions, be placed. To suppose that a successful farmer can have been either indolent or inattentive, argues an entire ignorance of the practice of agriculture. There is, in fact, no employment where intelligence, industry, and that prompt activity "which has no such day as to-morrow in its calendar," can be less dispensed with. Those who enter on this business in the view of making it profitable, must be ready to say with the poet—

> ——— Steriles transmisimus annos,
> Hæc ævi mihi prima dies, hæc limina vitæ.

And even with the greatest attention and industry, it is but rarely that farmers make a fortune. The great majority merely manage to live respectably, and to bring up their family. "The few," says the ablest agricultural writer of the present day, "who do more than this, will be found to have had leases at low rents; indulgent landlords; to have profited by accidental rises in the market or depreciation of currency, or to have become dealers in corn or cattle; and rarely indeed to have realised aught by the mere good culture of a farm at the market price."* The opinion of Mr. Burke, who, in the estimation of those most capable of judging, stood high both as a scientific and practical farmer, is to the same effect. "In most parts of England," says he, "which have fallen within my observation, I have rarely known a farmer (I speak of those who occupy from 150 to 300 or 400 acres), who to his own trade has not added some other employment or traffic, that, after a course of the most unremitting parsimony and labour (such for the most part is theirs), and persevering in his business for a long course of years, died worth more than paid his debts, leaving his posterity to continue in nearly the same equal conflict between industry and want, in which the last predecessor, and a long line of predecessors before him, lived and died."†

* Loudon's "Encyclopædia of Agriculture," p. 719.

† "Thoughts and Details on Scarcity," p. 21.

CHAPTER VII.

Division of the Produce of Industry, under Deduction of Rent, between Capitalists and Labourers—Definition of Profits—Mr. Ricardo's Theory of Profits; Sense in which it is true—Causes which occasion a Rise or Fall of Profits—Accumulation not the Cause of a Fall of Profits—Influence of the decreasing Fertility of the Soil, and of Taxation on Profits—Influence of Loans to Government and of Changes in the Value of Money on Profits.

BEFORE attempting to investigate the circumstances which determine the rate of profit, it is necessary to be aware of those which determine the proportions in which the whole produce of industry, under deduction of rent, is divided between labourers and capitalists.

This preliminary inquiry may be disposed of in a few words. We have seen that the whole produce of the land and labour of every civilised society is always divided, in the first instance, into *three*, and not more than *three*, portions; the *first* of which goes to the labourers, the *second* to the capitalists or proprietors of stock, and the *third* to the landlords: and we have also seen, that the portion of the produce of industry, or of rent, which belongs to the landlords, as proprietors of the soil, and not as capitalists, is altogether extrinsic to the cost of production; and that the circumstance of the landlords consenting to give it up, would not occasion any change in the productiveness of industry, or any reduction in the price of raw produce. Supposing, then, that rent is deducted or set aside, it is obvious that all the remaining produce of the land and labour of every country must be primarily divided between the two great classes of labourers and capitalists. And it is further obvious, that were there no taxes in a country, or were the rate of taxation invariable, the *proportion* of the whole produce of industry, under deduction of rent, falling to the share of the labourers could not be increased except by an equivalent reduction in the *proportion* falling to the share of the capitalists, and *vice versâ*. Suppose, still better to illustrate this proposition, that the whole produce of industry in Great Britain is represented by the number 1000: suppose, farther, that the landlords get 200 of this sum as rent, and that the remaining 800 is divided, in equal portions, between labourers and capitalists. Under these circumstances, it is quite obvious that nothing could be added to the proportion of the produce, or to the 400 falling to the labourers, except at the expense of the capitalists; nor to the proportion, or 400 falling to the latter, except at the expense of the former.

Whether the 800 were increased to 1600 or reduced to 400, so long as those between whom it must be divided receive each a half, their *relative* condition must continue the same. And hence the propriety of the distinction between *proportional* and *real* wages, or wages estimated in parts of the produce raised by the labourer, and those estimated in definite quantities of money or produce. If the productiveness of industry were to diminish, proportional wages might rise, notwithstanding that real wages, or the absolute quantity of the products of industry received by the labourer, might be diminished; and if, on the other hand, the productiveness of industry were to increase, proportional wages might be diminished, while real wages might, at the same time, be increased.

It is plain, therefore, that were taxation unknown or constant, the whole produce of industry, under deduction of rent, would be divided between capitalists and labourers; and that the proportion of that produce falling to either party, would vary inversely to the proportion falling to the other—that is, the proportion falling to the capitalists would be increased when that falling to the labourers was diminished, and diminished when it was increased.

Profits must not, however, be confounded with the produce of industry primarily received by the capitalists. They really consist of the produce, or the value of the produce, remaining to those who employ capital in industrious undertakings, after all their payments to others have been deducted, and after the capital wasted or used in the undertakings has been replaced. If the produce derived from an undertaking, after defraying the necessary outlay, be insufficient to replace the capital expended, a loss will have been incurred; if the capital be merely replaced and there is no surplus, there will neither be loss nor profit; and the greater the surplus, the greater, of course, will be the profit. Profits are not measured by the proportion which they bear to the rate of wages, but by the proportion which they bear to the capital by the agency of which they have been produced. Suppose an individual employs a capital equivalent to 1,000 quarters of corn in the cultivation of a farm, and that he expends 700 quarters in the payment of wages, and 300 in seed and other outgoings: suppose now that the return to this capital is 1,200 quarters. Under these circumstances, the proportion of the produce falling to the labourers as wages will be to that falling to the capitalist as 7 to 2; for, of the 1,200 quarters that fall, in the first instance, to the capitalist, 200 only are profits, 1,000 being required to replace the capital he has expended. In this case, therefore, the *rate* of profit would be said to be 20 per cent; meaning, that the *excess* of produce belonging to the cultivator, after the capital employed in its production was fully replaced, amounted to 20 per cent upon that capital.

I have been thus particular with respect to the definition of profits, because, from not keeping it sufficiently in view, Mr. Ricardo has been led to contend, that the *RATE of profit* depends on the *proportion* in which the produce of industry, under deduction of rent, is divided between capitalists and labourers; that a rise of profits can never be brought about except *by* a fall of proportional wages, nor a fall of profits except *by* a corresponding rise of proportional wages. It is evident, however, that this theory is true only in the event of our attaching a radically different sense to the term profit from what is usually attached to it, and supposing it to mean the *real* value of the entire portion of the produce of industry falling, in the first instance, to the share of the capitalist, without reference to the proportion which this produce bears to the capital employed in its production. If we understand the terms in this sense, Mr. Ricardo's theory will hold universally; and it may be affirmed, that so long as the proportion in which the produce of industry, under deduction of rent, is divided between capitalists and labourers, continues the same, no increase or diminution of the powers of production will occasion any variation in the rate of profit. But if we consider profits in the light in which they are invariably considered in the real business of life,—as the produce accruing to the capitalists after the capital expended by them in payments and outgoings of all sorts is fully replaced, it will immediately be seen that there are innumerable exceptions to Mr. Ricardo's theory.

It will facilitate the acquisition of clear and precise ideas respecting the circumstances which determine the average rate of profit in different employments, as that term is commonly understood, if we confine our attention, in the first place, to those that determine profits in agriculture,—both because the latter admit of being accurately measured, and because they may be taken as representing profits in other businesses. Agriculture is a branch of industry that must be carried on at all times, and under all circumstances: but it would not be carried on, if it did not, at an average, yield as great a return to the capital vested in it as other businesses; nor would these other businesses be carried on, if they yielded a less return than is derived from agriculture. It necessarily follows, therefore, that the returns obtained from agricultural industry, or agricultural profits, may, in ordinary cases, be considered as identical with the returns or profits obtained from other businesses. Whenever, for example, the average return to an outlay of capital or labour worth 100 quarters of wheat, employed in the cultivation of the soil, amounts to 110 quarters, we may safely infer, that 100*l.* employed in manufactures is also yielding 110*l.*: for, a regard to their own interest will not permit those engaged in such departments, to prosecute them for *less* profit than is obtained in agriculture; and the competition of the agriculturists will not permit them to obtain more.

Taking, then, as we are entitled to do, agricultural profits as a standard of all other profits, let us suppose that a landlord employs a capital equal in value to 10,000 quarters, or 10,000*l.*, in the cultivation of an estate; that he expends 5,000 quarters, or 5,000*l.* of this capital in seed, in the keeping of horses, and in defraying the wear and tear of implements and machines; and 5,000 quarters, or 5,000*l.*, in paying the wages of his labourers. Suppose, now, that the return obtained by this landlord is 12,000 quarters, or 12,000*l.*; of which 10,000 quarters, or 10,000*l.*, go to replace his capital, and 1,000 quarters, or 1,000*l.*, to pay his taxes, leaving 1,000 quarters, or 1,000*l.*, as profits, being 10 per cent on the capital employed. It is plain from this case, (and this case is, in point of principle, the actual case of all cultivators,) that the rate of profit may be increased in *three*—but only in one or other of three—ways, viz. (1) by a fall of wages, (2) a fall of taxes, or (3) an increased productiveness of industry.

Thus, it is obvious, (1) that if wages were reduced from 5,000 to 4,000 quarters, profits, supposing other things to be invariable, would be increased from 1,000 to 2,000 quarters, or from 10 to 20 per cent: if (2) the burden of taxation were reduced from 1,000 to 500 quarters, profits would be increased from 1,000 to 1,500 quarters, or from 10 to 15 per cent: and if (3), owing to the introduction of an improved system of agriculture, the return to a capital of 10,000 quarters were increased from 12,000 to 13,000 quarters, profits, supposing wages still to amount to 5,000 and taxes to 1,000 quarters, would be increased to 2,000 quarters, or to 20 per cent: and though, in this last case, after the productiveness of industry had been increased, wages would form a less proportion of the whole produce of industry than they did previously, it is to be observed, that this diminished proportion is the *consequence*, and not the cause of profits having risen; and therefore, in such cases as this, and they are of very frequent occurrence, it is true to say, that proportional wages fall because profits rise, but the converse of the proposition is not true; for the rise of profits was occasioned by causes that had nothing whatever to do with wages, and which were, in fact, totally independent of them.

It is, indeed, true, inasmuch as the rise of profits is the result of an increased productiveness of industry, that the *real* value of the 13,000 quarters will not exceed the *real* value of the 12,000 previously obtained by the same quantity of labour: but profits, in the sense in which they are practically understood, and as I understand them, do not depend on real values, but on the excess of the commodities produced above the capital expended in their production; and whenever this excess is augmented without any *previous* depression in the rate of wages, the rate of profit must evidently be increased by the operation of causes extrinsic to variations in that rate.

Nor is this all. The rate of profit may remain stationary, or rise though the *proportion* of the produce of industry falling to the share of the labourer be actually increased. Suppose, to exemplify this, that a landlord employs 1,000 quarters of wheat as a capital, 500 of which are expended in seed, keep of horses, &c. and 500 in paying wages; if the produce be 1,200 quarters, and the taxes to which he is subjected 100, his profits will amount to 100 quarters, or 10 per cent: suppose now that, owing to the introduction of improved machinery, or improved methods of culture, he only requires to expend 400 quarters in seed, keep of horses, &c. but that wages rise from 500 to 550 quarters, and that the same return is obtained: in this case, supposing taxation to be constant, the profits of the landlord will be increased from 10 to 15¾ per cent, though proportional wages have risen from 5-12ths to 5½-12ths of the whole produce.

It may be said, however, that if this increased productiveness were confined to agriculture, and did not extend to most other important businesses, the price of agricultural produce would fall, while that of other produce would remain stationary; and that, in such a case, the profits of agricultural industry, if estimated in money, or in any commodity other than corn, would be diminished in consequence of the rise of wages. This is true; but Mr. Ricardo has made no exception, in laying down his theory, in favour of those possible, and indeed frequently occurring cases, when, from any single circumstance, or combination of various circumstances, industry becomes generally more productive, and when, consequently, profits, estimated in money, corn, cloth, or any commodity in extensive demand, would have risen, without their rise having been occasioned by a fall of wages. And it is also true, that an increased productiveness of agricultural industry, whether it has been caused by the introduction of an improved system of agriculture, or by the repeal of restrictions on the importation of corn into a comparatively populous country, most commonly extends itself to other businesses, and has the effect of bringing about a universal rise of profits: for, as raw produce forms the principal part of the labourer's subsistence, and as he obtains a larger quantity in exchange for the same amount of money, after it has fallen in price, his condition is in so far improved; and a stimulus being, in this way, given to population, and the supply of labour increased, wages are reduced, and the rate of profit universally raised.

When industry, instead of becoming more productive, becomes less so, the opposite effects follow. Profits then fall, without any fall having previously taken place in the rate of wages.

It is evident, therefore, that the proposition that a rise of profits cannot be brought about otherwise than by a fall of wages, nor a fall of profits otherwise than by a rise of wages, is true only in those cases in which the productiveness of industry and the burden of taxation remain constant. So long as this is the case, or, which is the same thing, so long as the same capital is employed, and the same quantity of produce has to be divided between capitalists and labourers, the share of the one cannot be increased without the share of the other being equally diminished: and it is also true, that if profits depended on the *proportion* in which the produce of industry is divided between capitalists and labourers, they could not be affected by variations in its productiveness, but would be determined wholly by the state of proportional wages. But profits depend, as has been already seen, on the proportion which they bear to the capital by which they are produced, and not on the proportion which they bear to wages. Suppose an individual employs a capital of 1,000 quarters, or 1,000*l.* in cultivation, that he lays out the half of this capital in the payment of wages, and obtains a return of 1,200 quarters, or 1,200*l.*; in this case, assuming he is not affected by taxation, his profits will amount to 200 quarters, or 200*l.*, being at the rate of 20 per cent, and will be to wages in the proportion of 2 to 5. Suppose, now, that the productiveness of industry is *universally doubled,* and let it be farther supposed that the additional 1,200 quarters, or 1,200*l.*, is divided between the capitalist and his labourers in the former proportion of 2 to 5, or that the capitalist gets 343 quarters, or 343*l.* of additional profits, and the labourers 857 quarters, or 857*l.*, of additional wages: in this case, both parties will still obtain the same proportions of the produce of industry as before; and if we look only to them, we must say that neither profits nor wages have risen. But when we compare, as is invariably done in estimating profits, the return obtained by the capitalist with the capital he employs, it will be found, notwithstanding the constancy of proportional wages, that the *rate* of profit has increased from 20 to 54 per cent.

Thus, then, it appears, as was previously stated, that profits *rise* in one or other of the three following ways, viz. (1) from a fall of wages, or (2) from a fall of taxes directly or indirectly affecting capitalists, or (3) from an increased productiveness of industry; and they *fall*, (1) from a rise of wages, or (2) from an increase of taxes, or (3) from a diminished productiveness of industry. But they can neither rise nor fall, except from the operation of one or more of the causes now stated.

It is consistent with universal experience, that profits are invariably much higher in colonies, and thinly-peopled countries, than in countries that have been long settled, and where the population is comparatively dense; and that (referring to periods of average duration) their tendency is to fall in the progress of society. This sinking of profits in rich and populous countries has been ascribed by Dr. Smith to the competition of capitalists. He supposes that, when capital is augmented, its owners endeavour to encroach on each others' employments; and that, in furtherance of their object, they are tempted to offer their goods at a lower price, and to give higher wages to their workmen; which has a twofold effect in reducing profits. This theory was long universally assented to. It has been espoused by MM. Say, Sismondi, and Storch, by the Marquis Garnier, and, with some trifling modifications, by Mr. Malthus. But, notwithstanding the deference due to these authorities, it is easy to see that competition can never bring about a general fall of profits. It prevents any one individual, or set of individuals, from monopolising a particular branch of industry; and reduces the rate of profit in different businesses nearly to the same level; but this is its whole effect. Most certainly, it has no tendency to lessen the productiveness of industry, or to raise the average rate of wages or the rate of taxation; and if it can do none of these things, it is quite impossible it can lower profits. So long as an individual employing a capital of 1,000 quarters, or 1,000*l.*, obtains from it a return of 1,200 quarters, or 1,200*l.*, of which he has to pay 100 quarters, or 100*l.*, as taxes, so long will his profits continue at 10 per cent, whether he has the market to himself, or has 50,000 competitors. It is not competition, but it is the increase of taxation, and the necessity under which a growing society is placed of resorting to soils of less fertility to obtain supplies of food, that are the great causes of that reduction in the rate of profit which usually takes place in advanced periods. When the last lands taken into cultivation are fertile, there is a comparatively large amount of produce to be divided between capitalists and labourers; and both profits and *real* wages may, consequently, be high. But with every successive diminution in the fertility of the soils to which recourse is had, the quantities of produce obtained by the same outlays of capital and labour necessarily diminish.* And this diminution will obviously operate to reduce the rate of profit—(1) by lessening the quantity of produce to be divided between capitalists and labourers, and (2) by increasing the proportion falling to the share of the latter.

* This supposes, of course, either that no improvements are made, or that their influence has been taken into account.

The effect of the decreasing productiveness of the soil, as well on the condition and fortunes of society, as on the rate of profit, is so very powerful, that I shall endeavour to trace and exhibit its operation a little more fully. It has already been shewn, in treating of population, that the principle of increase in the human race is so very strong, as not only to keep population steadily up to the means of subsistence, but to give it a tendency to exceed them. It is true that a peculiar combination of favourable circumstances occasionally causes capital to increase faster than population, and wages are in consequence augmented. But such augmentation is rarely permanent, at least to the whole extent; for, the additional stimulus it is almost sure of giving to population seldom fails, by proportioning the supply of labour to the increased demand, to reduce wages to their old level, or to one not much above it. If, therefore, it were possible always to employ additional capital in raising raw produce, in manufacturing that raw produce when raised, and in conveying the raw and manufactured products from place to place, with an equal return, it is evident, supposing taxation to continue invariable, that, speaking generally, the greatest increase of capital would not occasion any considerable fall in the rate of profit. So long as labour may be obtained at the same rate, and as its productive power is not diminished, so long *must* the profits of stock continue unaffected. It is evident, then, that the mere increase of capital has, by itself, no lasting effect on wages, and it is obviously the same thing, in so far as the rate of profit is concerned, whether ten or ten thousand millions be employed in the cultivation of the soil, and in the manufactures and commerce of this or any other kingdom, provided the last million so employed be as productive, or yield as large a return, as the first. Now this is invariably the case with the capital employed in manufactures and commerce. The greatest amount of capital and labour may be employed in fashioning raw produce and adapting it to our use, and in transporting it from where it is produced to where it is to be consumed, without a diminished return. Whatever quantity of labour may now be required to build a ship or construct a machine, it is abundantly certain that an equal quantity will, at any future period, suffice to build a similar ship or to construct a similar machine; and, although these ships and machines were indefinitely multiplied, the last would be as well adapted to every useful purpose, and as serviceable as the first. The probability, indeed, or rather the certainty, is, that the last would be much more serviceable than the first. It is not possible to assign limits to the powers and resources of genius, nor consequently to the improvement of machinery, and of the skill and industry of the labourer. Future Watts, Arkwrights, and Wedgwoods, will arise; and the stupendous discoveries of the last and present age will doubtless be equalled, and most probably surpassed, in the ages that are to come. It is, therefore, clear, that if equal quantities of capital and labour could always raise *equal quantities of raw produce,* the greatest additions that might be made to them could not lessen the capacity of employing them with advantage, or sink the rate of profit. But here, and here only, the bounty of nature is limited, and she deals out her gifts with a frugal and parsimonious hand.

> "————Pater ipse COLENDI
> Haud facilem esse viam voluit——"

Equal quantities of capital and labour do not always produce equal quantities of raw produce. The soil is of limited extent and limited fertility; and it is this limited fertility that proves the real check — the insuperable obstacle — which prevents the means of subsistence, and consequently the inhabitants, of every country, from increasing in a geometrical proportion, until the space required for carrying on the operations of industry has become deficient.

But it is plain, that the decreasing productiveness of the soils to which every improving society is obliged to resort, will not, as was previously observed, merely lessen the *quantity* of produce to be divided between profits and wages, but will also increase the *proportion* of that produce falling to the share of the labourer. It is quite impossible to go on increasing the cost of raw produce, the principal part of the subsistence of the labourer, by forcing good, or taking inferior lands into cultivation, without increasing wages. A rise of wages is seldom indeed exactly coincident with a rise in the price of necessaries, but they can never be very far separated. The price of the necessaries of life is in fact the cost of producing labour. The labourer cannot work if he be not supplied with the means of subsistence; and though a certain period of varying extent, according to the circumstances of the country at the time, must generally elapse, when necessaries are rising in price, before wages are proportionally augmented, such an augmentation must, in all ordinary cases, be brought about in the end.

It is plain, therefore, inasmuch as there is never any falling off, but a constant increase, in the productiveness of the labour employed in manufacturing and commercial industry, that the subsistence of the labourer could not be increased in price, and consequently that it would not be necessary to make any additions to his *natural* wages, or the wages required to enable him to subsist and continue his race, were it not for the diminished power of agricultural labour, originating in the inevitable necessity under which man is placed, of resorting to inferior soils to obtain larger supplies of raw produce. *The decreasing fertility of the soil is, therefore, at bottom, the great and only necessary cause of a fall of profits.* The *quantity* of produce forming the return to capital and labour would never diminish but for the diminution that uniformly takes place in the productiveness of the soil; nor is there any other physical cause why the *proportion* of wages to profits should be increased, and the *rate* of profit diminished, as it uniformly is, in the progress of society.

I have thus endeavoured to exhibit the ultimate effect which the necessity of resorting to poorer lands for supplies of food has on profits and wages. But though this cause of the reduction of profits be "of such magnitude and power as finally to overwhelm every other,"* its operations may be, and indeed commonly are, counteracted or facilitated by extrinsic causes. It is obvious, for example, that every discovery or improvement in agriculture, which enables a greater quantity of produce to be obtained for the same expense, has a similar effect on profits as if the extent of superior soils were increased, and may, for a lengthened period, increase the rate of profit.

Had the inventive genius of man been limited in its powers, and had the various machines and implements used in agriculture, and the skill of the husbandman, speedily attained to their utmost perfection, the rise in the price of raw produce, and the fall of profits consequent to the increase of population, would have been so apparent as to force themselves on the attention of every one. When, in such a state of things, it became necessary to resort to poorer soils to raise an additional quantity of food, a corresponding increase of labour would have been required; for, supposing the perfection of art to be attained, nothing except greater exertion can overcome fresh obstacles. Not only, therefore, would additional labour have been necessary to the production of a greater quantity of food, but it would have been necessary in the precise proportion in which the difficulty of its production was increased. So that, had the arts

* Malthus's "Principles of Political Economy," &c. p. 317.

continued stationary, the price of raw produce would have varied directly with every variation in the qualities of the soils successively brought under tillage.

But the circumstances which really regulate the value of raw produce are extremely different. It is true, indeed, that even in those societies that are most rapidly improving, it has, as was previously shewn, a constant *tendency* to rise; for, the rise of profits consequent to every invention, by occasioning a greater demand for labour, gives a fresh stimulus to population; and thus, by increasing the demand for food, again inevitably forces the cultivation of poorer soils, and raises prices. But it is evident that improvements render these effects of this great law of nature, from whose all-pervading influence the utmost efforts of human ingenuity cannot enable man to escape, far less palpable and obvious. After inferior soils are cultivated, more labourers are, in most cases, required to raise the same quantities of food; but as the powers of the labourers are gradually improved in the progress of society, a much smaller number is required, in proportion to the whole work that is performed, than if no such improvement had taken place. The natural tendency to an increase in the price of raw produce is in this way counteracted. The productive energies of the earth gradually diminish, and we are compelled to resort to less fruitful soils; but the productive energies of the labour employed in their tillage are as constantly augmented by the discoveries and inventions that are always being made. Two directly opposite and continually acting principles are thus set in motion. From the operation of fixed and permanent causes, the increasing sterility of the soil is sure, in the long run, to overmatch the improvements that occur in machinery and agriculture, prices experiencing a corresponding rise, and profits a corresponding fall. Occasionally, however, these improvements more than compensate, during pretty lengthened periods, for the deterioration in the quality of the soils successively cultivated; and a fall of prices and rise of profits take place, until the constant pressure of population has again forced the cultivation of still poorer lands.

In so far as the general principle is concerned, the previous reasoning is applicable alike to the commercial world, or to a single nation. It is plain, however, that the fall in the rate of profit, and the consequent check to the progress of society, originating in the necessity of resorting to poorer soils, will be more severely felt in an improving country, which excludes foreign corn from her markets, than in one which maintains an unfettered intercourse with her neighbours. Were a highly manufacturing and commercial country, like England, to deal with all the world on fair and liberal principles, she might avail herself of all those capacities of production which Providence has given to different countries; and, besides obtaining supplies of food at the cheapest rate at which they can be raised, the numberless markets to which she could resort would prevent her from feeling any very injurious consequences from the occasional failure of her own harvests, or from deficiences in one or a few of the sources whence she drew her foreign supplies; so that she would thus go far to secure for herself constant plenty, and, what is of hardly less importance, constant steadiness of price. Such a nation would have the foundations of her greatness established on a broad and solid basis; for they would rest not on the productive powers of her own soil only, but on those of all the countries of the world. And supposing her not to be involved, to an unusual degree, in war, or subjected to comparatively heavy taxes, her profits would not be reduced, nor would she get clogged in her progress, until the increase of population forced the cultivation of inferior soils in the countries from which she had been in the custom of importing corn. And even then, she would not be surpassed by her neighbours; her progress being retarded by a cause which must equally affect them, her *relative* power would not be impaired; and should new markets be opened, or new discoveries made, in any quarter of the world, she would reap her full share of the advantage, and be renovated and strengthened for a new career of exertion.

But the case would be very different were foreign raw produce excluded from the markets of a nation like England, which has made an unusual progress in commerce and manufactures, and whose population is, therefore, comparatively dense. A government which prevents its subjects from exchanging their manufactured goods for the corn of more fertile or less densely-peopled countries, compels them prematurely to resort to poor soils at home; and profits being consequently reduced, the country is made to approach the stationary state at a period when, had the legislature acted on more enlarged principles, she might have been advancing with the same rapidity as before in the career of improvement.

I have briefly adverted, in a previous chapter, to the influence of restrictions on the corn trade in aggravating the evils of scarcity, and occasioning ruinous fluctuations of price. Although, however, they had no such influence, it is obvious, for the reasons now stated, that they are in the last degree injurious. It may, one should think, be laid down as an axiom, that government should not interfere at all with industrious undertakings, or interfere only in the view of rendering them more secure or more productive. But to exclude any article, and particularly one so important as corn, when it may be imported cheaper from abroad than it can be raised directly at home, is really to adopt the means most effectual for rendering industry least secure and least productive! It is not merely contradicting the best-established principles, but it is employing the power of government to arrest the natural progress of opulence and prosperity; and to accelerate the period of old age, decrepitude, and decay! If we could, by laying out 1,000*l.* on the manufacture of cottons or hardware, produce a quantity of these articles that would exchange for 400 quarters of Polish or American wheat, and if the same sum, when expended in cultivation in this country, would not produce more than 300 quarters, the prevention of importation occasions an obvious sacrifice of 100 quarters out of every 400 consumed in the empire; or, which is the same thing, it occasions an artificial advance of 25 per cent in the price of corn. It is not even true that a system of this sort is, in any respect, advantageous to the landlords or farmers; and to suppose that it can be advantageous to those who are obliged to buy their produce, is too ludicrous to merit one moment's attention.

Practically, however, I am disposed to think that the injurious influence of the existing restrictions on the importation of corn will gradually become less perceptible, and that, at no very distant period, they will scarcely be felt, except in unusually bad years, the evils of which they will necessarily continue to aggravate. The improvement now begun in Ireland may be expected to bring about this result. Previously to 1806, when all restrictions on the corn trade between Ireland and Great Britain were abolished, the imports of corn from the former into the latter did not exceed 400,000 quarters, whereas they now amount to 1,600,000 quarters, exclusive of about 600,000 cwts. of flour and meal. Every one, however, who has been in Ireland, or has any acquaintance with that country, must be aware that agriculture is there at the lowest possible ebb, and that, considering the extraordinary natural fertility of the soil, a very small advance towards a better system of farming would enable Ireland to export five or six times the quantity of produce she now sends to us. And it is satisfactory to know, that a spirit of improvement has been excited. The settlement of the Catholic question has done much to promote public tranquillity;

while the disfranchisement of the forty shilling freeholders, and the conviction now so generally entertained of the injurious consequences of the minute division of the land, will not only tend to prevent that splitting of farms which has been so fatal to Irish agriculture, but will most probably lead to the gradual consolidation of the small occupancies. This tendency has, indeed, been strongly manifested in several parts of the country; and it may be expected that, according as experience discloses the benefits of which it will doubtless be productive, it will acquire new strength. On these grounds, it would seem that a very great increase in the imports of corn and cattle from Ireland may be rationally anticipated. Nor should it surprise any one who considers her vast capacities of improvement, though we become, in a few years, an exporting people. That this would be " a consummation devoutly to be wished," is most certain. During the period while prices are sinking to the continental level, the agriculture of Great Britain must, indeed, be more or less depressed; but there can be no question that in the end such a fall would be highly beneficial to the community. It would either raise the rate of profit, or check its decline; and would consequently contribute, in no ordinary degree, to widen and consolidate the foundations of our prosperity. As respects the landlords and agriculturists of Ireland, the advantage would be immediate, and without alloy; and it is abundantly obvious, for the reasons stated in a previous chapter, that the same classes in England would reap far more real benefit from the improvement that could not but take place in the state of the country, should these anticipations be realised, than they can reasonably expect from a continuance of comparatively high prices, originating in oppressive restrictions.

But to return:—An unusually low rate of profit in a particular country not only lessens its power to accumulate capital, and, by consequence, to add to its population, but it also creates a strong temptation to transmit portions of its capital to other countries. The same principle that would prevent the employment of capital in Yorkshire, if the return to it were less than in Kent or Surrey, regulates its distribution among the different nations of the world. It is true that the love of country, the thousand ties of society and friendship, the ignorance of foreign languages, and the desire to have our stock employed under our own inspection, render a greater difference in the rate of profit necessary to occasion the transfer of capital from one country to another, than from one province of the same country to another. But this love of country has its limits. The love of gain is a no less powerful and constantly operating principle; and whenever capitalists feel assured that their stock may be laid out with tolerable security, and considerably greater advantage in foreign states, its efflux, to a greater or less extent, invariably takes place.

When the taxes which affect the industrious classes are increased, such increase must either immediately fall wholly on profits or wages, or partly on the one and partly on the other. If it fall on profits, it makes, of course, an equivalent deduction from them; and if it fall on wages, it proportionally depresses the condition of the great mass of the people. There are limits, however,—and those in most countries, are not, unfortunately, very remote,—to the power of the labourers to pay taxes; and were their situation more improved, were they habituated to comforts, and tolerably intelligent, the increased pressure of augmented taxes, by giving additional strength to the principle of moral restraint, and retarding the increase of population, would most probably raise wages to about their old level, throwing the taxes affecting them either wholly or principally on the employers.

The excessive weight of taxation has been the real cause of the lowness of profits in the United Provinces, during the last two centuries, and of the decline of their manufacturing and commercial prosperity. Notwithstanding the rigid and laudable economy of her rulers, the vast expense incurred by the republic in her revolutionary struggle with Spain, and in her subsequent contests with France and England, led to the contraction of an immense public debt; and, in order to provide for the payment of interest and other necessary charges, she was obliged to lay heavy taxes on the most indispensable necessaries.* Among others, high duties were laid on foreign corn when imported, on flour and meal when ground at the mill, and on bread when it came from the oven. Taxation affected all the sources of national wealth; and so oppressive did it ultimately become, that it was a common saying at Amsterdam, that every dish of fish brought to table was paid once to the fisherman and *six times* to the state! Wages being necessarily raised so as to enable the labourers to subsist, the weight of these enormous taxes fell almost wholly on the capitalists. And profits being, in consequence, reduced below their level in other countries, the prosperity of Holland gradually declined; her capitalists choosing rather to transfer their stocks to the foreigner than to employ them at home. "L'augmentation successive des impôts, que les paymens des intérêts et les remboursemens ont rendu indispensable, a détruit une grande partie de l'industrie, a diminué le commerce, a diminué ou fort altére l'état florissant où étoit autrefois la population, en resserrant chez le peuple les moyens de subsistance." †

* In 1579, at the Union of Utrecht, the interest of the public debt of the province of Holland amounted to only 117,000 florins; but so rapidly did it increase, that in 1655, during the administration of the famous John de Witt, the States were compelled to reduce the interest from 5 to 4 per cent, and yet, notwithstanding this reduction, it amounted in 1678 to 7,107,000 florins! See Metelerkamp, "Statistique de la Hollande," p. 203.

† "Richesse de la Hollande," tom. ii. p. 179. This work is full of very valuable information. The author, (M. de Luzac) mentions, that the Hollanders had, in 1778, about 1,500 millions of livres (62 millons

In the previous statement I have endeavoured to shew how variations in the rate of taxation, affecting those engaged in production, would affect the rate of profit; but I have said nothing as to the influence which loans to government exercise over that rate. Indeed, as they seldom occur except during war, and are consequently of an incidental character, they could not properly be classed among the circumstances that permanently influence profits, however deserving of a separate investigation.

If the loans made to government were of trifling amount compared with the disposable capital of the country, they would either exercise no influence, or next to none, over the rate of profit. But if they were large, and particularly if they were negotiated during two or three successive years, their influence could hardly fail of being very sensibly felt. When government comes into the market for money, it necessarily offers such a rate of interest as is sufficient, all things considered, to procure the sum which it wants. Now it is plain, that if the rate offered by government be greater than the rate at which money was previously obtainable on good security, and if it continue for two or three years to negotiate fresh loans on the same or higher terms, the rate of interest will be universally raised; for individuals would be unable to obtain loans, except on the same terms as government.

This, however, is not the only effect that would result from loans to government. Had the latter abstained from borrowing, the stockholders would either have employed the capital which they have lent to government in

sterling) in the public funds of France and England!—See also, as to the taxation of Holland, "A Memoir on the Means of Amending and Redressing the Commerce of the Republic," drawn up from information communicated by the best-informed merchants, and published by order of the Stadtholder, William IV. Prince of Orange, in 1751. This "Memoir" was translated into English, and published in London in the same year.

industrious undertakings, or they would have lent it to others who would have so employed it; and hence the negotiation of the loan, by causing the immediate consumption of a quantity of capital that would otherwise have been reserved as a fund to employ labourers in all time to come, will have an injurious effect upon the rate of wages. Capital and population always bear a certain relation to each other; the latter being, in the vast majority of instances, stationary when the former is stationary, or varying at the same rate and in the same way that it varies. It is, therefore, clear, that the negotiation of a loan, or the diversion of a portion of stock that has, or would, partly at least, have been employed in industrious undertakings, to military purposes, must unavoidably change the existing relation of stock and labour. Capital is, on the one hand, either actually diminished, or the rapidity of its increase checked, while, on the other, the population is not diminished, nor the rate of its increase retarded; for, it has been already shewn, that neither the number nor the habits of the people can be sensibly affected, except by slow degrees. The immediate effect of loans is, therefore, to render population redundant as compared with capital; and, by depressing wages, to raise, for a while at least, the rate of profit.

Such a rise cannot, however, be permanent. The distressed condition of the labourers naturally adds new strength to the principle of moral restraint; and by retarding the progress of population, gradually raises wages to their old level, or to one not much inferior. It is, however, easy to discover that there are other circumstances that conspire to produce this result, and which are powerful enough not only to occasion the reduction of profits to their old level, but to one still lower. It is difficult to imagine that it would be practicable, were the attempt made, so to impose the taxes required to defray the interest of loans, that a considerable portion of them should not fall either directly or indirectly on profits. But, however imposed, the pressure of these new taxes would naturally tend, as was formerly explained, to infuse a greater spirit of industry and economy into those on whom they fell, and, consequently, to occasion a more rapid accumulation of capital when government ceases to borrow. The growing demand for labour, resulting from the operation of this principle, combined with the more powerful influence of moral restraint on the supply of labour, could not fail of ultimately raising wages to about their old level; and when this is done, profits (supposing, of course, the productiveness of industry not to have varied) will be depressed, because of the increased weight of taxation, to a lower level than they stood at previously to the negotiation of the loans.

These conclusions seem to be fully verified by what has taken place in this country. According to the researches of Arthur Young, to whom we are indebted for much valuable information respecting the rate of wages at different periods, the medium price of agricultural labour in England in 1767, 1768, and 1770, was very nearly 1*s*. 3*d*. a day; and he further states, that its medium price in 1810 and 1811, when money wages were at the highest elevation to which they attained during the war, amounted to about 2*s*. 5*d*. being a rise of nearly, though not quite, 100 per cent. But the price of wheat, according to the account kept at Eton College, during the first mentioned years, was 51*s*. a quarter; and during 1810 and 1811 its price was 110*s*., being a rise of 115 per cent; and Mr. Young estimates that butcher's meat had, during the same period, risen 146, butter 140, and cheese 153 per cent; being, at an average, a rise of 138½ per cent, shewing that wages, as compared with these articles, had declined in the interval 38½ per cent, or considerably more than a third; and if the increased cost of beer, leather, and some other necessary articles, had been taken into account, the fall in the rate of real wages would have appeared still more striking. There are, it is true, some articles of clothing, particularly cottons, to which Mr. Young has not alluded, which fell very greatly in price during the period in question. These, however, do not form very prominent articles in the consumption of the working classes; so that, notwithstanding what they gained by their fall, it is abundantly certain that real wages sunk very considerably during the latter years of the war; and this fall satisfactorily accounts for a part, at least, of the rise that then took place in the rate of profit.

The circumstances that have occurred since the termination of the war, and the return to specie payments, appear equally consistent with what has previously been advanced. Wages not having fallen in the same proportion as the prices of corn and most articles of subsistence, profits have been consequently depressed; and they have also been depressed from the operation of the taxes imposed during the war to pay the interest of the loans.*

It has sometimes been stated, that a loan occasions, while government is spending it, a greater demand for labour than it would have afforded had it continued in the possession of individuals. I confess, however, that I have not been able to discover any grounds for this opinion. If the government expend the loan in the purchase of military stores, they will not, by doing so, give any greater stimulus to labour than the capitalists who have made the loan would have given had they employed it to purchase raw or manufactured goods: and suppose government employ it in hiring soldiers and sailors, they will not thereby occasion a greater demand for labour than would have been occasioned by employing it to hire common labourers. That there is frequently a very brisk demand for labour during periods of war is, no doubt, true; but we shall certainly find the cause of it in something else than the

* See "Edinburgh Review," vol. xl. p. 28.

mere substitution of government employment for that afforded by individuals.

Mr. Ricardo has shewn that the demand for labour may be increased, for a while, at least, by the imposition of taxes falling principally on luxuries.* Most rich men expend a considerable portion of their revenue on costly furniture, splendid mansions, horses, &c., employing, in the acquisition of these articles, the same amount of labour that they would have employed had they bought provisions or machinery. But when different articles have been acquired, the use or consumption of some of them occasions the employment of a considerable quantity of labour, while others may be used without any such effect being produced. Suppose a nobleman gives 500*l.* for a cabinet: as much labour will have been employed in its production as in the production of an equivalent quantity of food and clothes. When, however, he gets the cabinet, it affords no farther means of employing labour; whereas, had the 500*l.* been laid out on food and clothes, they would have afforded him the means of employing, and, indeed, could only have been bought in order to enable him to employ, an additional number of servants.

Seeing, therefore, that the produce of such taxes as tend to check the demand for articles of furniture and luxurious accommodation is, for the most part, employed to pay the wages of soldiers and sailors, it may be concluded that they tend to increase the demand for labour. It is, however, very doubtful whether the taxes imposed in this country have ever had any material or, indeed, sensible operation in the way now pointed out; and it would seem that the principal cause why the heavy taxation to which we were subjected during the war, and the loans then contracted, did not more seriously injure the labourer, is to be found in the influence of taxation in stimulating industry and economy.

* "Principles of Political Economy and Taxation," third ed. p. 476.

Besides being affected by variations in the burden of taxation, and by the negotiation of loans on account of government, the rate of profit is affected by changes in the value of money—increasing when it falls, and diminishing when it rises.

Mr. Hume has observed, in his "Essay on Money," that "in every kingdom into which money begins to flow in greater abundance than formerly, every thing takes a new face; labour and industry gain life, the merchant becomes more enterprising, the manufacturer more diligent and skilful, and even the farmer follows his plough with greater alacrity and attention. But when gold and silver are diminishing, the workman has not the same employment from the manufacturer and merchant, though he pays the same price for every thing in the market. The farmer cannot dispose of his corn and cattle, though he must pay the same rent to the landlord. The poverty, beggary, and sloth that must ensue, are easily foreseen."

Mr. Hume supposed that the stimulus he has so strikingly described, given by an influx of money to industry, originates in the circumstance of the additional money coming first into the hands of capitalists, and consequently enabling them to employ more workmen, and to increase their demand for the products of industry. Mr. Mill has, however, shewn that an influx of money could not operate in the way now alluded to, so as to have any material influence upon industry.* But although Mr. Hume seems to have mistaken, or rather overlooked, the mode in which an increase of money principally contributes to excite industry and enterprise, there is not, I apprehend, the shadow of a ground for doubting his statement as to such being its effect. Periods when the quantity of money and the prices of commodities are increasing, are invariably distinguished by a comparatively brisk

* Mr. Mill contends, in his able work, "Elements of Political Economy," 2d ed. p. 160, that it would have *no* influence; but this, were the point worth investigating, might, I think, be shewn to be an error.

demand for labour and an unusual degree of activity and invention among the industrious classes; nor is it at all difficult to discover why such is the case. Variations in the value of money obviously influence the rate of taxation, as well as rents and other fixed money payments. When its value declines, all the fixed and ascertained burdens affecting the productive classes decline in the same proportion. The fundholder, the annuitant, the person deriving a determinate income from mortgages or any other source, the landlord during the continuance of his lease,—all suffer in proportion to the fall in the value of money; their money incomes remaining the same, while the price of all articles is raised: but the farmer, while he pays the same rent to his landlord, the same taxes to government, and, most probably, the same composition for tithes, sells his produce for a price increased proportionally to the reduced value of money. In like manner, the merchant, the manufacturer, and the tradesman, pay the same duties on their goods, the same port dues, the same tolls, the same rent for shops and warehouses, the same rate of interest for capital borrowed, while they all obtain increased prices for whatever they have to sell. Their profits are, therefore, universally raised in proportion to the amount of the fixed charges falling upon them, and the fall in the value of the currency in which they are paid. The revenues of all those who do not employ their capital themselves, but lend it to others, and of all professional persons, being for a while universally, and in some instances perpetually, reduced;* while those whose revenues are derived from interminable or life annuities, payable by the state or individuals, sustain a permanent injury commensurate with the decline in the value of money.

Now, when we consider the immense number of individuals in Great Britain, such as landlords, fundholders,

* Those who had made advances on loan would get back less than they really lent when money fell in value, and would, therefore, be permanently injured.

annuitants, persons living on the interest of money, persons who, having retired from business, receive a fixed salary from their successors, clergymen, &c., it is evident that the total aggregate loss they would sustain by any considerable fall in the value of money would be exceedingly great. But it is also evident that what is thus lost by these classes is gained by others, — by those who are actively employed in industrious undertakings, and whose prosperity is always assumed to be the measure of that of the public.

A depreciation of the currency must, therefore, by lightening the pressure of taxation and of all fixed charges affecting individuals engaged in agriculture, manufactures, and commerce, proportionally increase their profits; and it is hardly necessary to add, that this increased profit must operate as a spur to production, that it must quicken all the operations of trade, and occasion an increased demand for labour.

Precisely the opposite effects will, of course, follow when, instead of falling, the currency becomes more valuable; all taxes and fixed charges being then augmented in an equal degree, the profits of those by whom those taxes and other fixed charges are borne are necessarily reduced in the same proportion. Here, then, is a key by which we may readily explain many apparent anomalies. The prosperity of the country during the latter years of the war, and its more recent prosperity in 1824 and 1825, was undoubtedly owing, in a very considerable degree, to the fall in the value of money, originating in the great additions that were then made to the paper currency; and the peculiarly severe distresses to which the industrious classes were exposed in 1815 and 1816, in 1819, and in 1826, are chiefly ascribable to the reductions that were then made in the quantity of money afloat, and the consequent increase of its value. There can be no doubt, indeed, that a rapid reduction of the quantity, or a rapid increase of the value of money, by giving a sudden shock to industry, and vitiating the basis on which innumerable contracts have been entered into to the prejudice of the industrious classes, has, in the first instance, a far more pernicious influence than can be fairly ascribed to the mere increase of the burdens affecting them. Still, however, the effects of an increase of this sort are always obvious, and are disastrous according to the degree in which the value of the currency may be raised.

I should be sorry were it imagined, from any thing now stated, that I am an advocate for the expediency of reducing the value of money by a legislative enactment, in order to lighten the pressure of taxation and the burdens of the industrious classes. My object has merely been to explain the operation and effect of such changes in the value of money, as originate either in variations in the cost of the precious metals, or in such political or financial measures as may affect, without its being intended, the value of money. An avowed reduction of the standard would have the effects already mentioned; but it would also have others, which it is essential not to lose sight of in estimating its probable influence. Besides diminishing the weight of taxation, and the burdens laid upon the industrious classes, it would partially subvert the right of property, and would go far to annihilate all confidence in the acts of the legislature. Whatever, therefore, might be gained on the one hand by such a measure, would, there is every reason to think, be more than lost on the other. Public and private credit would, for a while, be destroyed; and a large amount of capital would be transferred to foreign countries, as to places of security. In this respect a degradation of the standard would be worse than a voluntary public bankruptcy, to the same,* or even to a greater extent; seeing that the latter would affect the creditors of the state only, whereas the former would, besides them, affect the creditors of all private individuals.

* By the same extent is meant, that if the standard be reduced any given amount, as 10 per cent, the sums due the public creditor should be reduced in the same proportion, and conversely.

Perhaps, as Hume conjectures, credit might, at no distant period, grow up again, even after so flagrant a breach of faith; but such a result could hardly be expected, unless the country were to continue at peace, and to become decidedly more prosperous. Should we be involved in war, or should the measure not be followed by the anticipated effect in relieving the national distresses, it is very unlikely that credit would revive; for, in the former case, few would be willing, unless they were tempted by the offer of a large bonus, to lend to a government which had so strikingly evinced its contempt for the most sacred engagements; and in the latter, the continuance of the distress would naturally excite a fear lest it should lead to a repetition of the same violence of which it had already been made the pretext. It is clear, therefore, that nothing but the most overwhelming necessity can ever justify a measure of this sort. The benefits that a change in the value of money has occasionally conferred on the industrious classes, are the result of natural or fortuitous causes. They cannot be secured by voluntarily enfeebling the standard; for this being a scheme to benefit one part of society by defrauding another part, is sure to bring along with it evils that will not merely neutralise, but very greatly overbalance its advantages. At bottom there is no real distinction between what is just and what is useful. The accidental conflagration of the fleets of their rivals would no doubt have increased the power of the Athenians; but had they adopted the advice ascribed to Themistocles, and attempted to secure their ascendancy by the basest treachery, they would certainly have missed their end, and have become objects of universal hostility as well as of contempt. "*Nihil est quod adhuc de republicâ putem dictum, et quo possim longiùs progredi, nisi sit confirmatum, non modò falsum esse illud, sine injuriâ non posse, sed hoc verissimum, sine summâ justitiâ rempublicam regi non posse.*"*

* Cic. Frag. lib. ii. de Repub.

The statements now made sufficiently shew, that loans to government, and changes in the value of money, affect profits only by affecting wages, or the taxes, or other fixed charges which enter into the cost of production: so that whether government is borrowing or paying off debts, and whether the value of money be rising, falling, or stationary, it is still true that profits do not rise except when industry becomes more productive, or when wages or taxes are reduced; and that they do not fall except when industry becomes less productive, or wages or taxes are augmented.

No people have any reason whatever to be alarmed at the effects of competition in any department of industry, for instead of losing, they are always sure to gain by every discovery which tends to facilitate production or reduce cost. It is not by improvements among their neighbours, but by a decline in the productiveness of industry at home—a decline which will always be indicated and correctly measured by the fall of profits it must occasion—that either their absolute or relative situation can be injuriously affected. But every such fall will undoubtedly tend to sink them in the scale of national power and importance, and to enable their rivals to outstrip them in the career of wealth and greatness. Neither the skill and industry of the most intelligent and laborious artisans, nor the possession of the most improved and powerful machinery, can permanently withstand the paralysing influence of a relatively low rate of profit: and it should not be forgotten, that such relative lowness must necessarily be produced by every system or regulation which, by excluding foreign corn or otherwise, forces the premature cultivation of poor soils, and artificially raises prices; and can only be prevented by acting on a liberal commercial system, and enforcing the strictest economy in the public expenditure.

CHAPTER VIII.

Interest and Nett Profit identical — Circumstances which occasion Variations in the Rate of Interest — Impolicy of Usury Laws.

WHEN an individual, instead of directly employing his own capital, lends it to another, he stipulates for a certain annual premium or return, which has been denominated interest.

In the preceding chapter we have considered profits as they are practically considered, or as consisting of the produce, or the equivalent of the produce, remaining to the capitalist who undertakes any sort of work, after all his outgoings have been replaced. But to ascertain the relation of profits and interest, this residue must be still farther analysed. Now it is obvious, that it consists partly only of a return to the capital employed, and that it is partly formed of the wages or remuneration of the capitalist for his skill and trouble in superintending its employment, and of a compensation for such risks as it might not be possible to provide against by an insurance. Hence the distinction between *gross* and *nett* profits. The first comprises the wages of the capitalist, the return to his capital, and the compensation now alluded to, while the second consists of the return to capital only. In laying it down, when treating of the "Accumulation and Employment of Capital," that high profits are the best criterion of national prosperity, I had gross profits only in view. And it is, indeed, evident, that the condition of those engaged in industrious undertakings depends on the magnitude of the produce or sum remaining to them, after their various expenses have been deducted, without being in any degree influenced by the names they may give to portions of it.

When the parties to a loan are left, without any sort of interference, to adjust its terms, and when the security offered by the borrower is unexceptionable, and payment may be had on the shortest notice, the interest that will, under such circumstances, be stipulated for the capital or money advanced will be identical with the rate of nett profit at the time. The lender having nothing to do with the employment of the loan, is not entitled to any compensation on that head; but he is entitled to all that can fairly be considered as the return to it after the risks, wages, and necessary emoluments of those who undertake its employment, are deducted; and this much he will get and no more. Whatever else may be realised by the investment of the loan in an industrious undertaking, will belong either to the borrower, or the individual to whom he may have assigned the loan, and will form the wages or compensation due to him for his skill and trouble in superintendence, &c. I have the satisfaction of being able to quote the opinion of Mr. Tooke, who is not more distinguished as a profound economist than as an able practical merchant, in favour of what I have now stated. "The rate of interest," says he, "*is the measure of the nett profit on capital.* All returns beyond this on the employment of capital, are resolvable into compensations under distinct heads for risk, trouble, or skill, or for advantages of situation or connexion."*

Whatever, therefore, may at any time occasion a brisk demand for capital, without also occasioning an increase in the productiveness of industry, or a fall of wages or taxes, may raise the rate of interest, or of *nett* profit, without affecting *gross* profits, or profits in the customary acceptation of the term. And this, as has been already observed, is most commonly the immediate effect of government loans. They raise the rate of interest without affecting profits; the rise merely diminishing that part

* "Considerations on the State of the Currency," 2nd. ed. p. 12.

of the total produce falling to the employers of capital which is to be considered as their wages, and making a corresponding addition to the other part, or that which is to be considered as the nett return or interest of capital.

Hence the advantage of a loan to the monied interest, or to those who have capital to lend; and hence, also, its universally remarked injurious operation upon those who are employing borrowed capital.

The rate of interest is not, therefore, as has sometimes been supposed, always a correct test of the rate of profit. When, however, allowance is made for the disturbing effects of government loans, and other accidental causes of variation, the rate of interest or nett profit varies, generally speaking, directly as the rate of gross profit. Whenever interest is low during a period of peace, it is found that profits are also low, and conversely.

There are comparatively few species of security to be obtained in which there is no risk, either as to the repayment of the loans themselves, or the regular payment of the interest. And as the trustees of many public bodies, as well as those of many private individuals, are obliged to invest in such securities only, the rate of interest which they bring is frequently very much depressed below what may be considered as the common and average rate of interest at the time. Government securities are liable to be deeply affected by political considerations, by the greater or less latitude for a rise or fall in the capital sum invested, and by a variety of circumstances which it is always very difficult, or rather perhaps impossible, even for those most experienced in such matters, to distinguish and appreciate. Mercantile bills of unquestionable credit, and having two or three months to run, are generally discounted at a lower rate of interest than may be obtained for sums lent upon mortgage, on account of the facility they afford of repossessing the principal, and applying it in some more profitable manner. Other things being equal, the rate of interest must of course vary according to the supposed risk incurred by the lender of either not recovering payment at all, or not receiving it at the stipulated term. No person of sound mind would lend on the personal security of an individual of doubtful character and solvency, and on mortgage over a valuable estate, at the same rate of interest. Wherever there is risk, it must be compensated to the lender by a higher premium or interest.

And yet, obvious as this principle may appear, all governments have interfered with the adjustment of the terms of loans, some to prohibit interest altogether, and others to fix a certain rate which it should be deemed legal to exact and illegal to exceed. It is needless, however, to waste the reader's time by entering into lengthened arguments to shew the inexpediency and mischievous effect of such interferences. This has been done over and over again. It is plainly in no respect more desirable to limit the rate of interest than it would be to limit the rate of insurance, or the prices of commodities. And though it were desirable, it cannot be accomplished. The real effect of all legislative enactments having such an object in view, is to increase, not diminish the rate of interest. When the rate fixed by law is less than the market, or customary rate, lenders and borrowers are obliged to resort to circuitous devices to evade the law; and as these devices are always attended with more or less trouble and risk, the rate of interest is proportionally enhanced. During the late war it was not uncommon for a person to be paying ten or twelve per cent for a loan, which, had there been no usury laws, he might have got for six or seven per cent. It is singular that an enactment which contradicts the most obvious principles, and which has been repeatedly condemned by committees of the legislature, should still be allowed to preserve a place in the statute book.*

* The prejudice against taking interest seems to have principally originated in a mistaken view of some enactments in the Mosaical law,

(see Michaelis on the "Laws of Moses," vol. ii. pp. 327—353, Eng. edit.), and in a statement of Aristotle to the effect that as money did not produce money, no return could equitably be claimed by the lender! The famous reformer Calvin has the merit of being one of the first who saw and exposed the futility of such notions. "Pecunia non parit pecuniam. Quid mare? quid domus, ex cujus locatione pensionem percipio? An ex tectis et parietibus argentum propriè nascitur? Sed et terra producit, et mari advehitur quod pecuniam deindè producat, et habitationis commoditas cum certâ pecuniâ parari commutarive solet. Quod si igitur plus ex negotiatione lucri percipi possit, quàm ex fundi cujusvis proventu. An feretur qui fundum sterilem fortassè colono locaverit ex quo mercedem vel proventum recipiat sibi, qui ex pecuniâ fructum aliquem perceperit, non feretur? et qui pecunia fundum acquirit, annon pecunia illa generat alteram annuam pecuniam? Undè vero mercatoris lucrum? Ex ipsius, inquies, diligentiâ atque industriâ. Quis dubitet pecuniam vacuam inutilem omnino esse? neque qui à me mutuam rogat, vacuam apud se habere à me acceptam cogitat. Non ergo ex pecuniâ illâ lucrum accedit, sed ex proventu. Illæ igitur rationes subtiles quidem sunt et speciem quandam habent, sed ubi propiùs expendentur, seipsa concidunt. Nunc igitur concludo, judicandum de usuris esse, non ex particulari aliquo Scripturæ loco, sed tantùm ex æquitatis regulâ."— *Calvini Epistolæ*, quoted by Mr. Stewart in the notes to his "Preliminary Dissertation to the Supplement to the Encyclopædia Britannica."

PRINCIPLES

OF

POLITICAL ECONOMY.

PART IV.

CONSUMPTION OF WEALTH.

HAVING, in the previous parts of this work, endeavoured to explain the means by which labour is facilitated and wealth produced, and to investigate the laws regulating its distribution among the various classes of society, we come now to the *fourth* and last division of the subject, or to that which treats of the Consumption of Wealth.

Definition of Consumption — Consumption the End of Production — Test of advantageous and disadvantageous Consumption — Sumptuary Laws — Advantage of a Taste for Luxuries — Error of Dr. Smith's Opinion with respect to unproductive Consumption — Error of those who contend, that to facilitate Production it is necessary to encourage wasteful Consumption — Statement of Montesquieu— Consumption of Government — Conclusion of the Work.

IT was formerly shewn, that by the production of a commodity was not meant the production of matter, that being the exclusive prerogative of Omnipotence, but the giving to matter already in existence such a shape as might fit it for ministering to our wants or enjoyments. In like manner, by consumption is not meant the consumption or annihilation of matter, for that is as impossible as its creation, but merely the consumption or annihilation of those qualities which render commodities useful and desirable. To consume the products of art and industry, is to deprive the matter of which they consist of the utility, and consequently of the exchangeable value, communicated to it by labour. And hence we are not to measure consumption by the magnitude, weight, or number of the products consumed, but *by their value* only. Large consumption is the destruction of large value, however small the bulk into which it may be compressed.

Consumption, in the sense in which the word is used in this science, is synonymous with use. We produce commodities only that we may use or consume them. Consumption is, in fact, the end and object of human exertion. All the products of art and industry are destined to be made use of or consumed; and when a commodity is in a state fit to be used, if its consumption be deferred, a loss is incurred. Commodities or products are intended either to satisfy the immediate wants, or to add to the enjoyments of their producers; or they are intended to be employed for the purpose of reproducing a greater value than themselves. In the *first* case, by delaying to use them, we refuse to satisfy a want, or deny ourselves a gratification it is in our power to obtain; and in the *second*, by delaying to use them, we allow the instruments of production to lie idle, and consequently lose the profit that might be derived from their employment.

But although all commodities are produced only to be consumed, we must not fall into the error of supposing that all consumption is equally advantageous to the individual or the society. It is not always, however, very easy to distinguish between advantageous or disadvantageous, or, as it is more commonly termed, productive and unproductive consumption. In so far, however, as the public interests are involved, (and it is such only that we have here to consider,) it may be laid down, that the consumption of any given quantity of the products of art and industry is productive, if it occasion, whether directly or indirectly, the production of the same or of a greater quantity of equally valuable products, and unproductive if it have not that effect. A knowledge of the mode in which, or the purpose for which, wealth has been laid out or consumed, will not warrant our affirming any thing as to its consumption being productive, or the reverse. To decide as to this, we must look at the *results* of the consumption, and at them only. By fixing the attention on the *species* of consumption carried on, and not on its results, this part of the science has been encumbered with imaginary distinctions, and has been rendered, in no ordinary degree, obscure and unintelligible. It is plainly not enough, for example, to prove that a quantity of wealth has been productively employed, to be told that it has been expended in the improvement of the soil, in the excavation of a canal, or in any similar undertaking; for it may have been laid out injudiciously, or in such a way that it cannot reproduce itself. Neither, on the other hand, is it enough to prove that a quantity of wealth has been laid out unproductively, to be told that it has been expended in equipages or entertainments; for the desire to indulge in this expense may have been the cause that the wealth was originally produced, and the desire to indulge in similar expense may occasion the subsequent production of a still greater quantity.

Hence it is clear that, if we would come to an accurate conclusion upon such points, we must carefully examine not the immediate only, but also the remote effects of any expenditure; pronouncing it to be productive when it causes, either by its direct or indirect operation, the reproduction of the same or of a greater amount of wealth, and unproductive when it is not fully replaced. It is not practicable to adopt any other criterion of productive and unproductive expenditure, without leading to the most contradictory conclusions.

But, whatever may be the mode in which commodities are consumed, it is plain that it is on the balance between consumption and reproduction that the advancement or decline of every nation is dependent. If, in given periods, the commodities produced in a country exceed those consumed in it, the means of increasing its capital will be provided, and its population will increase, or the actual numbers will be better accommodated, or both. If the consumption in such periods fully equal the reproduction, no means will be afforded of increasing the stock or capital of the nation, and society will be at a stand; and if the consumption exceed the reproduction, every succeeding period will see the society worse supplied: its prosperity and population will evidently decline, and pauperism will gradually spread itself over the whole country.

It seems to be impossible to fix on any standard for the regulation of individual expenditure. The sentiments of no two persons will ever exactly coincide with respect to the advantage to be derived from any expenditure of wealth; and as each must be admitted to be the best judge of what is profitable and advantageous for himself, there are no means of deciding which is right, or which is wrong. The opinions of different individuals depend on the circumstances under which they are placed. The rich man is naturally inclined to give a greater extension to the limits of advantageous consumption than the man of middling fortune, and the latter than he who is poor. And it is sufficiently plain, that a man's expenses should always bear some proportion to the magnitude of his fortune, his prospects, and station in society; and that what might be proper and advantageous expenditure in one case, might be highly improper and disadvantageous in another. These, however, are matters with respect to which individuals ought to have full liberty to use their own discretion; and though a few may waste their fortunes in wanton and unprofitable expense, we may be assured that the efforts of the vast majority will be directed to their increase.

Governments have been generally, or rather, perhaps,

it should be said, universally, more profuse than their subjects; but they have, notwithstanding, very frequently enacted *sumptuary* laws, to restrain what they were pleased to consider the improper expenditure of the latter. These laws were long popular in Rome, and were formerly enforced in this and most other European countries; but it may be safely affirmed that they have not, in any instance, been productive of any good effect. They are, in truth, a manifest infringement of the right of property; and no legislator can ever fetter his subjects in the disposal of the fruits of their industry, without rendering them less zealous about their acquisition, and in so far paralysing their exertions.

Sir Dudley North has set the effect of sumptuary laws in its true light. "Countries," he says, "which have these laws are generally poor; for, when men are thereby confined to narrower expense than they otherwise would be, they are at the same time discouraged from the industry and ingenuity which they would have employed in obtaining wherewithal to support them in the full latitude of expense they desire. It is possible, families may be supported by such means, but then the growth of wealth in the nation is hindered; for that never thrives better than when riches are tossed from hand to hand. The meaner sort, seeing their fellows become rich and great, are spirited up to imitate their industry. A tradesman sees his neighbour keep a coach; presently, all his endeavours are at work to do the like, and many times he is beggared by it; however, the extraordinary application he makes to gratify his vanity is beneficial to the public."*

The public interest requires that the national capital should, if possible, be kept constantly increasing; or, which is the same thing, that the consumption of any given period should be made the means of reproducing a greater amount of useful and desirable products. But it

* "Discourses on Trade," p. 15.

has been sufficiently proved that this cannot be brought about by a system of *surveillance* and restriction. Industry and frugality never have been, and never can be, promoted by its means. To render a man industrious, secure him the peaceable enjoyment of the fruits of his industry; to wean him from extravagance, and to render him frugal and parsimonious, allow him to reap all the disadvantage of the one line of conduct, and all the advantage of the other.

Besides, it is clear that sumptuary laws, even were they in other respects advantageous, must necessarily be partial and oppressive in their operation. What would be wanton and ridiculous extravagance in one man, may be well-regulated moderate expenditure in another. If, therefore, for the sake of the prodigal, this expense be proscribed, the other is deprived of those gratifications to which his fortune entitles him; and if it be allowed to those who *can afford it*, then, in order to ascertain to whom the regulation is applicable, an odious and generally ineffectual investigation must be instituted into the circumstances of individuals. Certainly, however, it is no part of the business of government to pry into the affairs of its subjects. It was not framed for the purpose of keeping their accounts and balancing their ledgers, but in order to protect the equal rights and liberties of all. "If its own extravagance do not ruin the state, that of others never will." The poverty and loss of station which is the inevitable result of improvident and prodigal consumption, is a sufficient security against its ever becoming injuriously prevalent; and wherever the public burdens are moderate, property protected, and the freedom of industry secured, the constant efforts of the great body of the people to rise in the world and improve their condition, will insure the continued increase of national wealth. It is idle to expect that all unproductive expenditure will ever be avoided; but the experience of every tolerably well-governed state proves, that the amount of the produce of industry productively expended is always infinitely greater than that which is expended unproductively.

It was long a prevalent opinion among moralists, that the consumption and consequently the production of luxuries, was unprofitable and disadvantageous. If a man wished to get rich, his object, it was said, ought not to be to increase his fortune, but to lessen his wants. "*Si quem volueris esse divitem*," says Seneca, "*non est quod augeas divitias, sed minuas cupiditates.*" Had these opinions ever obtained any considerable influence, they would have formed an insuperable obstacle to all improvement. Those who are contented with the situation in which they are placed are without any motive to aspire at any thing better; and hence it is to the absence of this feeling of contentment, and the existence of that which is directly opposed to it, —to the desire to rise in the world, to improve our condition, and to obtain a constantly increasing command over the conveniences and luxuries of life, that society is indebted for every improvement. It is not matter of blame, but of praise, that individuals strive to attain to superior wealth and distinction; that they scruple not

> "Contendere nobilitate
> Noctes atque dies, niti præstante labore
> Ad summas emergere opes, rerumque potiri."

Ambition to rise is censurable only when, in order to forward our object, we resort to means injurious to the welfare of others. So long as we depend for success on the fair exercise of our talents and industry, it is deserving of every commendation. Until it has been excited, no progress can be made in civilisation; and the more powerful it becomes, the more rapid will be the accumulation of wealth, and the more prosperous will every individual be rendered. The mere necessaries of life may be obtained with comparatively little labour; and those uncivilised tribes who have no desire to possess its comforts, are proverbially indolent and dissipated. To make men industrious—to make them shake off that lethargy which benumbs their faculties when in a rude or depressed condition, they must be inspired with a taste for the comforts, luxuries, and enjoyments of civilised life. When this is done, their artificial wants become equally clamorous with those that are strictly necessary, and they increase exactly as the means of gratifying them increase. Wherever a taste for comforts and conveniences has been generally diffused, the desires of man become altogether unlimited. The gratification of one leads directly to the formation of another. In highly civilised societies, new products and new modes of enjoyment are constantly presenting themselves as motives to exertion, and as means of rewarding it. Perseverance is, in consequence, given to all the operations of industry; and idleness, and its attendant train of evils, almost entirely disappear. "What," asks Dr. Paley, "can be less necessary, or less connected with the sustentation of human life, than the whole produce of the silk, lace, and plate manufactory? yet what multitudes labour in the different branches of these arts! What can be imagined more capricious than the fondness for tobacco and snuff? yet how many various occupations, and how many thousands in each, are set at work in administering to this frivolous gratification!" The *stimulus* which the desire to possess these articles gives to industry renders their introduction advantageous. The earth is capable of furnishing food adequate for the support of a much greater number of human beings than can be employed in its cultivation. But those who are in possession of the soil will not part with their produce for nothing, or, rather, they will not raise at all what they can neither use themselves nor exchange for what they want. As soon, however, as a taste for conveniences and luxuries has been introduced, the occupiers of the ground extort from it the utmost that it can be made to produce, and exchange the surplus for the conveniences and gratifications they are desirous of obtaining; and, in consequence, the producers of these articles, though they have neither property in the soil nor any concern in its cultivation, are regularly and liberally supplied with its produce. In this way the quantity of *necessaries*, as well as of useful and agreeable products, is vastly increased by the introduction of a taste for luxuries; and the population is not only better provided for, but rapidly augmented.

Mr. Locke has given the sanction of his authority to this doctrine. "What," says he, "would a man value ten thousand or an hundred thousand acres of excellent land, ready cultivated, and well stocked, too, with cattle, in the middle of the inland parts of America, where he had no hopes of commerce with other parts of the world, to draw money (or the conveniences and luxuries produced by others) to him by the sale of the product? It would not be worth the enclosing, and we should see him give up again to the wild common of nature whatever was more than would supply the conveniences of life, to be had there for him and his family."*

And yet there is hardly a single article among those that are now reckoned most indispensable to existence, or a single improvement of any sort, which has not been denounced at its introduction as a useless superfluity, or as being in some way injurious. Few articles of clothing are at present considered more essential than shirts; but there are instances on record of individuals being put in the pillory for presuming to use so expensive and unnecessary a luxury! Chimneys were not commonly used in England until the middle of the sixteenth century; and, in the introductory discourse to "Hollinshed's Chronicles," published in 1577, there is a bitter complaint of the multitude of chimneys lately erected, of the exchange of straw pallets for mattresses or flock-beds, and of wooden platters for earthen-

* "Second Treatise concerning Government," cap. 5.

ware and pewter. In another place, he laments that nothing but oak is used for building, instead of willow as heretofore;—adding, that "formerly our houses indeed were of willow, but our men were of oak; but now that our houses are of oak, our men are not only of willow, but some altogether of straw, which is a sore alteration!"

Many volumes have been filled with lamentations over the prevalence of a taste for tea, sugar, coffee, spices, and other foreign luxuries; and the idea that their consumption is prejudicial to the increase of wealth, is still very common. Voltaire, whose opinions on such subjects are, for the most part, very correct, has in this instance given currency to the prevailing delusion. "Henry IV." says he, "breakfasted on a glass of wine and wheaten bread; he neither used tea, nor coffee, nor chocolate; whereas the products of Martinique, Mocha, and China, are now served up at the breakfast of a lady's maid! And if we reflect that these products cost France upwards of 50 millions a-year, we must obviously be carrying on some very advantageous branches of commerce to enable us to support this *continued loss*." But the gold and silver exported to India are procured in exchange for commodities produced in France; and what is the motive for the production of these commodities? Evidently, that they may be employed as means to obtain the tea, coffee, sugar, &c., for which there is a demand. Take away the taste for these articles, or prohibit their importation, and the export of the precious metals to India will immediately cease; but so will also the production of the commodities with which these metals are purchased; for, to suppose that they should still be produced, would be to suppose that men may be industrious without an object! Instead, therefore, of being enriched by the cessation of the demand for the articles in question, France would be rendered so much the poorer. She would retrograde in the scale of civilisation. Her inhabitants would be less industrious, and enjoy fewer gratifications.

"Un préjugé vulgaire," says the Marquis Garnier, "porte à regarder comme désavantageux l'échange dans lequel on donne un morceau de métal qui peut durer des siècles, pour avoir une denrée que la consommation va détruire en une minute. Cependant, le métal, ainsi que la plante, n'ont de valeur qu'en raison du travail qu'ils ont coûté ; l'argent ne manquera pas plus que le thé au travail qui voudra l'extraire du sein de la terre ; et de ces deux substances, celle qui se consomme le plus rapidement est, par cette même raison, celle qui tient plus de travail en activité. Une révolution qui abîmeroit sous les eaux toutes les mines de l'Amérique appauvrirait fort peu les nations de l'Europe. Mais si le sucre, le café, le thé, &c. venaient à perdre tout-à-coup leur saveur et leur arôme, s'ils n'avaient plus la propriété de charmer le palais, ils cesseraient de tenir rang parmi les richesses ; alors s'arrêterait le travail qui les produit dans les deux Indes, et, par contre-coup, tout le travail qui s'exerce en Europe pour les acheter." *

It is not meant, by any thing now stated, to imply that the stimulus given to industry and invention by a desire to indulge in luxurious gratifications, is the best imaginable stimulus. Undoubtedly, it were far better were the immense sums that are so often lavished on the most ridiculous frivolities, applied to promote some useful art, science, or industrious undertaking, or expended in re-

* "Richesse des Nations," tom. v. p. 509. The excessive indolence of the Mexicans has been ascribed partly to the facility of obtaining supplies of food by the cultivation of the banana, and partly to the mildness of the climate, which renders clothing and lodging of inferior importance. Humboldt mentions, that it is a prevalent opinion, that nothing short of the extirpation of the banana will ever render them industrious. It may, however, be expected that the altered circumstances under which Mexico is now placed, the many new avenues the revolution has opened to wealth and consideration, and the desire that will most probably be excited to obtain those European commodities which the freedom of commerce will pour into the country at a comparatively cheap rate, will infuse a spirit of industry into the inhabitants.

lieving those whom accident or misfortune has involved in unmerited distress. But we have to deal with man as he is, and not as we might wish him to be. And so selfish is human nature, that the desire of doing good to others, or of promoting the interests of science, has never, generally speaking, influenced man half so strongly as the desire to command some additional, though perhaps trivial, personal indulgence. The selfish passions are not, however, strengthened by a taste for luxurious accommodations. On the contrary, experience shews, that when this taste is comparatively feeble, sloth and barbarism uniformly usurp its place; and that the more generous sympathies are always most powerful in opulent, industrious, and refined communities.

The supposed pernicious influence which moralists have so often ascribed to luxury and refinement in the arts, seems to have principally originated in their contrasting the rapid growth of the Roman republic during the period of its rusticity and poverty, and the disinterestedness then so frequently displayed, with the decline of the martial spirit, the loss of liberty, and the venality that universally prevailed after the revenues and refinements of Greece and Asia had been introduced into Rome. But these disorders really arose from the defective nature of the government at home, the too great extension of the territory, and the oppressions exercised upon the provinces. "Refinement," says Mr. Hume, "on the pleasures and conveniences of life, has no natural tendency to beget venality and corruption. The value which all men put upon any particular pleasure depends on comparison and experience; nor is a porter less greedy of money, which he spends on bacon and brandy, than a courtier who purchases champagne and ortolans. Riches are valuable at all times, and to all men, because they always purchase pleasures such as men are accustomed to and desire; nor can any thing restrain and regulate the love of money but a sense of honour and virtue, which, if it be not nearly equal at all times, will generally abound most in ages of knowledge and refinement."*

It is plain, therefore, that the consumption of luxuries cannot, provided it be confined within proper limits, be justly considered as disadvantageous either in a moral or political point of view. If, indeed, a man consume more luxuries than his labour or his fortune enable him to command, his consumption will be disadvantageous. But it will be equally disadvantageous if he consume a greater quantity of *necessaries* than he can afford. The mischief does not consist in the *species* of articles consumed, but in the *excess of their value* over the means of purchasing them possessed by the consumer. This, however, is a fault which ought always to be left to be corrected by the self-interest of those concerned. The poverty and degradation caused by indulging in unproductive consumption is a sufficient guarantee against its ever being carried to an injurious extent. And to attempt to lessen unproductive consumption by proscribing luxury, is in effect attempting to enrich a country by taking away the most powerful incentives to production!

Dr. Smith has given another criterion of productive and unproductive consumption; but his opinions on this subject, though exceedingly ingenious, and supported with his usual ability, appear to be destitute of any solid foundation. He divides society into two great classes. The *first* consists of those who fix, or, as he terms it, "realise their labour in some particular subject, or vendible commodity, which lasts for some time at least after that labour is past;" the *second*, of those whose labour leaves nothing in existence after the moment of exertion, but perishes in the act of performance. The former are said by Dr. Smith to be productive, the latter unproductive, labourers. Not that, in making this distinction, Dr. Smith meant to undervalue the services

* "Philosophical Works," vol. iii. p. 310.

performed by the unproductive class, or to deny that they are often of the highest utility; for he admits that such is frequently the case: but he contends that these services, however useful, do not augment the wealth of the country; and, consequently, that the commodities consumed by this class are unproductively consumed, and have a tendency to impoverish, not to enrich. But to avoid the chance of misrepresentation, I shall give Dr. Smith's opinions in his own words.

"There is one sort of labour," says he, "which adds to the value of the subject upon which it is bestowed; there is another which has no such effect. The former, as it produces a value, may be called productive; the latter unproductive labour. Thus, the labour of a manufacturer adds, generally, to the value of the materials which he works upon, that of his own maintenance, and of his master's profit. The labour of a menial servant, on the contrary, adds to the value of nothing. Though the manufacturer has his wages advanced to him by his master, he, in reality, costs him no expense, the value of those wages being generally restored, together with a profit, in the improved value of the subject upon which his labour is bestowed; but the maintenance of a menial servant never is restored. A man grows rich by employing a multitude of manufacturers; he grows poor by maintaining a multitude of menial servants. The labour of the latter, however, has its value, and deserves its reward, as well as that of the former. But the labour of the manufacturer fixes and realises itself in some particular subject, or vendible commodity, which lasts for some time at least after that labour is past. It is, as it were, a certain quantity of labour stocked and stored up, to be employed, if necessary, upon some other occasion. That subject, or, what is the same thing, the price of that subject, can afterwards, if necessary, put into motion a quantity of labour equal to that which had originally produced it. The labour of the menial servant, on the contrary, does not fix or realise itself in any particular subject or vendible commodity. His services generally perish in the very instant of their performance, and seldom leave any trace or value behind them for which an equal quantity of service could afterwards be procured.

"The labour of some of the most respectable orders in the society is like that of menial servants, unproductive of any value, and does not fix or realise itself in any permanent subject or vendible commodity, which endures after that labour is past, and for which an equal quantity of labour could afterwards be procured. The sovereign, for example, with all the officers both of justice and war who serve under him, the whole army and navy, are unproductive labourers. They are the servants of the public, and are maintained by a part of the annual produce of the industry of other people. Their service, how honourable, how necessary, or how useful soever, produces nothing for which an equal quantity of service can afterwards be procured. The protection, security, and defence of the commonwealth, the effect of their labour this year, will not purchase its protection, security, and defence, for the year to come. In the same class must be ranked some both of the greatest and most important, and some of the most frivolous professions: churchmen, lawyers, physicians, men of letters of all kinds; players, buffoons, musicians, opera-singers, opera-dancers, &c. The labour of the meanest of these has a certain value, regulated by the very same principles which regulate that of every other sort of labour; and that of the noblest and most useful produces nothing which could afterwards purchase or procure an equal quantity of labour. Like the declamation of the actor, the harangue of the orator, or the tune of the musician, the work of all of them perishes in the very instant of its production." *

But though these statements are plausible, it will not, I apprehend, be difficult to shew the fallacy of the distinc-

* "Wealth of Nations," vol. ii. pp. 93—95.

tion Dr. Smith has endeavoured to establish. To begin with his strongest case, that of the menial servant: He says, that his labour is unproductive, because it is not realised in a vendible commodity, while the labour of the manufacturer is productive, because it is so realised. But of what is the labour of the manufacturer productive? Does it not consist of comforts and conveniences required for the use and accommodation of society? The manufacturer is not a producer of matter, but of utility only. And is it not obvious that the menial servant is also a producer of utility? It is universally allowed, that the labour of the husbandman who raises corn, beef, and other articles of provision, is productive; but if so, why is the labour of the menial servant who prepares and dresses these articles, and fits them for use, to be set down as unproductive? It is clear to demonstration, that there is no difference whatever between the two species of industry—that they are either both productive, or both unproductive. To produce a fire, it is quite as indispensable that coals should be carried from the cellar to the grate, as that they should be carried from the bottom of the mine to the surface of the earth: and if it be said that the miner is a productive labourer, must we not say as much of the servant who is employed to make and mend the fire? The whole of Dr. Smith's reasoning proceeds on a false hypothesis. He has made a distinction where there is none, and where it is not in the nature of things there can be any. The end of all human exertion is the same; that is, to increase the sum of necessaries, comforts, and enjoyments; and it must be left to the judgment of every one to determine what proportion of these comforts he will have in the shape of menial services, and what in the shape of material products. It is true, as has been sometimes stated, that the results of the labour of the menial servant are seldom capable of being estimated in the same way as the results of the labour of the agriculturist, manufacturer, or merchant: but are they, on that account, the less real or valuable? Could the same quantity of work be performed by those who are called productive labourers, were it not for the assistance they derive from those who are falsely called unproductive? A merchant or banker, realising 5,000*l.* or 10,000*l.* a year by his business, may perhaps be expending 1,000*l.* on his servants: now, suppose that he tries, by turning his servants adrift, to save this sum; he must henceforth, it is obvious, become coachman, footman, cook, and washerwoman, for himself; and if he do this, he will, instead of making 5,000*l.* or 10,000*l.* a-year, be most probably unable to make even 50*l.*! No doubt a man will be ruined if he keep more servants than he has occasion for, or than he can afford to pay; but his ruin will be equally certain if he purchase an excess of food or clothes, or employ more work-men in any branch of manufacture than are required to carry it on, or than his capital can employ. To keep two ploughmen when one only might suffice, is as improvident and wasteful expenditure as it is to keep two footmen to do the business of one. It is in the extravagant quantity of the commodities we consume, or of the labour we employ, and not in the particular species of commodities or labour, that we must seek for the causes of impoverishment.

The same reasoning applies to all the cases mentioned by Dr. Smith. Take, for example, the case of the physician. We are told that he is an unproductive labourer, because he does not directly produce something that has exchangeable value: but if he do the same thing *indirectly*, what is the difference? If the exertions of the physician be conducive to health, and if, as is undoubtedly the case, he enable others to produce more than they could do without his assistance, it is plain that he is indirectly at least, if not directly, a productive labourer. Dr. Smith makes no scruple about admitting the just title of the workman employed to repair a steam-engine to be enrolled in the productive class; and yet he would place a physician, who had been instrumental in saving the life of Arkwright or Watt, among those that are unproductive! It is impossible that these inconsistencies and contradictions could have occurred to Dr. Smith; and the errors into which he has fallen in treating this important branch of the science, shew, in the strongest manner, the absolute necessity of advancing with extreme caution, and of subjecting every theory, how ingenious soever it may appear when first stated, to a severe and patient examination.

An occupation may be futile and trifling to the last degree without being unproductive. We are entitled, at once, to affirm, that an individual who employs himself an hour a day in blowing bubbles, or building houses of cards, is engaged in a futile employment; but we are not, without further inquiry, entitled to affirm that it is unproductive. This will depend on a contingency: the employment will be as unproductive as it is frivolous, if it do not stimulate the individual to make any greater exertion during the remaining twenty-three hours of the twenty-four than he did previously; but if, in order to indemnify himself for the time that is thus spent, he produce as many useful and desirable commodities during the period he can still devote to that purpose as he previously produced, the employment will *not* be unproductive; and if the desire to indulge in it lead him to produce more commodities than he did before, it will be profitable.

Dr. Paley had a distinct perception of this doctrine, and has stated it with his usual force and clearness. "A watch," he observes, "may be a very unnecessary appendage to the dress of a peasant; yet if the peasant will till the ground in order to obtain a watch, the true design of commerce is answered; and the watchmaker, while he polishes the case and files the wheels of his ingenious machine, is contributing to the production of corn as effectually, though not so directly, as if he handled the plough or the spade. The use of tobacco is an acknowledged superfluity; but if the fisherman will ply his nets, and the mariner fetch rice from foreign countries, in order to procure to himself this indulgence, the market is supplied with two important articles of provision by the instrumentality of a merchandise which has no other apparent use than the gratification of a vitiated palate."*

It is on this principle that the productiveness of players, singers, opera-dancers, buffoons, &c. depends. A taste for the amusements they afford has exactly the same effect on national wealth as a taste for tobacco, champagne, or any other luxury. We wish to be present at their exhibitions; and, in order to get admittance, we pay the price or equivalent demanded by them for their services. But this price or equivalent is not a gratuitous product of nature—it is the result of industry. And hence it is, that the amusements afforded by these persons—how trifling soever they may seem in the estimation of cynics and *soi-disant* moralists—create new wants, and by so doing necessarily stimulate our industry to procure the means of gratifying them. They are unquestionably, therefore, a *cause* of production; and it is very like a truism to say that what is a cause of production must be productive.†

Our great moralist, Dr. Johnson, has maintained the same doctrine. "Many things," he observes, "which

* Works, vol. ii. p. 80, ed. 1819.

† The doctrine now laid down has been enforced with considerable ability in a work entitled, "Théorie du Luxe," published in 1771. "Celui qui veut avoir le bijou le plus frivole, ou le meuble le plus utile, ne peut acquérir l'un ou l'autre que par son travail, ou en payant le travail d'un ouvrier. S'il travaille lui-même la chose, soit utile soit frivole, qu'il veut avoir, il doit être précédemment pourvû de sa subsistance et des autres besoins: s'il emprunte la main d'un autre, il doit pourvoir de son côté à la subsistance et au reste des besoins de cet autre, ou lui donner un équivalent au prorata du tems que la chose exige. Dans les deux cas, il n'y a d'employés que du tems et des soins qui ne sont point soustraits au necessaire. Les deux habitans sont entretenus;

are false are transmitted from book to book, and gain credit in the world. One of these is the cry against the evil of luxury. Now, the truth is, that luxury produces much good. Take the luxury of the buildings in London: does it not produce real advantage in the conveniency and elegance of accommodation, and this all from the exertion of industry? People will tell you, with a melancholy face, how many builders are in gaol. It is plain they are in gaol—not for building, for rents have not fallen. A man gives half-a-guinea for a dish of green peas. How much gardening does this occasion! how many labourers must the competition to have such things early in the market keep in employment! You will hear it said, very gravely, 'Why was not the half-guinea thus spent in luxury given to the poor?' Alas! has it not gone to the *industrious* poor, whom it is better to support than the *idle* poor? You are much surer that you are doing good when you pay money to those that work, than when you give money merely in charity."*

The productiveness of the higher class of function-

les charges de l'état sont acquittées; le produit de ce travail, soit dans un genre soit dans l'autre, augmente également la masse des richesses nationales. Les superfluités ont au prix comme les choses utiles.

"Supposons les superfluités défendus ou ignorées; et supposons, ce qui est aujourd'hui bien éloigné de la réalité, que chacun ait la liberté de tirer de la terre ses besoins: alors l'homme actif, qui par le produit de son travail seroit en état de se procurer des superfluités, et qui n'est pas tenté d'autre chose, ne sachant que faire du fruit de ses peines, ne travaille plus tant. Celui qui se seroit addonné à fabriquer les superfluités, cultive pour obtenir sa subsistance, et ne va pas au-delà. Voilà donc deux habitans seulement entretenus, comme dans l'hypothèse contraire. L'état a de moins une place dans l'agriculture, et la valeur des superfluités qui auroient été fabriquées.

"Il en est de même des satisfactions que l'on tire des choses nonmatérielles; telles que la danse, la musique, &c. Supprimez ces plaisirs, les hommes qui y sont employés cultivent la terre; ceux qui les employoient cultivent moins. Il n'y a ni plus d'hommes ni plus de produits, et la société a moins d'arts et de jouissances."—P. 64.

* Boswell's "Life of Johnson," vol. iii. p. 52.

aries mentioned by Dr. Smith is still more obvious. Far, indeed, from being unproductive, they are, when they properly discharge the duties of their high station, the most productive labourers in a state. Dr. Smith says, that the results of their service, that is, to use his own words, "the protection, security, and defence of the commonwealth, any one year, will not purchase its protection, security, and defence, for the year to come." But this is plainly an error. Every one will allow that the corn and other commodities produced by the society this year form, along with portions of those produced in previous years, its capital, or its means of producing a supply of necessaries, conveniences, and enjoyments, for the ensuing year. But without the security and protection afforded by government, this capital would either not exist at all, or its quantity would be very greatly diminished. How, then, is it possible to deny that those whose labour is necessary to afford this security are productively employed? Take a parallel case, that of the labourers employed to construct fences: no one ever presumed to doubt that their labour is productive; and yet they do not contribute directly to the production of corn or of any other valuable product. The object of their industry is to give protection and security; to guard the fields that have been fertilised and planted by the husbandman from depredation; and to enable him to prosecute his employment without having his attention distracted by the care of watching. But if the security and protection afforded by the hedger or ditcher justly entitle him to be classed among those who contribute to enrich their country, on what pretence can those public servants who protect property in the mass, and render every portion of it secure against hostile aggression, and the attacks of thieves and plunderers, be said to be unproductive? If the herdsmen who protect a single corn field from the neighbouring crows and cattle be productive, then surely the judges and magistrates, the soldiers and sailors, who protect every field in the empire, and to whom it is owing that all classes of inhabitants feel secure in the enjoyment of their rights and privileges, have a good claim to be classed among those whose services are super-eminently productive.

That much wealth has been unproductively consumed by the servants of the public, both in this and other countries, it is impossible to doubt. But we are not to argue from the abuses extrinsic to a beneficial institution against the institution itself. If the public pay their servants excessive salaries, or employ a greater number than is required for the purposes of good government and security, it is their own fault. Their conduct is similar to that of a manufacturer who should pay his labourers comparatively high wages, and employ more of them than he had occasion for. But, although a state, or an individual, may act in this foolish and extravagant manner, it would be rather rash thence to conclude that *all* public servants and *all* manufacturing labourers are unproductive! If the establishments which provide security and protection be formed on an extravagant scale,—if we have more judges or magistrates, more soldiers or sailors, than are necessary, or if we pay them larger salaries than would suffice to procure the services of others, let their numbers and their salaries be reduced. The excess, if there be any, is not a fault inherent in the nature of such establishments, but results entirely from the extravagant scale on which they have been arranged.

But, in shewing that Dr. Smith was mistaken in considering the consumption of menial servants, and of lawyers, physicians, and public functionaries, unproductive, we must beware of falling into the opposite extreme, and of countenancing the erroneous and infinitely more dangerous doctrine of those who contend that consumption, even when most unproductive, ought to be encouraged as a means of stimulating production, and of increasing the demand for labour! The consumption of the classes mentioned by Dr. Smith is advantageous, because they render services which those who employ them, and who are the only proper judges in such a case, consider of greater value than the wages they pay them. But the case would be totally different were government and those who employ labourers to do so, not in order to profit by their services, but to stimulate production by their consumption! It is absurd to suppose that wasteful consumption can ever encourage production. A man is stimulated to produce when he finds a ready market for the products of his labour, that is, when he can readily exchange them for other products. And hence the efficient and only real encouragement of industry consists, not in an increase of wasteful and improvident consumption, but, as was formerly shewn, in an increase of production.

It must, however, be remembered, consistently with what has been previously advanced, that in deciding as to the character of the consumption or expenditure of any quantity of wealth, we must look at its indirect and ultimate, as well as its direct and immediate effects. An outlay of capital or labour which, if we take its immediate results only into account, we should pronounce improvident and unproductive, may yet be discovered, by looking at it in its different bearings and in its remote influences, to be distinctly the reverse; and it is also true, that cases frequently occur in which that expenditure which is ruinous to the individual may not be injurious, but beneficial to the state.

Montesquieu has said, "*Si les riches ne dépensent pas beaucoup, les pauvres mourront de faim.*"* The truth of this proposition has, however, been disputed; nor is this to be wondered at, as it may be either true or false according to the sense in which it is understood. If it be

* "Esprit des Loix," liv. vii. cap. 4.

construed to mean, that a rich man will be able *directly* to employ a greater number of servants or labourers if he spend his revenue in luxurious accommodations, than if he lay out a part of it on the improvement of his estate, or accumulate it as a provision for his younger children, it is plainly erroneous. The demand for labour cannot be sensibly increased without an increase of capital; and it is quite impossible for those who spend their whole revenue on immediate gratifications to amass any capital, or, consequently, to employ an additional individual. But the proposition advanced by Montesquieu should not be interpreted in this confined sense, or as referring only to the influence of the expenditure of wealthy individuals on their *own* demand for labour, but as referring to its influence on that of the society: and if we so interpret it, and suppose it to mean, that the lavish expenditure and luxury of the great and the affluent becomes a means of materially benefiting the poor by exciting the emulation of others, who cannot expect, except through an increase of industry and economy, to be able to indulge in a similar scale of expense, it will, I apprehend, be found to be perfectly correct. To suppose, indeed, that the passion for luxurious gratifications should decline amongst the rich, and that men should, notwithstanding, continue equally industrious, is a contradiction. Riches are desirable only because they afford the means of obtaining these gratifications; and so powerful is the influence of a taste for them, that it may be doubted whether the extravagance which has ruined so many individuals, has not been, by giving birth to new arts and new efforts of emulation and ingenuity, of material advantage to the public.

These remarks are not made in the view of countenancing extravagant expenditure, but merely to shew that those who attempt to decide as to the influence, in a public point of view, of any outlay of wealth, without endeavouring to appreciate and weigh its remote as well as its immediate effects, must, when they are right in their conclusions, be so only through accident. But, without insisting further on this point, it is abundantly certain that there is nothing to fear from the improvidence of individuals. There is not, as has been already observed, an instance of any people having ever missed an opportunity to save and amass. And in all tolerably well-governed countries, the principle of accumulation has always had a marked ascendancy over the principle of expense.

Individuals are fully sensible of the value of the articles they expend; for, in the vast majority of instances, they are the produce of their own industry and frugality; and they rarely consume them unless in order to subsist, or to obtain some really equivalent advantage. Such, however, it must be allowed, is not often the case with the consumption of governments and their servants. They do not consume their own wealth, but the wealth of others; and this circumstance prevents them from being so much interested in its profitable outlay, or so much alive to the injurious consequences of wasteful expenditure, as their subjects. But economy on the part of governments, though more difficult to practise, is of infinitely greater importance than economy on the part of individuals. A private gentleman may, inasmuch as he is the master of his own fortune, dispose of it as he pleases. He may act on the erroneous principle of profusion being a virtue, or he may attempt to excite the emulation and industry of his fellow-citizens by the splendour of his equipages and the magnificence of his mode of living. But government can, with propriety, do none of these things. It is merely a trustee for the affairs of others; and it is, consequently, bound to administer them as economically as possible. Were the principle admitted, that government might raise money, not for the protection and good government of the state, but in order to excite industry and ingenuity by the pressure of taxation, or the luxury of public functionaries, an avenue would be opened to every species of malversation. It is, indeed, pretty certain that no people would submit to be taxed for such purposes; but if they did, the flagrant abuses to which it would inevitably lead could scarcely fail of ending either in revolution or in national poverty and degradation. Economy in expenditure is, upon all occasions, the first virtue of government, and the most pressing of its duties.

I have now brought this view of the Principles of Political Economy to a close. I have endeavoured to shew the indissoluble connexion subsisting between private and public opulence,— to shew that whatever has any tendency to increase the former, must, to the same extent, increase the latter; and that SECURITY OF PROPERTY, FREEDOM OF INDUSTRY, DIFFUSION OF SOUND INFORMATION, AND MODERATION IN THE PUBLIC EXPENDITURE, are the only, as they are the certain, means by which the various powers and resources of human talent and ingenuity can be called into action, and society made continually to advance in the career of wealth and civilisation. Every increase of security, freedom, and intelligence, is a benefit, as every diminution, whether of one only or of all, is an evil. I have endeavoured to shew, that there is no real opposition of interests amongst the various classes of the community; that they are all mutually dependent upon each other; and that any favour or advantage given to one class, at the expense of the rest, is not only immediately injurious to the latter, and subversive of that equality of protection which every just government will always grant indiscriminately to all who are under its protection, but that it is not either really or lastingly beneficial to those whose interests it is intended to promote. The true line of policy is to leave individuals to pursue their own interest in their own way, and never to lose sight of the maxim *pas trop gouverner*. It is by the spontaneous and unconstrained, but well-protected efforts of individuals to improve their condition, and to rise in the world, and by them only, that nations become rich and powerful. The labour and the savings of individuals are at once the source and the measure of national opulence and public prosperity. They may be compared to the drops of dew which invigorate and mature all vegetable nature: none of them has, singly, any perceptible influence; but we owe the foliage of summer and the fruits of autumn to their combined action.

APPENDIX.

Note A. Page 53.

That M. Quesnay is entitled to the merit of originality, cannot be disputed. It is certain, however, that he had been anticipated in several of his peculiar doctrines by some English writers of the previous century. The fundamental principles of the economical system are distinctly and clearly stated in a tract entitled, "Reasons for a limited Exportation of Wool," published in 1677. "That it is of the greatest concern and interest of the nation," says the author of the tract, "to preserve the nobility, gentry, and those to whom the land of the country belongs, at least, much greater than a few artificers employed in working the superfluity of our wool, or the merchants who gain by the exportation of our manufactures, is manifest—1. Because they are the *masters and proprietaries of the foundation of all the wealth in this nation, all profit arising out of the ground, which is theirs; 2. Because they bear all taxes and public burdens;* which, in truth, are only borne by those who buy, and sell not; all sellers raising the price of their commodities, or abating of goodness, according to their taxes."—P. 5.

In 1696, Mr. Asgill published a treatise entitled, "Several Assertions proved, in order to create another Species of Money than Gold," in support of Dr. Chamberlayne's proposition for a Land Bank. The following extract from this treatise breathes, as Mr. Stewart has justly observed, in his "Life of Dr. Smith," the very spirit of Quesnay's philosophy:—

"What we call commodities is nothing but land severed from the soil—*man deals in nothing but earth.* The merchants are the factors of the world, to exchange one part of the earth for another. The king himself is fed by the labour of the ox: and the clothing of the army and victualling of the navy must all be paid for to the owner of the soil as the ultimate receiver. All things in the world are originally the produce of the ground, and there must all things be raised."—(This passage has been quoted in Lord Lauderdale's " Inquiry into the Nature and Origin of Public Wealth," 2d ed. p. 109.)

These passages are interesting, as exhibiting the first germs of the theory of the Economists. But there is no reason whatever to suppose that Quesnay was aware of the existence of either of the tracts referred to. The subjects treated in them were of too local a description to excite the attention of foreigners; and Quesnay was too candid to conceal his obligations, had he really owed them any. It is probable he might have seen Mr. Locke's treatise on " Raising the Value of Money," where the idea is thrown out that all taxes fall ultimately on the land. But there is an immeasurable difference between the suggestion of Locke and the well-digested system of Quesnay.

I subjoin from the work of Dupont, " Sur l'Origine et Progrès d'une Science Nouvelle," a short statement of the various institutions the Economists held to be necessary for the good government of a country.

" Voici le résumé de toutes les institutions sociales fondées sur l'ordre naturel, sur la constitution physique des hommes et des autres êtres dont ils sont environnés.

" *Propriété personnelle*, établie par la nature, par la nécessité physique dont il est à chaque individu de disposer de toutes les facultés de sa personne pour se procurer les choses propres à satisfaire ses besoins, sous peine de souffrance et de mort.

" *Liberté de travail*, inséparable de la propriété personnelle, dont elle forme une partie constitutive.

" *Propriété mobiliaire*, qui n'est que la propriété personnelle même, considérée dans son usage, dans son objet, dans son extension nécessaire sur les choses acquises par le travail de sa personne.

" *Liberté d'échange*, de commerce, d'emploi de ses richesses, inséparable de la propriété personnelle et de la propriété mobiliaire.

" *Culture*, qui est un usage de la propriété personnelle, de la propriété mobiliaire, et de la liberté qui en est inséparable: usage profitablé, nécessaire, indispensable pour que la population puisse s'accroître, par une suite de la multiplication des productions nécessaires à la subsistance des hommes.

" *Propriété foncière*, suite nécessaire de la culture, et qui n'est que la conservation de la propriété personnelle et de la propriété mobiliaire, employées aux travaux et aux dépenses préparatoires indispensables pour mettre la terre en état d'être cultivée.

" *Liberté de l'emploi de sa terre*, de l'espèce de sa culture, de toutes les conventions relatives à l'exploitation, à la concession, à la rétrocession, à l'échange, à la vente de sa terre, inséparable de la propriété foncière.

" Partage naturel des récoltes, *en reprises des cultivateurs*, ou richesses dont l'emploi doit indispensablement être de perpétuer la culture, sous peine de diminution des récoltes et de la population et *produit net*, ou richesses disponibles dont la grandeur décide de la prospérité de la société, dont l'emploi est abandonné à la volonté et à l'intérêt des propriétaires fonciers, et qui constitue pour eux le prix naturel et légitime des dépenses qu'ils ont faits, et des travaux auxquels ils se sont livrés pour mettre la terre en état d'être cultivé.

" *Sûreté*, sans laquelle la propriété et la liberté ne seraient que de droit et non de fait, sans laquelle le *produit net* serait bientôt anéanti, sans laquelle la culture même ne pourrait subsister.

" *Autorité tutélaire et souveraine*, pour procurer la sûreté essentiellement nécessaire à la propriété et à la liberté ; et qui s'acquitte de cet important ministère, en promulguant et faisant exécuter les loix de l'ordre naturel, par lesquelles la propriété et la liberté sont établiés.

" *Magistrats*, pour décider dans les cas particuliers quelle doit être l'application des loix de l'ordre naturel, réduites en loix positives par l'autorité souveraine ; et qui ont le devoir impérieux de comparer les ordonnances des souverains avec les loix de la justice par essence, avant de s'engager à prendre ces ordonnances positives pour régle de leurs jugemens.

" *Instruction publique et favorisée*, pour que les citoyens, l'autorité, et les magistrats, ne puissent jamais perdre de vue les loix invariables de l'ordre naturel, et se laisser égarer par les prestiges de l'opinion, ou par l'attrait des intérêts particuliers exclusifs qui, dès qu'ils sont *exclusifs*, sont toujours malentendus.

" *Revenu public*, pour constituer la force et la pouvoir nécessaire à l'autorité souveraine, pour faire les frais de son ministère protecteur, des fonctions importantes des magistrats, et de l'instruction indispensable des loix de l'ordre naturel.

" *Impôt direct*, ou partage du produit net du territoire entre les propriétaires fonciers et l'autorité souveraine, pour former le revenu public d'une manière qui ne restraigne ni la propriété ni la liberté, et qui par conséquent ne soit pas destructive.

" *Proportion essentielle et nécessaire de l'impôt direct* avec le produit net, telle qu'elle donne à la société le plus grand revenu public qui soit possible, et par conséquent le plus grand degré possible de sûreté, sans que le sort des propriétaires fonciers cesse d'être le meilleur sort dont on puisse jouir dans la société.

" *Monarchie héréditaire*, pour que tous les intérêts presens et futurs du dépositaire du l'autorité souveraine, soient intimement liés avec ceux de la société par le partage proportionnel du *produit net*."

NOTE B. Page 195.

Mr. Barton, in an ingenious pamphlet, published in 1817, entitled, "Observations on the Circumstances which influence the Condition of the Labouring Classes," has contended, in opposition to the principles laid down in this work, that the introduction of machinery most commonly occasions a decline in the demand for labour. Mr. Barton has illustrated his argument by the following statement, which I shall take the liberty briefly to examine:—

"As the doctrine, that the progress of population is measured by the increase of wealth, does not appear to be true in fact, so, on the other hand, it seems to me not consistent with sound reasoning. It does not seem that every acoession of capital necessarily sets in motion an additional quantity of labour. Let us suppose a case: A manufacturer possesses a capital of 1,000*l.*, which he employs in maintaining twenty weavers, paying them 50*l.* per annum each. His capital is suddenly increased to 2,000*l.* With double means he does not, however, hire double the number of workmen, but lays out 1,500*l.* in erecting machinery, by the help of which five men are enabled to perform the same quantity of work that twenty did before. Are there not, then, fifteen men discharged in consequence of the manufacturer having increased his capital?

"But does not the construction and repair of the machinery employ a number of hands? Undoubtedly. As in this case a sum of 1,500*l.* was expended, it may be supposed to have given employment to thirty men for a year at 50*l.* each; if calculated to last fifteen years (and machinery seldom wears out sooner), then thirty workmen might always supply fifteen manufacturers with these machines; therefore, each manufacturer may be said constantly to employ two. Imagine, also, that one man is employed in the necessary repairs; we have then five weavers and three machine-makers where there were before twenty weavers.

"But the increased revenue of the manufacturer will enable him to maintain more domestic servants. Let us see, then, how many. His yearly revenue, being supposed equal to 10 per cent on his capital, was before 100*l.*, now 200*l.*: supposing, then, that his servants are paid at the same rate as his workmen, he is able to hire just two more. We have then, with a capital of 2,000*l.* and a revenue of 200*l.* per annum,

5 weavers,
3 machine-makers,
2 domestic servants.
—
10 persons in all employed.

"With half the capital, and half the income, just double the number of hands were set in motion."—pp. 15, 16.

But plausible as this statement may at first sight appear, it will not, I apprehend, be very difficult to shew, that the conclusions at which Mr. Barton has arrived, are not fairly deduced from the premises he has laid down, and that, in the case supposed, there would not be a diminution, but an increase of the demand for labour.

In the *first* place, supposing, with Mr. Barton, profits to be 10 per cent, the goods produced by the capital which the manufacturer laid out upon the twenty weavers must have sold for 1,100*l.*, viz. 1,000*l.* to replace the capital, and 100*l.* as profits.

In the *second* of the supposed cases, the manufacturer employs a capital of 1,500*l.* in the construction of a machine: now, as this machine is fitted to last *fifteen* years, the goods produced by it must sell (exclusive of the wages of the men employed to attend to it) for 197*l.*; for a part of this annuity (47*l.*) being accumulated for fifteen years, at the rate of 10 per cent, will replace the capital of 1,500*l.* at the expiration of that period, while the other part (150*l.*) will pay the profits of the proprietor; and, adding to the annuity of 197*l.* the wages of the five weavers, and of the person employed to repair the machine, at the rate of 50*l.* a year each, and profits on them at 10 per cent, the total cost of the goods will be—

Profits of machine, and sum to replace it	£197	0	0
Wages of six men, at 50*l.*	300	0	0
Profits on wages	30	0	0
Prices at which the goods are now sold	£527	0	0

But, previously to the introduction of the machine, the same quantity of goods cost 1,100*l.*: the consumers will consequently have the difference, or 573*l.* to lay out on other things; the production of which will afford immediate employment for between eleven and twelve men. But this is not all. According to the principle explained at p. 194, a portion of this saving, —perhaps 250*l.* of the 573*l.*—will, in future, be employed as a capital in carrying on industrious undertakings; and in this way a fresh fund will be provided that will furnish wages, or the means of subsistence, for a number of individuals, (most probably *five*,) at the end of the first year, more than would otherwise have been employed; and supposing, as we ought, that this fund goes on increasing at the rate of 10, or even that it increases only at the rate of 5 per cent, compound interest, it would very soon afford the means of employing a vast number of individuals.

There is also another fund, of the existence of which Mr. Barton appears to have been as completely unaware as of the latter. It has been seen that of the 197*l*. produced directly by the machine, 150*l*. only are profits; the surplus 47*l*. being the annuity which is to replace the capital of the machine when it is worn out; but as this annuity is to be accumulated at the rate of 10 per cent, it will afford employment, in the first year, for one individual; in the second for two; in the third for more than three; in the fifth for nearly six; and in the fifteenth year for upwards of eight-and-twenty individuals!

It will be observed, too, that in the second case supposed by Mr. Barton, there is 200*l*. not employed at all; and which, if employed, would afford wages for four individuals. Instead, therefore, of a single labourer being turned out of employment, in the case supposed, or in any similar case, it admits of demonstration, that the demand for labour would be much more than doubled.

INDEX.

C.

F.

G.

Q.

R.

S.

THE END.

LONDON:
J. MOYES, TOOK'S COURT, CHANCERY LANE.

Printed in the United States
by Baker & Taylor Publisher Services